CW01371999

Jungle Ghosts

Walking Point in Vietnam

Ed Mann

Pen & Sword
MILITARY

AN IMPRINT OF PEN & SWORD BOOKS LTD.
YORKSHIRE – PHILADELPHIA

First published in Great Britain in 2025 by
Pen & Sword Military
An imprint of
Pen & Sword Books Ltd
Yorkshire – Philadelphia

Copyright © Ed Mann, 2025

ISBN 978 1 03611 742 9

The right of Ed Mann to be identified as the Author of this work has been asserted by him in accordance with the Copyright, Designs and Patents Act 1988.

A CIP catalogue record for this book is available from the British Library.

All rights reserved. No part of this book may be reproduced, transmitted, downloaded, decompiled or reverse engineered in any form or by any means, electronic or mechanical including photocopying, recording or by any information storage and retrieval system, without permission from the Publisher in writing. NO AI TRAINING: Without in any way limiting the Author's and Publisher's exclusive rights under copyright, any use of this publication to "train" generative artificial intelligence (AI) technologies to generate text is expressly prohibited. The Author and Publisher reserve all rights to license uses of this work for generative AI training and development of machine learning language models.

Typeset in INDIA by IMPEC eSolutions
Printed and bound in England by CPI (UK) Ltd.

The Publisher's authorised representative in the EU for product safety is Authorised Rep Compliance Ltd., Ground Floor, 71 Lower Baggot Street, Dublin D02 P593, Ireland.
www.arccompliance.com

For a complete list of Pen & Sword titles please contact:

PEN & SWORD BOOKS LIMITED
47 Church Street, Barnsley, South Yorkshire, S70 2AS, England
E-mail: enquiries@pen-and-sword.co.uk
Website: www.pen-and-sword.co.uk

or

PEN AND SWORD BOOKS
1950 Lawrence Rd, Havertown, PA 19083, USA
E-mail: uspen-and-sword@casematepublishers.com
Website: www.penandswordbooks.com

Contents

Foreword	x
Vietnam, Near the End of 1969	xi
Introduction	xiii
Chapter 1	**1**
1968	1
Enlisting	2
January 1969, Army Training	4
June 1969, The Presidio	5
Chapter 2	**11**
Vietnam	11
1st Air Cavalry Division	13
Chapter 3	**19**
B Co, 1/12th Cav at LZ Grant	19
Chapter 4	**25**
In a Meadow off LZ Grant	25
Chapter 5	**43**
Treated and Back to the Company	43
Sugar Bear's Radio	54
Chapter 6	**60**
Beyond the Wire Again	60
Chu Hoi	64
Arc Light	66
In the Column	69
First Time on Point	70
Lizard's Call	72
Walking Point Again	73

Chapter 7 — 75
Adapting — 75
Taking Over Walking Point — 79

Chapter 8 — 83
The Bunker Complex — 83
Moving Lighter and Quieter — 86
Bomb Crater Bathing — 88
The Majestic Jungle — 90

Chapter 9 — 93
Three Steps Away — 93
Repeating Days — 97
Tracking on Point — 99
Back to the LZ — 101

Chapter 10 — 103
No John Wayne — 103
Kill Counting — 107
Click — 110
Jay's Seizure — 112
Bodies, Jay, and Sugar Bear — 115
Claymore — 118

Chapter 11 — 119
Dark Days — 119
Leach Inchworms — 123

Chapter 12 — 124
Another LZ Break — 124
Back to the Jungle — 125
Captain Jones and the Tracker Dog — 127
Wounded Soldier's Tracks — 129
The Bucks in Trinity — 130
Cloverleaf Patrols — 132

Chapter 13 — 133
The Gold Pendant — 133
Johnny Ciulla — 134
Mike and Getting High — 134

Chapter 14   137
    Pushing the Limits   137
    Swamp   138
    Dead Log   142
    The Leaf Toter Ant   144
    Sick Jungle   145

Chapter 15   148
    Rising Out of the Jungle   148
    Stolen Steaks   149
    Sniper School   150

Chapter 16   153
    Return to the Jungle   153
    An Army of Pillaging Ants   154
    Sam   155

Chapter 17   157
    The New Lt.   157
    The Inspection   158
    Patrol off LZ Grant   161
    The Loach Pilot   165

Chapter 18   167
    A Ticket Out of the Jungle   167
    The Colonel's Orderly   170
    The Colonel's Driver   172

Part Two, The Central Highlands

Chapter 19   176
    Rejoining My Platoon   176
    Lt. Colclough   178
    Jim Quinlin and Me   179
    The New Squad   181
    The Central Highland Jungle   184
    Walking the NVA's Trails   187

Chapter 20 — **191**
    Christmas in the Jungle off LZ Lee — 191

Chapter 21 — **193**
    An Instant of Forever — 193

Chapter 22 — **203**
    Malaria — 203
    The 1970 State of the Union Address — 205
    Cam Rahn Bay — 207
    The Colonel on the Bus — 209
    Sugar Bear's Stolen Three-Day RxR — 213
    Combat Leader's Course — 215

Chapter 23 — **219**
    Mad Dog — 219
    Under a Distant Star — 223
    The Fruit Tree — 223
    A Second Gramps — 224

Chapter 24 — **227**
    An Ending Written in Bones — 227
    Letters From Home — 232
    Gramps and the Quiet — 233
    God in the Jungle — 234

Chapter 25 — **236**
    The Jolley Trail — 236

Chapter 26 — **258**
    Malaria Relapse — 258
    Some Things Have to Be Lived With — 260

Chapter 27 — **264**
    A Place Called Bù Gia Mập — 264
    Day 1 — 266
    Day 2 — 277
    Days 3 and 4 — 282
    Day 5 — 284

Chapter 28	**288**
LZ Snuffy	288
RxR	290
Reaching for Redemption	291
Sydney, Australia	292
Chapter 29	**296**
Return From RxR	296
The Door Gunner	297
Bravo Company Headquarters	299
The Drowned Rat	300
The Company Sergeant	301
Chapter 30	**303**
Back to the Jungle	303
Transitions	304
The Last Lt.	305
The Nightmare	305
Ending	307
Glossary	**308**

Foreword

I'm George Colclough, retired CEO of Smith & Wesson and retired colonel in the Army Reserve. As a young man, I completed Officer Candidate School and Ranger School at Fort Benning. In November of 1969 I was a second lieutenant assigned as a platoon leader for the 3rd Platoon of B Company, 1st of the 12th Battalion, 1st Air Cavalry Division. The unit was operating in the jungles of Vietnam, 8,000 miles from home and living in some of the harshest conditions imaginable.

That has been by far the most important post I've ever held, and I remember the events of those months well. The ever-changing thirty or so "grunts" in my platoon were Black, white, Latino, Asian and who knows what else, and they came from every corner of our land, the Bronx, the Heartlands, the shores of the Pacific. I suspect it's always that way: soldiers from all over the country coming together and fighting as Americans.

This book was written by Ed Mann, one of those grunts. I want you to know that the events Ed describes and the role he played during the time I was his platoon leader are exactly as he portrays them in this book. Although I can't attest to the events that predated my arrival, I saw the respect his fellow soldiers held for him when I arrived, and in a combat setting that level of respect speaks volumes.

Let me be clear: this is not a war story book. This is an accurate account of actual events, actual people, even down to actual conversations. It's told from Ed's unique perspective, but I strongly believe that it conveys a universal truth about the collective experience of many of us who served in that war. It's that good.

I've been very fortunate in my civilian and army careers. There were times when I was driving to work early in the morning, I would look in the mirror and wonder if this life was really happening. I've been extremely fortunate that way, but of all the things I'm truly thankful for, the best of the best is the great honor of being a platoon leader for that group of resolute and courageous men. They have forever earned my deepest respect. I can't tell you how grateful I am that Ed has captured so vividly our time together in the jungle.

George Colclough

Vietnam, Near the End of 1969

The colors of his uniform blended with the hues of the earth and the distant line of vegetation so that it seemed he was a piece of the jungle, but I could make him out. He led a short file of men walking from the LZ, well beyond the wire now, moving slowly, halting often, and surely sensing ahead for lurking dangers. The afternoon heat was oppressive and where the leaden mass of his pack pressed against his torso he'd be sweating dark patches onto his shirt. I knew every detail intimately, what he was thinking and what he was feeling. I could even feel the heat burning through him, and as his silhouette grew smaller I imagined that under the mottled green of his helmet his hair was brown, like mine.

The sun's rays burned against the bare ground that encircled the LZ as if to punish the very existence of that unnatural clearing. Layers of heat reflected off the red dirt, and the soldier's distant silhouette began to shimmer and distort, as though I were viewing him through a gently oscillating piece of warped glass. I'd learn nothing from him but something compelled me to watch his distance-silenced figure creep ever closer to the dark green line that marked the undisturbed edge of the jungle, its thickness shrouding all that lay beyond. Before he entered the jungle his image wavered, and then he passed into the tree line and silently and forever disappeared into the overheated, shimmering nothingness of Vietnam.

Would he survive his one-year cycle of the sun, trek full circle, and reach out to grasp the threads of civilized life again, or would he bleed out in the dimness of the jungle? Who would know? He was just a fleeting image who'd melted soundlessly into the dense green canopy. I had no reason to care about him, but something like anger came unbidden and swelled my lungs with air. The thick air suddenly seemed unbearable, and I turned my face from the distant line of trees and edged under the shadow of the makeshift poncho awning. A rivulet of sweat inched its way down the hollow of my back. A stray movement of the heavy air flapped the sagging poncho lazily, shaking loose specks of dust that hung silhouetted against the sun-bleached gray of the sandbagged bunker. I watched them float aimlessly.

"*Fuck that guy,*" I told myself, and I meant it. In a day or two we'd disappear into another distant piece of merciless jungle and fight for our survival. I was twice wounded already, and the only things I needed to care about were the ones that could keep us alive.

I'd have felt differently once, but that was long, long ago.

Introduction

"What Was it like in Vietnam?"

Vietnam was many things to many soldiers. Most of them completed their tours performing jobs that didn't expose them to close-quarters combat but a small percentage weren't that fortunate. The majority of those were infantry soldiers, men who viewed themselves as "grunts." Some of them fought in the rice lands of the Delta and some fought in the dense inland jungle areas. I served in the jungle, and this is how I viewed that after a couple of months:

We weren't the only company that was suffering casualties. Several men in our sister C and A Companies had recently been killed and as we prepared to leave I was seeing an increasing number of guys with pen and paper in hand, almost surely reaching out to their loved ones for what might be their last time.

I wasn't one of them. I wasn't going to share any of this with the people who cared about me...the thick jungle, the hiding, the whispering, every step taking me to unfamiliar vistas and potentially lethal sight lines, the bugs, the littered night perimeters permeated with the odors of feces and urine, the weight of our packs, the wet, the heat, the hunger, the weekly, stomach-churning orange malaria pills, and the threat of getting wounded or killed that never, ever, released its toxic grip, especially on point days when we knew that if anyone was fated to die it would probably be one of us. We were bitching about the weather, the way they were using us, the food...all kinds of things...but we never talked about the scary stuff; nothing about our fears, our thoughts of our loved ones, our thoughts of death, the terror of being hunted that left us with joyless faces sometimes etched with naked fear, all of us moving slowly, cautiously, fearfully, and forever aware that death was lurking somewhere in the shadows of the dense foliage.

That was the reality that had brought so many awake screaming in the night, but there was another side to that deadly peril; the jungle was the place where adrenalin pumping, heart thumping, and breathlessly vital moments awaited us, and the thrill of that was pulling at me.

Why I Wrote This Memoir

The war was winding down when I arrived home, already yesterday's news that most Americans wanted to put behind them. I'd wanted that too, but I couldn't leave it behind. Vietnam held too much fear, sadness, anger, bitterness, regret, pride, camaraderie, and wonder, and images from that faraway place kept finding their way into my everyday thoughts and dreams. When those memories grew too powerful I'd try to write them out of the shadows, not to explain or justify what I'd seen and done but just letting the experiences write themselves out of me. Maybe I did that because I'd left too many questions unanswered and the only person I could talk to about Vietnam was myself, or maybe I did it because those of us who'd fought the war had been so poorly caricatured by both those for and against the war. Whatever the reasons, I kept writing, trying to convey the experience as authentically as I could.

I hope I've done that. The physical conditions, the people, the conversations, and the events that I've chronicled here are all factual, including one experience that was so uncanny it won't seem credible. I recognize that but I've chosen to recount that event exactly as I perceived it then. That's an imperative for me. I'm no longer the 20-year-old who fought in Vietnam but I know what he saw and I know what he felt, and the accounts that I've written here are factual to him. Even the bugs that I've singled out did what I've written they did because I remember…

Chapter 1

1968

It was December of 1968. Dr Martin Luther King and Robert Kennedy had been assassinated and President Lyndon Johnson had declined to run for reelection. The Democratic National Convention in Chicago had erupted in chaos, and the newscasts had been filled with images of police beat-downs of dazed and bloodied protesters. Richard Nixon was poised to assume the presidency after an extremely close election that had been tainted with allegations of fraud on both sides, an election where more than 13% of voting Americans had cast their ballots for an unabashed segregationist candidate, George Wallace. Racial tensions were running dangerously high and parts of the deep South were on fire.

The war in Vietnam was ongoing and the national network news shows were broadcasting the reported enemy and American weekly kill counts like they were scores in a game, one that our team was always winning. Despite their kill counts, the bloody NVA and Viet Cong Tet offensive from early in the year had fully debunked America's military and political leaders' long-standing claims that victory in Vietnam was on the near horizon. Faced with increasing opposition to the war, the army was trying to suppress the fact that an Americal Division company had massacred several hundred men, women, and children in the remote South Vietnam hamlet of My Lai, and all the while the bodies of hundreds of young American soldiers were arriving home to their families every month.

Anti-war students and others were clashing with pro-war supporters and police forces in cities across the US. The widespread and persistent unrest was threatening the control of those who'd long held power and energizing those who'd long chafed at the status quo. "Love it or leave it!" had become the rallying cry of many of those who supported the war, and young people were symbolizing their demands for an end to the war and for sweeping societal changes by the way they dressed or wore their hair, and, at times, by publicly burning their draft cards or their bras.

2 Jungle Ghosts

The year that history would ultimately recognize as one filled with momentous events was ending. I hadn't played a part in those historic events but virtually every able-bodied young man who wasn't swimming against the strong currents of that era was destined to be swept up in them. That was me, drifting aimlessly in the slow water that was circling at the edge of the vortex; waiting to get sucked in.

Enlisting

My dad made a living working road construction jobs and when the jobs hadn't been there he'd worried himself sick trying to make ends meet for our family. I'd seen how miserable he'd been and I'd enrolled at my local Junior College hoping that an education would safeguard me from that. My intentions had been good but I'd wasted my time playing sports and partying, and at the end of my first year I'd been on academic probation with a 1.7 GPA. I'd started my third semester needing to up my GPA to a 2.0 to keep my student draft deferment but I hadn't attended classes in weeks, and now it was a cold December, the draft was looming, I had no job skills and no plan, and, of course, there was the girl.

I'd seen Barbara standing on the other side of a dance floor two years earlier, a tall, slender, straight-standing girl with long dark hair. The way she'd smiled and the way she'd carried herself had captivated me so powerfully that I don't think I'd have had the nerve to ask her to dance if my friend hadn't known the girl she was with. I'd been a senior in high school and she'd been in her first year of college but she'd danced every dance with me that night, and when it had ended I'd walked her to her car and surprised both of us by leaning forward and kissing her forehead. That moment's feeling had stayed with me, and when my mom had asked if I'd met someone special I'd said I had and that, "Someday I'm going to marry a girl like that."

We'd started dating. Three months later we'd gone to a drive-in movie and when I'd walked her back to her mom's house I'd had a sudden appreciation of how hard I was falling for her. She'd been a thoughtful girl with a separate college life and I'd been a reckless teenager afraid of getting hurt and unprepared for a committed relationship. That had terrified me, and in the faint glow of her porch light I'd told her that I was going to stop seeing her because I was starting to like her too much. She'd breathed a soft, "OK," and I'd left wondering if she'd cared. Several months later we'd started seeing each other again but I hadn't stopped blowing off my college classes, cruising town with my friends, meeting up with other girls, and getting into occasional street fights with violent older guys. I think both of us knew I didn't deserve her affection but neither of us had been willing to let go of the other. I couldn't see that lasting and I couldn't see a path forward so I took the easy way out.

One afternoon I was driving past the army recruiting office in downtown Redding and I spontaneously pulled over. The recruiters had my army qualification test results on file and they assured me that my scores would qualify me for any military specialty I'd want. A guarantee required a three-year enlistment so I opted for a two-year enlistment with a reporting date in three weeks.

When I told my family that I'd enlisted my WWII combat-veteran dad clenched his jaw and nodded, my sister yelled that I was an idiot, and my mom blinked away tears. I told Barbara and she hugged me tightly for a long while. I held her too, knowing that two years was a long time and this might be the end for us.

I didn't want to give my friends an incentive to enlist so I waited until I had a handful of days left before I told them. I should have waited longer because Johnny Ciulla and Sonny Hoyer rushed down to the recruiter's office. Sonny was rejected because he had a history of asthma. Johnny qualified but he said he wouldn't enlist unless they'd guarantee that he'd go through basic training with me. The recruiters made the deal, and on a gray-skied morning in the first week of January of 1969, Johnny Ciulla and I boarded a Greyhound bus bound for Oakland, California.

We passed out physicals and traveled by bus up I-5 to Fort Lewis, Washington. During orientation, I was told that my test scores had qualified me for Officer Candidate's School or a potential appointment to the West Point Academy. I wasn't interested but I did consider a warrant officer program to become a helicopter pilot. I tested too red/green color insensitive to qualify so Johnny and I started basic training with no assurances of any military specialties.

January 1969, Army Training

The army shaved our heads and outfitted us with olive green military clothing, and in less than an hour we'd become fifty bald and clean-shaven soldiers with nothing to suggest who we'd been as civilians. On our second day as a unit my drill sergeant pulled me aside and told me that I'd be the platoon leader. I asked him to choose someone else and he stuck his face inches from mine and screamed that this was the army and declining wasn't an option. There was no arguing that, and in the evening I gathered the others and told them that I hadn't wanted the job but I'd do the best I could. The next day we started our eight weeks of basic training, berated by the screaming tirades of drill sergeants who made it painfully clear that everything we were doing and everything we knew was unacceptable and punishable.

At the end of our basic training there was apprehensive speculation regarding which MOS (military occupation specialty), each of us would receive. The most dreaded one was 11b40 (infantry) which virtually guaranteed a combat tour in Vietnam. I was worried that Johnny would get infantry but he got orders to transfer to another fort for radio school training and I got orders to report to the old section of Fort Lewis for ten weeks of advanced infantry training, (AIT).

In the frigid cold of Washington's extended winter I continued training for the war in the tropics. The miserable cold made AIT difficult but I'd always been confident that I could withstand the physical rigors of army life. What I hadn't known was how well I'd handle the bullying and harassment I'd be subjected to during my five months of training and the remaining year and a half of my enlistment. That hadn't been a problem during basic training because our platoon had excelled and our drill sergeant had been happy to step back and take the credit, but that changed in AIT.

One of our trainers was a universally detested man who belittled soldiers at every opportunity, and after an incident when the trainer laughingly blared his bullhorn in our ears about half of my company stood together and yelled an obscenity at him. That sent him into a rage and he ordered everyone to drop to the dirt and assume a pushup position. I stayed on my feet. When he repeated his order I told him that he'd gotten what he deserved, and that led to a series of clashes that led to him telling me that he hoped I'd die in Vietnam.

When we arrived back at our barracks the head drill sergeant called me into his office, stuck his face in front of me, and told me to go ahead and hit him. I was as mad as he was and I told him, "You think you'll move your face before I hit you but you won't. I'll hit you so hard that I'll break your jaw and then I'll get court-martialed." I don't know if he believed me but we never came to blows and I managed to complete AIT without getting court-martialed.

And now I had five months of military training behind me and a year in Vietnam ahead of me. That's how I viewed my commitment, just getting through my two years of service one step at a time, and I left AIT believing I'd made it through to my year in Vietnam. I'd soon learn that I hadn't.

June 1969, The Presidio

We'd been told that we'd get thirty days of leave after completing AIT but the orders I received were for two week's leave and to then report to Oakland, California for transport to Vietnam. My sister's first baby was due within that two-week window, and when the baby was late I stayed longer. A series of *one more days* turned into two weeks of AWOL, and when the prospect of the army arresting me for desertion began to loom larger I gave up, caught a ride to San Francisco with my dad, and turned myself in at the Presidio Fort in San Francisco.

The clerk at a unit called "The Special Processing Detachment," typed up some papers, and then he called an MP to escort me to another building for *further processing*. The MP led me down some steps to a basement where two naked men were positioned in pushup positions with their fingers pressed against a narrow ledge inches above the floor. Both were quivering with fatigue, and one was sobbing. Club-wielding MPs were scattered throughout the room and a dozen or so naked men were sitting on benches facing a wall. Some of the men on the benches were crying openly and streaks of dried mucus were crusted on the faces of others.

I glanced back at the MP manning the desk. He was eyeing me with a curious expression, waiting for a reaction, I guessed. I didn't give him anything.

"What did you do?" he asked, his voice neutral.

"I had two weeks' leave. I took four."

"Strip and drop your clothes," he said, gesturing at the bundles of clothing crumpled on the floor behind him. I was tugging off my clothes when the sobbing guy on the wall collapsed. His body made a sound like a giant hand slapping cement when it hit, and two of the MPs sprinted at him screaming, **"I told you not to break your fall!"** He scrambled to regain his position but they got to him too quickly and they each grabbed an arm and slammed him against the wall twice, hard. When they released him he clawed his way back to a pushup position on the wall, but he was already on the verge of another collapse, his body shaking, snot flowing from his nose, and tears falling from his eyes and splattering against the cement floor creating dark dots; a frantic animal caught in a trap.

Naked, I followed the desk MP's directive and lowered myself into a pushup position an arm's length from the crying guy. Less than a minute later he uttered an anguished groan and collapsed. His chest and face hit the cement, harder than before, and the guards rushed forward, slammed him against the wall, and manhandled him to the bench. I heard him sobbing helplessly, and I resolved that I wasn't going to get that weak. *I'll drop before that happens, and I won't be scrambling to get up. If they want to slam me they'll lift 185 pounds off the floor without any help from me.*

I was on the wall with the other guy when two more detainees arrived behind us. The desk MP reported that one of them had been charged with rape. The rape guy tried to sound tough and the MP in my peripheral vision looked amused. The guy on the wall beside me uttered a low moan and collapsed. He tried to scramble up but the guards got to him and slammed him against the wall. He bore it with just a grunt, no sobbing and no whimpering, and he made it to the bench with his dignity intact.

The new detainees joined me on the wall. The tough-talking rape guy was the first to weaken. The MPs were waiting eagerly and when he hit the floor they rushed at him screaming at the top of their lungs. They kept screaming and slamming him until he was sobbing and begging them to stop; not so tough after all. Some of the other guards were laughing. One of them looked at me curiously; the guy who'd been on the wall for a long time, not trembling, poker-faced, just an AWOL. Maybe he'd had enough blood, I don't know, but he told the other guards, "The hell with him, he's been up there long enough," and he directed me to take a seat on the bench.

Three more guys endured the wall, and when the last one made it to the bench we started moving through the center of the basement and answering questions from club-wielding MPs who were filling out forms. I'd been keeping a tight rein on my temper but at the next-to-last station the most sadistic of the MPs was leaning back in a chair with his boots on the desk, and his aggressive eyes were fixed on me. I slid my eyes past his and tried to keep my face blank but the image of his arrogant, bullying face stayed with me and I could feel my heart thumping more powerfully with every beat. I knew what was coming but I couldn't control it, and then I didn't want to, and I thought, *Fuck you!* and stared straight into his eyes.

He stared back and we were locked eye-to-eye. His eyes started to glisten, and then a tear trailed down his left cheek. His eyes still held onto mine, surprising me, and then he couldn't do it any longer and he looked away. When he turned back my eyes were still there, challenging him, inviting him, inviting all of them, not caring about time in the brig or a bad conduct discharge, not caring about anything, just sending my eyes boring into that sadistic fucking face with my entire body expanding and contracting with every beat of my heart and one thought repeating over and over in my mind, *If you come for me I'll rip a club from one of you and I'll make all of you pay! And after this is finished I'll hunt you down!*

He exploded out of his chair, screaming, "I want him! I WANT THAT SONOFABITCH!"

The desk MP's head snapped up and when he saw what was happening he said, "OK, OK, let me finish with him first."

The sadistic MP stalked off to the far end of the basement. He stayed there while I finished processing and dressed, and when they led us out of the building I was relieved; not crazy anymore.

The SPD barracks were situated on the second floor of another old brick building. The entire floor was filled with bunks and about a third of them were occupied. A portable radio was resting on one of the bunks blaring music at nearly full volume. A few detainees were talking over the noise but most were lying or sitting on their bunks. I walked through the middle of the bunks to the farthest bunk in the southwest corner, and then I turned back and deliberately surveyed my surroundings and my fellow inmates. No one looked back. That's what I wanted.

8   Jungle Ghosts

I spent the rest of the week confined to those barracks and knowing that every day I was wasting here was one more day I could have had at home. The possibility that I might not survive Vietnam made them seem tremendously valuable and I decided that if they didn't process orders sending me to Vietnam before the weekend I'd try to spend it at home. The orders didn't arrive, and Friday after dark I hung from a second-story window, pushed off, and landed on the grass outside my barrack. My dad picked me up on his way home from his road job south of San Francisco and I spent two days with my family. On Sunday evening I rode back with my dad. We parked in front of the SPD barracks at about 10 pm and my dad walked around the hood of the car and stopped in front of me. He started to say something but he couldn't seem to find the words. My family nickname was "Bucky," and in a deep, gravelly voice he finally rumbled, "Bucky, don't try to be a goddamned hero!"

I said I wouldn't. He gave me a rib-crushing hug with his powerful arms, and without another word he turned away and climbed back in the car. The Rambler settled with his weight, and then the engine rattled and knocked lightly as it accelerated, the way it always did, and I watched it enter the shadows and disappear around the corner. I stood there for a few seconds, wishing that big-shouldered caring man was beside me still, and then I squared my shoulders and walked into the SPD's building.

When I told the night desk clerk what I'd done he warned me somberly that I'd have to face *discipline* when I *processed* in the morning. We both knew what those loaded words meant, and I climbed onto my still-vacant bunk thinking that my run-in with the MP would have been eating at him and wondering if he'd be there when they took me back to the basement.

In the morning a sergeant called me out and escorted me to their battalion sergeant major's office. He was seated behind an uncluttered desk, a solidly built and square-jawed man in his late 40s with the red-veined nose that's typical of long-term heavy drinkers. He stayed seated, dismissed the sergeant, and spent a few moments eyeing me slowly from head to foot.

"You were assigned here because you went AWOL?"

"Yes."

"You went through special processing?"

"Yes."

"And then on Friday you went AWOL again and reported back last night?"

"Yes."

"That's never happened here," he said, "do you want to explain yourself?"

He'd looked me in the eye and talked straight, and I responded candidly, "Look sarge, I'm waiting for orders to Vietnam. I don't mind going to Vietnam but I'm not going to sit here and listen to a bunch of deadbeats blast loud music when I could be home for the weekend. Just get me to Vietnam and I'll do a good job there."

He looked me over a second time, just as carefully, and then he nodded and said soberly, "I believe you will. I'll get you out as soon as I can."

And that was it; a "Good luck" dismissal with no second article 15 and no second trip to that basement.

June 29, 1969

Three days later two unsmiling MPs drove me across the Bay Bridge and then east on I-580 to the Oakland Naval Base.

An hour later I was sitting on my duffle in the warmth of the Bay Area's mid-morning sun, just one of the hundreds of young men scattered on the asphalt tarmac waiting to hear our names called for a seat on an airliner bound for Vietnam. They called my name and I took my place in the long line of men snaking along the side of the airliner that loomed high above us. Every seat was filled when the doors closed. The plane taxied to a runway, and then the engines roared and the jet rocketed forward and climbed into the sky, on its way to the place on the bottom of the world that we called South Vietnam.

Chapter 2

Vietnam

After twenty-plus hours in the air, I was half asleep when a scratchy intercom voice announced that we were approaching Vietnam's Tan Son Nhut Air Base. I caught brief glimpses of flat land and scattered buildings, and then our aircraft banked sharply and dove steeply toward the ground. We touched down hard and bounced twice, and then the thrusters roared desperately and we decelerated. The intercom voice warned us to prepare to exit quickly, and I followed the lead of the men ahead of me and stood in the aisle.

The plane lurched to a stop and the ground crew started positioning the exit ramp. A few minutes later the forward door opened and when Vietnam's bright mid-afternoon sunlight pierced the front of the cabin the men ahead of me started inching forward. The thin air we'd breathed throughout the flight grew progressively thicker as I neared the exit and when I reached the doorway the air was so liquid it felt like a wet blanket was plastered against my face. My reflexive breathing stopped and I had to force the thick air in and out of my lungs. Each breath carried the acrid stench of diesel exhausts, sunbaked asphalt, and an odor reminiscent of rotting vegetation and old outhouses.

I stepped onto the open ramp and the sunlight reflecting off the oil-slick asphalt and tin roofs of nearby buildings seared painfully into my squinting eyes. Service vehicles were darting around the tarmac in seemingly random patterns, and helicopters and planes were climbing into or dropping out of the sky. My ears recoiled from the jarring, throbbing, and discordant confusion of revving engines, barking loudspeakers, roaring turbines, and the slapping and thumping of helicopter blades hammering through the dense air. I'd never experienced anything like it, and I stood in that sauna-thick air appreciating why so many of us had hesitated at the airliner's threshold as if we could avoid passing through that arched portal into the cacophonous, sweltering, and confusing reality that awaited us on the other side of the doorway. But none of us could; Vietnam would swallow all of us, some of us forever.

I descended the ramp and joined the others standing on asphalt so hot I could feel the heat through the soles of my boots. After a few minutes, we joined 100 or so men who were sheltering under a tin-roofed open-sided structure beside the runway. All of us were waiting quietly with the exception of a group of eight or ten men wearing mismatched jungle fatigues who were animated and noisy, seemingly oblivious to those of us who were waiting so silently with them. Several of them had sun-bleached boonie hats on their heads and their faces were so darkly tanned that their teeth appeared starkly white when they smiled. I wondered if they'd have any advice for a new arrival, and I walked over and said, "Hello."

They quieted mid-sentence. One of them finally nodded, and then he turned back to the others. After a moment's hesitation, he turned back and asked where I was from and what my MOS was. I said I was an 11b40 from California. One of the others asked what part of California, and when I told him he nodded. That was it. I didn't know why my arrival would have dampened their high spirits, but it had, and I nodded goodbye and rejoined the new arrivals.

I wouldn't have believed it possible but the overheated air beneath the metal roof had grown thicker. I heard the rumble of thunder and I followed the sounds to a dark mass of swirling ground-hugging clouds laced with intricate webs of crackling lightning. The leading edge of the storm was moving our way and within minutes the overhead sky darkened menacingly and powerful gusts of wind began to buffet us. Peals of thunder rumbled and exploded with ear-splitting crashes and the runway was lit with flashes of brilliant white light. Torrents of warm rain collapsed from the sky, and sheets of water waterfalled off the tin roofs and created ever-widening pools on the asphalt. The fury of the storm continued unabated for ten or fifteen minutes and then patches of sun-yellowed sky peeked through the dark clouds and the lightning-lit edge of the storm roiled into the distance.

The incredible energy of the storm had brought the airport to a full stop, but within minutes wisps of steam were rising from the tarmac and ground crews were speeding through the puddles and mists as if such storms were everyday occurrences. Unnerved by how little I understood of this place, I sat on my duffle waiting for instructions from whoever would be directing me to wherever I'd be going. I didn't like feeling that overwhelmed and I glanced back at the small group of devil-may-care men whose casual presence seemed to create an island of assurance in a sea of uncertainty. They were smiling and laughing again, apparently unawed by the storm or the chaotic beehive of activity that had once again enveloped us. I assured myself that they must have once been wide-eyed arrivals feeling the way I was feeling, and I told myself, *if they could handle this place then so can I*, and I straightened up and sat a little taller.

We were still waiting under the overhang when those carefree men bounded up the steps of the ramp we'd descended. I saw them being greeted warmly by the stewardesses who'd seemed so distanced from us, and then I watched them disappear into the airliner that had borne us to Vietnam. I'd later know that those men could have told me that the small percentage of soldiers who ventured outside the wire were facing the most lethal odds and that most of them were serving in infantry companies. They could have let me know that Vietnam was a disorderly place where you could forge your own path to a safer place; "*Don't want to hump the jungle? Don't want to go to the 1st Air Cav, the Americal Division, the 25th Infantry Division, the 196th Infantry Division, the 101st Airborne, or one of the other infantry outfits where so many guys were getting zipped into body bags? All you had to do was ignore the men with the bullhorns and climb onto a bus that was heading to a better place, or better yet just step away and make your own way to wherever you wanted to end up.*"

They'd have known those things but telling me wouldn't have changed anything. I wouldn't have stepped out of line and forced someone to fill the slot that fate had chosen for me; I'd have done just what I did when they called my name, cramming myself in with the others sitting two and three to a seat in our sticky-hot, diesel-fume-reeking bus, none of us with the slightest idea where we were bound, and all of us facing our uncertainties and fears alone.

1st Air Cavalry Division

I'd pictured a war where danger would be lurking around every corner but it wasn't like that. Our unguarded buses exited through the gates of Tan Son Nhut and traveled down a two-lane paved road that was crowded with automobiles and a bevy of mopeds ridden by Vietnamese civilians. Flat landscapes often stretched green and empty into the distance, and in other places we passed by tacked-together, tin-sided shacks and Vietnamese bicyclists and pedestrians who traveled perilously close along the sides of the highway. Sprinkled among them were tiny women wearing wide-brimmed conical hats and satiny gowns that appeared strikingly out of place amid the squalid shacks that lined the sun-beaten road.

We drove that road until late afternoon, and then our bus rambled past a dense cluster of shacks to the gates of the Bien Hoa Army Base. The guards waved us through and we traveled a short distance down narrow streets lined with single-story tin-sided buildings. There were no grassy areas, no trees, and no bushes, just patches of dirt and those tin buildings. We arrived at a compound that was posted with a large sign that read, "First Air Cavalry Division." Another sign hung from the crossbar that framed the entry, proclaiming, "The best soldiers in the world pass under this sign." We passed under the sign, collected our gear, and joined a group of soldiers who were eating in a canvas tent.

Our sleeping quarters were cavernous tents filled with rows of double-decker cots, and I stowed my duffel under one of the lower cots and settled in with the blanket they'd given me. The canvas sides of the tent had been rolled up to allow the night air to circulate but the thick air wasn't stirring, and I lay in the heat and humidity of my first night in the tropics listening to the unfamiliar noises of the base and scenting the unfamiliar air with no idea what tomorrow would bring. It was scary and lonely, and at the same time it was challenging and exciting. Either way, there was no going back.

I awoke to the familiar sound of a bugle blowing reveille. We filtered out of our tents and made our way to a morning formation where we were told that we'd been assigned to the 1st Air Cav, and that we'd be undergoing four days of 1st Air Cav training and then sent to a 1st Air Cav company. Over the next three days they lectured us on procedures and tactics, issued us packs, jungle gear, and an M-16 rifle, and fitted us with a pair of canvas-sided jungle boots. On our forth day they marched us to the 1st Cav's tower. It was the tallest structure on the entire Bien Hoa Army Base, and specialized trainers took small groups of us to the top and gave us a quick lecture on the correct way to thread ropes through the rings that were affixed to rappelling harnesses. They assured us that applying pressure to one of the rope loops with our "braking hand" would arrest our free falls, and then they directed us to the edge of the tower and instructed us to face in and jump back into thin air.

Every instinct was telling me that launching myself into that void was suicidal but I'd seen others doing it and none of them had splattered on the ground. I gathered my nerves, sprang back, and allowed myself to free fall before I applied the pressure. I stopped a few feet short of the dirt, let the rope slip through my fingers, and slid the rest of the way down. The most cautious of us stopped just below the top of the tower and inched the rest of the way down. A few resisted the sustained yelling and ridiculing of the trainers and refused to jump. Those non-jumpers didn't *"graduate"* into the 1st Air Cav Division's ranks. I don't know where they sent them but I'm pretty sure the outfits they were assigned to didn't have "Air" in their division's names.

At the end of the 1st Cav's training about a dozen of us were held back and placed in a newly formed *Ready Response* group. We were told it was to guarantee that Cav-ready replacements would be on hand whenever a Cav company suffered what they euphemistically referred to as *a sudden loss of personnel*, but we knew what they meant. They directed us to a tent and I selected an upper bunk where the night air might circulate a little. A lanky, brown-eyed guy with jet-black hair and a high, wide forehead tossed his gear on the upper bunk next to mine. He turned to me with a smile, and in a clipped Rhode Island accented voice he introduced himself as Rene Gamache. I took one look at his friendly face and I knew I'd met my first friend in Vietnam.

The next morning the permanent cadre gave the latest cycle of 1st Cav's recruits the same first-day speeches they'd given us, and then they marched the new batch of soldiers off. When we had some free time Rene and I walked under the *best soldiers* sign and then up the narrow avenues that dissected Bien Hoa's tin-sided buildings. The streets were eerily empty until a middle-aged Vietnamese man came walking down our side of the street. We'd been told we were helping a grateful South Vietnamese people repel North Vietnamese Communist invaders and when he glanced up I gave him a friendly smile. The sullen expression on his face didn't change. We crossed paths with several other Vietnamese pedestrians that day and if any of them felt thankful for our involvement in their war they hid it well.

A small metal building situated in the middle of a dry and dusty lot had a sign that identified it as an enlisted men's club, and we walked through its crude wooden doorway into its shadowed interior. Three GIs were perched on bar stools at the far end of the wood-planked bar and a lone GI was sitting at a table butted up against the back wall. Rene and I took stools at the opposite end of the bar from the three GIs, and when the bartender walked over to ask what we were drinking we pulled out the monopoly-like, "military personnel currency," (MPCs) and, for the first time in our young lives, we lawfully ordered beers.

The GIs at the other end of the bar were boisterously discussing what they'd do when they went on leave. I didn't find them interesting but the soldier sipping a beer at the back wall caught my eye. He was a medium-small brown-haired guy with a lean build and the kind of face you might see more than once in a high school yearbook. I thought he looked a little raggedy, the way a baseball player might look at the end of a hot summer game, not truly dirty but not clean either. His eyes kept flicking to the doorway as though he expected someone to pass through it at any moment, and when the voices of the three GIs got louder he glanced their way with a look on his face that reminded me of the way I'd felt when I'd been the new kid in school. I wanted to know what his story was, and when he passed by on his way from the latrine I asked if we could buy him a beer.

"Hell, yes!" he said, and he invited us to join him at his table.

He told us he was from the Midwest and that he'd spent ten months as a grunt "humping the bush" with the 25th Infantry Division. He'd just been reassigned to a "rear job" in Bien Hoa but he said he was in no hurry to report to his new outfit, and then he asked about us. He was looking down at his beer when I told him that the 1st Cav was holding us in reserve for an infantry company that needed quick replacements. His head snapped up, and then he lowered his eyes and changed the subject. I waited until we'd shared a couple of beers and then I asked what it had been like for him, out there.

He literally stopped moving, and then he shook his head, paused, and shook it again. He stayed silent for so long that I thought he wasn't going to answer, and then in a voice that was almost a whisper, he said, "It's mostly hard humping, bugs, and waiting, but the gooks are tough. Just watch the guys that's been there and do what they do."

Rene asked how bad it had been and he said, "If it's your time, it's your time. Only don't listen to lifers that tell you to do something stupid."

And then he shook his head, looked straight at me and then straight at Rene, and muttered huskily, "Fuck it, man, you'll make it."

We knew we'd taken him to a place he hadn't wanted to go so we drank beers and talked about other things. He was slurring his words when we were leaving, and he wished us "good luck" so gravely that Rene felt a need to tell him we'd be OK. I never said anything to Rene but that guy knew a lot more about what lay ahead of us than we did and he sure as hell didn't see it that way.

Over the next days, Rene and I kept exploring the sprawling, wire-enclosed, and guard-tower-protected maze of narrow roads and temporary buildings that was Bien Hoa Base. The cave-like interior of the dingy enlisted men's club was the best refuge we found to escape the 100 degrees or higher temperatures and 90% plus humidity, and I sometimes whiled away a few hours there sipping a drink and observing the mix of soldiers who happened by. I never crossed paths with our first infantry friend again but a few of the men who stopped by were combat soldiers. Sometimes they'd relate a combat experience to me, and at other times I'd hear them talking about "the gooks" with a buddy they'd arrived with. I knew they were reliving real experiences because they'd get jittery and trembly in the telling, and I'd hang onto their every word seeking any hard-earned wisdoms I could glean from their encounters.

One day I crossed paths with my high school friend, Gary Taylor. Gary had only a few minutes to spend with me but he made a point of letting me know that his artillery unit had been on an LZ that had been attacked by waves of NVA soldiers. He said the NVA had suffered massive casualties but they'd continued their attack and a handful of them had breached the perimeter. He told me there'd been several earlier assaults on that same LZ, and he warned, "Whatever you do, don't go to LZ Grant!"

We'd been waiting for almost two weeks when one of our guys sprinted back from morning formation to tell us that five of us had been called. Rene and I were among the five, and the others were Merle Haben, Roger Allred, and a guy I didn't know by name. They crammed the five of us and our gear in a jeep and drove us to a chopper pad. The driver pointed to a chopper and we hustled over and climbed aboard. The chopper vibrated to the beat of its accelerating blades, and when they were hammering hard it lifted off, circled into the sky, and climbed until the air rushing through the belly of the open-doored chopper was cool. When Bien Hoa was far below we lined out and flew on as straight as an arrow, five young men completing the last leg of their long journey to their infantry unit.

The shape of a solitary mountain rose out of the flat land. A tiny group of huts was nestled against the base of its eastern slope, and our chopper passed directly over the huts and followed a strip of grassland toward what looked to be an oval construction site with dots at its epicenter. As we flew closer the dots materialized into bunkers and tents, and I called above the noise of the chopper to ask the door gunner what was there.

He yelled back, "LZ Grant!" and I looked down at the barren LZ perched in the middle of a dirt clearing that Gary Taylor had warned me about.

Chapter 3

B Co, 1/12th Cav at LZ Grant

The pilot landed the chopper on the dirt helipad and the five of us climbed off, instinctively stooping low as we passed below its still-turning blades. As the rotors slowed to a crawl I stood in the settling dust surveying an LZ rimmed by an earthen berm. Bunkers spaced in sequences of three were lined up along that berm. Two were low and squat but every third perimeter bunker had a tall guard platform that afforded an unobstructed view over the 30-meter-deep swaths of twisted concertina wire that extended from the outside edge of the berm.

To the southwest of the LZ the solitary mountain rose out of the flat terrain like a badly misshapen cone resting upside down on a table. Natural grasslands stretched in that direction, but on the other three sides of the LZ a massive expanse of earth had been bulldozed and sprayed clear of vegetation. At the edges of the cleared areas distant lines of thick vegetation created opaque walls of green that reached unevenly toward the sky. I surveyed the heavily sandbagged perimeter bunkers, the thick berm, and the twisted concertina wire, and considered the colossal effort it would have taken to clear the vegetation to that distant tree line, wondering what might be hidden there that had made those precautions so necessary.

About a half-dozen men appeared in the avenue that opened through the wire of LZ Grant. The group of them slowed as they neared us but a medium-short and rusty-haired guy walked straight to Rene and me, saying, "I'm Barry, the platoon sergeant for the 3rd Platoon. It's a good platoon. Do you want to go there?"

I liked the look of him and I never hesitated. Rene agreed, and we gathered our gear and followed him through the gap in the wire. I could see that his gait was fluid and the soles of his boots were well-worn, and I thought, *Outside the wire boots, outside the wire soldier*, certain that I'd arrived at the end of my journey.

We circled the inside of the berm to a mid-20s blond-haired man who was standing shirtless in the shade of an overhead poncho tied to the side of a bunker. Barry introduced him as "Lt. Jones," and the Lt. welcomed us to the platoon, assigned Rene and me to different squads, and asked Barry to get us situated. I'd have thought he'd say something about what he expected of us, but that was it.

LZ Grant had appeared deserted when we'd flown in but men were sitting or reclining under the makeshift poncho awnings that were affixed to every bunker we passed. All of them were wearing blousy, multi-pocketed pants with their pants legs string tied tightly over their boots and most were shirtless. Without exception they were young, and as we passed by they were surveying us with serious faces and measuring eyes.

Barry stopped at a bunker situated a few steps to the right of the LZ's gate and introduced the two men reclining in the shadow of its poncho-strung awning as, "Jay and Sam." He told them I'd be in their squad, and with an over-the-shoulder, "See you later," he and Rene continued down the perimeter. Sam was a little under average height, slim and wiry with brown eyes and dark hair that showed a sprinkling of the road dust that peppered it. Jay was about the same height but more solidly built. He had light brown hair, copper-toned skin, and a long face marked by a strong Roman nose. In a pronounced Southern drawl, Jay told me he was from Oklahoma and that although he had bluish-gray eyes he was a Cherokee Indian. Sam was also from the South but his accent wasn't as noticeable. We exchanged some casual information about ourselves and then they lay back in the shade.

I settled with my back braced against the bunker's sandbags and listened to the flies droning through the hot diesel-fumed air. Two hours ago I'd been anticipating another day of uncertainty in Bien Hoa, and now I was an infantryman perched on a desolate LZ at the edge of the jungle. It was apparent that we'd reached the war, or at least the edges of it. Rifles, grenades, and ammo belts were lying everywhere, and the LZ's artillery battery had sent rounds screaming away that I'd heard explode in the distant jungle. I thought about Gary Taylor's account of the attack on the LZ and I asked Jay and Sam what they knew about it. They told me they'd been in the jungle when it happened but they'd heard that hundreds of NVA had been killed just outside the perimeter. The bodies had been bulldozed into a pile and buried in a mass grave nearby, they said, except for one who'd been so entangled in the wire that they'd let his body rot there.

That night I stood watch on a guard bunker platform. It was a no-moon night and I was scanning the starlight-lit wired area that extended from the berm for any murky shadows that might have moved or changed shape. The LZ's artillery launched a flare and I looked up and watched it pop open. The burning orb swinging beneath the tiny parachute was emitting a harsh, white light that lit the area beyond the berm daylight-bright, and as the flare drifted slowly to earth I looked for any suspicious shapes or movements. The flare's light yellowed and burned out before it landed. I kept scanning for enemies until my turn on watch ended, and then I returned to our musty bunker, settled on a cot, and fell asleep.

I awoke to a dimly lit scene that was so eerily unfamiliar that it took a couple of seconds for me to realize I was inside a sandbagged bunker on the edge of the jungle. I slipped quietly to the blanket-draped opening and walked the perimeter road to the open-air latrine. I shooed away flies with my off hand and tried to ignore the stench as I urinated into the barrel of waste beneath the seating hole. I returned and settled beneath our poncho awning. A hint of movement at the edge of my vision drew my eye, and I watched a rat about the size of a small cat emerge from beneath one of the sandbagged sides of our bunker. It ambled unhurriedly along the base of the bunker and disappeared around a corner. I rose stealthily and slipped to the corner to see where it was going. It was nowhere in sight. I leaned in close and tracked its sharp-clawed prints to the side of another bunker, and then I returned and sat back against our sandbagged bunker as the sun climbed higher on the eastern horizon.

Occasional noises sounded from the interior of the LZ where the guys who cooked, worked the artillery, or did other jobs on the LZ were active. As the sun rose higher the canopied areas began to fill with guys sitting or reclining languidly on the perimeter. I ate at the mess tent, and then I returned and settled back in the shade. I ate lunch. Late in the afternoon the sauna-like conditions grew more oppressive. In the early evening the heat and humidity built to a sticky climax, and then the skies opened and buckets of warm monsoon rain turned the perimeter road to mud. I ate dinner. That was the entirety of my first full day on LZ Grant, just that.

Over the next few days, I settled in with the others and lived like a bat. We spent the daylight hours in shaded locations and rarely emerged until the sun had dropped below the perennially smoke-hazed western sky. My regular activities consisted of walking to the mess tent for three meals, using the water-barrel-supplied outdoor shower to wash the stickiness off my body, and an occasional light morning detail. Judged by almost any standards it was a miserable existence but the men who'd just returned from the jungle seemed to treasure their time on the LZ. I looked out at the line of green that pressed against LZ Grant's clearings again, wondering how bad it would be out there.

My company spent weeks and months' long intervals in the jungle and I wanted to know everything I could about what happened out there. I'd expected someone would clue me in or that I'd hear them talking about that but I'd never heard any of them discuss their time in the boonies. I didn't know why it was such a taboo subject, and one morning when Jay, Sam, and I were alone I asked why the company had so many casualties the last time they were out.

Jay's face tightened. "We was moving up a lil hill in some thick stuff. I was telling Sam it looked a bad place but the others dint seem to notice."

Sam sat up and planted his boots on the dirt. "I was jumpy too. The ones up front was careless and Jay and I was too far back to help out."

"You got to watch out fer yerself," Jay added, "Some of em, like Barry, think they know everything but they don't."

Sam nodded. "That's what got them guys hurt and kilt up ahead. We just kept going to the top of thet lil hill and then there was gook bullets flying right over us from everywhere. We couldn't move back cause they was behind us too. We'd walked past their bunkers and they just opened up on us."

Jay's voice was shaky, "It was real bad. Them up front was pinned behind a log and couldn't move back, is what I heard. Me and Sam started to work our way up to get em out but Lt. told us to stay where we was."

He shook his head from side to side. "We finally did git on the top of thet hill but there wasn't nothin we could do till they dropped a bomb in on top of them gook bunkers. It musta killed a bunch of em. Then we got out to where the birds could take them thet was dead and wounded. They was some good men got hit thet day."

He turned away for a long moment, and then he said, "And then they went and put in Little Joe fer a silver star fer droppin a frag'n thet bunker. He wasn't doin nuthin we wasn't doing cept he was so blind he ended up on top of a bunker he dint know was there and he had to frag it to get offa it."

"I thought we was going to have to pull him out too," Sam added.

The talk died. The whispers of a distant chopper's blades touched my ears. Someone was banging on something in the interior of the LZ, maybe a pot, but otherwise it was quiet. A shirtless guy trudged down the perimeter road. He was in our platoon but I didn't know his name.

After he passed by I asked what the NVA bunker complex had looked like, how close Jay and Sam had been to the bombs, and how long it had taken for the medevac to arrive. They answered my every question, telling me in their own words "how things was." Little Joe had a reputation as a standout guy so I was sure they were putting their spin on things but I didn't care. Just like the stories I'd heard in Bien Hoa, their accounts were opening a narrow window into the unseen world of the jungle and I was sorting through every word, searching for any lessons that might help me survive.

I was about to become a participant in the war in the jungle, and the import of that loomed larger that evening when the booms of explosions and the sounds of automatic weapons emanated from an area of jungle northeast of us. We learned that three of our sister companies were pinned down by a sizable NVA force, and that night I sat on my guard bunker listening to an almost unbroken succession of ear-shattering blasts as the LZ's artillery battery sent heavy rounds whistling away to the section of the jungle where the firefights were crackling. I could hear them exploding there, and I could see wavering lines of tracers flowing down from our aircraft and the lines of NVA tracers that were fired back at them.

We'd been told we'd be heading there at first light, and I sat watching and listening to the battles, envisioning the men who'd died out there and the men who'd killed them, and wondering how I'd measure up. A lot of our training had been designed to condition us to automatically obey orders, and the consequences of failing that had been drilled into us with absolute certitude; **"You'll do what your officers and NCOs tell you to do or you'll get yourself killed and your buddies killed. Follow orders, always follow orders!"**

They'd tried to drill that into us but I'd always had questions, and many times I'd been singled out for discipline and told, "Mann, you're the kind of guy who'll screw up and get your buddies killed."

Their certainty hadn't convinced me then, but as I listened to the deadly firefights raging deep in the jungle those dire warnings were echoing in my mind; *Were they right? Would I be the guy who failed to follow orders? Would I get someone killed?*

I sat atop that guard bunker in the darkness and weighed my inexperience and uncertainty against the cocky on-LZ demeanor of some of the experienced grunts in my company. The contrast was all too clear, and I resolved that when we left the LZ I'd do exactly what I was told. The sense of relief I felt at that moment made me certain that I'd made the right decision. When my guard duty ended I returned to our hooch. The intermittent ebbs and flows of the distant firefights were audible through the sandbagged thickness of our bunker, and before I fell asleep a popping burst of heavy firing sounded. It persisted for a while, and when it ended a voice out of the dark murmured very softly, "Poor bastards."

Chapter 4

In a Meadow off LZ Grant

The line of us began passing through LZ Grant's southern gate a little after first light, each of us carrying our weapons, ammunition, gear, and a three-day supply of food and water. One man after another, we entered the barren expanse that encircled the LZ, moving on until the tail end of our long column broke free of the concertina wire. Before we entered the foliage that pressed against the edge of the LZ's clearing I turned back for a last look at the LZ squatting lifeless beneath a clouded gray sky, the sun-bleached look of it reminiscent of an old black and white photo. The sight somehow generated the phantom odors of diesel-burned waste and men confined in airless bunkers.

I pulled in a lungful of the greenhouse-heavy air to clear my nose, and then I followed the lead men through a narrow gap in the dense wall of vegetation that I'd looked out at so often. The thick vegetation soon opened into another meadow, and we walked straight up the middle of that meadow and then down a series of loosely connected meadows for another hour or so. I knew we were so nakedly exposed that the noises didn't matter but I tried to step lightly on the balls of my feet, the way I'd slipped so quietly through the mountains back home.

I kept looking back to create a sight picture in case I needed to retrace my steps. Each time the silhouette of the Black Virgin Mountain's peak dropped closer to the top of the intervening foliage, and when I checked again the mountain was fully hidden. The disappearance of that sentinel mountain made it feel like we'd lost connection to the last vestiges of civilization and become an isolated company of men advancing ever deeper into a feral land where men killed other men on sight. The unfiltered danger of that was exhilarating, almost intoxicating, and then the gravelly voice of my dad echoed in my head. "Don't try to be a goddamn hero," he'd said, and I reminded myself that this wasn't one of the adventure books I'd read; tens of thousands of Americans had died doing what we were doing and there was no coming back from that.

Chapter 4

We trudged steadily northeast through knee-high grassed meadows and the low-brushed areas that separated them. I knew that we'd appear as three-quarter tall silhouettes to anyone who was lurking in the foliage, and I kept picturing myself lined up in an NVA rifleman's sights like one of the targets that slid along the rail in a carnival shooting gallery. If I'd been shooting I'd have dropped each one of us as fast as I could have pulled the trigger, and I tried to stay centered between the man ahead of me and the man behind so I wouldn't present a double target and draw a shooter's eye. I found myself hoping that they'd target someone else and give me time to drop out of sight in the grass. I felt guilty wishing that on someone else, but I was pretty sure I wasn't the only one with that thought running through his head.

Our Vietnamese scout, Buc, was walking at the head of our column, and his head was on a swivel scanning the opposing tree lines of the meadows we were walking. I'd been doing that too, but the vegetation that lined the meadows was so opaque that I thought any NVA hiding there would be almost impossible to spot. I wondered if Buc's experienced eyes might detect them but at the pace we were moving I didn't think that he would. I wondered, *Were they inviting the NVA to reveal themselves by opening up on us? Did they know something that made them believe we wouldn't be targeted? Were they trusting to luck?* I was sure there had to be an explanation but I couldn't shake the dread that the NVA were going to shoot into us at any moment. I told myself that it was out of my hands, and I palm-popped the base of my 18-round clip to be sure it was locked in place and kept moving.

We were exposed to the full burn of the sun, and the overheated and humid conditions were growing increasingly worse. Sweat was dripping off the tip of my nose and trailing down my neck, chest, and back. My heavy pack was pressing against my back and by late midmorning every place my sweat-soaked shirt touched my skin felt like a steaming towel was plastered against me. My thirst was raging and I sucked in a mouthful of warm water from my canteen and kept it in my mouth for a few steps before I swallowed. I craved more, but my water had to last and I slipped the canteen into its cloth holster.

The air trapped beneath my steel helmet was baking the top of my head, and the weight I was packing was squeezing my 4E-wide feet painfully into my jungle boots. I glanced down at the nickel-plated dog tags I'd threaded into the laces, remembering Barry telling me to lace them there so they wouldn't jingle or get blown off in an explosion and me thinking, *At least they'll identify my feet.* My steel helmet slipped down on my forehead. I nudged it up. My pack was riding low too, and I crouched down and straightened up fast to bounce it higher on my back. It settled there, hot and wet against my skin.

I glanced back at the men trailing me. Their steel helmets were wrapped in their multi-shaded camouflage covers, and their green packs and jungle fatigues were the same reddish tint from the jungle dirt that had been stained into them by the men who'd donned them before. They were all leaning slightly forward to balance the heavy loads riding high on their backs, and their helmeted heads were bobbing in unison as they trudged wearily toward an unknown fate; sweat-soaked and pack-burdened soldiers as identical as faceless pawns on a chessboard.

When we stopped for a break I shrugged out of my pack and tugged my sweat-soaked shirt off my skin. It let go with a sucking sound, and the moisture evaporating from my sweat-slickened skin created a few seconds of relative coolness. Minutes later a chorus of *saddle ups* came whispering down the column, and I replastered my sodden shirt against my skin, strapped on my pack, and continued following the men in front of me.

The explosive crack of a shot shattered the silence! I heard a burst of Vietnamese words on one of our radios as I dived down to join those who'd disappeared into the grass. Minutes later a message was whispered up the column that one of us had inadvertently triggered a shot from his M-16. A nearby NVA soldier had been monitoring our radio frequency and the shot had startled him into keying his talk button as he'd spoken. With the NVA nearby tracking our movements I thought we'd stop making easy targets of ourselves, but we didn't. Men started rising out of the grasses and we trekked single file down the middle of another meadow as if we were bulletproof. It was just another reminder of how little I knew about the war we were fighting.

Our company commander was "Captain Jones," (as distinguished from our Lt. Jones) a medium sized, mid-thirties guy with a crew-cut haircut who wouldn't have stood out if it weren't for his rank. Captain Jones called a halt early in the evening, and he had us establish a circular perimeter on a side of one of the largest meadows we'd encountered. My platoon's arc of the perimeter was closest to the tree line, and I paired up with two guys from another squad to dig a foxhole. Our little trenching tool made the digging slow but our pace picked up after we dug through the tough grassroots to the loamy dirt below. After I took my turn digging I opened a can of C-rations. I ate the contents cold, sitting on the edge of our sticky-humid meadow and scanning the tangled wall of foliage that loomed close by. I assured myself that we'd know what we were doing but sitting so exposed to that veiled foliage was spooky, and I shifted lower, trying to make myself less conspicuous.

Our foxhole was dug mid-calf deep when I was told I'd been selected to go on patrol. I emptied my pack of everything I didn't think I'd need and joined the patrol on the lower edge of the perimeter. Rene was there, dirt-streaked and somber, along with eight other guys. Our patrol leader was an E-6 squad leader on his second tour of Vietnam. He selected a guy to walk point and we followed the point man to the tree line that edged a tall section of jungle, and then we pushed through the brushy tree line and, for the first time in my life, I was moving beneath a dense jungle canopy. I'd been anticipating this moment for a long time, and like a boy kissing his first girl I experienced a rush of vivid impressions.

The hanging mass of intertwined foliage anchored high in the trees formed a thriving sea of green that almost fully obscured the sky. Long and leafy vines hung from that canopy like twisted ropes, and some of them stretched all the way down to the large-leafed, light-collecting shrubs that were reaching up from the jungle's shadowed floor. The lushness of the overhead canopy and the low vegetation created a confusing maze of browns and greens that limited visibility in every direction, and the sauna-heavy air it trapped was filled with the rich odors of damp earth and exotic scents that were new to me. The teeming vegetation, the strange scents, and the overhead canopy that seemed to have added a third dimension to the earth's surface made everything seem surreal...and then the haunting cry of an unknown animal sounded in the distance and I felt like I'd stepped onto the surface of an alien planet. Those moments forever imprinted themselves in my memory, and then, eyes wide with wonder, I followed the men ahead of me, moving deeper into that incredibly exotic world of sights, scents, sounds, and threats, just a jungle newbie trusting my life to men who knew so much more than I did.

The point man led us down a long-unused footpath that was so overgrown in places I had to use the barrel of my rifle to push my way through hanging vines that bristled with hooked barbs. The spongy carpet of rotting leaves and twigs that overlay the trail muted the sounds of our footsteps, and our only telltale noises were the sounds of the vegetation that brushed against our packs and the water sloshing inside our partially filled canteens. Just specks of yellowed sunlight showed through the green ceiling of overhead growth, and then we came to a ray of sunlight that had somehow found an avenue through the canopy to light a couple of steps of the trail, and when I moved into it I felt the radiant heat of the still-powerful sun. When men ahead of me paused I looked down at the minuscule movements of the insects that were crawling in the debris. Later, a chest-high termite mound took shape a few meters away and then disappeared when I'd moved a few steps beyond it. It was an ominous reminder that an enemy could lie undetected just a few steps away but I was too filled with excitement and wonder to feel much fear.

We slipped through about 300 meters of the heavily canopied jungle to the edge of another large meadow. A huge bomb had landed where the tree line bordered the meadow. The force of the blast had taken a crescent-shaped bite out of the jungle that edged the meadow, and an even wider-arced semicircle out of the head-high elephant grass that filled the main meadow. The blast-created crescents had filled in with low scrub grass, and the trail we'd followed ran through the scrub grass to the bomb crater and disappeared in the elephant grass of the main meadow. We walked the trail to the bomb crater that was about the size of a small backyard swimming pool. The basin was three-quarters filled with murky green water but there was enough space between the rim and the water to allow us to conceal ourselves. The patrol leader signaled us into the crater, and we climbed down its steep bank, shrugged out of our packs, and hid below the crater's rim. I positioned myself at the far edge of the crater and looked out over the half-moon section of scrub grass that extended about 25 meters and the wall of elephant grass that stretched 200 meters or so to a jagged tree line that framed the lower edge of the eastern sky.

I squatted at the lip of the crater, facing out at the distant, multi-hued, tree line and listening to the unfamiliar notes and cadences of some animals that were calling there while the patrol leader tried to reach the company using the little handheld radio they'd sent with us as. It felt almost tranquil with the sun dropping below the tops of the western horizon, the heat draining from my body, and the sound of the patrol leader's softly murmuring voice in my ear. And then the calls at the far tree line changed and my adrenalin surged!

I didn't know the faces of the animals that were calling and I didn't know the tones and cadences of their normal calls, but I felt the same innate sense of warning I'd felt when I'd heard the alarm cries of the scolding blue jays or the chattering squirrels that served as nature's tattletales back home. The patrol leader hadn't paused his murmurings. I glanced back to see if the men in the crater with me were sensing what I was, and they were sitting back against the sloped bank, all of them facing inside the crater and appearing unconcerned. Heart pounding, I felt like I was living in an alternate reality; *What do these guys know that I don't?* I scanned the tops of the elephant grass that stretched to the location of the animal calls, searching for any ripples that might unveil a line of travel. Seconds passed with nothing heard and nothing seen, and then a faint sensation tickled against my ears, *sh--, --ish, --sh*, impressions more sensed than heard. My mind formed the words, *What's making those wisps?* and at that instant I *knew*.

I hissed. The patrol leader's voice went silent. Without taking my eyes off the elephant grasses I made a *down*! motion with my left hand, and then a walking motion using two fingers. There were rustling noises and then everything behind me froze to silence.

The tickles of sounds grew to the distinct whispers of legs brushing through the high grasses. I soundtracked their course, and when I realized they would emerge at our crater my heart began pumping so powerfully that I could feel my entire body throbbing with every heartbeat. The blood that was surging through the capillaries of my ears grew stronger and faster until the roaring and whooshing sounds of the surging blood threatened to drown out the sounds of the unseen men who were pushing so relentlessly through the tall grasses. I forced myself to take a deep breath and tried to slow my racing heart, needing to hear, needing to breathe. Images were flickering through my mind of us pinned in the exposed crater and the enemy creeping unseen through the elephant grasses in front of us and the jungle behind us, encircling the crater and picking us off one by one, or crawling in close and hurling grenades that the walls of the crater funneled into us.

I didn't *think* those things, but the images that flashed through my mind created a certainty that the crater was a lethal trap. I knew we had to escape it before they broke through the elephant grass and pinned us down, but they were closing too rapidly for us to gather our gear and make it to the tree line unseen. The only option was to open up before they broke through the screen of elephant grass and sprint to the tree line before they could regroup. That was so crystal clear to me that it never even entered my mind that the patrol leader wouldn't see it that way, and as the approaching legs grew ever closer I waited for his signal to come up shooting.

As the sounds approached closer and closer my heart was pounding harder in my chest, and then they were *too close*. I glanced back at the others. Their faces were wrong and their bodies weren't positioned to rise up and shoot, and at that immensely perilous moment all the inexplicable things we'd done crystallized in my mind and written words printed in my head; *THESE GUYS HAVE NO FUCKING IDEA WHAT THEY'RE DOING!*

The words were irrefutable, almost biblical in their power, and I was freed to decide for myself.

I was starting to rise and spray bullets into the sounds of the oncoming men when the thumps of bodies dropping to the ground came. *What had they seen?* I glanced behind me and saw the corner of one pack protruding slightly above the crater's lip. Maybe that hadn't alerted them, but whatever it was they knew we were here. I unhooked a grenade from my pistol belt and tried to hear if they were crawling closer. Waves of blood were still whooshing noisily through my ears but it "*felt*" like they were crawling back. I thought we'd need help soon and I squat-stepped down the bank, retrieved the handheld radio the squad leader had placed on his pack, dialed the volume off, and started keying the speaker button to generate static in a repetitive short-long-short, SOS, pattern.

Minutes later the raucous calls at the far tree line intensified, and I thought that at least some of them had pulled back. The patrol leader stepped over, retrieved the radio, and tried to get through to the company again. He did, and it was apparent that the company hadn't received my squelch SOS signals, or they hadn't decoded them, and the words printed again, smaller but just as irrefutable, *These guys have no fucking idea what they're doing!*

I listened to the patrol leader giving an accurate account of our near contact and a detailed description of our position to our company commander. When he finished he started nodding his head and mouthing soft, "Uh-huhs" and "Oks," and then he signed off and whispered, "Unpack your claymores. We're setting an ambush here." After a moment's hesitation guys started pulling claymores and detonators out of their packs.

I didn't move. The NVA had three infantry companies pinned down in the nearby jungle and the ones hurrying through the meadow had been traveling on a line that pointed directly toward my company. They'd surely intended to attack our company, they had our location pinpointed, and they'd know we were a small force separated from our company by hundreds of meters of dense jungle. All those things should have been clear from the information our patrol leader had given over the radio, and yet they'd ordered us to stay in place and ambush them.

In Bien Hoa I'd listened to a couple of grunts with shaking hands and haunted faces telling me that if the gooks knew where you were they could drop a mortar "right on top of your head." Guys with shaking hands and haunted faces don't make things up. I'd believed it when they'd said it and I believed it now, the NVA knew we were here, the light was fading, our only link to artillery or air support was the little handheld radio that had proven itself unreliable, and the crater was a deadly trap. The patrol leader was bending over a tangle of claymore wires, and I stepped over, leaned in close, and asked if the company knew that we didn't have a machine gun and that our radio was unreliable.

He turned with a surprised look. "The company knows what equipment we have."

"What're we gonna do if they mortar this crater?" I asked.

His eyes widened slightly, and then his jaw tightened. "If we get hit the company'll come up and support us."

I said, "You're crazy if you think they're gonna crawl through the dark up hundreds of meters of twisting trail that they've never been on with bullets flying over their heads. They won't get here, and if they do it won't be in time to do us any good."

He was an E-6 squad leader on his second tour of Vietnam and I was FNG (a new guy) who hadn't carved out a place for himself. He whispered dismissively, "We've got our orders. We're gonna set up an ambush **right here**, just like the Old Man told us." And then he turned his back on me.

Maybe that's what set me off, or maybe it was because I was certain that what he was telling me to do was going to get me killed. Whatever the reason, I was suddenly furious and I snapped back, "**No! You're** going to stay here and get yourself killed. **I'm not!**" and without waiting for a response I turned and stepped back to my pack.

The others had to have heard some of our whispered words but no one said anything as I strapped on my pack and circled the inside of the crater toward the trail that led back into the jungle. Rene was on the exit side of the crater with his claymore in his hands. He met eyes with me but he didn't say anything. I thought he'd made his choice but as I was about to step over the crater's rim he whispered, "Ed, wait a minute. I'm going with you."

I crouched below the rim while he repacked his gear and saddled up his pack, and in the dusky light of the approaching dark the two of us crossed over the western lip of the crater and started through the scrub grass toward the tree line. We were several steps from the crater when the patrol leader hissed us to a stop and hand-signaled us to return to the crater's edge.

We slipped back and he whispered, "Fuck it, we're all going!"

There were murmurs of approval, and a voice from the other side of the crater said softly, "Fuckin' A right!"

Minutes short of full darkness, we climbed out of the crater and headed toward the jungle, just a line of vague shadows slipping unseen toward the inky outline of the tree line. Before we reached it the thumps of mortars launching off the bottom of their firing tubes sounded! I sprawled face down into the scrub grass and tried to burrow deeper into the earth, even an inch or two, as the whistling screams of the falling mortars grew insanely louder.

An instant later 3 or 4 mortars exploded in the crater behind us. There were brilliant flashes of white light, and the blasts thundered in my ears and the ground beneath me shuddered. Tracers were painting green lines over the top of the crater and bullets were snapping overhead, and when a voice hissed "Form an L-shaped ambush!" we crawled in the dark to try to position ourselves to stop any NVA that might come charging after us.

The bullets stopped snapping, and when another voice whispered huskily, "Let's go," we scrambled to our feet, bent low, and fled into the black wall of the tree line.

It was so dark that we had to fasten grips on the packs of the man in front of us to keep contact. I don't know how the guy leading us managed to find his way through the tangled foliage in that inky darkness, but we stumbled through it and emerged at the meadow near where our company was set up. Our point man thought they were a little to the north of us and we started feeling our way in that direction. We'd radioed that we were coming but we didn't want to get shot by our own guys, and every few steps we paused and called out softly to identify ourselves. A voice out of the dark finally responded, and we veered toward it and entered the perimeter. I could barely make out the shadowy outlines of the foxhole depressions and the packs resting on the ground as I moved through the perimeter whispering the names of my fellow foxhole diggers. After a few "Uh-uhs" and "Not heres" a voice replied, "Yeah, that's us," and I was back.

I'd seen what those mortars had done to that bomb crater, and I walked straight to the foxhole and lowered myself into it to see how deep they'd dug it. It was only waist deep. I told the others that the NVA who'd mortared our crater had been headed this way, and without a word one of them retrieved the trenching tool, climbed in the hole, and started digging it deeper. I was standing beside the foxhole waiting to take my turn when something enormous smashed into the left side of my body. I had a vague impression that I was flying through the air, and then I was lying flat on my back, slack-bodied and befuddled. The left side of my chest was throbbing, and I reached my right hand under my tattered shirt and touched a warm wet opening just above the level of my heart. Without giving myself time to anticipate the pain, I inserted my index and middle fingers into the opening. My fingers penetrated midway to my second knuckles and then the tips of my fingers encountered solid flesh. There was another opening a little lower on my chest, and when the tips of my fingers reached through to solid flesh and I knew that my chest cavity hadn't been penetrated an immense wave of relief flooded through me.

Weapons were firing at a frantic pace and muzzle flashes lit the flickering images of men dragging others to safety. I could hear the shooting and some yelling voices but the sounds seemed muted and distant. I realized that I was lying exposed but I felt detached, like I was dreaming. I told myself to wake up, that this was real and that I needed to get back to my foxhole. I was confused because I didn't know where my foxhole was, and then I realized that any foxhole would do and I rolled to my stomach, intending to crawl toward the nearest muzzle flashes. I reached out with my left hand, and when I started to pull myself forward a fiery, stabbing pain in my chest brought me fully awake. The pain took my breath away. I rolled to my side to recover, and then I steeled myself to accept the pain and started forward, pushing with my legs and pulling with my right arm to the edge of a foxhole. I rolled into it. Someone lying on the bottom of the hole grunted loudly when I landed on him.

The foxhole smelled of gunpowder, dirt, and blood, and I lay unmoving, gathering strength, waiting for my ragged breathing to steady, and trying to figure out how the guy on the bottom of the hole and I were tangled. I tried to work my way off him gently but I couldn't help kneeing, elbowing, or stepping on him. He gasped several times but he never complained. When I finally got my feet planted on the bottom of the foxhole I rose to a crouch beside the guy firing the M-16. I didn't know who he was until I heard Rene's voice asking if I was OK.

The flickers of his muzzle flashes illuminated the multiple weapons, packs, and bandoleers that were lying on the dirt outside our foxhole. I reached out my right hand, dragged in a M-16, and started shooting into the line of foliage that was less than 30 meters away. There was shooting from foxholes further up and down our perimeter but the explosions had targeted our section and the two foxholes on the left of us and the one on our right were unmanned. Those three and ours were the ones closest to the tree line, and if the NVA came charging out of it we'd be directly in their path.

Artillery flares launched from LZ Grant suddenly started whistling in and popping overhead. Their bright light wouldn't reveal any NVA shadowed in the tree line but they lit those of us in the open meadow as though it was daylight. An unbroken progression of them followed. I kept picturing an NVA sharpshooter sighting up a narrow sight avenue and targeting us and I kept my head down most of the time. I asked Rene to do the same but he was determined to keep a sharp lookout and he kept sneaking long looks at the tree line.

The man lying at the bottom of our foxhole was Ralph Bugamelli, a lean guy with dark hair, intelligent eyes, and a thoughtful demeanor. The flares illuminated a bloody gash above his right upper lip and a gaping wound in his thigh that wasn't pumping much blood. He'd been handling it stoically, but when a flare drifted directly overhead he asked, "How's my face? How do I look?"

We assured him that his face looked fine. The leg wound was the one that looked bad but he didn't ask and we didn't say anything.

Rene dragged in a radio and called for a medic. A voice responded and Rene told him we had a wounded man in our foxhole who needed medical attention.

The voice asked for a description of the wounds, and after Rene gave it to him the guy said he'd check with a medic. A few minutes later he radioed back for directions to our foxhole. After Rene gave him the directions he told us that it might be a while before they came and to be sure to keep Ralph talking so he wouldn't go into shock. Ralph had been acting groggy but Rene's friendly disposition got him talking, and Ralph was fairly alert when two bent-over men came running over to carry him away.

When I'd helped lift Ralph out of our foxhole the rivulets of blood that had been dripping slowly down my chest had started flowing more heavily. I didn't want to leave Rene alone on our poorly protected section of the perimeter but my shirt was heavy with blood and I wasn't sure how much more I could afford to lose. Rene assured me that he'd be OK, and when the light of a flare started to fade I climbed gingerly out of our foxhole and ran to the shallow depression where Captain Jones and the wounded were sheltering. Several medics were tending the wounds of the dozen or so casualties, and I told one of them that I needed to get bandaged up. He nodded that he'd heard me, and I moved out of their way. A few minutes later, he summoned me back and had me hold large pieces of gauze in place while he hurriedly taped them around my chest. When he finished he told me that a medevac chopper was inbound and that I needed to get on it.

I hurried back to our foxhole. The shooting had slowed but sporadic shots were still coming our way, and Rene and I periodically fired a few bullets into the tree line. Rene heard the medevac chopper coming but my ears were ringing so loudly that I couldn't hear it until it flew closer. The flares stopped popping overhead as it neared, and when the ones floating down burned out the meadow darkened. I was so light-blinded from the steady streams of bright flares that everything went black until someone came scrambling out of the security of Captain Jones's depression with a strobe light to mark the spot they'd selected to land the medevac chopper. The place they'd chosen was directly behind Rene and me, perilously near the tree line and just 10-15 meters from the site of the earlier explosions; the place I'd have wanted that chopper to set down if I'd been hidden in the tree line holding a rocket-propelled grenade.

The screaming medevac came thundering out of the night sky. It flared to a stop almost directly over our foxhole, hovering so close that I could feel the pressure of every whump of its thumping blades. The door gunner's machine gun was spitting bullets into the tree line and Rene and I ignored the pelting stings of the debris the churning blades were whipping at us and added our M-16s' bullets. The door gunner stopped shooting but we kept firing as the chopper settled slowly toward the ground. Before the runners touched the earth men rushed out of the swale bearing the first of our wounded. They kept bringing more wounded men to the chopper, and as the load grew heavier the pilot kept upping the tempo of the chopper's blades to keep the chopper's runners resting lightly on the ground. They kept loading wounded until the chopper's blades were hammering deafeningly and the body of the chopper was shuddering under the strain.

The distinct pings of bullets biting into the chopper's skin sounded and a voice on our radio yelled frantically, "Get up! Get up! You're taking fire!"

That pilot and his crew were sitting ducks for an RPG, but in a voice that suggested he had all the time in the world the pilot replied very, very slowly. "Aw thank we got ah lil mawr time, why doan ya jus load ah few mawr aw those boys awn heeyah."

They loaded two more wounded men on the chopper, and when the men who'd brought them scrambled back to the depression the medevac was isolated on the ground behind us with its 1,000-hp engine screaming at full power and its blades hammering so hard that air they were deflecting off the ground was shaking the chopper like it was a rag doll.

Bullets from the tree line kept pinging into the chopper. I emptied another magazine and when I snapped in another one the howling hurricane of noise coming from the chopper hadn't moved. I glanced back and saw the chopper's runners elevating an inch or two into the air and then collapsing back and hitting the ground hard. I turned and fired another magazine empty, and when I looked back again the machine was shuddering so violently that I expected it would break apart at any moment. I fired another magazine into the tree line, convinced that the medevac was too overloaded to get off the ground and that it would either break apart or they'd have to land it and take some of the wounded off, but the chopper's engine kept screaming maniacally and the next time I looked back the runners were bouncing higher and touching down more gently.

It took forever for that chopper to tiptoe a few feet into the air, and as it rose the tempo of the bullets biting into it increased. It was becoming an ever more exposed stationary target, and my shoulders tensed in anticipation of an RPG rocketing past us, blasting it apart, and sending broken pieces of it flying at us. Somehow the pilot coaxed the medevac a little higher, and then he tilted it nose-down and skimmed it just above the meadow's grasses. It crossed beyond the northern edge of our perimeter, and then he picked up enough velocity to slingshot that weighty bird into the starlit sky. I heard the sounds of that heroically crewed medevac chopper dim in the distance, and then there was just the NVA and us trying to kill each other in a deadly slice of nighttime Vietnam jungle.

The artillery flares started popping overhead again, and Rene and I were facing the same threats we'd faced before the medevac had arrived. The shooting had been coming from the tree line that lay directly in front of us but they still hadn't sent anyone to man the three foxholes that adjoined ours, and I surveyed the 30 or so meters of open meadow to the tree line and tried to estimate how many seconds it would take them to reach our foxhole. If a mass of them charged out of the trees I wasn't sure we'd have time to reload a magazine so Rene and I timed a dying flare and ventured out to gather the many weapons that had been abandoned near those foxholes. We checked to make sure they were fully loaded, set them within easy reach, and waited.

I thought we'd gained the ability to empty one M-16 and grab another, but if a lot of them erupted out of that tree line I couldn't see the two of us stopping them with bullets. Our other possibility was to trigger the claymores that the guys who'd dug this foxhole had placed at the tree line. They'd strung their detonation wires tightly so they'd twitch if anyone messed with the claymores, and I kept my fingers resting lightly on those wires like a fisherman trying to detect a fish nibbling on his hook. My heart leaped when I thought I felt a tiny tug, but I wasn't certain enough to squeeze the detonator. I felt it again a few minutes later and I thought, *the hell with it*, and squeezed the clacker. Nothing happened. Rene and I tried all the other detonators and none of the claymores exploded.

The possibility that the NVA had disabled those claymores to clear a path to us was spooky, but at least we knew where that path started. They'd have to mass to do that, and Rene and I decided to make that as hazardous as we could by firing bullets into the tree line there. I wasn't confident that the M-16s' lightweight .223-caliber bullets were penetrating the foliage deeply enough to force the NVA back far enough so we started using a M-79 grenade launcher we'd gathered in. The lower foliage was too dense to get a grenade through but we were able to lob them through some gaps in the thinner upper foliage. Two or three of the mini grenades detonated at the edge of the tree line, but the others made it through and exploded in the expanse of foliage that lay deeper. Those blasts must have been taking a toll on the NVA because they started firing from inside the tree line and bullets were whistling and snapping overhead.

The hollow depression where Captain Jones and his entourage were burrowed was lined up with the shooters and our foxhole, and within seconds our radio came alive with a voice yelling, "You're drawing their fire! Cease firing!"

Their bullets were telling us that we were making it costly for the NVA to mass on our vulnerable section of the perimeter, and we ignored the order and kept lobbing M-79 grenades. The radio came alive again, and a panicky voice screamed, **"This is Captain Jones and I'm ordering you to cease firing!"**

He wasn't isolated on a thinly guarded section of the perimeter in front of a tree line that might erupt with NVA at any moment, we were, and we turned the radio off to silence his frightened voice and fired more grenades through the seams. I was expecting a visit from someone in Captain Jones' group but none of them left the relative safety of the swale to enforce that order.

The NVA stopped firing, but we periodically laced the tree line with bullets or lobbed in a grenade to remind them our section of the jungle could be deadly. All the while an almost unbroken stream of flares lit up the meadow like it was daylight. We were making targets of ourselves every time we raised our heads so we waited until a flare was dying out and dragged in a section of a log and some dead limbs to create a blind. We got it done but the blind was so full of gaps that I barely had enough nerve to take an occasional peek over the rim of the foxhole. Rene was much braver, and the risks he was taking made me cringe. I asked him to keep his head down but he was determined to keep an eye on that ominous tree line, and he didn't.

We decided to dig in deeper to protect ourselves in case they shot in RPGs or tried to drop a mortar on us. We hadn't found a trenching tool so we removed the liners from our helmets and used our steel pots to scoop dirt out of the bottom of our foxhole. I kept at it for a while but pulling my helmet through the dirt lit up the pain from the shrapnel wounds. We weren't making much progress anyway, so we quit digging and folded our bodies as far beneath the foxhole's rim as we could and lay semi-reclined with our heads at opposite ends of the shallow hole. My angle gave me a clear view of the sky to the northeast where a fixed-wing airplane and three Cobra helicopter gunships were patrolling. The NVA in the jungle below had two .51-caliber machine guns that were intermittently firing wavering lines of green tracer bullets at our aircraft, and every time one of those lines of green tracers reached into the sky multiple lines of red tracer bullets tracked the path of the NVA's green tracers directly back to the gun crews that had fired them.

The most devastating response was from a high-circling fixed-wing aircraft known as Puff the Magic Dragon which was armed with three Gatling guns that could fire up to 6,000 rounds per minute. Every fifth bullet was a red-lit tracer round, and Puff's miniguns were spitting out bullets at such a lightning-fast tempo that their tracers appeared as unbroken streams of red light that widened and seemed to curve in midair as they sped from Puff's flight path. I didn't know those statistics but I watched those streams expand, and as they neared the jungle those undulating red swaths of light made it appear that Puff was literally breathing flames onto the earth. And it wasn't just Puff, the Cobras' miniguns were raining down bullets and launching rockets at the same sites.

I'd heard that Puff could carpet an entire football field with bullets and leave no one on it uninjured, but over the next hours those green tracers rose skyward several times and each time a retaliatory hailstorm of red tracer bullets and rockets tracked them to the precise locations where the NVA gun crews had been. I couldn't imagine those gun crews surviving that onslaught, and after several instances I decided that the NVA must have been replacing dead and injured firing crews with soldiers who were equally willing to sacrifice themselves. That pattern continued until a couple of hours before dawn when one of the NVA guns stopped firing. The other .51-caliber fired green tracers skyward two more times, and then it too went silent and our deadly aircraft patrolled the skies unmolested.

Rene and I had planned to alternate turns keeping watch and sleeping but when the morning dawned I don't think either of us had slept. I know I hadn't. I'd have expected my mind to have been dulled with exhaustion but my thoughts were racing. Less than 24 hours ago we'd walked off LZ Grant, and now I was lying cramped and wounded in a foxhole littered with shell casings and crammed full of the weapons of men who'd been wounded or killed. Those hours had been physically demanding, confusing, and at times terrifying, and I was trying to make sense of it. I'd seen the advantages our control of the sky afforded us, but our air superiority hadn't prevented the NVA from pinning three of our companies down, and it hadn't protected us from getting hit hard. We were ground-locked grunts and I'd passed beneath a curtain of jungle canopy that would have cloaked us from the sky. It would be just us and the NVA in places like that and I hadn't seen anything that made me believe we could match up with the NVA face-to-face in the jungle.

Unseen NVA soldiers would have wiped out our patrol if we'd stayed in the bomb crater a minute or two longer, and they'd wounded or killed more than a dozen of us by attacking our perimeter. I'd heard their determined push through the elephant grass and I'd seen their NVA gun crews invite the deadly bullets and rockets that had rained down on them. The prospect of combatting committed NVA soldiers in their native jungle was forbidding, and Captain Jones's incompetence and our carelessness made that prospect seem even more forbidding. I tried to tell myself that one day in the field couldn't foreshadow everything but I'd barely escaped death twice, and the light of the dawning day didn't lessen the thought that was pressing at the back of my mind, *How long will I survive?*

At full light men started climbing out of their foxholes, a few at first and then the rest of them. I watched them moving freely within the perimeter but that opaque tree line was still there, maybe still hiding something deadly, and I stayed in my foxhole and waited to see if any of them got shot. They didn't, and when a chopper flew in and landed I climbed gingerly out of our foxhole and stood erect for the first time in hours. The many unattended packs that littered our section of the perimeter were reminders of last night's casualties, and I scanned the nearby faces to see which of us remained. The two guys who'd dug the foxhole with me and the E-6 who'd led our patrol were nowhere to be seen. Sam and Jay were sitting further down the perimeter. Big Jack and Gramps were standing beyond them and Barry was walking away from us.

I was still looking for familiar faces when Captain Jones emerged from the safety of the hollow, trailed by the aide who perpetually shadowed him. They continued straight to the foxhole to the right of ours, one of the three they'd left unmanned throughout the night. Jones leaned over and peered in the hole, and then he straightened, turned to his aide and said derisively, "No wonder those men got hurt, they didn't dig their foxhole deep enough."

Every man in that hole had been wounded or killed, and now he was trying to lay the blame on them. Something inside me just exploded. I heard myself saying, "You stupid sonofabitch!" The words kept flooding out…our foxholes were too shallow because he'd sent us on patrol before we'd had a chance to dig in…all of us on that patrol would have died if we'd followed his orders and set an ambush at the crater…it had been stupid to light us up with flares all night when the NVA had the cover of the jungle…it had been stupid to leave the perimeter nearest the tree line undermanned and then scream at us to stop firing when we'd needed to stop the NVA from massing to attack. The words kept tumbling out, raw and unfiltered.

Captain Jones stood frozen in front of me, his face shocked and then impassive. I ran out of air, and when I stopped to take a breath he muttered, "No one would have gotten killed in that crater," spun on his heel, and hurried away with his aide trailing behind him, leaving me standing there with my M-16 dangling from my hand, bloody, bandaged, and shivering with anger. I was still shaking when the chopper lifted me off to LZ Grant.

Chapter 5

Treated and Back to the Company

The chopper settled on the helipad outside Grant. I lowered myself very carefully to the ground, tugged my pack to the edge of the deck, and slipped a strap over my right shoulder. I stood upright with my pack, picked up my rifle, and surveyed the LZ's sun-drenched homeliness through bloodshot eyes. I shook my head at the thought that I hadn't lasted two days in the field, and then I told myself *it is what it is* and turned to the gate. I was walking through the perimeter wire, and then I found myself sprawled face down in the dust with the echoes of an artillery blast ringing in my ears. The burst of pain that followed made me gasp. Too embarrassed to wait it out, I spit out the fine dust I'd stirred and gathered myself to rise. I was hoping that no one had noticed but a kindly voice behind me said, "It's just our own guns, buddy." I got a knee under me and pushed up with my right arm. I sent a smile in his direction without registering his face and moved on, trying to ignore the throbbing pain of my freshly pulled-open wounds and assuring myself that I'd get sewn up soon and the pain wouldn't last. When the artillery fired again I was halfway to the ground before I could stop myself. The burst of pain that followed left me lightheaded, and I paused to let it ebb, thinking that earlier the sounds of those artillery explosions had only made my ears wince.

The communications bunker's radioman told me he'd get me a chopper ride to the aid station at Tây Ninh as soon as he could. I thanked him, and then I stepped through the bunker's opening to the shadow of its awning and slow-motion lowered myself to the ground. The musty smell of the sandbagged bunkers and the mixed odors of diesel fuel and burning waste were familiar scents, safe scents, and I tucked my left hand into the waist of my pants to keep my wounds closed and lay unmoving on the warm earth. I fell semi-asleep, and then the radioman was standing over me saying he had my ride to Tây Ninh.

The LZ's fine dust was chalky in my mouth again. I pulled a canteen from my pistol belt and gulped a drink of the hot rubber-flavored water, remembering how I'd worried that I'd run dry before we were resupplied. The memory of that thirst made me drain the canteen, and then I stowed my pack, helmet, and rifle in a corner of the communications tent and walked to the chopper pad. A chopper was sitting there with its blades turning lazily. The door gunner perched in the open doorway confirmed that it was bound for Tây Ninh, and I stepped onto the skid, sat-pivoted on the deck, and inch-scooted my way to where I could get a handhold for my right arm. A few minutes later the lightly loaded slick sprang effortlessly into the air. It was a short ride to Tây Ninh but the chopper's vibrations had my wounds throbbing painfully when we landed.

The Tây Ninh aid station was a cavernous green tent filled with hospital-style beds, and its canvas walls were as dank and grimy as every tent I'd seen in Vietnam. A medic guided me to a bed near the entryway. He steadied me as I lowered myself into it and helped me remove my blood-encrusted shirt. He tugged off the dirt-darkened bandages that were fluid-glued to my chest and inspected the wounds, and then he rinsed them with a soapy concoction, rebandaged me, and told me I'd have to wait for a doctor. Cleaning my wounds had set them on fire, but after a few minutes the pain eased to a deep pulsing ache and I faded into a red-tinted, semi-sleep.

He returned with another medic and they wheeled my bed into a blanket-partitioned section of the tent. He removed the bandages he'd just applied and I sat up to get a first look at the angry-looking wounds on my chest. My movement up had made them gape open, and I lay flat and moved my left arm against my side to close them again. One of the medics soaked a towel with an evil-smelling soap and started scrubbing the skin around the wounds. That hurt, but the pain got a lot worse when he doused another cloth, pulled the wounds open, and started dabbing the raw flesh inside the gashes.

A young doctor walked through the blanketed partition with a friendly smile on his face. He greeted me with a casual hello and asked when I'd been wounded and how it had happened. As I answered he pushed and pulled here and there, inspecting the gashes in my chest and the multiple smaller entry wounds on my upper left arm. When he finished he told me that cutting out the small pieces of shrapnel that were embedded deep in my arm would do more harm than good. He assured me that those would heal on their own, but he said that he'd have to cut the dead flesh out of my chest wounds and then stitch them tightly so they'd heal cleanly. I told him to do whatever he thought was best, and he nodded and selected a syringe from the instrument tray beside my bed. He loaded it with liquid from a bottle and started inserting the needle and injecting the contents along the edges of the gashes. After multiple shots, he reloaded the syringe and started injecting the liquid inside the wounds. The earlier shots had hurt but the ones inside the open gashes were far more painful.

When he left to scrub up the medics draped weighted cloths around the open wounds. The doctor returned through the blanketed doorway with his scrubbed hands held shoulder high, selected a scalpel from the instrument tray, and leaned over me with an intent look on his face. His right shoulder was blocking my view but I felt the white-hot pain of severed nerves when he started cutting. I assumed that my wounds were in a place that was difficult to numb, and I locked my arms against my sides and tried to stop myself from flinching away from the slicing scalpel. Rivulets of blood started spurting about a foot into the air and then falling back and staining the white cloths on my chest a bright red. I asked if he needed me to apply some pressure so I wouldn't bleed to death and if he'd feel any remorse when he sobered up. He chuckled and said that he might.

I managed to hold still until he made a slice that was so searingly painful that I couldn't stop myself from jerking away. His face instantly snapped to mine. He asked if I was feeling anything, and I smiled and asked if all his patients lay tensed rock hard and pouring sweat while he sawed away on them. He apologized profusely, and then he reloaded the syringe twice and injected so much anesthetic that the liquid was oozing out of the punctures. When he finished, he told me that a small percentage of patients didn't numb easily and that if I got wounded again I needed to tell the doctor that I was one of those.

He left, and when he returned about 20 minutes later he pinched the flesh around the wounds to make sure I was numb. I barely felt the pinches, but when he picked up the scalpel I braced myself to endure the return of the white-hot pain. He cut for a few minutes and all I felt was a tugging sensation and a dull pain. When he finished he laid the scalpel aside and told me that he was going to stitch the flesh inside the wounds together and then stitch the surface of the wounds. He used his stitches to pull those long gashes into shorter ones, and then he shook my hand and wished me good luck.

The numbing agent was still working when the medics wheeled me back to the main tent area and, for the first time in almost 40 hours, I fell into a restless sleep. In the early evening, they transferred me to a recovery facility in Tây Ninh. The facility turned out to be two medics in a narrow canvas tent that had ten cots lined up on each side of it. I was their only patient. They gave me a cot in the middle of the side of the tent, set a pitcher of water on a bedside table, and asked if I was hungry. I hadn't eaten for a long while but the only thing I wanted to do was sleep the pain away. I got a few hours of restless sleep and awoke in pain and feverish. One of the medics took my temperature, fed me aspirin, and poked my finger to get blood for malaria testing. The test came back negative but my temperatures would often climb to 103 or 104 degrees, and as they rose I'd progress from feeling very hot to feeling icy cold. The medics fed me more aspirins but that usually didn't lower the fevers, so the medics would walk me to the outdoor shower. The shower water was lukewarm but it always felt like I was being showered with ice water, and I'd endure minutes of teeth-chattering misery before the water lowered my temperature enough for me to feel hot again.

The two medics were often gone, and there'd been times when my temperatures had risen dangerously high and I'd had to wait for their return. After a couple of those instances I asked them to give me a thermometer and a bottle of aspirin so I could take care of myself. They were more than happy to do that, and from that time forward I'd check my temperature whenever I felt my fever spiking. If it was 102 degrees or higher I'd swallow a few aspirins and recheck it 15 or 20 minutes later. Far too often it hadn't dropped, and I'd have to roll out of my cot and wait for the inevitable lightheadedness to subside, and then I'd reach from bunk to bunk and make my way to the shower. I knew the misery that was coming but there was no other option, and I'd strip out of my pajamas and sit under the water with chattering teeth until I felt the heat of the fever again. I was always steadier on the return trip, and I'd retake my temperature and fall into a fevered sleep that might last for several hours before I'd have to repeat the process.

I hated that persistent fever and the frigid misery of the showers, but what I dreaded most was the persistent recurrence of a fever dream of a massive flood at my grandmother's cabin. My grandfather had died when I'd been 12, and then my grandmother lived alone in their remote cabin on the east bank of the Trinity River. She didn't have electricity, running water, or any neighbors, and the only access to the cabin was the cable-suspended footbridge that my grandfather had strung across the river. No one liked her being alone there, and I'd spent many of my summer months and Christmas vacations in Trinity with her.

I'd been there when a freak rainstorm had swollen the river so high that huge razorback swells had been tossing massive trees in the air as if they'd been twigs. The river had jumped the far side channel, and the dark water had been surging through the trees there for as far as I could see. Our riverbank was higher but the relentless waters had been undercutting it and creeping ever closer to the cabin, and that night I'd lain in my attic bed listening to the ominous growls of the floodwater growing more insistent and coming ever closer. Several times I'd stepped down to the riverside porch and shined the dimming yellow beam of my flashlight through the pouring rain, and each time the maelstrom of black, roiling water had collapsed more of the bank and grown closer until that mountain of merciless water had been hurtling by less than three steps from the edge of the porch. The rain had slackened at dawn and the bridge had survived, but in my feverish nightmares the blood pounding in my head became the pulsating roar of floodwaters and my grandmother and I were trapped in a churning mass of dark water that was tumbling the cabin downriver and ripping it apart.

After several days I awoke fever-free. I forced myself to eat a couple of meals that had the bitter flavor of the aspirins I'd been swallowing, and I left 20 pounds lighter than I'd been when I'd been wounded. I got a ride to our battalion headquarters in Tây Ninh and told them I needed to get to LZ Grant. They said they didn't have a chopper heading there until the next morning. Shadowy rats were scurrying on the ground so I ended up spending the night on the sandbagged crown of a bunker beneath a sky layered with sparkling stars. In the morning choppers were flying to and from the chopper pad like bees to a hive. I plotted their paths, walked to the pad, and found a chopper that was hauling supplies to Grant. I told the door gunner I needed a ride and he waved me on, no questions asked.

The RTO (radio telephone operator) on duty at LZ Grant told me that my company would be walking into the LZ that afternoon, and I retrieved my pack, pistol belt, and rifle from the corner of his where I'd left them a week and a half earlier and returned to my old bunker. I dozed in the shade of its poncho awning, ate lunch, and showered under the black barrel. On my way back to my bunker I passed by the empty awnings that had sheltered the idle brown-skinned men of my company. Seeing them empty made me feel unsettled, maybe even anxious. I think it was because I knew that many of the men I'd seen languishing under those awnings were never coming back.

I was on our guard bunker platform looking out at the broad expanse of dirt that stretched beyond the wire when the lead men of my company emerged from the tree line. As the line of them crossed the open area I was struck by how much shorter the column was than it had been on the day we'd filed off the LZ. They picked up their pace as they neared the LZ, and then the men of Bravo Company filed through the gate and arrowed off to their home bunkers as purposefully as homing pigeons returning to their roosts. I met Jay and Sam at our bunker but we didn't linger. Dinner was being served and no one wanted to be stuck at the end of the chow line if they ran short of hot food. Rene spotted me and he stepped back in line and joined us. I nodded to some of the other guys in our platoon but all I got back were neutral glances. I felt like an invisible FNG again, but after a couple of minutes faces started turning my way and then Big Jack stepped back and apologized, saying that I was so pale and thin they hadn't recognized me. I'd only spent a single day in the jungle with these guys but I knew then that already I'd become one of *us*, and I realized how much that meant to me.

Rene and I sat with two guys who'd spent several months in-country. They'd have known the men who'd been wounded, and I asked if they knew how those guys were doing. They looked perplexed, or maybe even offended, and one of them answered brusquely that he hadn't heard anything. I'd expected it would be like it was back home where everyone wanted to track a friend's injury and recovery, but I realized that it wasn't. I was surrounded by guys from my platoon, their voices boisterous and their *LZ* spirits high, all of them seemingly unmindful of the 20% of our company who'd suffered unknown fates. I was reminded of herd animals returning to normalcy mere minutes after some of them had been culled by predators, and I wondered, *was that how it was here, just keep feeding, keep moving, and leave the past behind?*

I'd been wondering whether Captain Jones would try to discipline me for insubordination based on what I'd said just before I'd left, but I knew he wouldn't when Rene told me that Jones had sent a patrol back to check out the bomb crater we'd been in. Jones had told me, "No one would have died in that crater," but they'd found it pockmarked from the mortar blasts and most of the water had been blown out of it. Someone said they'd found a bunch of bodies in the stretch of jungle that lay in front of where Rene and I had been too, so maybe that was another reason that I never heard a word about it.

I was awakened for night watch, and I climbed atop our guard platform and gazed out over the wire at the lone sentinel mountain. The Vietnamese called it Núi Bà Đen but men in my platoon called it the Black Widow or the Black Virgin Mountain, both dark testaments to the many grunts who'd died in campaigns to drive the NVA from its jungled slopes and caves. None had succeeded. The NVA still controlled its jungled slopes but the army had leapfrogged the deadly hillsides and constructed an Americal Division LZ on the summit of the Black Virgin. And when the mountain's peak wasn't obscured by clouds the Americal Division's bunkers appeared like tiny warts on its barren crest.

On this moonless night the Black Virgin looked like a giant shadow looming against the backdrop of the starlit sky. On a previous watch I'd seen pinpoints of light flicker across its slopes and I was scanning its black shadow for glimmers of light when something zipped by overhead. An instant later I felt and heard the ear-pressuring roars of two low-flying jets. For one terrifying moment I thought the NVA were bombing us, and then strings of bombs began exploding on the near slopes of the Black Virgin. Each blast emitted a brilliant light and the frenetic pace of the progressing line of falling bombs created overlapping circles of bursting light so that it looked like a colossal arc light welder was spitting a weld across the side of the mountain. When the bombs stopped dropping a deep rumbling thunder of noise rolled over the LZ, the ground trembled, and then it was over. A handful of small fires glowed red on the side of the mountain for a few minutes, and then the fires burned out and the Black Virgin Mountain was once again squatting dark and unmoving against the night sky, a massive cone of rocky earth that was impervious even to the ferocity of our bombs.

I'd never spent much time with anyone but Sam and Jay, but that morning I rolled quietly off my cot, nudged the entryway blanket aside, and stepped from our dimly lit bunker into the bright light of the new day. John Glasshof and Ron Belin were sitting under their bunker's awning, and I joined them. John was our recently arrived squad leader and Ron was another of my squad members.

John was dark-haired with a solid frame and a darkly handsome, Burt Reynolds, kind of face. Ron was tall and lanky with straight brown hair and a softly angled even-featured face that could appear pouty, or maybe rebellious, but the thing that stood out to me were his thoughtful brown eyes that didn't miss much. John had somehow gotten a bottle of whiskey to the LZ and we found an unoccupied interior bunker and sat shirtless under the semi-cloudy sky, passing the bottle and telling each other about ourselves. John talked sports, girls, and cars, and all the while his socially alert eyes were weighing Ron and me, probably wondering whether we were the guys he'd want to get close to.

When John dozed off I asked Ron about his family. He told me they had a home near Washington DC and that his father was a retired military officer who held a senior position in the State Department. I'd never expected that the son of a politically connected family would end up as a grunt in the jungle, and I asked him straight out how that had happened. He said that he'd enlisted, and then, as if the two were somehow connected, he told me that his father had never been to war.

"He would have gone," he said, "but it never worked out and he always felt shorted."

A little later he added, "He's good at everything he does. I'd bring girls home and they'd end up talking about my dad. He just does things better than anyone else."

Those could have been the words of a proud son speaking of his father but Ron hadn't voiced them in that tone, and I was sure they weren't when he turned to me with a sad and introspective look on his face and said, "I never could do anything right."

My father's approval meant far more to me than anyone's but I'd never felt I'd needed to do something heroic to make him proud of me. In many ways it was just the opposite. I remembered an incident after one of my high school football games when I hadn't played well and we'd lost. My crowd-averse dad had always departed the stadium before the games had ended, but that night I'd been walking off the field feeling miserable and a shape had materialized on my right. I'd turned my head and seen my dad merging his path with mine, and without breaking stride he'd thrown an arm across my shoulder pads and said with a grin, "Hell, Bucky, everybody has a bad game sometimes." He'd peeled away before I'd had a chance to reply but from that moment my playing poorly and our losing that game hadn't seemed important.

Ron's dad was clearly a remarkably successful provider and mine had often struggled to provide some of the basic things in life, but I knew I'd been the one who'd grown up lucky. I wanted to tell Ron that he deserved better but he was sitting across from me with his face averted and I didn't think he'd want me to know how hurt he felt, so I changed the subject.

Before dark, Ron and I met up with about a dozen of our 3rd Platoon guys who were sitting in a circle on the dirt of the perimeter road. Two of them scooted apart to make space for us, and we sat and talked until full dark. When the LZ quieted a couple of matches flamed yellow and red-lit dots began floating in opposite directions around the circle. The scent of burning weed carried on the still-heated air, and then the sibilant sounds of air being drawn through pursed lips and the whooshing exhalations of long-held breaths came, sometimes followed by hacking coughs. The burning ends of the joints glowed brighter and dimmer on their start and stop paths through the darkness, like two fireflies wandering our circle and landing on each of us one by one. A few of us weren't smoking the weed but every one of us accepted the joints and each of us ceremoniously, maybe even ritualistically, passed them on to the next man in line. The serious tokers were tracking the progress of the red-lit joints, and if someone held a joint too long or tried to double-toke there were drawn-out laments of, "Hey maaaan, doan Bogart that joint!" which invariably drew giggles from out of the dark.

After the weed had made a couple of laps we played a game they called, "Bullshit!" It started with someone selecting a letter, and then each next player in the circle had to offer a next letter that could be used to spell a word without actually completing a word. The first two letters didn't matter, but beginning with the third letter the next player could call "Word!" if he thought the letters had spelled a word, or he could call "Bullshit!" if he thought the sequence of letters couldn't be used to spell a word. The darkness hid our facial expressions so all of us listened intently for any stumbling submissions of letters or subtle voice inflections that might indicate confidence, indecision, or bluffs. Boldly presented letter combinations that made no sense were greeted with spontaneous bursts of laughter but other times it wasn't that clear, and spirited disputes would arise concerning the correctness of a word's spelling or whether the proffered word was legitimate. If the bickering lasted too long the New York-accented voice of Barry Frost would often chime in, and his judgment was invariably accepted.

As the night progressed the letters came more slowly, especially from the heavy tokers, and the game trailed off. Those of us who weren't stoned talked and the stoners listened quietly, apparently content to simply share company with the rest of us. When shadowy forms began walking or stumbling off into the night I climbed to my feet and walked the road back to my hooch.

There were other diversions but mostly I had time to think about what was awaiting me when we went out again. I'd seen how easy it was to get killed but I'd hardly learned anything about how to stay alive, and I'd look out at the lines of distant vegetation and wonder about the enemy out there. I wanted to know everything about them; what they looked like, how they interacted with each other, what they believed, how they lived, what their tactics were, and even what they ate, and I didn't know where to find answers. The only Vietnamese people I'd been around were the three Vietnamese Kit Carson Scouts on the LZ with us. Two of them were so guarded they appeared timid and the third was just the opposite.

His name was Buc, pronounced "boo" with a "k" at the end. He was older than the other scouts, probably in his thirties, and he was reputedly a mercenary who'd fought for both sides of the war. Buc was shorter than most of us but nothing about him seemed small. His pronounced jaw muscles framed a hard-angled face and his eyes were cold and challenging, looking past most as though they were insignificant. I'd seen him bark harsh-sounding Vietnamese words at the other scouts and they'd responded meekly, maybe even fearfully, and it wasn't just the other scouts that walked carefully around Buc. I'd see eyes following him when he passed some of us by, the eyes of men who recognized strength. I didn't know anything about Vietnamese culture but the manifestations of male aggressiveness are universal and I'd sensed the danger in Buc at first sight. He must have seen something in me too, weighing me the way the tough guys who'd hung out in the Pine Street parking lot had, and then moving on.

I'd later appreciate something that Buc had given me; a thing that would help me survive. I hadn't been able to construct a mental image of the shadowy NVA soldiers secreted in the jungle, but after seeing Buc I visualized them with cold and brutal faces…the faces of men who knew a hell of a lot more about the jungle and killing than I did, and the kind of men that I could never, ever, dare to underestimate…deadly men like Buc.

After weeks of waiting my mail caught up with me. I had a letter from Johnny Ciulla telling me that he'd dropped out of radio school and he'd be on his way to Vietnam soon. One letter was from my mom, and my sister Evelyn had sent one enclosing a picture of the baby I'd so much wanted to meet before I'd left. She was a girl, and Evelyn and her husband David had named her Stephanie. I smiled at the picture of her cute little face, and then I slipped her picture opposite the one of Barbara that I kept in the alligator-skin wallet my dad had given me. I received a packet of letters from Barbara too. She'd written one every day, telling me about people we knew and the part-time jobs she was working to put herself through Chico State College.

One of her letters told me about her friend Loretta. Loretta was the twin sister of Barbara's best friend, Floretta, and Barbara had boarded with their family when her mom and stepdad had moved to Washington. Loretta was the quieter of the twins and everyone had been happy when she'd fallen in love and married Don Dunn. Don had recently graduated from the Army's Officer's Candidate School and a few weeks ago he'd been sent to Vietnam, and Barbara had written that Don had been killed in combat and they'd just returned his body to Loretta and their unborn child. Those people were real to me, and I tried to shut that news out of my mind as quickly as I could, thankful that I hadn't left a wife or a child back home to suffer the agonizing heartbreak that Don's death had left behind him. *Had Barbara been warning me to be careful?* I wasn't sure, but I wished I hadn't known.

My thoughts turned to my family. *Was it hot enough that the thumpity-thumpeting swamp cooler with the bad bearing would be running all night? Had my dad gotten work or was he struggling by on unemployment again?* I pictured my ancient grandmother rocking in the late afternoon waiting for the day's heat to dissipate. She'd have opened the cabin's living room door and windows and she'd be looking out through the window that faced the river and the hanging cable bridge, a bridge that no one had crossed in days. I had a memory of her standing on the other side of the Trinity River hiding her tears when I'd said goodbye and I wondered, *if I make it home will she still be alive?* I'd had that poignant thought before but it didn't tug at my emotions as strongly now. *Was it that way for the people back home? Was the hole I'd left in their lives already closing?*

I wrote letters to Barbara, my mom, and Evelyn, but I didn't have much to say. The embarrassing truth was that my letters could have been condensed to, "*The weather's hot. Looking forward to hearing from you. How's everyone? I'm just fine. Miss you. It's real quiet here.*"

That evening I reread Barbara's letters. I pictured her eyes reaching into mine the way they sometimes had and I wondered, *would she meet someone else?* I didn't like the way that made me feel so I walked the perimeter road to our guard bunker, climbed the platform, and looked out at the northeastern slopes of the mountain that rose so proudly above the flat jungle. It was so close I could have walked through the grasslands that extended to its base in an hour or two, and then I'd have climbed that green-carpeted mountainside to its sun-yellowed rocky summit, my legs carrying me higher with powerful thrusts the way I'd climbed so many higher mountains back home. I pictured myself sitting alone on its peak gazing out over the hundreds of square kilometers of jungle that extended to the north, east, and west of it, awed at how vast and exotic it was. But this wasn't Trinity. Deadly NVA soldiers were dug in on that mountain's slopes, and I scanned the lush green side of the Black Virgin wondering how many narrowed NVA eyes might be staring back at the wire-enclosed compound that was LZ Grant.

Sugar Bear's Radio

I had a history with a soldier in my squad named Lairn Schmidt that was the foundation of a relationship that would extend through many perilous months. It had started with an incident when I'd first arrived at the company, and I'd almost forgotten about it the day he sashayed toward our bunker carrying the little transistor radio he'd picked up somewhere. It was our only source of music and during our stay on the LZ he'd rested it on a sandbag outside his bunker so we could listen to its tinny speaker broadcast music from the Armed Forces Radio Station. He'd packed it through the jungle and back to the LZ again but this time its tiny earphones were piping music to his ears, and his ears only. To make it unmistakably clear that he was deliberately cutting us off from his music he'd sauntered by earlier with the same smirk on his face.

We all knew it was an act of revenge for some real or imagined slight but his flaunting behaviors were so obviously intended to stir our outrage that no one had given him the satisfaction of demanding an explanation.

Jay had finally had enough, and as Lairn walked nearer Jay yelled at him to take off his earphones so the rest of us could listen.

Without an instant's hesitation Lairn spun to face us and snapped.

"I'm tired of gettin screwed. You can all **go fuck yourselfs!**"

"What are you talkin' about?" someone asked.

"Why don't you go ask that fucking dink, John, and that FNG, Ed!" he sneered.

I knew then that it was about the shit burning detail. The long-standing practice in my platoon was that the FNGs, "funny, or fuckin, new guys," would be given the least desirable details. Lairn had come to the company a couple of weeks before I had but John had been assigning him the nasty "shit burning details." Lairn hadn't been happy about that, and he'd started complaining that I was the FNG and I should get those details. John couldn't dispute that so he'd sent me with Sugar Bear to learn the detail.

The thought of burning shit repulsed me but I had wanted to know more about Lairn. He had blue eyes and ringlets of dishwater-blond hair, and he was the only still-chubby guy I'd seen in our company. That made him stand out a little, but what really distinguished him was his churlish attitude. I'd seen him erupt at the slightest of provocations, real or imagined, lashing out with, "*Fuck you, you dink*," or "*fuck that dink*," retorts, and then stalking angrily away. I'd asked Jay and Sam about him, and they'd lit up and called him, "a chickenshit asshole." And it wasn't just Jay and Sam, Lairn was universally disliked and he'd isolated himself like a silent and frowning loner who didn't care what anyone thought about him. I wasn't sure about that. When John had told me to go on the detail with him a look that had crossed Lairn's face that had made me suspect he was glad for the company. He'd quickly replaced it with a frown and smirked, "You'll be the one gittin screwed now!" but the gloating had been so little-kid-nasty that I'd had to smile.

That morning I'd watched Lairn use a long pole to drag two half-barrels filled with sloshing human waste out from beneath the open-air, wooden-planked seats. When the containers had cleared the latrine, he'd poured diesel fuel into the stinking mess, and when he'd dropped a match in it the diesel had flamed up. We'd kept shifting positions to escape the swirling black smoke until the diesel fuel had burned out, and then Lairn had pole-pushed the barrels back under the latrine. The detail had been as disgusting as I'd feared but as I'd watched Lairn work I'd been reminded of the chubby "Sugar Bear" character depicted in the *Sugar Crisp* cereal commercials who was always trying to steal a bowl of sugar crisp from some clever little kids to the tune of "Can't get enough of that Sugar Crisp, Sugar Crisp, can't get enough of that Sugar Crisp." Sugar Bear's cereal pilfering schemes had invariably been foiled by the clever little cartoon kids but the cartoon Sugar Bear had always remained irrepressibly happy and optimistic. The blondish-haired, square-faced, and slightly chubby Lairn I'd watched burning shit on our desolate LZ could have been a caricature of the cartoon Sugar Bear, and the contrast between that character and Lairn's propensity to erupt in profane outbursts at the slightest provocation had amused me. I'd had to smother my laughter whenever Lairn had said something snarky, which was often, and I'd managed that until Lairn had gleefully reminded me that I'd be the one "gettin screwed now." He'd been so delighted at that prospect that I'd broken out laughing, and when Lairn had stared like there was something wrong with me I'd told him that he looked like the Sugar Bear on the Sugar Crisp cereal commercials and that from now on I'd be calling him "Sugar Bear." He'd snapped back, "Fuck you, you dink," but I'd thought he was considering it.

After that detail, I'd asked Ron Belin what he knew about Lairn. Ron had told me that Lairn had come to the company with one other guy and a few days later the two of them had been sent to man an observation post. They'd left the perimeter walking an arm's length apart, and when they'd gotten about 20 meters out there'd been a big explosion. He said the two of them had disappeared in a cloud of dust and smoke and Lairn had walked slowly out of it without a scratch on him but the guy beside him had been blown apart so completely that they'd had to pick up pieces to have something they could wrap in a poncho and send home to his family, including a fully severed leg. Maybe that's what had made him so churlish or maybe that's just who he was, but none of that mattered to me. I knew how it felt to be socially isolated and I'd already decided to befriend him.

That wasn't easy, and John hadn't helped when he'd assigned Sugar Bear the shit-burning detail again. Sugar Bear had snapped, "Why don't you send that fucking NG Ed?" and John had suggested that we "choose a number or something." We'd guessed numbers, and when John had announced that I'd won Sugar Bear had stormed off, red-faced and muttering curses. On our last day on the LZ Sugar Bear had insisted that John write the number down and John had scribbled something on a scrap of paper. We'd made our guesses and John had declared that I'd won. Sugar Bear had started to stomp off, and then he'd spun back and demanded angrily that John show him the paper. John had flashed the number too quickly for Sugar Bear to read and I'd realized that he'd cheated for me. I'd told Sugar Bear that I hadn't known and started off to work the detail, but Sugar Bear had jumped in front of me and snapped, "Fuck you, you dink! I'll do it my ownself." I'd tried to push past him a couple of times but he'd continued stepping in front of me, snapping that he'd do it himself. I should have insisted but it was a disgusting detail, and I hadn't.

I'd been sure the incident had moved me to the top of his, *guys I hate*, list, but I hadn't expected him to hold a grudge for weeks, plan his revenge, and make everyone suffer for it. So, yes, I knew it was about Sugar Bear getting stuck with the shit-burning details the last time we'd been on the LZ, but when the others turned to me with questioning looks I said innocently, "Who knows?"

A red-faced Sugar Bear yelled, "Fuck you!" and stomped off.

The next morning, Sugar Bear sauntered by with the radio pretending that he didn't know we existed. I said a friendly-voiced good morning, and he stopped dead in his tracks and glared at me hatefully. When I didn't react, he screwed his face up tighter. I wanted to keep a poker face but the look he'd pasted on his face was too much and I burst out laughing.

"You fucking dink!" he yelled, and he spun back toward his bunker and stomped away again.

One of the guys yelled at his back that he was an asshole, and I turned to him and said soberly, "Sugar Bear's OK. He's just Sugar Bear being Sugar Bear."

A few hours later the sounds of Sugar Bear's radio sounded from outside his bunker. I didn't know why he'd decided to relent but I knew it didn't include me. He made a point of telling me that he hadn't forgotten, "You gettin me screwed," and then for reasons known only to him he kept working the shit-burning detail without being asked. None of that seemed to moderate his other behaviors. He deliberately shunned me, but he continued to lash out at the others in our squad. That wasn't doing him any favors but I kept reminding them that he was "just Sugar Bear being Sugar Bear" and before long some of them repeating the refrain that he was "just Sugar Bear being Sugar Bear." Sugar Bear never acknowledged that he liked the nickname but he never objected to it. I think that oddly appropriate nickname was helping him find his place in our squad, and he deserved that. He was the most colorful personality of us all and his harmless contrariness and snarky antics afforded a welcome reprieve from the hours of LZ monotony…and those hours stretched long.

During the hot and humid daylight hours our trips to the mess tent or the shower were among the few things that could entice us to get moving. We usually got some relief from the heat after dark, but at night our only source of light was an occasional smoking candle behind the blanket-draped doorway of a dank bunker. We could talk, but nothing much changed on the LZ and there wasn't much to discuss that we hadn't already covered several times. We might have found more to do if we'd interacted with the men posted on the LZ, but I was beginning to realize that anyone who hadn't ventured outside the wire was virtually invisible to most of the guys in my company. I don't think that bothered them. I imagine they viewed us as uncouth, clannish, and uncivil, observations that I thought hit pretty close to the mark. The upshot was that most of the time we simply ate, slept, worked a few light details, and pulled guard duty while we waited out our handful of listless days before they sent us back to the jungle.

The next afternoon I was sitting shirtless in the shade. A blowfly was buzzing me and I leaned my shoulders against my pack, relaxed my arm, and waited for the persistent fly to buzz near. I was thinking that after dark I'd bait a blasting cap with C-ration food and try to ambush one of the red-eyed rats that brazenly faced off with us at times, seemingly aware of the caution their sharp teeth warranted. I'd stretch the wire to the blasting cap and when the rat tugged at the bait, I'd squeeze the clacker, and then…

Happy Together by The Mamas and The Papas came on Sugar Bear's radio and memories flooded in; the rain rattling on my car's roof, her face, the way she smiled, the way her kisses lingered, and later that night holding the phone to my ear and listening to her sleep-breathing on the other end of the line.

The fly buzzed near and my left hand snatched it out of the air. Its wings beat furiously in the hollow of my grip, and I opened my fingers and let it go. Maybe I didn't want fly parts smeared inside my hand, or maybe I didn't feel like crushing anything then.

The next morning Sugar Bear's radio played a song I'd never heard...

In the year seventy-five ten
if God's acomin'
he oughta' make it by then.

The song ended with the singer wondering if man will survive, a feeling I could relate to.

A month after I'd arrived in Vietnam, we'd broken free of the earth and set foot on a piece of the heavens, and all the while we were butchering each other as savagely as we had back in the dark ages. That dissonance was real to me, and the song's mournful melody, bleak lyrics, and allusion to senseless destruction resonated. I sat silently in the muggy heat, looking out at the distant line of the jungle and thinking about the world we'd left behind and the world we'd arrived to and wondering how the same civilization could foster both. I loitered near Sugar Bear's bunker for several more hours, hoping that the little radio would hold out long enough for me to listen to the words again. It did, and it seemed that the music captured the senselessness, despondency, and hell-bent destruction that pervaded this place better than words ever could.

That evening the batteries in Sugar Bear's radio weakened and the speakers began whispering too softly to be heard. I'd have regretted that a day or two earlier, but not now. The little radio's music had been pulling my mind back to a civilized time and place and I didn't want that. I'd lived for years internalizing the realities, norms, and standards of that relatively safe existence but this wasn't that place. Life or death could hinge on an instant's hesitation here, and I didn't need to have one part of my mind planted in that gentle world and the other planted in this deadly one. I didn't reason that out, but on that last afternoon on the LZ I think I knew that I needed to adapt every corner of my mind to the reality of this place, and this place only.

Chapter 6

Beyond the Wire Again

We filed through the LZ's gate with fully loaded packs on our backs and weapons in our hands. Ten or twelve Huey choppers were on the pad with their engines humming and their blades rotating lazily in the early morning light. All were open-bodied *slicks*, (choppers with their interiors emptied except for their door gunner and their guns.) We climbed into their open bellies and their turbines began to whine. Their blades strummed quicker and quicker and when the noise was almost deafening the thick-bodied choppers started rising into the sky like a covey of fat quail flushed out of a grassy meadow. They leveled out high above the LZ, and I sat in the open doorway with the cool, high-altitude air buffeting my body looking down on a vast expanse of green-blanketed jungle. No signs of human habitation showed but the NVA were down there somewhere, hidden beneath the canopied roof of the jungle.

When I felt the bird start easing lower I gripped the chopper's door frame, braced my feet on the skids, and leaned out to scan the lush jungle that was streaming beneath us. We dropped to just above the canopy and skimmed the treetops to a small meadow. Our chopper circled, and when our turn came it darted down and hovered just above the ground. I tossed my pack out, stepped off the skid, and plunged through the wind-whipped grasses. I landed on flexed knees, caught my balance, and hurried out from under the churning blades. A gust of rotor-driven wind pressed against my back and I glanced over my shoulder and saw my unburdened chopper leaping effortlessly into the air.

Several of my squad members were at the tree line, and I hurried over and took a knee between Ron and Sam. The sun's rays were filtering through the bamboo that lined the meadow's edge, creating dappled patches of light a few steps ahead of me. Beyond that everything was shadowed. Our noisy arrival had shocked the jungle into a cautious silence, and the only sounds were the rustlings of our movements and the droning and humming of insects. That silence felt slightly ominous, and it wasn't just the silence that seemed spooky; the tight faces and subdued movements of the nearby men were eerily reminiscent of frightened victims depicted in horror films. I guessed I was making too much of the moment, and then I looked into the shadowed depths and reminded myself that at any instant death could reach through some hidden avenue and I might never see it coming.

I folded my body deeper into the curvature of the earth and waited quietly with those silent grim-faced men until a whispered chorus of *saddle ups* made its way softly along the fringes of the meadow. We climbed to our feet, strapped on our packs, and began filtering onto the machete-slashed path the point platoon had cut. They'd forged a trail through 250 or 300 meters of untracked jungle but the spacing between us took up much of that distance and I was only about 75 meters from the meadow when the men ahead of me slowed to a stop. I unsaddled my pack, removed my bandoleers, and settled to the ground beside a large-leafed bush. I felt tender where my bandoleers had been rubbing against my chest. There was a dark spot on my shirt there, and I pulled my shirt aside and saw that my upper chest wound was bleeding. When he'd stitched me up the doctor had pulled my flesh and skin together to compensate for the dead flesh he'd cut out and my scar was much smaller than the initial gash. I didn't know if it was trying to stretch longer again but a corner of it had opened up and it was leaking blood. I guessed that the inside stitches were holding because most of it looked intact, and when word came to saddle up I repositioned my bandoleers, realigned my left shoulder strap so they wouldn't pull directly on the wound, and for the rest of the day I followed Jay: stopping when he did and moving when he did, just one link in a chain of silent men slipping down the trails the point squads hacked through the jungle.

When we stopped for the night the others started unpacking their claymores and setting them outside the perimeter. I carried mine to a ground-hugging plant about 15-20 meters beyond the perimeter, and I anchored the claymore's tiny tripod legs under the bush with the claymore's deadly half-moon crescent facing out to the jungle. I rearranged some leaves to camouflage its face, inserted the fuse, and let the detonation wire unroll behind me as I made my way back. When I reached the perimeter I placed the unattached detonator near the end of the detonation wire and searched for a place to bed down. I found a gap between two bushes. I used our squad's machete to open it up a little wider, and then I tugged my rubber air mattress out of my pack and started blowing air into it. I got a little lightheaded but I finally got it inflated. I surveyed the ground for crawling insects. A few bugs were crawling but I didn't see anything that looked dangerous, so I slid my air mattress into the gap and spread my nylon poncho liner over the air mattress, and my first jungle bed was ready.

I pulled a chunk of C-4 explosive out of one of the side pockets of my pack and pinched off a little piece to heat my C-ration meal. It had the consistency of silly putty and it felt slightly greasy as I rolled it between my thumb and fingers to create a ball the size of a tiny pebble. I brushed aside some debris and placed the ball of C-4 in the small patch of bare dirt that I'd cleared. I punched a circle of tiny cuts along the rim of my lima bean C-ration can using my paperclip-thin inch-long P-38 can opener. I left a section of the lid uncut, and I pried the cut section of the lid up and bent it back to serve as a handle. I had to hold the flame of my cigarette lighter against the C-4 for several seconds before it got hot enough to ignite, and then it sputtered and started spitting out a hissing blue flame like a mini torch.

I rocked the can of lima beans back and forth over the flame as it heated, and then I ate the lima beans with the plastic spoon I'd packed. I pulled the spoon through the bottom of the can several times to make sure I'd gotten every last drop, and then I sawed open a can of peaches and a tiny tin of pound cake. I ate a couple of bites of peaches to create some space and then I stirred in the airy pound cake. The combination tasted like peach cobbler and I ate every drop. I licked my spoon clean, and then I tucked the spoon, the lighter and the little can opener back into one of the pockets of my pack and set the empty C-ration cans under the bush where they wouldn't get stepped on. I was craving more food but I knew that if I ate more now I'd go hungrier later. I uncapped one of my canteens and pulled a mouthful of water slowly into my mouth. I let the water linger before I swallowed, and then I tipped the canteen back for another mouthful, recapped the canteen, and placed it on my pack.

My sweat-dampened shirt was hanging heavily on my shoulders but the bugs were intent on making a meal out of me so I kept it on. I was waiting for them to thin out after dark but after enduring a few minutes of their buzzing and biting I gave up and rubbed the army's chemical-smelling insect repellent over my face, head, and exposed skin. It burned my chaffed and bite-irritated skin but most of the bugs stopped landing.

I'd seen guys passing through the perimeter to shovel over a clump of dirt, defecate in the hole, and shovel dirt on top of it to hold down the stench, and I pulled some packets of toilet paper out of my pack and passed word that I was exiting the perimeter. I heard *"Man out, man out"* whispered along the near line of our perimeter, and I passed through it and made my way to a semi-private place. Being outside the perimeter with my pants pulled down around my knees was really spooky. I'd heard stories of men being killed with their pants down, and I'd heard of one similarly occupied grunt who'd been attacked by a tiger. His buddies had reportedly heard his screams and when the tiger had leaped away with him in its mouth they'd fired in the tiger's direction. The tiger had dropped that guy but I'd added tigers to the list of the ways I could get killed in Vietnam, and I scanned the nearby foliage and listened for stealthy sounds with my M-16 resting across my knees.

I returned through the perimeter, leaned back against my pack, and surveyed our section of the perimeter as far as the thick growth allowed. Gramps was cupping his hand to shield the glow of his lighter as he lit a cigarette. Seconds later his smoke drifted to my nose, the scent so distance-diluted that it was almost pleasant. Jay and Sam were sitting side by side a few steps beyond Gramps, facing out and not talking. I caught a glimpse of Big Jack farther down the perimeter, bareheaded with his butt resting on his inverted helmet. He was looking down at something, maybe a letter. I turned the other way. Sugar Bear was lying back against his pack, still ruddy faced from the stifling heat and carrying too much body weight; grimly facing this alone and probably hating the world even more now, especially me. An unseen man whispered "Man out," to warn that another of us was stepping outside the perimeter. I relayed the warning and Gramp's whispering voice passed it on.

In the early night I lay on my back looking up at the leaf and limb-etched moonlit sky. I had a lot to think about but I was so tired and muscle-sore after our pack-weighted and bug-bitten trek that I couldn't stay awake. I turned to my stomach and the air coursed through my air mattress with a loud *"whoosh"* that startled my ears. I was thinking that this would be the first night I'd sleep in the jungle, and the next thing I knew Sugar Bear was ungently nudging my foot to awaken me for my turn on watch. The moon had dipped below the horizon and the night was very dark. I felt my way to the edge of the perimeter and found a place to sit, and then I rested my rifle across my knees and listened for the soft sounds a creeping enemy might make. There was no berm in front of me, no concertina-wired barrier, and no open areas lit by occasional flares, just a darkened mass of thick foliage filled with exotic scents and sounds that were new to me. Throughout the day my eyes, ears, and nose had been frustrated by the novelty of the jungle, and that night I did something I'd repeat during the days and nights that lay ahead; I let my mind replay the day's sights, sounds, and smells, not focusing in on them but just letting them flow freely to whatever place my instinctive brain wanted to store them, hoping that maybe they'd one day coalesce into wisdoms that would help me to survive in a place where the tiniest inkling might be the one thing that could keep me alive.

The illuminated dials of the night duty watch that we passed from hand to hand signaled the end of my shift, and I woke Ron, transferred the watch, and climbed back atop my air mattress. The air swooshed through it again, loud in my ear, and someone sleeping nearby turned and murmured something. *Was he dreaming of home or was he dreaming of this place?* I breathed in the heavy scents that were so different from the sweet dry aromas of summer's sunbaked grasses back home, and I fell asleep remembering the times I'd slid thirstily off the steep slopes of the sun-heated Trinity mountains and sucked in deep gulps of the cool, crystal-clear water from the river that flowed beside the cabin my grandfather had built so many years ago…the place on the other side of the world that I called home.

Chu Hoi

In the morning the near jungle was cautiously quiet but calls were echoing from the distance. Most were melodious but a few were clamorous. *Were they early morning boisterous calls or were they alarmed?* I listened intently, feeling for patterns and internalizing the cadences and timbres of their habitual cries and hoots.

Others started retrieving their claymores, and I crossed through the perimeter to gather mine. As I neared the bush where I'd set it my eyes were drawn to a mark in the dirt that hadn't been there when I'd placed it. Instantly wary, I dropped to a knee and searched through the foliage for any flickers of movement or suspicious outlines. I didn't find any, and I moved up close. There was a single distinct print and a line of pressed humus and disturbed debris that unveiled the path of the man who'd created it. I sight-tracked his line of travel as far as I could, and then I listened beyond that. It felt empty there, but the man who'd left that track still felt deadly, like in a movie where a monster rustles the doorknob and scratches at the windows, and then everything gets still and it's even scarier because the monster's lurking out there somewhere and you don't know where.

I'd heard that the NVA's *Ho Chi Minh* sandals were cut from the treads of tires, but the tire-track impression printed on the floor of the jungle still seemed absurdly out of place in a stretch of primeval jungle that had appeared so untouched by man. I glanced back at our perimeter just 20 steps distant. He'd have known that one false footfall could have ended him and his heart must have been hammering. *What had he intended? Had he discovered the claymore and lost his nerve? Had he been testing himself? What could I learn from him?* The sign he'd left couldn't answer those questions, and I retrieved the claymore and rerolled my wire as I walked back to the perimeter, telling only Ron.

We were going to the site of a recent B-52 bomb strike to make a damage assessment, and then the battalion radioed that an NVA soldier had surrendered in a nearby section of jungle. He'd said that he knew the location of a big weapons and rice cache, and they were sending choppers to fly us there. The lead platoon immediately turned and cut a path to a clearing. A short time later the choppers flew in and started dipping into the meadow to pick us up. My turn came, and I hurried into the clearing, shoved my pack and rifle into the waiting chopper, and pulled myself aboard. By chance, I'd boarded the chopper that was carrying the NVA who'd surrendered, (the "*Chu Hoi*"), along with an interpreter and an American officer. I'd pictured NVA soldiers with the cold eyes and aggressive arrogance of our scout, Buc, but the slightly built NVA sitting across from me was soft featured and he kept his head down deferentially. I watched above the reach of his lowered eyes wondering, *Why had he surrendered? Who was he betraying? Could we trust him?*

We arrived at an area of jungle that was characterized by grasses and low brush and the other choppers circled higher while ours dropped lower and began zig-zagging about 100 meters above the foliage. Communicating through the interpreter, the Chu Hoi directed us on a wandering course above a succession of bamboo thickets and grassy patches. He pointed down several times, and we descended and hovered near ground level while he leaned out and inspected the terrain. Each time he shook his head "*no,*" and we moved on. After yet another of those instances the interpreter told the officer that the Chu Hoi was saying that everything looked different from the air and he didn't know if he'd be able to locate the cache. The officer's face darkened instantly, and in a voice thick with warning he growled at the interpreter to tell the Chu Hoi that he'd better find the cache and "**it had better be soon!**"

The Chu Hoi had been casting furtive side glances at the officer when he should have been scanning for the cache. I was pretty sure he wasn't going to lead us to anything until he pointed down emphatically and the interpreter relayed that he'd found the site. Our chopper settled in the grassy area he'd identified, and when we climbed out of the bird I followed the Chu Hoi with my thumb resting on my M-16's safety as he poked around the edges of the meadow. I never saw any tracks, lines of foot-pressed grasses, or trails that would indicate an NVA presence, and after a short search the translator relayed that this wasn't the site.

We lifted off and continued our low-level aerial search until the choppers ran low on fuel, and then they dropped us in another meadow and we waited in the muggy heat while they flew somewhere to refuel. The chopper I boarded when they came back wasn't carrying the Chu Hoi, and my chopper circled high above his until we ran low on fuel again. They must have decided that the Chu Hoi couldn't, or wouldn't, locate the alleged cache because the choppers deposited us in another meadow and hammered noisily away. As we waited for the point squad to cut another stretch of trail I was remembering the dark look on the officer's face when he'd warned the Chu Hoi that he'd better find the cache. I didn't know what he'd been threatening, but if I'd been that Chu Hoi I'd be dreading what was coming because that guy hadn't been bluffing.

Arc Light

We moved a short distance and circled up for the night. On my turn on watch beams of moonlight were penetrating through the uneven canopy and bathing patches of the jungle floor in a pale-yellow light. The stealthy NVA who'd left his sandal print beside my claymore was on my mind as I scanned the moonlit areas for movements and shapes and listened into the shadows for the sounds of a deadly creeper. When the jungle stayed quiet my anticipation of a lurking menace lessened and I relaxed into the silence. Midway through my watch I snapped alert, shocked that I'd started to doze. I reminded myself that the NVA could be creeping in but I had to struggle to stay awake.

My watch ended, and I woke Sam, crawled onto my air mattress, pulled my silken poncho liner across my chest, positioned my M-16 at my side with the barrel angled toward my feet, and fell asleep almost immediately. I awoke to the sounds of men climbing off the jungle earth. The dim vegetation, the scattered packs, and the rumpled figures of my rising squad members seemed jarringly surreal. I lay still for a moment and then I crawled off my air mattress, pulled the tab to let the air out, stuffed it and my blanket into my pack, and ate a C-ration, and after I dry brushed my teeth I was ready to move.

I'd been told that we'd reach the arc light site today, and some of the more experienced guys had been saying that if the bombs had missed their targets we might walk into a nest of NVA bunkers. It was my platoon's day on point and one of our squads led out with the rest of our platoon and company trailing in one long column. We traveled about an hour and arrived at a patch of jungle that was littered with torn branches and mud. The foliage ahead was even more ripped and shredded. Globs of mud were clinging to broken limbs and branches and thuds and plops were sounding randomly as lumps of mud and debris dropped to the ground. Beyond the torn section I could see lines of sunlight reaching unimpeded to the floor of the jungle. The point squad started heading there and the rest of us followed, stepping over shattered limbs and downed vegetation to reach the periphery of the blast area.

The bombs had burrowed deeply into the earth, and when they'd detonated they'd blasted the overlying dirt and vegetation high into the air. All of that had collapsed back to earth and created a tangled mass of torn logs, tree limbs, and foliage that stretched 20 meters or more from the rims of the overlapping craters. The rest of whatever had once existed near the epicenters of the explosions had congealed into the deep stew of watery muck that lay within the craters, and I stood in the thick air filled with the scent of explosives, torn earth, and ruined vegetation looking at the skeletonized lines of a few partially submerged limbs and pieces of brush extending just above the surface of that mucky mess, reaching up as though they were striving to break free of it. I felt I was witnessing a malevolent crime against the earth, and I was only seeing the surface, who knew what lay buried in that festering wound?

We continued bending, climbing, and crawling through the tangled mass of blasted vegetation to assess the destruction the blasts had created. It was impossible to know what had existed at the epicenter of the multiple craters we were paralleling but we waded mid-calf deep along the edges searching for any signs of what the bombs had destroyed. On the outside edge of one we discovered some shallow depressions that had been walled with pieces of logs. There was a suspicious-looking mound of dirt there and Lt. Jones told us to dig into it. I was dreading the possibility that I'd puncture a decomposing body when I took my turn. I didn't, but one of the others dug into something. I was anticipating the reek of death, but when he cleared the dirt away we found a plastic-wrapped cache of semi-automatic rifles smeared with grease.

Another squad wasn't as lucky. They dug up some freshly buried corpses, and I looked down the long path of devastation, wondering who'd buried the rifles and the bodies. I thought back on the surreptitious glances of the Chu Hoi who'd said he'd lead us to the alleged NVA cache. *Had that been a ruse to delay us so the NVA could get here ahead of us? Were the NVA sophisticated enough to manipulate us? Were they familiar enough with our thinking and our likely responses to react that quickly?* Maybe not, but the day we'd spent searching for that phantom cache had given them more time to clean up whatever had survived the B-52s' bombs.

We left whatever was buried at the arc light site and spent the rest of the day cutting through a short section of intact jungle. When I squatted with Jay and Sam a few minutes before dark Jay glanced around to ensure no one would overhear, and then he leaned in close and whispered that a squad in another platoon had seen a few dazed NVA soldiers with blood oozing out of their ears stumbling down a trail they'd been watching. He asked me to "keep it quiet," because they'd allowed the "poor bastards" to pass by. I pictured the scene. *Had our guys shown them mercy because the shell-shocked NVA soldiers hadn't posed a threat? Had they done it to avoid a firefight that might have gotten some of them killed? Had they balked at killing another human being? What would I have done?* I didn't know, but if it was true then the shellshocked NVA soldiers who'd walked down that trail were all alive this evening and so were the guys who'd allowed them safe passage. It was hard to argue with that.

In the Column

In the morning we started moving through single and double-canopied patches of jungle led by point squads alternating turns forging trails through 250-300 meters of jungle. In some places the foliage was almost impossible to pass through without using a machete, but even when it wasn't the sections of trail that point squads created were called *cuts*. At the end of each cut the point squad's platoon would leapfrog up to the point squad, another squad would begin another cut, and the remainder of the company would link up with the tail end of the point platoon.

I was moving in the main column when the men ahead of me accordioned slightly and came to a stop. Ron was a few steps ahead of me, Jay was in front of Ron, and I could see Sam drifting back to wait out the break with Jay. There was a stir of movement from a vaguely shaped someone further up the trail but the foliage was so thick I couldn't make out who he was. I moved to the right of our trail and checked the ground for biting bugs or snakes. I didn't find any, and I settled into a sitting position, unstrapped my pack, let it drop free behind me, and tugged the back of my fatigue shirt from my sticky skin. The air that circulated against my sweat-slickened skin felt almost cool, and then a host of no-see-ums and mosquitoes homed in on me and I fumbled my bug juice out of my baggy pants pocket and slopped it on my face, my hair, the back of my hands, and the open-shirt-exposed areas of my chest.

It was like that all day, moving and stopping with no relief from the hot humid air, always grateful when I could shrug out of my pack and let the heat drain from my torso, eating the contents of a small C-ration tin for lunch and drinking a few swallows of water, constantly hungry, thirsty, and aware that deadly men could be laying hidden a stone's throw away. That's how miserable it was for those of us moving in the main column but we knew that the men cutting trail for us were enduring the greatest hardships and facing the greatest peril.

First Time on Point

I'd never gone out with a cutting squad. The day my platoon had been on point we'd moved to the arc light site and my squad hadn't walked point. That was going to change because tomorrow was another point day for our platoon and my squad would be alternating turns cutting trail. I'd been anticipating the experience from the day I'd been assigned to the infantry, I imagine every infantryman had and that most of us had been dreading it. We'd have been foolish if we hadn't. The long history of the infantry in Vietnam had made it unquestioningly clear that at any given moment the men who were most likely to die were the ones cutting trail and the man walking point was facing the greatest risk of death. That grim actuality formed the bedrock of a tenet of grunt lore that the average life expectancy of a point man who encountered the NVA was less than three seconds. I didn't know how they'd arrived at that number but every war story I'd heard of a grunt outfit walking into the NVA had started with words to the effect of, "That time when ----- got killed, or got wounded, on point." I was new to the jungle but I'd seen enough to know why that would be and I'd been turning it over in my mind; *What would it be like forging a path through the jungle with my squad, how would the animals react to the presence of a handful of us, how would we navigate the foliage, what could we do to lessen our risks, and how frightening would it be?*

The morning sun had risen, a few flies were droning and the mosquitoes were already buzzing. Our morning preparations were the same, eat, repack, and saddle up, and then it was my squad's turn to venture out and cut trail. I'd known that everyone except the M-60 gunner, the RTO, and the squad leader alternated turns walking point but I'd never pictured our easy-going, dope-smoking Gramps leading out. He had the first turn on point, and when he turned to the jungle his face was tight with fear, unmistakable palpable fear, maybe even terror. I told myself *everybody has to take their turn*, and then I stepped into the third-man-back slot and followed him into the panorama of greens and browns that stretched in every direction, including overhead.

I'd expected that we'd creep cautiously through the thick growth but Gramps never paused to listen or to peer ahead, and he only slowed when he had to cut a path through the foliage with the machete. The possibility that he'd lead us blindly into an ambush seemed very real and I kept searching the foliage in front of him for lethal enemies I was certain he wouldn't detect. They weren't there, and when we made it to the end of Gramp's cut he sank to the ground panting, his clothes sweat-soaked and his face ashen. Jay was next. He moved with a wooden-legged gait and he had a hollow look on his face that he didn't try to disguise. Sugar Bear turned a ghostly pale but he did it, tramping heavy-footed through the jungle with his jaw clenched and his chest heaving with his labored breaths. John had declared that I was too new to take a turn on point but I was certain I was as capable of identifying outlines and movements as those I'd followed and I didn't think it was fair to have the others shoulder my share of the risks. I told John that I wanted to take my turn, and when he nodded a thoughtful "OK" Ron moved up to walk backup for me.

I compass sighted along the azimuth they'd given us and took my first lead step into the shadowed jungle that loomed ahead. I'd many times envisioned doing that but I hadn't had any idea how all alone I'd feel or that the prospect of a violent death would strike me as intensely as it did. Those emotions were almost overwhelming, and then I took some deep breaths and started slipping from one piece of foliage to another. I was acutely aware that the jungle might erupt on any next step and I constantly scanned through the tangled webs of branches, leaves, and vines seeking any unnatural shapes or movements that weren't consistent with the stirrings generated by the slight breeze. I paused just short of a denser patch of thicketed growth and peered into it, listening for any threatening sounds. The host of biting bugs that were buzzing my head zoned in on me, and I moved on more quickly than I would have if the bugs hadn't been that bad, angling for seams I could use to work my way through the thicket quietly. I'd envisioned myself moving silently on point but the seams petered out and I had to push through vines and branches and step over, on, and under denser vegetation with an 80-pound pack riding on my back. It was miserably tiring work, and I was painfully aware that I was making far too much noise. And it wasn't just me, the men following me were negotiating the same obstacles and generating the same branch-snapping, foliage-brushing noises.

I rarely perspired heavily but the effort, the tension, and the stifling heat had me dripping with sweat. My thirst was raging, and I uncapped a canteen and took a generous swallow of water, not caring if I went dry later. The bugs continued their buzzing and biting and I moved ahead, trying to keep on the azimuth I'd been given without using the machete. I came to a patch of foliage I couldn't push through and I yielded to the jungle and started hacking a path through a maze of tangled vines and branches, acutely aware that the whacks and thuds that were echoing ahead would announce my presence and reveal my line of travel to deadly enemies who might be waiting in ambush.

I'd watched the others push through the jungle resignedly, accepting that if he was walking into an ambush he wouldn't detect it until he'd come too close to survive it. I didn't think I'd detect an ambush in time to survive it either but I wasn't willing to place my life solely in the hands of fate. I listened into the abnormally silent jungle that stretched ahead, hoping that its cautious silence was just a reaction to our noisy progress, and then I gathered my resolve and moved on. As I neared the end of the thicket I peered through the leaves and branches, searching for foreign shapes or movements in the thinner jungle that lay beyond it. I didn't detect anything, and I pushed through the thicket into foliage that I could negotiate more quietly. That felt safer, but I knew that our noises had carried far ahead and that any NVA lying in wait would know I was coming. They weren't, and I finished my miserable and demoralizing first turn on point uneventfully; an experience so frighteningly intense that every step of it seemed to have blurred into a heart-pounding haze of indistinct shapes and nerve-cringing noises.

That evening's dying light found us scattered on our night perimeter, our clothes damp with sweat, our gear littering the ground, and all of us squatting or sitting on the spongy leaf-littered earth eating end-of-day meals from C-ration cans. It could have been just another whispering end-of-day scene except that Sugar Bear's, Gramp's, and Jay's unguarded hands were trembling like wind-stirred leaves, the way my grandmother's age-blotched and palsied hands had fluttered as she'd rocked away the late evenings in her chair. There wasn't anything I could say to change that, and I leaned over my hissing C-4 flame and quartered away, pretending not to notice.

Lizard's Call

I had the first watch, and just short of nightfall I moved to the perimeter and settled in with my rifle resting across my lap. Minutes later the voices sounded just beyond our perimeter, close in and startlingly loud,

"FukYuuuuuuuu"

"FukYuuuu"

"FukYuuuuuuuuuuuuuuuuuu"

"FukYuuuu"

"FukYuuuuuuuuuu"

Heart pounding, I dropped flat on my stomach and searched for flickers of movements in the dim light that was filtering down from a sliver of a moon.

The long, trailing, and slightly accented intonations kept coming, one here and one there, sounding the way I thought taunting NVA voices would sound. I heard Big Jack whispering to someone that it was just lizards but I couldn't imagine lizards making such human-like calls, and I listened like a musician searching for a false note, marking their changing locations and trying to gauge whether they were coming closer. After about a half-hour the calls slowed to isolated *"Fuck Yu's,"* and then stopped.

At dawn I passed through the perimeter to where the calls had sounded. If the NVA had been there I'd have found prints or their leaf-disturbed trails in the rain-dampened earth, and when I didn't I accepted Big Jack's wisdom that it had, after all, been a gaggle of Vietnamese lizards telling us to go fuck ourselves…even the lizards.

Walking Point Again

Two days passed and it was another point day. As the light dawned the foliage turned a lighter shade of gray and then the natural hues of the jungle emerged. My squad members started crawling off their air mattresses and dismantling their poncho tents, but I lay nestled in the earth. The smell of urine wafted to my nose. I turned my head and saw Gramps pissing against a bush. That got me up.

Ron had the first turn walking point, and he moved like a hunted deer creeping through cover. He had deer eyes too, big and wide. Sam led out next, walking with his head turning alertly from side to side, and then it was my turn. The foliage was open enough for me to slip ahead quietly in places, and in other stretches of foliage I had to push through stickery vines that tugged and scratched at my clothes, my pack, and the exposed skin of my hands, neck, and face. I'd been determined to forgo the noisy machete but I had to hack my way through a tangled thicket that I couldn't sidestep. Some of its ropy vines were inches thick, and when I cut through them they bled bitter-smelling milky fluids. If I had to hack more than once their juices would splatter back and leave a sticky residue on my shirt, and when I reflexively wiped a stinging rivulet of sweat from my right eye with my shirt sleeve it felt like my eye had caught fire. I stopped to blink the irritant away and a host of mosquitoes attacked my face and neck. Half blinded, I reached into my pants pocket for my bug juice and rubbed so much of it on my arms, face, neck, and hair that the air reeked of it. It didn't deter the hungry bugs from buzzing my head but most of them stopped landing.

I ignored my blurry eye and moved on, judging distances through one eye as I machete-hacked my way ahead. My *Whack, whack, whip, whack, thunk*! sounds were echoing insanely loudly in the cautiously silent jungle that surrounded us, and I ignored the buzz-whirring bugs and paused to listen into the now-quiet jungle and peer through blurry eyes for anything that might signal an ambush. I found nothing, and I continued bending, pushing, and cutting my way through the thicket of poking, pricking, and tugging foliage that was filled with biting bugs. I was acutely aware that my repetitive cutting was broadcasting my presence, direction, and pace far into the looming jungle ahead but I'd grown so sweat-soaked, exhausted, and massively thirsty that I abandoned all caution and cut on heedlessly.

That evening I eased my heat-exhausted body to the ground and thought back on the times I'd walked blindly into what could have been lethal ambushes. I wasn't alone in that, we all had, but what dispirited me most was that I'd been so overwhelmed by the jungle that I'd virtually given up caring whether I'd lived or died. Quitting didn't fit my image of who I was and I took it personally, as though the jungle was an entity that was trying to crush my will. I was resolved to fight back but I'd learned that the weight I was carrying and the jungle's sweltering heat, humidity, and dense vegetation were too formidable. I couldn't change the conditions but I could lighten my load, and on our resupply day I sent my heavy air mattress and two of my canteens back and packed less food, determined to endure whatever it took to adapt to a harsh jungle that would give no quarter.

Chapter 7

Adapting

I'd spent more than a week in the jungle and I woke up knowing what to expect on a normal day. Every hour and a half or so we moved up in a company-long column to reconnect with the point platoon, and an hour or so before dark we formed a night perimeter. I found a sleeping spot and spread my nylon blanket on some nearby brush to air out. The bugs were biting, and I squirted a puddle of bug juice into the palm of my hand and rubbed the repellent on my arms, face, neck, and head. The pungent chemical scent lessened after a minute or so and the buzzing bugs stopped biting. A whispered "*man out*" signified that someone had passed beyond the perimeter to relieve himself. I passed it on.

The hissing sounds of C-4 fires and the chirpings of inch-long, lever-like, can openers slicing through the lids of C-ration cans started. The scents of heating C-rations began to drift to me, canteens gurgled, gear rustled, and men whispered. It was the noisiest we'd been all day. The sounds wouldn't carry very far through the thick foliage but I'd heard of companies who'd unknowingly stopped just short of NVA trails or bunkers, and I stepped to the perimeter and listened into the opaque jungle beyond where our guys had set claymores. When I turned back one of the guys was watching. He mouthed, "Did you hear something?" and I shook my head and returned to my sleeping spot.

I took two sips of warm water, and then I recapped the canteen, squatted on my heels, and pinched a fingernail-sized chunk off the edge of the little piece of C-4 explosive I carried. I rolled the C-4 into a tiny ball and placed it in the middle of the small circle of dirt I'd cleared, and then I sawed ¾ of the way through the lid of a C-ration spaghetti can, pried the cut part open, and bent it back to serve as a handle. I held the flame of my lighter against the C-4. It got hot enough to sputter, and then it caught fire and spit out blue flame like a tiny blowtorch. The spaghetti was so dense that the bottom heated and the top didn't. I tried to stir it but my plastic spoon snapped in half. I tried again with a twig but it was too supple, and I gave up and used the remnant of my spoon to dish it out. The spaghetti from the bottom was singed and the stuff on top rested stuck lard-like in my mouth but I scraped the can clean and ate every morsel.

I brushed some harmless bugs off my nylon blanket, and then I settled on top of it, rested my head on a corner of my pack, and let my tired body go slack. Gramps was sitting a few steps away smoking a cigarette. Big Jack was beside him cleaning his M-60; peering at the mechanism so closely that I thought his eyes must be crossed. Ron was further down the perimeter heating his tin cup over a C-4 flame, probably making hot chocolate. Sugar Bear was off by himself in the other direction, frowning like a winter bear that wanted to be left alone. He'd tried to be less unpleasant lately but he hadn't managed to maintain even that level of awkward civility, and when he'd snapped I'd reminded them that he was just Sugar Bear being Sugar Bear. It must have been hitting home because some of them had been smiling at his antics. I liked to believe I'd helped make that happen but Sugar Bear had a mental list of real and imagined incidents where he felt I'd screwed him over and he'd let me know that he wasn't forgetting or forgiving. I didn't care, trying to puzzle out how he thought was one of the things that made Sugar Bear so interesting.

I had no idea what tomorrow would bring. I'd expected we'd return to the jungle and encounter aggressive NVA who were looking for any opportunity to attack us, but we'd been the ones hunting them. The fact that we hadn't yet *found* them didn't make me feel less threatened. I knew what happened to grunt outfits ambushed by the NVA, and I had months of walking through sections of jungle that would be filled with ambush sites ahead of me. They'd be there one day, and when it happened we'd probably be moving through foliage so opaque that the first warning we'd have would likely be the snap of bullets coming our way. I'd been searching for strategies that might allow me to survive that deadly moment, and the only thing I'd come up with was my decision to pack less weight.

That had helped. I hadn't been packing enough food to regain the fever weight I'd lost and I'd been suffering increased thirst, but lightening my load had helped me stay alert during the hard going and the increased hunger and thirst hadn't beaten me into submission the way exhaustion had. The other thing that helped was that I was acclimating, regaining my strength, conserving energy, and perceiving the jungle more clearly. I guess that must have shown because an old hand from another platoon asked how *short* I was. A grunt was considered short when he neared the end of his one-year tour of duty and when I told him I'd only been in Vietnam for a few weeks he thought I was joking. After he realized I wasn't he told me, "You carry yourself like you've been here forever."

I thought about that, and I realized that in some ways I was still the new guy on the job learning the ropes but when it came to fitting into the jungle, I wasn't. The other thing I knew was that my ability to adapt to the jungle could help me survive and that it could also put me more at risk of dying. I knew that because I understood that our instinctual urge to help each other survive was inducing us to assume the roles we were best suited for, and I'd grown up doing the kinds of things that enhanced the skills a point man needed.

From the age of 7 or 8 I'd spent most of my free time slipping quietly through nature with a BB gun or a bow and arrow. From the age of 9 or 10 I'd done the same with a .22-caliber rifle, tracking animals and following game trails through mountain terrain that had been largely untouched by man. In the summers with my grandmother I'd been free to hunt and explore the huge expanse of uninhabited mountains that rose from her side of the river. I'd always been alone, and I'd often felt I was a part of nature, absorbing the sights and sounds with no ego and no sense of self, just a pair of legs, a nose, and a set of eyes and ears sneaking up to new sightlines and drinking clear water from secret springs and seeps that were known only to me.

On many days I'd hiked through gullies and climbed mountain slopes that probably hadn't been marked with a human footprint for years. I'd had my .22-caliber rifle but wandering such a huge expanse of rugged terrain alone had been a little scary at first. I'd worried I'd meet up with an aggressive mountain lion, a mean bear, a rattlesnake, or some wild-bearded crazy-eyed man, and if I got hurt no one would know where to find me. I had crossed paths with my share of rattlesnakes and bears, and I'd seen mountain lion tracks, but in all the years I'd hiked those remote Trinity mountains I'd never once encountered another human being.

There'd been no mirrors, no people, and no responsibilities to focus my thoughts inward, and I'd opened my mind to nature's subtle secrets....the smell of water bubbling from a spring, the scents of the animals and the plants and bushes they fed on, the movements of the wind-stirred leaves and branches, the warning snorts of alarmed deer, the barks of foxes, the huffing warnings of a bear, the piercing screams of high-soaring hawks, the scolding chatters of squirrels, the caws of curious crows, the hoots of owls, the *woo-wooings* of pigeons perched high in the needled branches of evergreen trees or lined up along the barren limbs of dead snags, the chirps, twitters, and whistles of the many varieties of birds, the raucous complaints of the perpetually overly dramatic blue jays, and the relaxed notes of their calls when they felt everything was OK again.

The jungle's exotic ecosystem was far different than the one I'd known but many of the abilities I'd sharpened and the habits I'd formed were transferable, things like how to read terrain, how to use cover for concealment, how to move through vegetation quietly, how to detect and identify vaguely unnatural shapes or movements in the foliage, how to isolate specific noises, how to read sign, how to put aside short-term thirst and hunger, and how to pace myself when the going was tough. Unfortunately, the skill that was most critical to my survival was the ability to intuit what nature's subtle sounds and scents were signifying, and that one wasn't transferring easily.

I knew the messages were there because the jungle was talking, a lot. Its thick air held exotic scents, its ambient silences amplified other noises, and its overhead layers of growth created a vast expanse of habitat for a multitude of hooting, whistling, and screeching animals whose collective voices generated multi-tiered symphonies that changed with the time of the day, the weather, and even the temperature. The canopy-dwelling animals had eyes on the jungle floor and they didn't miss anything. If they saw something unusual or threatening their calls would reverberate out like concentric circles from a pebble dropped in a still pool, repeated for a distance and then ebbing to silence after they'd reached the ears of those too distant to feel endangered. When they no longer felt curious or threatened their normal calls would return and the symphony of gentler, safer sounds would make me feel more secure. I didn't know the names and I rarely knew the faces of the animals that were doing the talking, but I didn't need too. I just needed to familiarize myself with the undisturbed cadences and intensities of their normal calls and then *feel* when they changed to warning calls or quieted to cautious silences. Most of all, I needed to intuit when those warning calls or silences hinted at the presence of the NVA.

The animals in Trinity had taught me that was possible, and the jungle's animals were schooling me here, calling genially to each other in the distances, changing their calls to warn of our approach, marking our progress with bubbles of wary silence that moved with us, and then calling out to announce our departures. And it wasn't just the animals. I was intensely attuned to the nuances of the natural jungle; the way the plants were spaced in the dim light, the way the leaves of different plants moved with the wind, the patterns of insect life that thrived underfoot and in the air, the arrays of exotic smells, the way the air flowed during the heat of the day and in the less heated nights, all of it meant something and I was sucking it in because my life depended on it.

I'd always been the guy who hadn't felt a need to do his homework, the one who hadn't trained for the sports that he'd played, the one who'd never fully committed and never felt driven to do more, but that had changed. The jungle had become the most riveting, fascinating, and magnetic force imaginable and I was always reaching out to it. When we stopped on the trail my mind was sifting through the most minute details of the jungle's sounds, sights, smells, and feels, and at night I'd lie on my earthen bed and mentally backtrack our movements through the dangerous sight avenues we'd crossed through, replaying the jungle sounds that had preceded us, the zones of silence that had surrounded us, and the notes and cadences of the calls that had announced our presence and our leaving. I didn't try to catalog that, it was too nuanced and vast to wrap my thinking mind around and I just let my survival mind carry it to wherever it needed it to go. I don't believe that stopped when I slept because I'd sometimes awaken vaguely aware that I'd been dreaming the jungle's sights, sounds, and smells; trying to get everything right in a complex and deadly jungle where I knew that wasn't possible.

Taking Over Walking Point

I wasn't the newest guy in our squad anymore, Walter Morris was. Walter was just short of medium height with a square body and a face that told you he was Irish. He was New York City direct, and he carried himself in a way that let you know that he could do the job, whatever it might be. Sugar Bear learned that Walter had worked as a mailman back in the world, and when he started calling him "Walter the Mailman" the name stuck. Shortly after he'd arrived, he'd come running up the trail when a few shots had been fired. A new guy who'd do that was someone I'd have wanted close behind me but I'd heard that Walter was married. I'd thought of Loretta living on without Don Dunn and that evening I'd squatted beside him and whispered that those of us who weren't married were the ones who needed to be up front. I didn't think my words were going to change anything Walter would do, but I felt better for trying.

Walter's arrival made me think back on the weeks I'd been in the jungle. I'd been hot, muggy, wet, bug-bitten, thorn-scratched, exhausted to the point of giving up, dirty, itchy, hungry, thirsty, and living with the unrelenting threat of being killed or wounded. Those miseries were inherent to the jungle but the jungle was more than that. It was vibrant and alive, and in some places it was majestic. We'd passed through sections of it marked by giant trees that had layers of vines and plants clinging high up their massive trunks to form weighty canopies that sucked up moisture, light, and carbon dioxide. Those tons of vegetative mass hanging suspended over our heads had sometimes made it seem that we were tiny beings inching under a sky of green, and there'd been moments when I'd felt we could have been transported to a far darker planet than the one I'd been born to; one filled with alien sounds, sights, and scents, and one where something dreadful was perpetually on the verge of happening.

We weren't walking the surface of another planet but the threats were incredibly real. I felt that, and the faces and movements of the men with me laid bare their fears that the jungle could erupt at any moment and darken their lives forever. I believe that had awakened primal survival instincts that had lain dormant deep inside me. I'd become incredibly attuned to the whispering men who were walking the jungle with me, automatically differentiating their distinct strengths and weaknesses from the way their bodies reacted to the smallest of things and weighing them from one perspective; what could they do that would help us survive? Even more remarkably, nature's sights, sounds, scents, and feels had more and more often been flowing through my mind untethered to words; just vivid impressions streaming one after another or all at once, coming too rapidly for my thinking brain to analyze, catalog, or weigh. I could sort back through some of those impressions when we were stopped in the column or at night before I slept, but in real time I just opened my mind to the jungle, unquestioning, unanalytical, and uncritical, absorbing what I could and trusting to intuition, especially when I was walking point.

Maybe those survival instincts were inhibiting me from taking over the point-walking duties for my squad, or maybe it was the opposite, maybe my survival instincts were prodding me to do it and my analytical mind was pushing back. I couldn't have said, but I'd seen it coming from the first day I'd cut trail with my squad. And now, with just weeks of actual time in the jungle I was poised on the brink of a death-defying precipice; the leap across it terrifying but ultimately inevitable. And one evening I did what I'd known I'd do, slipping from man to man along our evening perimeter and clearing it with the guys who'd been sharing the risks of point. Only Ron hesitated, weighing the risks I'd be taking, and then he nodded and it was no going back done.

I told John and Big Jack what we'd decided, and then I assured myself that I'd be less likely to get killed walking point than trailing behind another point man. I believed that but I knew the odds, and I talked with my squad members one by one, telling them that if there was shooting up front I needed them to spray bullets in my direction. I asked them to aim high, but not too high because I needed their shots to hit close enough to force the NVAs' heads down. They knew I was asking them to take the risk of hitting me, and I explained that I'd rather risk getting shot by them than face an almost certain death at the hands of the NVA. Each of them listened soberly, and every one of them assured me that he'd do what I was asking. I knew it wasn't much of a lifeline, but I left believing that if I survived the initial bullets their covering fire might give me time to toss a grenade and create an opportunity to escape their kill zone when it exploded.

The intermittent monsoon storms gave way to a steady rain that lasted almost two days. The rain stopped mid-morning of the second day, and I pulled off the rubber poncho that had kept me partially dry, shook the water off, and stuffed it into my pack. *Saddle ups* came whispering down the column, and I strapped on my pack and struggled to my feet. Seconds later the line of us started up the meandering path the second platoon's point squad had cut. With each step our boots pressed the decaying overburden deeper into the rain-sodden ground so that those at the back of our column were stepping in sucking mud while those of us nearest the front walked whisper-quiet on the damp carpet, passing through the dim, rain-soaked jungle like silent green ghosts.

When our column slowed to a stop big water droplets were working their way through the canopy, plopping or smacking against leaves and landing on the debris-carpeted ground. I looked up to see, and I had to smile at myself when a large drop targeted the middle of my forehead and splattered my face. The drops soon stopped falling, and when the quiet of the jungle returned I sat solitary in the dappled sunlight that filtered through the green of the canopy, listening to the soothing sounds of the breeze pushing through the leaves and the in-and-out whirring and droning of insects. In the sun-warmed aftermath of another sleep-interrupted night the effect was as hypnotic as the voice of a teacher droning on in a warm afternoon classroom and I awoke to familiar *saddle up* whispers and the scuffs, creaks, and thuds of nearby men shrugging into their packs, unsure of how long I'd slept or what the jungle might have signaled. The gap in my sentience spooked me, and I resolved that I wouldn't sleep on the trail again.

Chapter 8

The Bunker Complex

I was walking point through a low-treed and vine-impeded patch of foliage carrying three days of food and water on my back. A hint of a line of thinner foliage appeared a few meters to my left, and I edged in that direction and discovered a long-overgrown footpath that led to a less foliaged area. I looked and listened there for 2 or 3 minutes. I didn't sense anything, and I was creeping into it when a shocking hiss sounded behind me!

I dropped to the ground and searched feverishly for the threat. I didn't find it. I glanced back and saw a guy who'd just returned to complete the last days of his tour lying flat with a terrified look on his face. I followed the angle of his gaze to a termite mound that was jutting out of the earth ahead of me and a little to my left. I'd glanced past it earlier, but this time the outline of the rectangular firing port that peered out of it filled my eyes. I frantically scanned the shadows behind that sinister opening searching for any hint of movement. I didn't find any movement, and I freed my eyes to search for other threats.

The silhouette of that deadly firing port had printed itself in my eyes, and they darted to another firing port peering out of another mound. I waited fateful seconds with my body tensed in anticipation of tearing bullets and when they didn't come I shrugged out of my pack and crab-scuttled back from the yawning voids that lay behind those narrow firing ports. My squad retreated with me, all of us moving back until we were screened from the bunkers. From that safer distance, I weighed the signs of disuse and listened into the silence. My panic lessened, and when I decided that the bunkers were deserted I crawled forward and flipped a grenade through the firing port of the lead bunker. It exploded with a thudding boom and dust and smoke boiled out of the port. There was no reaction in the nearby jungle and I rose to my feet and got my first look at an NVA bunker complex.

A handful of bunkers were spread throughout the foliage. Their interiors measured about 4 1/2 feet from their dirt floors to their log-supported ceilings, about 3 feet from front to back, and about 6 feet from side to side. Their firing ports were situated just above ground level, and their dirt roofs and walls were thick enough to stop M-60 bullets. Each bunker had two openings. One was a short entry trench that they'd dug with a 90-degree bend to block blasts or bullets and the other was the approximately 4-inch high, 14-inch wide, and 8-inch-deep firing port that peered through one of their thick walls.

I'd heard accounts of how difficult it was to detect NVA bunkers but I hadn't realized that they could make them disappear into the natural jungle. Like hunters creating a blind, the NVA had sacrificed the occupants' fields of vision and firing angles to keep their bunkers hidden, and the only feature that distinguished the above-ground section of the bunkers from the many termite mounds that dotted the neighboring jungle was the narrow firing port that faced out from just one side of each bunker. The other telltales were the shadowed hints of the below-grade trenches that accessed their interiors and the places where they'd strategically thinned the low vegetation to open ankle-high sightlines that anyone moving to the bunker would have to cross, cuttings so innocuous that you'd never notice them unless you were searching for them with savvy eyes. And I hadn't had savvy eyes, not for the narrow firing ports, not for the shadows of the entryway depressions, and not for the ankle-high sightlines that opened from the other bunkers' firing ports.

I could have assured myself that abandonment and the passage of time had concealed this bunker complex to the point of near invisibility but I'd have been deluding myself. The complex had been so artfully designed to blend into the jungle that if the NVA had been in it I might have slipped past the point of no return before I'd realized what awaited me. That was frightening enough, but what that complex was telling me about the men who'd created it was far more terrifying. I'd viewed the NVA as aggressive cold-eyed killers like Buc, but the men who'd built this killing field were far more deadly than that. These men had labored for days constructing bunkers that almost perfectly mimicked the appearance of termite mounds and then they'd left themselves blind to approaching enemies on three sides to better conceal their existence, all based on the slim chance that we'd one day appear in this remote section of jungle. I stood in that complex picturing shrewd, patient, and committed to the death enemies like them, and, for the first time, I think I fully appreciated the lethality of the enemy I was facing.

I'd known that a point man's odds of surviving contact were dismal but I'd thought I could see through the foliage more clearly, listen better, read sign better, and move through the jungle more silently than most of the point men who hadn't survived. I'd had a vague expectancy that the natural jungle would alert me, too, but the bunker complex drove home the lesson that I'd been too ignorant to accord the NVA the lethality they merited and too slow to recognize the ingenuous ways they could use the jungle as a weapon.

I had no excuse for being that ignorant because I should have learned that lesson when I'd been hunting with my dad at the age of 13. We'd hiked to a ridge that had overlooked a slope filled with chest-high manzanita brush. My dad had led the way noisily to the rocky outcropping that had squatted in the middle of it, and we'd sat atop the outcropping for 10 or 15 minutes scanning for deer in the manzanita thicket below. I hadn't detected any shapes or movements, and when I'd whispered that there weren't any deer down there my dad had smiled and said, "Bucky, there's probably a deer or two down there watching us right now." I'd felt pretty smug about how sharp my eyes were and how wrong he was, and then a deer had flicked an ear and her head had taken shape in the middle of that confusing tangle of manzanitas, right where it had been the entire time we'd been sitting on that outcropping. I'd spotted another deer's head a few feet to her left and, just as my dad had predicted, both of the deer had been staring at us.

I'd learned two things on that rock. First, that for the last few years I'd spent a lot more time hiking the mountains than my dad had, but he'd spent a lot more years living off venison and he knew more about hunting than I did. The second thing I'd come away with was the humbling realization that I hadn't appreciated the innate canniness of a species that had survived for countless generations using nature to conceal themselves from predators or ambush prey, just as our ancient human ancestors had. I don't know why I'd needed to relearn that in this place where it was so critical to my survival but I had, and I left that complex knowing that my survival depended on my detecting the tiniest of off-key sounds, scents, sights, or movements.

That night I sat-squatted on my inverted helmet in the no-moon starlit night, listening into the closeting jungle that enveloped us. A tiny noise conjured up the specter of a crawling enemy, and my heart beat a little harder. The noise didn't repeat but it was a few minutes before I recaptured the sense that nothing deadly was stirring. When my watch ended I woke Sam and laid back on my earthen bed. I brushed my fingers lightly against my M-16 to be sure it was on safety, and then I laid it against my right side with the barrel angled down my leg, shifted my body to conform to the gentle hollows and ridges of the natural earth, and thought about what I had to do, certain that if I didn't change things I'd someday die without hearing the shots that killed me.

Before I fell asleep I wondered again, *what did he believe, how did he live, how did he think*, and for the first time I asked the questions I should have been asking long ago; *how would the men who'd built that complex expect me to move, look, and sound, and how would they expect me to think?*

Moving Lighter and Quieter

On our next log day I emptied my pack and sorted everything into a keep pile and a go-back pile. I knew I'd have to endure some miserably wet days and nights without my rubber poncho, but it was heavy. I tossed it on the go-back pile. I'd suffered more thirst after I'd discarded two of my eight canteens but water was weighty. I told myself that I'd probably get some rainwater or groundwater and that I could survive a waterless day if I had to, and I dropped 2 of my 6 canteens on the go-back pile. I took a long look at my claymore and its clacker and wire. I decided that decreasing the odds that I'd lead us into an ambush was more valuable than the loss of one claymore, and those went into the go-back pile.

I'd shed a total of 10 or 12 pounds of weight, and when the log bird landed I ate and drank as much as my shrunken belly would hold, refilled my four canteens, and packed lighter on C-rations. I picked up two of the grenades they'd sent out and when I left I was carrying 4 grenades, 360 rounds of M-16 ammo, a plastic bottle of bug repellent, a plastic spoon, a toothbrush but no toothpaste, a plastic handled razor, a lighter, an inch-long P-38 can opener, a few packages of plastic-wrapped toilet paper, my lightweight nylon blanket liner, and a finger-sized slice of C-4 explosive for heating C-rations. My personal items were a few pieces of writing paper, a stub of a pencil, and the thin alligator-skin wallet my dad had handed me before I'd left. I had a few MPC notes and two pictures in that wallet, one of Barbara and another of Stephanie Wilder, my little niece who'd been born after I'd left for Vietnam.

When word came to move out guys started sitting on the ground to strap into their 80-plus pound log-day-heavy packs. Some of them shared a pull-up with a buddy and others rolled to a knee and levered themselves up to a standing position, but not me. I leaned over and threaded one arm through a shoulder strap, and then I straightened upright and slung it across my shoulders, wondering if I'd packed enough food and water to navigate the next three days.

It turned out to be yet another hot and muggy day where the heat and the humidity combined to make the conditions equate to temperatures of more than 120 degrees, but my legs never felt tired. That evening I ate the contents of a single C-ration tin and retired to my blanket with a gnawing ache in the pit of my shrunken stomach and a nagging thirst that was worse than usual. A warm monsoon rain started after dark, and I drank my canteen dry and refilled it with the water that was draining off the poncho tent Big Jack and Gramps had strung. I felt my way back to my blanket, settled onto the wet earth, and wrapped my now-sodden blanket around me. It started raining harder, and I rested my head on the corner of my pack, tugged my nylon blanket up to shield my face from the rain splatters, pulled my knees to my chest, and fell asleep. The rain had cooled when I took my turn on watch, and I sat guard on my inverted helmet shivering, and then I returned to my sleeping nook and wrapped my wet blanket around me. I woke the next morning soaking wet and bleary-eyed from lack of sleep. Ron held one end of my blanket and we twisted it as dry as we could, and then I stuffed it in my pack, wondering whether the damp blanket was heavier than the poncho I'd sent back.

Two days later I walked to the resupply site with 4 empty canteens and a feather-light pack slung loosely over one shoulder. I'd lived with a gnawing ache in the pit of my ever-gaunter stomach for almost two full days and I'd had just a few sips of water over the last several hours, but I'd made it through our 3-day log cycle. I'd been uncertain if my body could endure that level of deprivation and still function but the additional thirst and hunger hadn't reduced my alertness, my connection to the jungle, or my will to survive, and the lighter load had allowed me to slip ahead more quietly through dense foliage. That ability to move more silently had encouraged me to distance myself from the telltale noises of the guys behind me and I'd lengthened the gap between me and the rest of my squad. Their sounds had carried beyond me at times but I'd hoped that if any ambushers were tracking their noises my unexpected arrival might create a moment of startle and a split second more time for me to take cover before they opened up. I knew that was a stretch but I was willing to employ any possible strategy and pay any price to up my odds, even a little.

I'd once been a new guy packing heavy, succumbing to exhaustion and resigning myself to suffering an almost certain death if the NVA were waiting in ambush. The jungle had overwhelmed me then but I'd gotten on my feet and fought back, and I left our next log site packing ultra-light again, determined to accept hunger and thirst and do whatever I could to make it to another log day.

Bomb Crater Bathing

Our column threaded its way into a sunbaked clearing dotted with old bomb craters. My section of the column slowed to a stop near a large crater that was three-quarters full of algae-tinted water. I unsnapped a canteen and gulped down the last of its tepid water. It had its customary hot-plastic taste but the gulps of water that were coursing down my throat were incredibly pleasurable. I climbed down and rinsed my canteens in the brown-tinted water at the crater's edge, and then I submerged each of them beneath the sun-heated surface water as far as I could reach. The air bubbled out until they were filled to their brims with the muddy water created by the wind that was lapping it against the crater's banks. I didn't care, the mud would settle to the bottom of the canteens and I'd drink the water and rinse the mud out later.

I knew we'd be clear targets to anyone who might be in the trees at the edge of the meadow but I had weeks of heat and dirt behind me. I climbed back up the bank and laid my M-16 on top of my pack, and then, for the first time since we'd left the LZ, I removed my boots and socks. I barefooted gingerly down the side of the crater to the water's edge and walked in, clothes and all. The surface water was warm but the water beneath that layer was progressively cooler, and when I'd waded in neck deep I could feel the cooler thermal layers sucking the heat out of my body.

I luxuriated in that for a few minutes, and then I started kicking my legs and circling my arms to agitate some of the dirt out of my shirt and pants.

The movements generated a slowly expanding circle of muddy water that was countering my crude laundry efforts, so I stripped off my pants and shirt and tossed them over the lip of the crater. Jay was looking down, and I asked if he'd toss down the cake of soap that he packed. He disappeared. A few seconds later he reappeared and tossed the soap. I lathered the jungle-rotted patches that were starting on my legs, left shoulder, and chin. When I thought I'd gotten as clean as I was going to get I laid the soap on the bank, dog-paddled to the middle of the crater, and dove under the muddy water to rinse away the suds.

I climbed up to the rim of the crater and borrowed Jay's tiny mirror so I could shave. The lean, sun-darkened, and whiskered visage that looked back from the mirror had a wolfish cast. For a moment it was a stranger's face, and then my brain accepted it and I dug my disposable razor out of my pack and started pulling at the whiskers. The dull razor tugged painfully at the crusted areas where the jungle rot had started and I had to shave twice to get all the whiskers off. I surveyed my scraped-pink face when I finished. *I look like a kid*, I thought, but I didn't feel that way; I felt like the stranger who'd stared back at me when I'd first looked in the mirror.

I climbed back down to the water to rinse my socks. The woolen ones the army supplied made me itch and I'd been wearing the pair of nylon dress socks that I'd had on when I'd arrived. I'd covered a lot of jungle wearing those socks and now they were worn so thin they were almost sheer in places. I rinsed them and twisted them drier very gently, and then I climbed to the rim and laid them on my pack to dry. I'd sunk ankle-deep in mud climbing the bank so I spaced some debris on the bank as I made my way down. Rene was swimming in the crater and when I dog paddled out he splashed water at me like we were kids in a pool. We tread water for a while, relishing the relative coolness of the bomb crater's muddy water in the glare of another miserably hot and muggy day.

I used the debris I'd placed as stepping stones and climbed to the rim almost mud free. Sam held one end of my soaked clothes and we twisted them as dry as we could. The column started saddling up, and I pulled on my pants, shirt, socks, and boots and caught up with the tail end of my platoon as it entered the tree line, mercifully cooler and wearing bomb-water-rinsed clothes that might have been a little less filthy.

The Majestic Jungle

A day or two later I was walking point. The foliage was wet from the earlier rain and the sunlight that filtered down through the single canopy made the water-slick greenery glisten. I slipped silently through the damp jungle with my squad trailing somewhere behind me. It was quiet jungle with no signs of an entrenched NVA presence, the good kind of quiet, and then I ducked beneath a branch and the red ants kamikazed me.

Most of the jungle ant species had relatively compact bodies but the red ants had long legs, long antennae, and slender bodies that gave them an almost delicate appearance. They nested in the overhead leaves, and when my helmet brushed the foliage beneath their nest they launched themselves onto my neck and back, biting. Ron came on me when I was brushing at them, and he rushed up and grabbed the back of my pack. I felt him take the weight, and I unsnapped my hip belt and slipped out from under it. Freed of the pack, I pulled my shirt off and started slapping the biting ants away, even then anticipating that Ron's account of me slapping at myself like a crazy person would be good for a few laughs.

I'd heard that the red ants' bites were the most painful, but they weren't. Shortly after I'd come to the jungle a line of night-marching army ants had crawled onto my air mattress. The mattress had amplified the sounds of their tiny creepings, and I'd held very still, wondering where the sounds were coming from and what they signified. Still uncertain, I'd raised onto an elbow, and when I'd moved the ants had attacked in unison. They'd stopped biting when I'd rolled off the mattress and stood, but those army ant bites had burned longer and hurt a lot worse than red ants' bites had.

Little events like that marked a few of our days but on most days nothing unusual stood out. Despite that almost every moment was significant, or at least it was to me. I'd been in Vietnam a little less than three months but my life before I'd arrived was seeming less and less real while everything that had happened here seemed to have printed vividly in my mind. I never questioned that, it just was, but I think my brain was turning away from memories and understandings that had little value here. And I think it was enhancing memories and understandings that matched the imperatives of the ecosystem that now governed my survival, an ecosystem whose ever-flowing instants were filled with the tiniest of things and the most massive of things…like the meters-long tree root tendons that swelled out of the rich earth beside me and flowed into the meters-thick trunk that was towering arrow-straight through the triple canopies. The vine-tethered masses of vegetation clinging to its stovepipe-straight trunk created a sea of reaching, climbing, and drooping greenery that blocked my view of the massive tree's emergence into the sky, but I knew it would be one of the monarchs I'd viewed from the choppers piercing through the rolling green of the jungle's ceiling. I guessed it must have taken 1,000 years for that mighty tree to have grown so thick and reached so high, and I envisioned it towering over this small section of jungle canopy for many more of our generations before its gargantuan weight toppled it back to the earth. I don't know why the prospect of that mighty tree's long reign made my potential death seem less important, but at that moment it did.

It wasn't only the extraordinary aspects of the jungle that fascinated me, almost everything about it seemed to fill my mind; how it smelled, sounded, and looked, and how everything connected. I don't know if all those things were crowding out memories of the past but I knew the past was dimming and I accepted it. I think I even welcomed it. Memories of the past generated yearnings and regrets that I didn't want, and they could inspire hope. In the short time I'd been here I'd learned that hope's inseparable companion was the fear that my hopes would never be realized, and I wanted as little of that pressing at the back of my mind as possible. I thought I'd done a pretty good job of pushing that away but at times murmurs of a different place and a different me would find their way to the front of my mind, and one moonlit night the jungle carried me there.

When I was awoken for my night watch a full moon was shining bright above the broken canopy, and I found a shadowed nook and watched the moonlight crawl in and out of shadowed patches of foliage as the moon drifted slowly up the limb-etched night sky. When the moon had risen directly overhead the slowly creeping moonbeams that had found a path through the canopy were lighting pieces of the jungle floor so brightly that the shadowed areas appeared unbelievably black. Spellbound, I sat beneath that exotic, canopy-etched moonlit sky watching those moonbeams wander through the reaching, trailing, and shrubbery growth that thrived beneath the canopy; witnessing the breathtaking night beauty of a living, breathing, three-dimensional ecosystem filled with vibrancy and life. The wonder of it inspired emotions I'd long suppressed, and I imagined that someone back home was gazing up at that yellow moon and thinking of me.

I fumbled a piece of notepaper and a stub of a pencil out of my baggy pants pocket and positioned the paper in a narrow beam of moonlight that reached down beside me. The light that had appeared so bright in the shadowed jungle was barely strong enough to show the marks of my pencil, so I wrote in sprawling letters, "Dear Barbara." And then I sat for long minutes searching for words that might convey the splendor I was witnessing. The words wouldn't come, and I sat in that ancient jungle beneath the light of a timeless moon knowing that the exotic beauty that enthralled me would be mine, and only mine. Disheartened, I scribbled a few lines that said nothing, and then I stuffed the letter in my pants pocket and sensed out for any NVA who might be using the expanding shadows to creep in on us.

In the morning I read what I'd written. It was so banal that I considered burning it. I didn't, because I knew that any letter I'd write to replace it would be just as empty. I hated the way I was feeling and I turned my thoughts to this day. I was starting the day thirsty and we had hours of bug-filled and humid heat ahead of us. If I didn't find water it was going to get a lot worse but the jungle didn't give anything to anybody and the water would be there or it wouldn't. Either way, I'd handle it. A deep-throated fly droned nearby and a lone ant was negotiating its way through the debris-littered jungle floor, forging a path through the maze of this place and accepting it uncomplainingly, just surviving.

I watched Gramps pull a C-ration out of his well-stocked pack. He packed heavy and he had a sweet tooth. When we made it to our night perimeter maybe I could trade him my last tin of pound cake for some dense calorie-laden meal he'd have buried in that pack, maybe even a beans and wieners one. The thought brightened my mood. Living in the moment was better, memories of the past and dreams of another life were just too fucking hard to bear.

Chapter 9

Three Steps Away

I squatted motionless on the edge of another slice of jungle that buffered an arc light site, reaching into the torn remnants with my ears and my nose like a blind man relying on those senses to guide him. They weren't telling me much. Clumps of goop were dropping from partially intact shrubs and branches, each one sending my never-sure ears and eyes darting, seeking threatening movements or a note of something deadly, and all the telltale calls of the animals had been silenced. I inspected the floor of the jungle for signs of what may have been here and what might still be here, but the debris-covered earth wasn't revealing anything. I scanned ahead, and then I moved further into the plopping sounds of falling mud, and the scents of explosions, torn earth, and weeping vegetation.

A slender concussion-downed tree was held partially aloft by its springy branches. I slipped up to the base of the tree, peered through its uplifted branches, and listened. I didn't detect any warnings, and I bent low to keep my head and shoulders from rising and stepped over the downed tree. My right foot cleared cleanly but my trailing foot brushed the trunk of the tree lightly. The touch created barely a whisper of sound but it was so delicately suspended that the full 10-meter length of it trembled. At that instant I had the oddest impression of someone seeing the log quiver, and I froze mid-step and sensed out for the source. And then I felt a powerful urge to distance myself from the tree and I glided ahead three long steps.

Partially hidden, I searched the shadowed depths for any sightlines that opened back to the downed log and felt for any subtle changes in the nearby jungle. The disordered jungle didn't reveal anything but I couldn't shake the uncanny sense that a stranger's eyes had seen the log quiver, and I held motionless in the knocking, plopping, rustling, cordite-smelling foliage for a long while. I heard Ron closing up behind me, and I motioned him to stillness. Nothing seemed to have changed, and I put aside my unease and slipped forward another few steps. My next move covered 4 more meters, and when I didn't sense anything I angled slightly left and ghosted to the side of a termite mound that was more than 2 meters tall and almost as thick. The twinge of unease I'd felt when I'd sent that shudder down the full length of the downed tree had dissipated and I was once again moving instinctually through the bomb-shredded patch of jungle.

I stepped out from beside the termite mound with my M-16 angled slightly to my left and my right index finger resting lightly on the trigger. And then I was hurtling backward with my arms stretched full length in front of me. I could see my M-16 in my extended hands when the bullets started coming from the right of me, snapping through the air where my torso had been. I could feel my feet still touching the ground, and then I was airborne with my body stretched out horizontally and flying away from the line of snapping bullets. I hit the ground flat on my back with the termite mound between me and the shooter, already triggering my M-16 to the left side of the mound. I expected a burst of bullets, and when the M-16's action locked open after a single shot I felt like my head exploded. I jammed the palm of my hand against the butt of the magazine to lock it back in place. I felt it seat and I snapped the bolt shut and lay there with my eyes darting from one side of the mound to the other, terrified that at any moment they'd be darting around the sides of it shooting, waiting for my squad's covering fire, needing it desperately, counting on it. It didn't come.

I pulled a frag from my pistol belt and scrambled to a knee, and then I popped the frag's handle, cooked it off for a three count, and lobbed it high over the top of the mound. I watched it clear and I was moving when it exploded. I took two leaping steps at an angle that would keep the mound between me and the shooter and at the end of the second step I dove as far as I could. I landed on my belly and spun around to see if anything was coming after me. Nothing appeared, and I pulled another frag off my pistol belt and did it again. The next time I landed the lead men of my squad were crouched a few meters back, wide-eyed and unmoving. I motioned them into a line that faced the mound and we sprayed a multitude of bullets that zipped through the foliage like swarms of enraged bees. When we paused we heard crashing noises moving from our left to right and we opened up in that direction. The second time we stopped the only sounds I heard were the plops and thumps of falling mud. We waited another couple of minutes and then we hurried back to our platoon.

I hadn't noticed during the adrenalin pumping frenzy of the incident, but both my forearms were powder burned and my right forearm had been grazed by two bullets. Doc White cleaned the bullet grazes with a sticky yellow soap and applied a greasy ointment to the burns and the grazes, all the while telling me how lucky I'd been. I knew how right he was. When my body had launched me backward my extended arms had stayed in the path of the shooter's bullets, and the fraction of a second it had taken my torso to clear the space where my arm had been had surely made the difference between my living or dying.

After Doc finished Lt. Jones asked if I could find my way back to the ambush site. I told him I could and he asked if I would. Rene had come over to check on me, and when I said that I'd do it he insisted on walking backup for me. We circled wide of the termite mound with our entire platoon trailing behind us, and when I'd traveled far enough to approach the mound at an angle that would open a sightline to the area where the shooter had been I started creeping back. After I slipped through about 40 meters of foliage the vague outline of the mound began to take shape and I settled on my left knee and searched through the vegetation for any NVA that might be there. I was so concentrated on that disarrayed patch of jungle that I didn't know Rene was working his way up until he slipped in beside me. I indicated the location of the mound and Rene immediately elevated his head to get a better look. I warned him to keep his head down but once again Rene was courageous and curious, and he didn't. We searched for a long while, and when neither of us detected any signs of an NVA presence we pushed up to, and then beyond the termite mound.

When we were confident the near jungle was clear we turned back and inspected the site. The dozen or so .30-caliber casings we found scattered on the torn jungle floor were less than three steps from where I'd been when I'd stepped out from my side of the mound, and the end of the barrel that had powder burned me had been a little closer. He'd left a few smudges where he'd stood. That little sign indicated a lone shooter, so maybe he'd been checking out the bomb site like we were, or maybe he'd been posted as a lookout for something nearby. I had no way of knowing, but he must have been expecting me to appear because the split second that had elapsed between my stepping out from behind the mound and the triggering of those bullets was too short a time for him to have recognized and reacted to an unexpected target. There wasn't any sign of an established trail where he'd crashed through the torn jungle, and I angled away from the direction he'd fled and led the rest of the way to the epicenter of the arc light. It wasn't as massive as the first arc light site we'd surveyed and we didn't find anything to suggest that there'd been an NVA bunker complex there.

In the afternoon we set out through the jungle again, and at the tail end of the day I pulled out the C-ration meal I'd been hoarding from myself and heated it slowly, savoring the scent of the warming contents. I hadn't dwelled on how near to death I'd come but every bite I spooned out of that C-ration beans and wieners tin made me think of what a waste it would have been if I'd died and left it uneaten. I knew how skewed it was to treasure such a trivial thing on a day so filled with significance, but my half-starved self didn't see it that way. I'd been enduring hunger, thirst, and the threat of impending death for a long while and my pleasures had been few and far between, and on this heat-lessening jungle evening a still-alive me found immense pleasure in each bite of a favorite meal that had nearly gone uneaten.

A few guys stopped by to ask what had happened. I told them that I'd stepped past a termite mound and the next thing I knew I'd been flying backward and bullets had started zipping in front of me. They wanted to know what had warned me and I had to tell them that I'd just stepped out from beside the termite mound and then my body had been flying backward. My inability to answer that question puzzled them but it was tormenting me. I wanted to learn something that might help me survive again, and I sorted through my memories searching for something that might give me a little more control over my living or dying.

I had a perfect recall of utilizing the best cover, avoiding potential sightlines, and reaching out for sounds and scents on my path to the fallen tree. I had a shockingly vivid recollection of feeling someone seeing the tree shudder when I'd brushed against it. I could envision almost every leaf and branch I'd passed on my way to the termite mound, and I had crystal clear recollections of the partially tangled foliage and debris that had lain beyond the mound. I could even recall the stray movements of the leaves and the scents of shredded vegetation and torn earth that had wafted to my nose just before I'd stepped out from beside the termite mound. I had a vague sense of my left boot reaching for the dirt that I wasn't sure was real, and then I was traveling backward with my arms outstretched and the bullets were snapping through the air where my body had been. There had to have been a warning, but if I'd seen or heard anything why had I been so amazed to find myself flying backward? And if I hadn't had a warning then what could have triggered that explosive leap that had kept me alive?

I couldn't find it, and I decided that the answers had been lost in the chaos of the moments. I accepted that, but I'd spent a lot of time sorting through those memories and the thing that stayed with me was how strongly I'd *felt* someone seeing the downed log quiver as I'd brushed against it. Logic was telling me that had to have been generated by my fear that someone could have seen it but I couldn't dismiss that feeling, and I decided that if I ever felt anything like that again I'd accept it as real no matter how fantastic it might seem.

I learned other lessons that were much clearer. My guys had intended to open up if I walked into contact but in the chaos of the moment they hadn't, and I'd wasted precious seconds anticipating covering fire that hadn't come. Maybe it wouldn't work out that way next time but I wasn't going to chance it. I wasn't going to count on anyone doing anything to keep me alive and I sure as hell wasn't going to continue carrying a rifle with a magazine that wouldn't stay locked.

Repeating Days

The following days were so similar that I felt like I was reliving the same three-day pattern over and over again. Each day the battalion would radio out a new azimuth for us to follow. We were never told who'd planned the routes or what they thought we'd find when we got to wherever it was we'd be going, but we faithfully tracked their azimuths on dawn-to-dusk, hot, sticky, and bug-bitten marches that were followed by sleep-interrupted turns-on-watch nights. Resupply days came and went and we continued taking our malaria pills, dealing with the bug-caused maladies of the jungle, and whispering a few soft messages to each other. The humid monsoon weather was unrelentingly oppressive and we stayed filthy, thirsty, hungry, weary, and forever aware that the jungle could erupt at any moment with bullets or explosions triggered by the deadly NVA we'd been sent to hunt and kill.

That's what the army had sent us to do and yet the NVA who'd been so aggressive when I'd first come to the jungle hadn't engaged us, and other than the day I'd been bullet grazed my company hadn't *found them*. That didn't surprise me. I didn't have any idea what the army strategists might know about the NVA's whereabouts but I knew how to hunt and I knew the terrain. Unless the NVA were deaf, dumb, and blind they'd almost certainly hear, see, or smell our presence long before we could sneak up on them. And in dense jungle foliage where soldiers lying a few steps to the sides of our path would be nearly invisible why couldn't they choose to ambush us or slip away?

The *kill* element of their *search and destroy* strategy seemed just as simplistic. It was based on the premise that we'd outkill the NVA to the extent that they'd have to stop fighting, but any NVA we encountered would likely be familiar with their area of the jungle and they could choose the time and place to engage us. In a jungle setting that offered multiple ambush sites they'd have the advantage, and I couldn't imagine why anyone would expect the number of their deaths to exceed ours. That's how I viewed it but no one was asking the opinions of those of us who were pushing through the jungle. Our fates had been placed in the hands of others so we kept moving through the jungle searching for deadly men who'd choose a place to ambush us.

The cadence of the slowing steps of the men ahead of me signaled a routine closing of the gap between us and the point platoon. A wind was whispering through the tops of the canopy but the cloying ground-level air was listless. My shirt was clinging hot and wet against my skin but I took a long look at the leaf-littered earth before I shed my pack. I'd seen a scorpion crawl out from under a leaf at an earlier stop that had been two or three times the length of the ones back home. The heavy stinger curled behind it had looked like it could have done some serious damage, and it wasn't just that scorpion. I'd seen tarantulas as big as the palm of my hand, centipedes the length of some of the big blue belly lizards in Trinity, and termites close to an inch long with pincers so oversized and powerful that if you picked one up by its pale globular body and leaned in close you'd hear its pincers "*click, clicking.*" None of those bugs had shown signs of aggression but I hadn't liked that big-stingered scorpion crawling nearby and I'd crushed it under my boot heel. I'd had to spin my full weight on it before it had stopped moving and then I'd felt guilty as it had lain twitching, like I'd wasted its life for no good reason. There'd been no taking it back, though, and it hadn't been wasted; the ever-foraging ants had been making a hearty meal of it when we'd moved on.

Reassured, I dropped my pack, slipped my bandoleers over my head, and removed my weighty pistol belt that held two grenades and a canteen. They hadn't choppered out clean clothes for days and I could feel where my stiff dirt and salt-encrusted shirt had chaffed my armpits. A faint scuffling sounded behind me and when I twisted to make sure it was one of our guys it felt like someone started running a pin-bristled roller up and down the side of my back. I tugged off my shirt, and when I didn't find any bugs I twisted to see if the pinpricks would return. When they did I knew I'd finally developed the prickly heat rash that so many others had been suffering.

The thought that my pores were so dirt-encrusted and irritated that they'd pop open when my skin stretched wasn't pleasant, but I couldn't complain. Some of the others had oily ringworm circles and deep pockets of jungle rot, and all I had were a few shallow patches of jungle rot on my face and a few more on my legs where I'd pulled off leeches. Still, I sat in the muggy heat imagining what I'd give to dive into the clear, cold, waters of the Trinity River. I couldn't hold that thought so I pictured myself standing under the black-barrel shower on Grant with a thin stream of the sun-warmed water trickling over my dirt-darkened, chafed, and itchy skin and soaking the filth off me. I yearned for that moment, and I leaned back against my pack and promised myself that when we got back to the LZ I'd head straight to that shower, whenever that would be.

Tracking on Point

I squatted at the edge of the small meadow in the early midmorning, scanning the path of the NVA trail that passed through it. High above the single-canopy jungle white clouds were drifting across a sun-yellowed sky but the low air was still. A few small birds were twittering companionable notes on the other side of the meadow but their amiable tweets didn't reassure me. Even from a distance the sign that marked the surface of the NVA trail looked fresh, and I traced the line of it a few meters through the meadow and into the low brush. The twittering birds were flitting undisturbed there, and I finally accepted their assessments and crossed through the meadow. My squad followed, and we set up at the far edge and radioed back the existence of the NVA trail.

Minutes later they radioed back that they were sending Buc up to check it out. That was a surprise. Buc had led the day we'd walked off LZ Grant but Captain Jones had kept Buc at his side since then, maybe as an adviser or more probably, as a protector.

As we waited I leaned over the trail and inspected the sign. Partial Ho Chi Minh tire tread prints showed in places but mostly it was just scuffs and smudges. The marks were well centered on the trail so they'd had decent light when they'd passed through. I isolated the marks the best I could and counted 6 or 7 footfalls within the length of a short man's stride. The smudges had exposed damp dirt that was darker than the undisturbed dirt on the trail. I wanted to get some idea of how fast the earth they'd uncovered might be drying, so I dragged my fingers along the surface of the trail. The marks I created were much darker than the sandal-smudged soil, but even as I watched the rising heat was drying my marks to a lighter shade. During the morning's less heated hours the tracks would have dried more slowly, but as I waited for Buc my marks grew so close in shade to the NVA's smudges that I wondered if we'd missed each other by hours or less. The thought stirred me to look up and listen for any bubble of quiet in the jungle where the trail was pointing.

The distinct cadence of Buc's footfalls sounded behind me. He walked casually past the kneeling members of my squad to where I crouched, and then he leaned over to inspect the sign. After a mere second he straightened, pointed down at the scarred surface of the trail, and said brusquely, "NVA, two-three days." His English was rudimentary so I scraped another line in the dirt and pointed at the lighter dirt of the undisturbed trail, the intermediate shade of the NVA tracks, and the darker line that I'd created.

He shook his head, "No," impatiently.

I hand signaled that the line of footfalls was tracking the center of the trail and said, "Today."

He shook another, "No," emphatically, and then he said, "Old, old," and dragged the side of his foot across the trail to obliterate the marks.

I sent him a look that should have told him I didn't appreciate that, and I shook my head to let him know I wasn't taking his word for it.

We'd have never been sure which of us had been right if Lt. Jones hadn't sent us a short way down the trail to determine its general compass bearing. After about 15 meters we discovered a pile of morning-fresh excrement. Buc's face stayed impassive but we both knew he'd misread the sign, or maybe he'd read it right and reported it wrong. Either way, it was another reminder that relying on the judgment of another could get me killed, even someone as reputedly expert as Buc.

We backtracked to the meadow and continued on our previous azimuth, leaving our boot prints overlaying the sandaled prints of the NVA squad of soldiers we'd almost encountered.

Back to the LZ

A poker game awakened our sleepy LZ perimeter one morning. The sweltering heat and the loss of their pocket money sent a succession of players and observers scurrying back to the shade of their poncho-awned hooches, and by midafternoon the only ones playing were me, Jay, and two guys who'd just joined our squad. One of them was Larry, a lean, brown-haired, and quick-eyed guy. The other was the even-keeled guy he'd arrived with, Vern. Larry was dealing. The humid air had made the cards sticky and he carefully selected each one and tossed it on the blanket we were using for a table. I picked up two aces in a five-card draw game and when I bet the other three called. I held the aces, and when I edged my three new cards apart I discovered four aces and a deuce. The odds were that none of the others would have betting hands, but Jay bet out, Vern called, and I raised. Larry re-raised, Jay called the raises, and when Vern folded I raised Larry's re-raise. Larry and I kept raising and Jay kept calling until almost all of our collective money was scattered on the poncho liner. When we finished betting Jay showed a flush, Larry had a full house, and I flipped over my four aces. Larry's face tightened and then he laughed. I liked that.

The $30 of MPC I'd won was as worthless on the LZ as the monopoly money it so closely resembled. I didn't care about the money but Big Jack Billups had been standing at the doorway of the hooch with a pen and a piece of paper, and before he ducked out of it he handed me the sketch he'd drawn. With a dismissive laugh that suggested he didn't think it was a big deal, he told me that I could keep it. He left, and I looked down at the ink-drawn caricature he'd sketched. It depicted the final three of us playing poker, ourselves and yet not ourselves, me with four aces and a throbbing middle finger extended to the world and the others holding losing hands. I held it pinched between the thumb and forefinger of my sweat-dampened hand, sensing that the drawing was more honest than a photograph…that it was like getting an unexpected glimpse of your reflection in a window or a mirror, the one where for an instant you see yourself through the eyes of a stranger, and at that moment you know that the you that's looking back is more authentic than the one your insecurities and vanities have painted in your mind.

He'd captured the essence of the inner Jay with the far-off look and the jaw-clenching grimness that masked the deep-seated fear he tried so hard to hide. Larry's caricature reflected his inquiring intellect and uncertainty. The image I had of myself wasn't the guy in the drawing. The caricatured me seemed older and less vulnerable, projecting an aura that said he was supremely confident, or maybe that he just didn't care, but I cared about everything, a lot. Those aspects of Jack's sketch were immediately apparent to me but there was something about the entirety of the drawing that struck me as even more discerning. Big Jack might have been a little high on weed so maybe that's how it found its way in, but I felt that the fullness of the caricature captured the essence of our bizarre existence here…all four of us leaning a little off-kilter, living a succession of corrosive moments and maybe truly on our way to becoming caricatures of the men we'd have been if we'd never come to Vietnam. I'd *sensed* that, but as I looked at the drawing Big Jack had so deftly created I was wondering if he could *see* it.

The next morning, I mailed Jack's sketch to Barbara, hoping it might convey something of the strangeness of this place, and of us, to her.

Chapter 10

No John Wayne

The dense jungle gave way to long stretches of grassy meadows, and we slowed to a stop with a wide strip of sun-drenched, semi-open grassland on the left of our column and a long line of single canopy foliage on our right. A few wide-spreading trees were dotting the open area, and I watched some medium-sized birds fly-hopping from branch to branch in one of the distant ones. The single-canopy jungle that stretched to the right of me was midday quiet, and I shrugged out of my pack, moved a little closer to the foliage, and settled into a patch of its dappled shade. Dark clouds were roiling beyond the savanna-like grasslands but they were moving away, and I thought I'd stay dry, or at least into the early night. A stray wisp of wind came whispering through the foliage. I stilled my breathing and tracked its progress. The breeze died and the rustling noises stopped. A blowfly's lazy dronings grew louder, and then it buzzed away fast, maybe scenting a C-ration that someone was heating. The distance-muted calls of the fly-hopping birds and the quiet hums of flying insects made the early afternoon seem normal, and I relaxed my overheated body and stretched out on my back with my head resting on the edge of my pack.

Minutes later a burst of AK-47 shots shattered the silence! The popping sounds of our M-16s answered and then one of our M-60s joined the AKs to create the thunderous frenzy of a frenetic close-quarters firefight in the single canopy jungle about 150 meters distant. A message was passed from man to man that the 2nd Platoon's point squad had run into bunkers and that some of them were dead, and our company saddled up and moved toward the firefight. The sounds of the firefight grew louder, and when it seemed we were going to walk straight into it the 1st Platoon veered to the right and my platoon veered a little to the left. We continued past the location of the firefight, and then we stopped and formed a line that faced the sounds of the chaos. I thought I could have thrown a rock to where the firefight was raging but I couldn't see through the thick foliage. I pictured NVA soldiers materializing out of the foliage and

I settled deeper into cover and searched the leafy growth for anything that seemed out of place in the natural jungle.

The shooting trailed off to sporadic bursts of gunfire for a brief interval, and then another sustained burst of frenzied shooting started. I could distinguish the flat cracking sounds of shots fired in our general direction but I didn't hear any bullets ticking through the nearby leaves or branches. Men started yelling. I couldn't make out the words but I thought it was our guys. The stressed-out timbres of their voices made my adrenaline surge higher, and then the furious firing ended with no tapering off, just stopped. I heard movements and cautious murmurs, and then the voices went silent and the site where the firefight had raged became deathly quiet. About 10 minutes later I learned that the company had radioed asking for help cutting a place to land a medevac and I collected our machete and got directions to Captain Jones' position.

He'd positioned himself as far from the firefight as he could get without exiting our perimeter, but before I got there I heard machetes hacking. I followed them to where 8 or 10 guys were trying to open up a site that was filled with low brush and a few trees. Cutting a landing pad out of the low brush looked doable but when I started cutting I discovered that the twisted trees and low-slung shrubs that choked the site were iron-hard. I kept cutting as fast as I could but before long my arm was getting rubbery and my machete was so slippery with sweat that I had to be careful to land every stroke cleanly so it wouldn't slip out of my hand and spin into one of the nearby guys. I could see that the others were working just as hard and yet we were hardly making a dent in that brushy jungle. I think all of us realized how futile our efforts were but we kept cutting as hard as we could until they sent someone out to tell us to stop.

I trailed that messenger back to Jones' position. As I approached I saw a wounded man lying motionless on his back. Two medics were leaning over him working feverishly to try to slow the blood that was leaking from his torso. I'd stopped well short of them but I was sure the wounded guy was the big athletic-looking guy who'd choppered out from the Ready Response Group with Rene and me. He clearly needed a lot more help than the medics could give him and when I heard the medevac chopper arrive I expected it to drop down quickly. But it didn't; it stayed incredibly high and circled overhead. I heard Captain Jones' RTO ask the pilot to bring it down and the pilot's radio voice demanding assurances that the area was "clear of hostiles" before he'd drop any lower.

I couldn't fucking believe what I was hearing. There hadn't been any shooting for at least 15 minutes and our guy was leaking blood like a sieve and bleeding out as we waited, but the RTO kept pleading with the pilot to bring the medevac down and the pilot kept demanding assurances that it was safe. I felt like I was caught up in a nightmare where something horrendous was happening and there was nothing I could do to stop it. It seemed like that continued forever, but it might have been as little as 3 or 4 minutes before the medevac pilot started bringing the chopper lower. Even then, he ratcheted it down with a series of starts and stops that told me he intended to bolt at the slightest hint of danger.

The words, *"Come on! Come on!"* kept repeating in my head but that fucking chopper just kept inching its way down. When it had finally descended to just above treetop level the medevac crew kicked out a harness chair and started hand winching it toward the ground. The chair dropped slowly, hanging up on tree limbs, breaking free, hanging up, and finally reaching the waiting hands that guided it to the ground. Four men gripped the corners of the poncho they'd spread under the wounded guy, and then they hoisted him off the ground and hustled him to the chair. As they were strapping him to the chair the wind from the chopper's blades wind-whipped his bandages loose but they left him unbandaged and kept strapping him in and when they finished the medevac crew started winching him up. The dangling chair swung from side to side as it ascended. Before it cleared the foliage the chopper tilted a little to one side and then corrected. The length of the cable amplified that slight movement and the chair swung into a tree and hit hard. It was lodged in the crotch of some branches for a second or two, and then it broke free with a sharp jerk. Our wounded guy's chin had been resting on his chest and his body had been still as they'd winched him up but when that chair jerked free I saw his body go limp and his chest deflate as if all the air had left his lungs. It felt like something had burst inside me too, and I was infused with rage, grief, frustration, and contempt. If that chickenshit pilot had mustered the little courage it would have taken to bring that medevac down sooner then maybe our guy would have made it to the chopper alive, and maybe the medics inside it would have gotten some fluids into him, and maybe he'd have survived long enough to make it to an aid station and gotten some treatment that would have gotten him home alive. But he hadn't. We'd needed a different breed of man piloting that medevac, a man like the slow-talking Southerner who'd roared his chopper into that bullet-pinging nighttime meadow off LZ Grant, spitting in death's face and doing the fucking job instead of some lily-livered, rear echelon motherfucker posing as a soldier.

    I watched them winch his airless body the rest of the way up, and then they pulled him inside, circled higher, and thumped away. I felt light-headed then, the about-to-pass-out kind of light-headed, and I took a deep breath to steady myself and looked up at some wispy clouds drifting above a jungle that was heavy with silence. A few guys were making their way back to their squads. Captain Jones' group was huddling together, whispering about something. None of that had anything to do with me, and I took another deep breath and turned back to rejoin my squad. On my way there I saw several guys standing beside two poncho-covered bodies and I stopped to ask who the dead were. I couldn't place one of the names but the other was Merle Haben, the wiry and energetic guy who'd come out from the Cav's Ready Response Group with me, Roger Allred, Rene, and the guy who'd gone up in the harness chair.

    The last time I remembered seeing Merle he'd been talking with one of the guys in his platoon. I'd been walking by and he'd glanced up and given me a friendly nod. I'd smiled back, thinking of how wide-eyed the 5 of us had been just weeks earlier and how self-assured he'd seemed. And now Merle was a body wrapped in a poncho with its boots poking out. An hour later his platoon filed by with two men carrying each of the corpses, one gripping the poncho-wrapped head and the other gripping two booted feet. When the last of their platoon passed us by we filled in behind them.

    We established a night perimeter about a half-klick from the bunker complex, and that night I lay on my blanket remembering the guy in the harness chair and Merle. All five of us had surely known we might die when we'd ridden the chopper to LZ Grant but I doubted that any of us had *felt* it would be him. I know I hadn't, but the prospect of dying felt so real now that my thoughts of Merle were tinged with guilty relief that it hadn't been me. I didn't want that emotion connected to Merle's death but I couldn't unfeel it, and I sure as hell couldn't undo his dying. I turned to my stomach, shifted to conform to the uneven contours of the still-warm earth, and tried not to think of them, wanting to, needing to, focus on staying alive.

Kill Counting

We'd abandoned the area of the bunker complex and given the NVA hours to prepare for our return but the next morning Captain Jones ordered my platoon back to it, just us, he'd be holding back at a safe distance with the rest of the company. Going back was scary as hell but Lt. Jones assigned my squad the point and we picked up our weapons and headed out. We neared the complex without encountering any NVA and I started creeping back to the ground we'd occupied hours earlier. *Were the NVA still there?* I glanced back and saw my fears reflected in the faces of the others, and I resolved that I'd move ahead but if I got the slightest inkling the NVA were there I'd stop; I wasn't going to get us killed by fucking around with NVA soldiers dug into their deadly little bunker fortresses.

I angled toward the site where I'd heard Merle's platoon getting shot up, moving one or two steps and then pausing and searching for sightlines that looked back at me and any warning movements, noises, or scents. The patch of jungle where Merle had died stayed silent, eerily silent, so still that the slight noises we'd make would carry to any waiting NVA, the sloshing of water, maybe even the sounds of our breathing. Their sounds would carry too, but if they hunkered unmoving in their bunkers there might not be any sounds.

Bullet-shredded boughs were sagging brokenly in the jungle ahead. I knew I was close and my adrenalin surged. Everything was coming very, very, clearly, and I squatted in the shadows and sensed ahead for a tiny tug of something that might indicate their presence. My heart was beating powerfully but my breathing was steady. Time passed, and the jungle in front of me began to *feel* deserted. I couldn't have explained why but I went with it, slipping a step or two ahead, once, and then again, hearing, scenting, seeing, and feeling my way closer to the bunkers I knew were there.

I took another step, and my eyes guided my mindfulness through 30 meters of tangled leaves and branches to the almost fully obscured corner of a firing port. Heart pounding, I tried to see through the foliage into the shadow that

108 Jungle Ghosts

lay behind that port. I didn't detect any flickers of movement but I wasn't sure I'd have detected them if they'd been there.

I was in the same situation Merle had been in when he'd been ordered to check out a bunker, maybe the same bunker I was looking at, but my sense of the near jungle was so vivid that I felt I could sense the NVA and stop short if they were still there. Ever aware of the firing port of the bunker I'd identified, I inch-crawled ahead to identify the bunker that would be covering the one I'd spotted. Something pulled at me, and my eyes found their way up a subtle line of thinner growth to the shadow of the almost fully obscured firing port of a bunker on my left. I reached out to it with my ears and eyes. It felt as lifeless as the first. I motioned Ron up, and I scanned from one port to the other as he crept forward. I hadn't detected any movement in their shadowed recesses and when Ron was in position I took a deep breath, aimed through the first bunker's port, and pulled the trigger. Ron fired into the other bunker. The reports of our M-16s were obscenely loud but when we stopped shooting there was no reaction from the jungle.

I popped in a fully loaded clip and inched toward the first bunker, staying far to the right to stay hidden from the bunker on my left and restrict the shooting angle of anyone who might be lurking behind its port. I didn't detect any other bunkers, and when I was about 7 meters short of the firing port I pulled the pin of my grenade and released the spoon. The spoon sprang free and went spinning away. I held the grenade for a long two-count and then I levered up on my left elbow and lobbed it at the firing port. The frag landed at the opening and rolled inside. When it exploded a cloud of dust and smoke boiled out of the firing port. The dust and smoke dissipated. The surrounding jungle hadn't stirred but I wasn't sure the clever NVA hadn't left the initial bunkers empty to lure me in, so I crawled through the complex, collecting grenades and fragging the half a dozen bunkers that were there. One of my frags missed the firing port, but I buried my face in the dirt before it exploded and I wasn't hurt.

After we'd cleared the bunker complex Lt. Jones told us that Captain Jones wanted a body count of the NVA that Merle's platoon had killed, so we established a perimeter and started searching the complex. There was a big dirt-darkened bloodstain about 20 meters in front of the first bunker I'd fragged but I was sure it was Merle's. There wouldn't have been a reason for an

NVA to have exposed himself there and the location was consistent with what the second platoon's guys had been saying about Merle's death. According to them, their West Point-trained Lt. had ordered Merle to check out the bunkers and Merle had refused, telling him, "I ain't no John Wayne." But the Lt. had insisted and Merle had done it, and now a foliage-thinned sightline led directly from that bunker's firing port to that bloody patch of dirt. If that's the way it had happened then the NVA who'd killed Merle had paid a heavy price because I looked through that bunker's firing port and its walls and ceiling had been drenched with blood. I couldn't imagine anyone surviving after losing that much blood but there was no blood trail leading away from it and I couldn't see a body inside it. I wanted to know why, and I crawled through the small entry trench and squeezed into the bunker to find an answer.

The interior was infused with the acrid scent of my frag's blast and another stench that might have been a mix of urine, the smell of blood, and the mustiness of long-damp dirt. The ceiling was so low that I had to stay crouched and the bunker was so narrow that I couldn't turn without brushing against the dirt walls. I was nearly blinded by my entry into the shadowy interior and then my eyes adjusted to accept the dim light that was coming through the firing port, and I surveyed a bunker that was bare-dirt empty except for a bamboo-woven 2-foot-square mat that was leaning against one of its dirt walls. I knelt gently in front of the mat and edged it aside very, very, carefully. The gaping entrance to a down-sloping tunnel began to appear, and when I slid the mat aside a little further the bunker's dim light illuminated the first 2 or 3 meters of a bloodstained tunnel floor. Everything beyond that was pitch black, and those dark recesses reeked of death, soulless, rattlesnake-coiled-inches-from-your-face death. I didn't want anything to do with that, and I repositioned the mat to conceal the entrance and squeezed out into the light. John Glasshof had been watching through the firing port, and he met eyes with me and nodded his approval.

One of the other bunkers had a length of thin fishing line strung across its interior. I couldn't see where either end of the line was attached and I backed away and kept a safe distance from that one. None of the other bunkers showed any evidence of a tunnel or any gore that would suggest an NVA soldier had been killed or wounded inside. At the far end of the complex I picked up signs of travel that made me suspect the NVA had another destination close by, but

I didn't want to be asked to check that out and I didn't mention it. We told Lt. Jones what we'd found and I heard him radio in that we'd confirmed a single NVA KIA. He signed off and we got the hell out of there and, for the third time, retraced the path we'd taken when we'd first left the complex.

We made it back safely but a lot of things could have gone wrong. We'd invited an ambush by retracing our route to the complex and when we'd been there we'd been in the same deadly predicament that Merle's platoon had faced when they'd been ordered to approach the bunkers. Whoever had sent us had to have understood how perilous that was and yet their only justification for ordering us to take those risks was that they'd wanted a count of the NVA's dead. I looked over at Captain Jones and his command group with narrowed eyes, remembering how careful they'd been to keep themselves safely out of the line of fire and hoping that Jones and the platoon leader who'd ordered Merle to his death would have to pay a price for being on the losing end of their fucking body count scorecard.

Click

Captain Jones directed our company on a heading that led away from the bunker complex, and our long column made its way through several hundred meters of relatively open terrain with the unbroken tree line that led from the complex looming on our left. We halted in the open area early in the afternoon and I settled in the grass. I'd just finished drinking a few swallows of water and eating the unheated contents of a C-ration tin when we got word that Captain Jones was sending our platoon into the tree line. I surveyed the 150 meters of grass and the 70-meter fringe of low brush that stretched to that tree line. We'd walked in full view of it the entire distance we'd traveled from the complex and the NVA could have been tracking us every step of the way. If they were there we'd be open targets as we neared the tree line, and if they weren't there then probing the tree line would be a waste of time. That's how dumb-shit-crazy I thought it was but I buckled on my pistol belt, slung my two bandoleers, and scanned the looming tree line, wondering if they were looking back.

My squad was assigned point again. We led to the 70-meter-deep fringe of sparse brush that buffered the tree line, and Lt. Jones placed us in a slightly curving line facing the trees with my squad situated in the center and the rest of our platoon spaced about 5 meters apart on both sides of us. I was at the apex of the curve and I approached the tree line slowly, bending at the waist to lower my profile and meandering a little to utilize any brushy cover I could find. At times I moved a step or two and knelt in the brush for a long pause, and sometimes I moved a little further or took a shorter pause; knowing they could be waiting and not wanting them to anticipate when we'd appear and how long we'd be exposing ourselves.

I covered about half the distance to the tree line. The unshielded midday sun was burning down on me and the air trapped beneath my steel helmet was baking my head. Trickles of sweat were running down my face, and I tilted my helmet back to let some of the heated air escape and surveyed the dense foliage that loomed in front of me. It would be less heated in the shadowy dimness there but I wasn't in a hurry. Every additional moment I took would increase my odds of detecting any NVA who might be lurking there, and I squatted on my heels watching and listening into the veiled jungle for a telltale inkling. The men on either side of me were waiting too, timing their movements with mine and keeping our curved line as intact as possible.

I moved ahead a couple of steps. About 40 meters away the multi-hued foliage was very quiet. *Was our presence that heavy? Had the shooting and fragging at the bunker complex silenced this section of the jungle too, or was the jungle telling me that they were hidden there and waiting for us to move closer?* I couldn't find an answer, and I rose to a crouch and started moving again. I was mid-step when an incredibly faint noise reached me. It was so fleeting and so subtle that I sensed more than heard it but my mind isolated and amplified that tiny resonance so that it registered like a nerve-shattering alarm. I was halfway to the ground before I categorized it in words but I'd recognized it wordlessly the instant it had sounded; *the click of a weapon levered off safety.*

The guys on either side of me followed me down like lines of falling dominoes, and then all of us were lying prone searching for the threats. Sugar Bear spotted them first, and he yelped, "In the tree! Gooks! They're in the trees!"

Someone bolted and that set off a chain reaction, or maybe everyone bolted at once. I didn't know because it was happening behind me, but when I looked back I saw our entire platoon sprinting back toward the company. I turned and followed at a full run, expecting that at any instant the NVA would start shooting and I'd be the closest target. They didn't, and we sprinted unharmed through the brush and then the grassy area like frightened rabbits, never slowing until we reached the company.

I settled in with thoughts flying through my head. Getting the hell out of there had been the right thing to do but the way we'd done it had reeked of panic and I couldn't get that picture out of my mind. I'd been in street fights with some guys who'd been a lot bigger and older than me. If those guys had landed a punch I'd have taken a severe beating but I'd dodged their first punches and ended those fights before they'd had time to throw more. I knew that it needed to be that way here, that we had to react to their initial bullets and shoot back fast enough and straight enough to put them down before their next bullets could find us, and the way we'd panicked and fled made me doubt we had the resolve and toughness that required. The odor of the decomposing bodies we were carrying wafted to my nose. *Did those corpses have something to do with the way we'd panicked?* I didn't know about the others but their presence always reminded me that any of us could have been wrapped in those ponchos.

I looked back out at the tree line wondering, *why hadn't the NVA started shooting when they'd known their ambush had been blown? How close had they intended to let us come before they'd have sprung that ambush?* My mind kept looping through those questions. No answers came. I was weary, I guessed, and I leaned back against my pack and ignored the merciless heat as we waited to be told where we'd go next.

Jay's Seizure

The *search and destroy* war strategy the army had settled on was premised on our ability to locate and kill the NVA. We'd spent weeks trying to locate them and now we'd found them entrenched in the section of jungle that ran to the bunker complex but the course Captain Jones chose led directly away from the NVA who'd proven their determination to stand and fight. We traveled a couple of klicks through open areas that gradually filled with patches of brush and late in the afternoon we circled into a night perimeter. There were a few hours of daylight left and Lt. Jones assigned my squad a patrol. We dropped our packs, looped our bandoleers across our chests, and wound our way through 300 or 400 meters of semi-brushy terrain that provided good cover. We were moving stealthily and for the first time in a long while I felt more the hunter than the hunted. I think that's why I decided to sneak a look into the tree line etched in the sky about 200 meters in front of us.

When I was about 30 meters away I saw a segment of a trail running inside the growth. I looked and listened for a long while. I was pumping a lot of adrenaline when I edged up to the tree line, and when I slipped through to the interior my senses were intensified. I'd anticipated stepping into the far different bionetwork the canopied foliage created but the scene that greeted me was remarkable. In the diffused light of early evening the pastel greens and browns of the tiered jungle's leaves and branches created a watercolor-painted almost dreamlike panorama that felt incredibly peaceful, and I took a knee in the shadowed stillness of the lush foliage, calmed by its serenity and feeling as though this jungle nook was providing a respite from the life-threatening storms I'd endured throughout the day. Those dreamlike moments imprinted themselves in my memory, and then my eyes took me to the line of the NVA trail and I was once again seeing a dispassionate jungle that protected nothing and favored no one. I sensed deeper into the foliage that hung unmoving in the humid air, and the only threat I found was the footstep-compacted line of the NVA trail. It ran straight for about 15 meters to my left, and then it cornered sharply and disappeared into the foliage. On my right, it curved gently into the trees and disappeared. I crept up closer and found its surface marred with scuffs and smudges, some of them fresh.

The NVA would expect us to have circled into our night perimeter, and if they wanted to get someplace before dark they'd be moving soon. I envisioned a line of NVA soldiers rounding one of the corners and walking into us unaware, the way I'd so many times feared I'd walk into them, and I slipped back to my guys and whispered that I wanted to ambush the trail. No one protested, and we set up an L-shaped ambush with each arm of the L covering one of the trail's corners. I was positioned at the junction of the L with sightlines in both directions and the guys in my squad were facing one or the other corners of the trail. I'd been feeling vulnerable and hunted for weeks but we had the advantage here, and I waited silently, edgy but confident. I glanced back at the others. Their tense faces appeared more resolute than frightened, and I quieted my thoughts and reached back to the jungle.

Ten or fifteen minutes later a slight knock-like noise sounded in the veiled jungle in front of us and to our left! I couldn't catalog the sound but some part of my mind had perceived it as a *man* sound. I trusted that and I put my left hand behind me and signed walking steps, and then I slowly angled my left ear to where the sound had been. The jungle felt alive there and when seconds passed and no NVA rounded the corner I had the sinking feeling that we'd been detected. Or *maybe they were just wary of a section of trail that approached the edge of the tree line?* Either way, they weren't going to be coming around that corner unaware.

I looked back to make sure everyone was warned. Sugar Bear was staring to his right, and I looked in that direction and saw Jay lying face up with his back arched, the tendons of his neck corded like ropes, and his jaw working soundlessly. I feared that he'd break silence at any moment and draw their fire, and I low crawled toward him. When I reached him his eyes were rolled back in his head and his teeth were grinding so hard I thought they'd shatter. I cupped his face in my hands to bring him out of it, and when he didn't respond I picked up a stick and tried to work it between his teeth. His jaw was clenched so tightly that I couldn't get it in until John crawled over and held the top of Jay's head while I pulled down on his chin.

A couple of guys were watching us, and I shook my head emphatically and motioned toward the trail. At that moment Jay's body started bucking up and down, thumping each time it hit the ground. I put my full weight on his chest to restrict his movements and muffle the noises, and after a minute or so his face started to relaxx, his pupils dropped into view, and his body stopped slamming against the dirt. He regained some level of awareness, and with a guy on each side of him we backed out of our ambush site with our fingers on our triggers. When we'd put enough distance between us and the tree line for me to feel we'd escaped a wave of relief flooded through me that equaled anything I'd felt throughout the entirety of our threat-laden day.

After we rejoined the company John took Jay over to Doc White. I held back at the perimeter and watched our back trail to see if someone had trailed us in, maybe a hyper-alert NVA point man who'd sensed our presence from beyond that bend in the trail, or maybe just a rabbit-cautious one who'd appreciated the threat of that short section of the trail that ran so close to the edge of the tree line. Or maybe the noise hadn't been made by any NVA coming down

Packing up to leave LZ Grant.

Above left: Me sitting on sandbags on LZ Grant.

Above right: Fresh bomb crater.

Above: Choppers carrying us over lowland jungle on an insertion.

Below: Helicopter insertion into elephant grass.

Above left: Lairn Schmidt (Sugar Bear).

Above right: Walter, me, Vietnamese scout, and Quinlin on LZ Grant.

Eight insertion helicopters.

Above: Crossing a rare jungle stream.

Left: A log day chopper.

Walter sharing a care package on log day. John Glasshof and I are closest to him.

Above left: A picture of me that brought Barbara to tears.

Above right: Ralph Bugamelli and Al Gilmore.

Puerto Rican born Freddy, John Glasshof, and Fuji from Guam.

Dennis Rydgren.

Automatic ambush killed tiger with M-16 on ground in back right.

Right: Kenny, Henry, and me joyriding a Mule on an LZ.

Below: Lt. Colclough, Walter, and me.

Above: David Tedford (Henry), me, and Rene.

Below: Long shot of Black Virgin Mtn. taken from a helicopter.

that trail? I wondered about those things but it never entered my mind to question why I'd ambushed that trail. I know I hadn't done it because of any hatred of the NVA, and I sure as hell hadn't done it to further the *search and destroy* strategy that the military had decided on. The premise that we'd be able to hunt down and kill so many committed NVA soldiers that they'd run out of replacements or quit fighting now seemed so dimwitted that I couldn't imagine any rational person entertaining it. I think I'd simply *felt* like doing it, and whatever had generated that feeling must have endured because I never second-guessed that choice.

The other thing I didn't question was why Lt. Jones had assigned our squad to lead into the bunkers, lead toward the tree line, and take the late afternoon patrol, all on the same day.

Bodies, Jay, and Sugar Bear

In the morning we made our way to the log site carrying the bodies of our fellow soldiers who'd been killed almost 48 hours earlier. I'd helped pack the booted end of one of them on the evening they'd died but I'd avoided looking at the dog tag laced into the exposed boot because I hadn't wanted to know if it had been Merle. I'd tried to handle it gently and yet each time we'd laid the sagging poncho down the body had settled awkwardly and I'd felt like I'd dishonored the gurgling still-limp corpse that had been entrusted to my care. The guys in their platoon had been packing those grisly burdens through another day and a half of putrefying, hothouse heat and I pitied them for what they'd endured. The bodies had smelled of fresh gore when I'd helped, but the stench that had drifted to my nose had grown so overpowering that my memories of them would be forever linked to that putrid odor. *And why?* They could have sent a chopper to retrieve their bodies that first evening, or at least by the second morning, revering our dead and leaving us with our memories of them alive. Anyone who'd truly cared about them or us would have felt compelled to do that but Captain Jones hadn't insisted, or the REMFs in the rear hadn't agreed.

That gruesome ordeal was finally going to end because the log day chopper was taking the corpses out. Sugar and Jay were getting out too. Jay was leaving because of his seizure, and Doc White was saying that he wouldn't be coming back. Sugar Bear was getting sent back because his stomach was covered with oily ringworm circles and Doc White had decided that he needed a few days of drier conditions to clear it up. Sugar Bear had been crowing that he'd be eating hot meals and sleeping in a hooch while we were out humping the bush but Jay's reaction was just the opposite. I think all of us would have liked to have basked in his good fortune but any mention of him getting a ticket out of the jungle had been met with dead silence and an expression on Jay's face that told you how terrified he was that something would leap out and take his life at the last instant.

I didn't expect to see Jay again, and when I heard the chopper coming I made my way to the log site to see him off. They'd deposited the bodies at the side of the landing pad and as the chopper neared the ground the downdraft from its rotors started buffeting the poncho-wrapped corpses. I saw a corner of one of the ponchos tear loose, and before the chopper settled the entire poncho was flapping in the wind. A couple of guys ran out to rewrap the corpse and I turned away, disgusted and repulsed. He'd been left to rot in the jungle and now his decomposing corpse had been nakedly exposed to those of us who'd known him, another hellish chapter in the sordid saga of his death. I wondered if it was Merle, and then I wondered if Merle's family would know the full story. *Would I tell them if I could*? I guessed not, the truth was too motherfucking painful and what difference would it make?

They rolled the heavy water bladder out and began unloading cases of C-rations, munitions, and the ammo cans they'd filled with what they inaptly referred to as our *hot meals*, and then they loaded the bodies and lifted off. Sugar Bear and Jay hadn't been on the chopper. I found Jay standing beside his pack with a worried look on his face, and when I asked why he hadn't left he clenched his long jaw and gave me an incredulous look that suggested he thought I was dimwitted, and then he said heatedly, "I'm not getting on no chopper with no dead men!"

I didn't know if it was superstition or the stench of those dead bodies that had generated his passionate response, but I knew he was right about me being an idiot; I wouldn't have shared a chopper ride with those stinking bodies unless my life had depended on it.

I saw Sugar Bear loading C-rations into his pack as though it was just another log day. I said, "I thought you were getting out to get your belly treated?" and he looked up with a trace of a grin and told me, "It ain't so bad

I can't carry no pack." and then the always lurking frown appeared and he snapped, "It's none of your damn business anyhow!"

I knew what that meant but after all his gleeful crowing he'd chosen to stay with us. I didn't want to call him on it, so I told him that I hoped his belly would rot off. For once he took it the right way, saying "Fuck you, you dink," and smothering a grin.

The resupply bird returned and after they loaded the empty canisters, water bladder, and unused supplies Jay climbed onboard and positioned himself in the middle of the chopper's belly. It was as far as he could get from anything that might reach out from the jungle to get him, and as the bird climbed into the sky the only part of Jay that showed was the vibrating sole of his right boot. The unexpected sense of loss I felt as the chopper shrank in the distance made me think of how Sam must be feeling, and I circled the log day perimeter to him and sat an arm's length away in case he wanted to talk. He didn't say anything, and after a few minutes I returned to the log site.

On my way there I crossed paths with Captain Jones' RTO, and I asked him if the battalion was unhappy with Captain Jones and Merle's Lt. because of the kill-ratio loss we'd suffered in the bunker complex. Before the words were fully out of my mouth his head jerked back reflexively and he barked out a coughing laugh and said, "No! Jones claimed we'd killed a bunch of gooks. It was a fucking victory!"

I looked into the twisted expression on his face and at that moment I knew. The success or failure of the war was being measured based on the relative numbers of those of us who died versus the number of enemies that we'd reportedly killed, and those kill-count numbers were being reported on the nightly network news broadcasts like they were the scores of a game we were always winning. The same numbers were being used to evaluate the performance of every combat officer up the army's entire chain of command, as well as the effectiveness of the civilian leadership of the war, and on each step up the ladder from the boonies to the news broadcasts that data was passing through the hands of those who had personal incentives to create or rubber stamp inflated numbers. *Jones had lied, but would his superiors at the battalion level know that he was lying? Would any of them care? How many other officers were sending those same lies up their chains of command? Was that how it worked, were streams of little lies merging into a massive lie to paper the war records of officers and support the bureaucrats and politicians who were intent on justifying the hundreds of us who were dying every month? Who would stop them from lying? Who would even know?*

It had never occurred to me that any officer would lie about the single metric the army was using to assess the success or failure of the war, but I knew better now. Captain Jones' RTO was staring at me, each of us detesting Jones' incompetence and the lies that had covered it up and each of us powerless to do a damn thing about it. "Fuckin' REMFs!" I said bitterly, and I left him standing there nodding his head.

REMFs was an acronym for "rear echelon motherfuckers." It could be uttered pridefully and a little disdainfully if it was directed at the everyday REMFs who worked in the rear areas but it could have far darker overtones when it was directed at the REMFs who were directing the war from their safe perches in the rear, and whenever we'd gotten news of a grunt outfit getting hit hard I'd witnessed experienced grunts with grim faces and shaking heads bitterly echo two epithets; "poor bastards" and "fuckin' REMFs." I hadn't felt their level of hostility then but the dead had faces now, the faces of men I'd known, and the self-serving men who'd disrespect our dead and lie to distort the reality of the war would forever be fuckin REMFs.

Claymore

We left that log site traveling in a company-long column that was heading toward the back side of the slice of jungle where Merle had died. After a couple of kliks the lead platoon spotted an American-made claymore mine sitting at the end of a patch of low foliage. Its lethal face was pointing back at us and that stopped us dead in our tracks. About ten minutes of waiting followed, and I made my way up the column to see what they were doing. The NVA had set the claymore above the foliage in plain sight. They could have concealed it but they must have wanted to use it to warn us away. If that had been their intent it was working with me because seeing the killing face of that claymore looking back at me was scary as hell. Several guys who were lying prone about 35 meters short of the claymore started shooting and after a few shots one of their bullets turned the claymore's face to the sky. I thought we'd be moving ahead then but Captain Jones heeded the NVA's in-plain-sight-warning and we turned back, conceding that lethal slice of enemy-occupied jungle to the NVA who'd killed Merle.

Chapter 11

Dark Days

My hostility toward the REMFs didn't change anything. I didn't feel any sense of duty to them but I had to accept their decisions just as I had to accept the incessant heat, thirst, hunger, bugs, and threats that the jungle imposed. They radioed their orders to Captain Jones, he conveyed them to Lt. Jones, and, like pawns in a deadly game, we played our parts, following seemingly random azimuths and pushing through patches of jungle vegetation like hunting dogs hand-signaled to flush out birds. None of that was new to me but the days felt darker, like a big storm was gathering or a grim winter was approaching.

I'd always been able to envision myself stepping through a freedom bird's life-affirming portal that would lead back to the world, the way I'd seen those exuberant old hands do on the day I'd arrived in Vietnam. That had been my light at the end of the tunnel but I'd seen firsthand that death could come from any direction at any instant, just *crack* you're gone, and that it didn't care how jungled you'd become or whether you thought good thoughts. Images and impressions were circling through my head...Merle's death, the tangled jungle, my near-fatal experiences, what we were doing and how we were doing it, and the months of walking point that lay ahead of me. I think all those pieces must have coalesced in my deep sleep because one morning I woke in the predawn darkness imbued with an intuitive certainty that I wasn't going to survive Vietnam. I hated the emptiness and despair that followed but I'd come too close to death to disbelieve it, and when I realized that it wasn't going to change I did what most people ultimately do when their doctor tells them that they have a short time left to live; I looked back on my life and thought about the loved ones I'd leave behind. I hadn't done that in a long while.

When I'd first arrived in Vietnam I'd seen things through back-home lenses, automatically comparing the weather, the sights, the scents, the sounds, and how people behaved to the way things were back there. Distinct pictures of my friends, my family, and Barbara had come to mind and I'd often wondered what they'd be doing and whether they might be thinking of me. And then I'd entered the jungle, and being in the jungle had been a little like being in a perpetual slow-motion car wreck where your nonessential thoughts fall away and your entire focus narrows to the most minute details of what's happening around you. The longer I'd been here the more remote I'd felt from my earlier life and the people who'd cared for me, but my certainty of death turned my thoughts back, and I revisited memories and tried to envision a post-grief future for those I'd leave behind.

My mom and dad had wanted my sister and me to go through high school without being the perpetual new kids and when I'd been 13 we'd settled in the town of Central Valley, California. Over the next four years there'd been sports, girls, nights cruising downtown Redding, and memorable days spent on Lake Shasta. We'd usually cruised up the lake's Sacramento arm to the railroad bridge at Lakehead. A long rope had been tied to one of the bridge beams and we'd swung off it and dropped into the water or we'd climbed to the road that crossed the lake and launched ourselves off it. When the lake had been low the drop to the water had been heart-stopping and the force of the impact had plunged us through the lake's thermal layers to waters so frigid it had taken our breaths away.

My friend Dave had an older brother, Jim, and from the age of 15 I'd sometimes snuck out of my house and cruised the Market Street to Pine Street loop with Jim, Dave, and Bob Piercy. Young people had been entering and exiting the cruise and we'd never known when a mysterious carload of girls might pull up and smile at us. On rare nights some of us had experienced the magical touch of a girl who'd trusted us to hold her close, but mostly there'd been the chirping tires of throatily revved cars, our hit-and-miss attempts to buy alcohol, and our stops at Pine Street parking lot number 5; the place where the tough guys congregated and hard looks or aggressive words could lead to bloody street fights.

I'd met Barbara at a local dance hall in February of my senior year. That fall I'd enrolled at Shasta Junior College, and over the next two years I'd made the choices that had led me to Vietnam. And now the only legacy I'd be leaving were the memories the people who'd grieve my death would carry and the suffering my death would cause them. I didn't want to end my life with thoughts of their grief etched in my mind so I tried to envision them having moved beyond their suffering.

Before I'd turned myself in at the Presidio I'd driven to Trinity to say a last goodbye to my 87-year-old grandmother. She hadn't hugged often but at the cabin end of the bridge she'd clutched me tightly in her age-wasted muscle and bone arms. I'd hugged her back and she'd smelled like the cedar that lined the old oak dresser at the foot of her iron bed. I'd crossed the walking bridge and when I'd looked back I'd seen my slightly stooped grandmother standing on the same riverbank where she'd stood to say goodbye to my dad when he'd left to fight in WWII. She'd had her arms folded across her chest and she'd tried to hide it but I'd seen that iron-tough old lady crying. She wouldn't have cried for long. She never did. She'd buried my grandfather and four of her children and she'd set her jaw and tell herself, *if it has to be, it has to be*, and then she'd live her life one day at a time, the way she always had. I didn't know how much longer she'd live, and I'd sent her happy letters about how safe I was and when I'd be home so she wouldn't end her life worrying about me.

My sister Evelyn would fault me for the poor choices I'd made but it wouldn't last. Her husband and daughter would fill her days and she'd move on, missing me and telling my little niece about the person I'd been and the life we'd shared.

My mom's belief in a far better afterlife would help her, but I couldn't see past my dad's pain. The only thought that gave me any comfort was that he'd seen a lot of death in North Africa and Europe and he'd have surely steeled himself to hear the worst.

Saying goodbye to Barbara was the hardest. The summer after we'd met I'd worked at the icehouse in Redding. Some days she'd brought me homemade lunches, and sometimes after I'd gotten off work we'd gone to the drive-in movie. At intermissions we'd walked hand in hand to the concession booth to buy little parfait ice creams, and we'd eaten them in the car with tiny wooden spoons that had felt rough on my tongue when I'd licked the last sweet drops scraped off the bottom of the cup. With her face softly illumined in the glow of the movie she'd been amazingly beautiful, and I'd held her close and breathed in the scent of her perfume. A few times we'd dialed down the volume of the window-hung speaker and held each other until everything had given way to our shared warmth and the sounds of our breathing. I'd have given almost anything to spend one more summer evening like that, with her.

We'd never spoken of a future together but I'd thought about it and I felt sure she had too. The thought of my death casting an enduring shadow over her was hard to bear, and it wasn't just her suffering that haunted me. Imagining what she might feel she'd lost was focusing my thoughts on what I might have lost, and I was grieving for myself too. I knew what a rabbit hole that was and I told myself that she'd meet someone and fall in love, and then I said a deep aching goodbye and tried to put it behind me.

Throughout those days I kept my dark thoughts to myself, believing that in the whispering solitude of the shadowed jungle my gloom would go unnoticed, and then on an evening perimeter Sugar Bear sneered, "What's wrong with you? Did that pretty girl of yours wise up and send you a dear John letter?"

The snarky delight he took in his nastiness had often amused me but that evening I stared hard into his smirking face, and when I whispered, "Go fuck yourself!" he stepped back, knowing I meant it.

A couple of days later Sugar Bear was sitting on my right reading an outdated *Stars and Stripes* newspaper as we awaited the return of the log day chopper when he suddenly twisted my way and started slapping my leg with the paper. I looked down at the agitated 3-inch-long black scorpion clinging to my pants with its stinger curled for a strike. I kicked it off, and then I stood and crushed it with the heel of my boot. Sugar Bear was on his feet too, staring at me red-faced and waiting for me to thank him. We'd always messed with each other, and the expectant look on his face prompted me to ask why he'd tried to get the scorpion mad enough to sting me.

He hissed, "Fuck you, you dink! I should'a let the damn thing crawl up your pants. Next time I will!" and then he spun on his heel and made his signature exit, stomping away with nowhere to go and his gear spread on the ground beside me.

I knew he'd be back soon, and then he'd be giving me the silent treatment and a succession of nasty looks until he decided I'd been punished enough or something happened to redirect his peevishness. Anticipating that made me smile and suddenly the world felt brighter than it had in days. I didn't know why it changed so fast but it was like a switch had flipped. My feeling that I'd someday walk that dim jungle path to my death didn't change but the unrelenting gloom that had darkened my days never returned. I guess that like many people who get a fatal medical diagnosis I'd found a way to accept it, and

I reimmersed myself in the succession of hot, thirsty, hungry, and threat-laden moments we were living, each one of them now even more precious.

Leach Inchworms

I'd led through about 300 meters of the dense jungle, and I stopped at the base of a huge tree to wait for our platoon to leapfrog up. The massive tree was anchored by root tendons that fingered out of the ground and swelled to a head-high level at its trunk, and I shrugged gratefully out of my pack and settled on the moist ground between two of its thick tendons. The tendons and trunk that screened me from sight in three directions were muting my sense of the near jungle. The nagging sense of unease that generated made me consider moving but the walls of my nook were thick enough to block AK-47 bullets so I decided to stay.

A pattern of movements crystallized on the lower edge of my vision, and when I looked down the jungle debris seemed to come alive with a multitude of gray leeches pulling their back ends to their front ends and then extending their front ends forward. All of them were moving at a frenetically fast leech pace, and all of them were arrowing directly toward me. The horde of single-mindedly looping and unlooping leeches converging on me created the impression that I was being attacked by an army of slinky toys but I was badly outmatched by the voracious little bloodsuckers and I rose to my feet, gathered my gear, and made a hasty retreat.

From a safe distance, I finger-flipped the two leeches that were slinking on my pack onto the soft debris. I tried to crush them with my boot heel but they proved too rubbery-tough to squish, so I picked up a twig and flipped them as far away as I could. I inspected the ground, settled down again, and looked back at the well-protected nook I'd abandoned thinking how ironic it would be if I got zipped because that army of tiny leeches had driven me from my shelter. It stayed quiet, and after our platoon linked up with us we moved on, leaving a disappointed multitude of tiny ghouls waiting hungrily for that mighty tree to lure in another blood source.

Chapter 12

Another LZ Break

We'd been out for about six weeks when the choppers plucked us out of the jungle and lifted us high above the canopy. As we neared the LZ their engines eased and, like water swirling down a drain, our covey of choppers corkscrewed out of the sky and settled on the dirt pad of LZ Grant. I was fully one of us now, exhausted, eagerly anticipating the reprieve that the hot, ugly, and rat-infested LZ offered, drinking in its overheated and foul-smelling essence, and exulting in its promise of ample water, food, and a chance to scrub clean. Grateful too, that the concertina wire that encircled it guaranteed that no NVA would be lying hidden a few feet distant, his face twisted with deadly intent and his finger tightening on the trigger of his AK-47.

The meal from their makeshift kitchen wasn't anything special but after weeks of semi-starving on limited C-rations it tasted delicious. I filled my shrunken stomach, and then I wound my way back to our section of the perimeter and leaned back against the sandbagged exterior of our bunker. Ron, Sam, and John were lazing under the canopy with me, all of us returned from treading the same stretches of jungle, often literally walking in each other's tracks, and I relaxed in the warmth of their camaraderie, appreciating this day and looking forward to the handful that would follow.

Each day on the LZ passed slowly and all of them passed by way too fast. Six days of sleeping on a canvas cot or the dirt floor of our hooch bunker, six nights of guard duty, eighteen hot meals, and all the water we wanted. We'd had a few light details but mostly we'd loitered carelessly, assured that no deadly enemy was lurking nearby. That was ending, and we knew what that meant. Several men in our sister companies had been killed recently and as we prepared to leave I'd seen an increasing number of guys with pen and paper in hand, almost surely reaching out to their loved ones for what might be their last time.

I wasn't one of them. I wasn't going to share any of this with the people who cared about me. Not the thick jungle, the hiding, the whispering, every step taking me to unfamiliar and maybe lethal sight lines, the bugs, the littered night perimeters permeated with the odors of feces and urine, the weight of our packs, the wet, the heat, the hunger, the weekly, stomach-churning orange malaria pills, and not the threat of getting wounded or killed that never, ever, released its toxic grip. We bitched about the weather, the way they were using us, and the food but we never talked about our fears, our thoughts of death, or the terror of being hunted that left us with joyless faces sometimes etched with naked fear, all of us moving slowly, cautiously, and fearfully knowing that death would be lurking somewhere in the shadowed foliage.

That was the reality that had brought so many awake screaming in the night but there was another side to that; the jungle was the place where adrenalin pumping, heart thumping, and breathlessly vital moments existed, and as we prepared to leave I could feel that pulling at me.

Back to the Jungle

We loaded onto the choppers in the early morning light, many of us with the same questions running through our heads; *Where were they sending us? Would all of us make it back? Would I?*

I was sitting in the slick's open doorway and I found a handhold and braced my feet on the skid as our chopper lifted off. It climbed into the sky and then we lined out over the jungle with the other choppers flying beside, behind, and ahead of ours like oversized and fat-bellied green birds. The lead choppers hit some upper-air turbulence and took turns bobbing up and down like boats cresting separate ocean waves, and then we passed through the turbulence and flew noisily on, hammering high above the green of the jungle.

I felt a gentle falling sensation as we eased down, and I leaned out and surveyed the multi-hued greens of the jungle's roof streaming by below, wondering how many NVA listening ears and watching eyes might be tracking our path. A natural clearing appeared ahead of us, and our choppers started dropping into it. Our turn came, and I stepped off the rails, dropped through the grass, and moved to the brush at the edge of the meadow. About an hour later the cutting squad radioed back, and when the man ahead of me moved out I let him take a few steps and then I followed. Throughout the day we start-and-stop advanced behind the lead platoon's cuts, and about an hour before dark we set up in as close to a circle as the foliage would allow. There was a little twilight left so I picked up my M-16 and circled to Rene's section of the perimeter. He was sitting with a brown-haired Kentuckian named Jim Quinlin, a guy who'd taken over walking point for his squad shortly after I'd done the same for mine.

Quinlin was slightly taller than average with long arms, ropey muscles, and straight hair that was a little lighter shade of brown than his dark Indian-looking eyes. None of those things made him stand out but if you had jungle eyes you'd notice him. His shirt was perpetually dark with sweat but the muggy wetness never seemed to bother him, maybe because he'd grown up on the banks of the great Ohio River where the summers were hot and humid. He moved loose-limbed and stealthily, although at times he'd surprised me by spinning on his heel or swatting at something like a man who needed to shed some excess energy. He smoked his cigarettes that way too, sucking in the menthol-filtered smoke hard and then snatching the cigarette out of his lips with an eye-catching movement that made me feel uneasy for him. I'd read a lot of old paperback westerns and Quinlin's woodsy jargon and ease in the jungle made it easy to imagine him stepping seamlessly into the pages of one of those books.

They touched on the usual things; the weather, the LZ days that had just ended, the bugs, and whether there were NVA in our new section of the jungle, speaking in whispering voices that sounded accented to my ears, Rene's clipped and fast-paced and Quinlin's slow and drawling. When full dark neared I circled back to my sleeping nook. Most of my squad had settled under the shelters they'd made by tying their ponchos to the foliage but I lay beneath the canopy, an inconspicuous lump on the night-shadowed earth. I heard the night rustlings of a turning body and the careful steps of someone feeling his way a short distance along our dark perimeter. They were reassuring sounds, and I turned my face to the canopy-etched night sky and let my mind wander an intuitive path through the day's steps, sights, sounds, and scents; always seeking, always learning.

Sugar Bear woke me at 2 am in the morning, or at least that's what the luminous dials of the watch indicated. I thought the watch kept accurate time but there'd been times when the last guy on watch had realized that someone had wound the hands of the watch forward and he'd been stuck with an extended turn on guard. Or maybe it hadn't been just one guy, maybe it had been a few guys shaving 10-15 minutes off their turns on watch? There'd been a fair amount of speculation concerning who could have done it. Sugar Bear's name had been whispered most often, but not by me. I'd seen a few hints cross his face, maybe smugness or amusement, but it wasn't the kind of thing you'd lay on somebody unless you knew for sure it was true, and I wasn't that sure.

I caught a few hours of sleep and in the morning we started working our way through the jungle again. In some places we walked through savannah-like meadows filled head-high with elephant grass and fringed by bamboo thickets or brush, and at other times we pushed through bamboo thickets or wandered beneath moderately tall trees that shaded brushy, big-leafed, and stickery-vined growth which limited visibility to a handful of steps. In a few sections of the jungle we crept ant-sized beneath towering trees whose mighty roots rose out of the earth and flowed into massive trunks. Multiple canopies interwoven with thick vines were anchored to those trees and their masses of overhead foliage trapped the humid air and off-gassed the water vapor that nurtured the ground-hugging big-leaved ferns, shrubs, and bushes that competed for the diffuse light that filtered through the canopies. All of the jungle areas we passed through were vibrant with life but those big-treed, high-reaching, and multi-dimensional sections of canopied jungle were literally teeming with it, and as we threaded our way through them I'd often feel the sense of wonder I'd felt when I'd gazed down at the world from the high mountains in Trinity and realized how infinitesimally insignificant I was.

Captain Jones and the Tracker Dog

I was angling up the moderate rise of a low ridge when a faint scent reached my nose. I recognized it at a gut level, and I dropped to a knee and listened into the terrain above. All I heard were the sounds of my breathing and the droning of insects. I crept higher and a slice of an NVA trail began to appear. I slipped the rest of the way up to the trail. I couldn't get a good read on how fresh the scuffs that marked its surface were but the warning scent was still there. My squad secured the opposing corners of the trail and we radioed the discovery in. A few minutes later the company radioed back that a *tracker team* was on the way and for us to sit tight and wait. We heard the chopper set down and a few minutes later I heard them coming up the rise. Captain Jones must have wanted to impress whoever had sent the tracker team out because when they topped the rise I saw that Jones and his RTO were with them.

The tracker team turned out to be one handler and a friendly German shepherd dog. The handler led the dog to me and Jones and his RTO followed. In a whispery voice, the dog handler asked what we had. I told him I'd smelled gooks when I'd neared the trail, and I was about to ask if the dog could distinguish older scents from the scents of a nearby NVA when the handler hissed, "He's got something!"

Captain Jones' face contorted, and without a word he spun around and sprinted full speed back down the trail. He covered about 20 meters with his helmet bouncing crazily on his head and his canteen flapping on his hip, and then he disappeared off the side of the ridge leaving his suddenly deserted RTO standing red-faced and listening to snorts of derision from the dog handler and the rest of us. No one added anything to that, no one needed to.

We started up the trail with the handler and the dog in the lead. I was right behind them, and I kept scenting that faint odor I associated with the NVA. The dog's nose was many times keener than mine and he was alerting on almost every step. After about 40 meters of that the handler conceded that too many warnings were as useless as no warnings and we turned back. The dog team made their way back to the chopper, and when the chopper lifted off Captain Jones pulled us off the ridge and set a course that led away from the trail. I was certain he'd chosen that course to assure his own safety but his *let's get the hell out of here* decision was fine with me. Captain Jones was far more eager to fabricate phony kill counts than he was to engage in deadly firefights that would have truly generated a lot of dead bodies, both theirs and ours. And that was a gift to me because I was given more time to look at, listen to, analyze, and absorb the amazingly subtle things I'd need to internalize in order to survive. That would ultimately turn out to be even more critical than I could have foreseen because Captain Jones would eventually be replaced by a battlefield commissioned warrior willing to walk us through the gates of hell to engage the NVA, and I'd often be leading the way.

The days continued to pass by in a progression of evening meals, night watches, and days spent moving through the closeted jungle. We stayed anxious, itchy, thirsty, hungry, tired, sleep-deprived, sweat-sodden, rain-soaked, jungle-rotted, ringworm-blotched, bug-bitten, prickly heat rash-tormented, leach-sucked, and unwashed. We hadn't had any recent contacts with the NVA but reports of the deaths and injuries suffered by our sister companies kept coming. On two occasions the outlines of a lone bunker's firing port seemed to leap out to me through the tangled foliage. Each time I'd reached back for any hint of life. I hadn't found it but I'd made sure by tossing grenades through their ports.

The first had gone smoothly but at the second bunker I'd cooked my frag off for a 3-second count, and when I'd flipped it away the grenade had exploded the instant it had cleared the firing port. I couldn't understand how that could happen, and then the battalion radioed that we'd received a batch of grenades with three-second fuses instead of the 5-8-second ones we should have had. They never told us how they'd discovered the defect but if I'd held that grenade a split second longer it would have exploded in my hand, and it wouldn't have surprised me if someone had gotten blown up cooking one of them off.

Wounded Soldier's Tracks

I was walking point in a dim section of low canopied jungle with some sight avenues that stretched as far as 30 meters, and that's about how far I was from the meter-long segment of an NVA trail that was peeking through a tangled maze of leaves and branches. Everything had suddenly seemed to grow more vivid, and I eased to a knee and listened into the foliage where the trail ran. It was quiet there, maybe unnaturally quiet, and I stayed unmoving on my knee. I was still there when my squad began to close up behind me. I hand signaled them to go to ground, and when they'd settled I ghosted up to just short of the trail, scanning for movements and reaching out for sounds. All I found was silence.

The tracks of a lone traveler were printed clearly on the well-worn trail's damp surface. His left sandal prints had pressed deeper than his right ones and he'd left a third line of indentations that ran along the outside of his right sandal's prints. I leaned in close to one of the indentions and saw that he'd been using the butt end of his rifle as a cane or a crutch. His strides and the spacing between the rifle butt marks had lengthened as he'd moved down the trail to my left; the marks of a hobbled NVA who'd detected our presence and rushed away. The area of jungle where he'd headed felt different, heavier maybe. I wasn't sure what that meant but it felt like a warning.

There was good cover in the direction he'd gone, and I used that and tracked his prints down 35 meters of the trail to an arbor-like archway of leafy vines that reached across the trail and obscured whatever lay on the other side. It was an obvious danger point, and I squatted at the side of the trail for several minutes. The foliage on the far side of the arbor still had that heavy feel but I was intensely curious, and I gathered my courage and parted the viny growth with the tip of my rifle barrel. The tiny sight avenue I'd opened revealed a muddy depression that had been hollowed out by the footfalls of the many travelers who'd pushed through the vines and stepped onto the trail. The partially crippled NVA had left muddy footprints in the depression that were pointing in all directions, and one of the prints at the periphery of the mudhole was still filling with seeping water. Those prints told me what he'd done, and I was pretty sure they were telling me what he'd been thinking.

He'd been on the trail and he'd seen or heard us coming. He'd moved away as quickly as he could but he was pretty badly crippled because he'd had to continue using his rifle as a crutch. A seriously hobbled NVA probably wouldn't have traveled far, so maybe he'd been posted as a sentry. He'd been limping badly so maybe it was a hospital bunker complex. I surveyed the muddy prints he'd left as he'd shifted positions on the blind side of the arbor, knowing that he'd paused his flight and lingered there deciding something. I'd tracked him to the mudhole thinking he was a runner but the time he'd hesitated there indicated he almost surely wasn't. I knew the answer was lying on the other side of that arbor, and I knew I wasn't going to step through that arbor to find it.

Lt. Jones leapfrogged up with the rest of the platoon. He radioed in the trail's coordinates, and then we crossed it and continued on our previous azimuth, leaving me to forever wonder whether that injured VA had been secreted somewhere on the other side of that vine-leafed arbor with his finger on the trigger; maybe an NVA impelled by a sense of duty, maybe a hot-blooded warrior with a lust for blood, or maybe a soldier so wearied by pain, starvation, and misery that he no longer dreaded death.

I'd been none of those, I'd only tracked him because I'd been curious.

The Bucks in Trinity

I didn't know why the jungle beyond that arbor had "felt heavy" but it reminded me of something I'd seen long ago. I'd been hunting above my grandmother's cabin one late afternoon at the very moment two bucks had poked their heads over a ridgeline. Their necks and heads had been sky-lined more than 200 yards above me and the sunlight had glinted off their horns as they'd turned their heads to scan the ravine where I'd been standing. I'd been almost fully hidden beneath the boughs of a fir tree but both of the bucks had instantly reared back on their hind legs. They'd wheeled out of sight before their front hooves had touched down, and I'd heard them clattering and thumping full speed up the hidden side of the ridge as though a leaping mountain lion had been hot on their heels.

Their ability to sense my presence and the speed of their responses had astonished me then, but not now. I was incessantly sensing for any sound, scent, silence, or any nudge of a feeling that might suggest the lethal presence of killers hidden in the foliage, and I think that unrelenting threat was reawakening latent abilities that had allowed my ancestors to survive in a primeval world filled with predators. Maybe that wasn't how it was happening, but something was changing. I'd grown up in a world where words were useful tools and predictable paths often led to logical endpoints, but countless instants could pass unremarkably here and in the next mercurial instant everything could explode with life-or-death meanings. My step-by-step logical brain was too slow to keep pace with that and I was starting to think in pictures, sounds, scents, and feels that flashed through my mind unfettered by words. Even more remarkably, I sometimes *knew* things without thinking. And I was feeling more inexplicable tugs and pulls, especially when I was walking point. Those tiny nudges felt a little like the sense of unease you might ignore at the moment you lost something; an unease that you might vaguely recall when you were looking for it, and then maybe you'd let some part of your mind nudge you toward the place where you'd felt it and that lost item would be right where some hidden part of you had been telling you to look. My mind was learning how to collect bits and pieces of objects through a myriad of tiny foliage peepholes and combine those bits and pieces into shapes I could recognize too, the way your mind will fill in the gaps and allow you to *see* hidden objects as you hurry along the slats of a picket fence.

I didn't know where all that was coming from. I don't think I even questioned it because I was becoming more and more like those two bucks I'd seen poking their heads over that ridge in Trinity so many years ago; a wild and skittish animal relying on his intuitive brain to survive in an ecosystem that was filled with lethal threats.

Cloverleaf Patrols

Our straight-line treks apparently weren't creating enough opportunities to generate kill counts so they decided to have us periodically halt our daily straight-line searches, set up temporary perimeters, and send four squads on simultaneous patrols. Each patrol was supposed to conduct a 250-meter loop through the adjacent jungle and the composite paths of the loops were intended to create the outline of a four-leafed clover. It was a workable plan in theory, but whoever came up with it couldn't have had the faintest idea of how difficult it was to forge a looping path through a section of unfamiliar jungle and arrive back at the starting point. We did, and we knew that sending 4 hair-trigger squads simultaneously wandering through dense foliage was inviting a deadly friendly fire incident, but no one asked us.

The only squad that made it back to the perimeter unaided on our first cloverleaf patrol was ours. The other three got lost and our company spent more than an hour trying to talk them in. When that didn't get the job done they called in an artillery marker round to sound-pinpoint our location. The round exploded overhead and about twenty minutes later two of the patrols tracked it back to us. They had to call in another marker to guide the third patrol back.

Those three patrols hadn't been anywhere near where they were supposed to have been, and we'd been lucky we hadn't run into any of them. I guess the REMFs were willing to accept that risk but we weren't. Whenever we were sent on a cloverleaf patrol we traveled just far enough to be screened from the company. At regular intervals we'd radio-whisper in progress reports, and after an appropriate amount of time we'd reenter the perimeter at a slightly different location. I was pretty sure that the squads in our other platoons were doing the same thing, so our company was traveling shorter distances and covering less ground than before. I was fine with that but I didn't like the way we were doing it. The jungle was our domain, and sneaking around their orders instead of outright refusing to follow them was an implicit acknowledgment that we couldn't. I hated giving them that but survival overshadowed pride and I didn't object.

They stopped the cloverleaf patrols after a couple of weeks. No one told us why.

Chapter 13

The Gold Pendant

The choppers thundered down and we lifted out of the jungle again. That evening I stood beneath the thin stream of sun-heated water from the overhead shower barrel on LZ Grant scrubbing my irritated and jungle-rotted patches of skin. I deposited the clothes I'd worn for so long in one pile, and then I picked through the cleaner clothes they'd dumped in the dirt, dressed, and waited in line for a hot meal, not needing more, just that.

The listlessness of the LZ was temporarily interrupted by another poker game that included Quinlin, Sugar Bear, me, and the three Kit Carson scouts. The scouts were often barking harsh bursts of Vietnamese words at each other, and when Buc barked something and one of the scouts discarded his hand before anyone had bet I knew the scouts with the worst hands weren't going to be contributing anything to the pot. It handicapped the three of us, but the alternative was tedium so I stayed in the game.

Sugar Bear and Quinlin soon lost their pocket money and dropped out. About 15 minutes later Buc started haranguing the other scouts and they stopped sharing information and started betting against each other. Within an hour Buc and I had cleaned out one of the scouts. The other scout quit playing and then we eyed each other cautiously and wordlessly ended the game. Buc ended up with a slightly larger share of the MPC money and I had the rest of it along with a thumb-sized ivory and gold-faced pendant that one of the scouts had wagered.

I'd never worn a piece of jewelry, but that night I strung its leather cord around my neck and let the finely carved golden-white pendant dangle beneath the front of my fatigue shirt. Over the next days I'd often find myself sliding the pads of my fingers over its weighty gold and ivory face, enjoying the worn-smooth feel of it and envisioning the many Vietnamese men and women who must have done the same over many decades to have created such wear on its ivory face. I don't know why having that ancient pendant dangling against my chest made me feel connected to all the previous wearers of that precious little piece of jewelry and a little less of a stranger in their faraway land, but it did.

Johnny Ciulla

Johnny had written earlier that he'd dropped out of radio school and gotten orders for Vietnam and I'd written him a list of infantry outfits he should try to avoid, including the 1st Air Cav. This letter said that when he'd arrived in Vietnam he'd claimed that he and I were half-brothers and he needed to join my outfit. They'd informed him that they weren't allowed to assign brothers to the same outfit and assigned him to another infantry division. He'd posted this letter from a stateside hospital where he was recovering from a serious knee wound but I didn't feel sad; Johnny Ciulla was safe at home and he wasn't coming back.

Mike and Getting High

I was bored enough to join several weed smokers behind the blanket-draped doorway of a bunker after dark. I wasn't a smoker so they loaded the weed into a pipe, lit it, and blew backward through the pipe's bowl into the blanket we'd draped over our heads. A thick line of smoke streamed through the pipestem and the blanketed space filled with smoke. After a few smoke-filled blankets we were all on the same wavelength, or maybe not, but I was so caught up in a sense of shared intimacy that I thought we were, all of us talking, bursting into laughter, and then laughing at our laughter. When it became too much the laughter died and we sat long silent in the dimly lit interior of the LZ Grant perimeter bunker, each of us lost in our slowly moving thoughts. Caught up in the grip of that gentle contemplation I felt a sense of *wow*, because for the first time in a long while my senses weren't reaching out for what might be creeping behind me or beside me, and man that felt good.

And then someone found Mike's letter; cocky, twitchy-nerved, small-man-complexed Mike who'd carelessly left the letter he was writing home sitting out for someone to grab. Mike tried to wrestle it back but he couldn't, and the letter was read aloud with its *real bad over here* accounts of implausible firefights Mike claimed to have *been in*. Mike, who'd been on the LZ while we'd spent weeks or months in the jungle, Mike, who'd never been anywhere near a firefight, Mike the liar.

A deep feeling of wrongness permeated the brain-clogging smoke I'd inhaled. The words for the wrong of it were beyond the reach of my muddled thoughts, but I knew how wrong it was. The others were laughing at what Mike had written but I wasn't, and in the candle-flickering interior of the bunker my eyes narrowed until the only thing in them was Mike's thin face. I heard my voice saying, "You look like a rat, Mike. A beady-eyed, rat-faced, sharp-toothed-rat living off what we leave."

Mike tried to giggle it off but a couple of the others picked it up, intoning, "Rat-faced Mike, rat-faced Mike."

Mike giggled again, weak and helpless. A part of me knew I should be pitying him but I was too screwed up, or too numb, or maybe it just wasn't in me, and in the shadowy light of the flickering candle I stared into his sharp-featured distressed face without mercy. I'd seen the John Wayne movies and I'd heard the gung-ho cheers of those who'd sent us, and I knew that their depictions of war and the soldiers who endured it had been glorified to cartoonish lengths. We weren't fantasized soldiers heroically ready to die fighting for a cause we believed in; we were frightened young men fighting to stay alive and protect each other. Those two things and how we did them were everything to us, the rest was like their lying kill counts, just smoke and mirrors bullshit to make the hundreds of us who were dying every month more palatable to the people back home. Fantastic accounts like Mike's were feeding those myths and promoting the war and I sat fucked up on weed in our smoke-filled bunker sickened by the lies.

Mike was facing away but the others were looking at me. I knew they were awaiting my words but I had no words in me. I turned my face to the corrugated wall of the bunker. Everyone quieted. My thoughts carried me deeper into melancholy. In the long silence that followed each of us drug-dreamed our mildly hallucinatory thoughts. Someone left. One by one the others drifted into restless sleeps and when the candle burned out and I was alone in the darkness. Eventually, I fell asleep. The next night I got high again, but not with Mike.

Even before that our brief LZ break had felt different. I don't know if I'd done it intentionally but I'd had fewer thoughts of home. Maybe my sense that

I wouldn't return had made those thoughts too painful, or maybe I'd sensed that I didn't need two divergent realities rattling around inside my instinctive mind. Whatever the reasons, I'd been replaying what I'd seen and felt in the jungle, searching for parallels and connections that might help me dodge death or deal death; compelled to extract every moment of life I could from that merciless place.

Chapter 14

Pushing the Limits

Barry wasn't with us when we climbed into the waiting choppers. He'd been in-country for a lot of months so maybe he'd wrangled a rear job, or maybe he'd taken his 7-day RxR. Whatever the reason, he'd been the cornerstone of our platoon and I felt less secure leaving without him. John Glasshof filled his platoon sergeant slot and Lt. Jones made me the squad leader. I hadn't spent much time in-country and I was outranked by almost all of them, but everyone seemed fine with it except for Sugar Bear who hissed that I was a "kiss ass."

The choppers lifted off, and I was once again looking down on a carpet of jungle that stretched in every direction. Skimming high above the hidden world that lay under that canopy had always energized me but I felt a vague sense of detachment, and that feeling lingered during the day as we leapfrogged up behind the point platoon. I might not have noticed it if I'd been in a place where the tiniest of things hadn't meant so much, but this was the jungle and I had an unsettling awareness that I wasn't attuned to the messages it was sending. I'd hoped things would change but I walked point the next day with no feeling for the rightness or wrongness of the living jungle that stretched ahead. The possibility that I'd lost that connection forever terrified me, but two or three days later it was back. Getting high had been the only thing I'd done differently, and I thought the weed I'd sucked into my body might have dulled the part of my mind that could read the jungle. Maybe not, but I wasn't going to risk losing it again. I was through with getting fucked up on weed.

Being the squad leader didn't change anything. My guys kept doing what they'd been doing and I packed light and walked point. I'd proven to myself that physical exhaustion dulled my senses in a way that going hungrier and thirstier didn't and I'd have cut more weight if I'd thought I could make it from log day to log day on less food and water. I didn't think I could, and then one log day I opened a C-ration box and found a hidden treasure.

Hash was the least desirable meal, and the dense fruitcake dessert that came with it was so disliked that the box was usually looted for sundries and discarded. I was looting one of the two I got and I found an unlabeled desert tin that was too light to contain a fruitcake. There was a pound cake inside. The other hash dessert was a fruitcake but I scavenged through my platoon's discarded C-rations and found another hash meal with an unlabeled pound cake. The airy pound cakes were the most desirable food trading items and I ignored the curious looks and walked the perimeter sifting through discarded box meals. I found another, and I packed two pound cakes, two half-sized tins of canned chicken, and one heavy main course meal, picked up my light pack, and left, wondering if I'd gone too far.

I ate my main course meal on our evening perimeter. In the middle of the next day I ate the contents of one of the small tins of chicken, and with about 48 hours of hard going ahead of me I was left with the pound cakes and one half-sized tin of chicken. That evening I asked if anyone wanted to trade for a pound cake. The meal I was offered wasn't my favorite but I ate every bite of it and went to sleep hungry. I opened the second half-sized chicken tin in the middle of the next day, and that evening I traded my final pound cake for another heavy meal. Midmorning of the following day I walked to the log site with no water, no food, and a virtually empty pack. It hadn't been easy but I'd made it work.

The unlabeled pound cake tins were probably from stockpiles of WWII or Korean War C-rations. If that was it, then they were mixing in a fair amount of those decades old tins because I was finding two or three of them ever log day. I traded every one of those delicious pound cakes for a heavy meal that someone had humped through the jungle for a day or two, and I never felt guilty about that. I was going hungrier and thirstier than the guys I was trading with, and I was so thin that Barbara burst into tears when she saw a photo of me with my shirt off. Being thin didn't bother me because I knew what was awaiting me in the weeks and months ahead and I was determined to be who I'd need to be when it happened.

Swamp

The gentle night rain intensified to a drenching rain that felt as cold as the late fall rains back home. I pulled my rainwater-slickened M-16 closer to my side, wrapped my sodden nylon liner around the two of us, and curled into a fetal position to try to fight off the cold. The pool of water beneath me rose higher and I propped my head on my arm to keep it out of the puddle. It started downpouring and I gave up and wormed my way to slightly higher ground. The movements brought a rush of cold water that displaced the body-warmed water that my blanket liner had trapped, and I elbowed into a sitting position, rewrapped my soaked liner around me, and sat with chattering teeth, paying a price for giving up my poncho liner.

I looked up, hoping I'd see the day beginning to dawn, but it was pitch black. I decided I had too many night hours remaining, so I felt my way toward the sound of the rain drumming on the poncho-tent shelter that Sugar Bear, Ron, and Walt the Mailman had tied. They'd worked their way to the higher end of their sheltered nook to escape the water pooled at the lower end of their tent, and I slipped under the poncho and eased my body into the shallow water. One of them stirred. I whispered, "It's just me," and he mumbled something and started sleep breathing again. I pulled my liner over my head to capture the warmth of my breath, and then I positioned my arms to create a breathing pocket and lay shivering. Someone pushed his feet against me to create a little more leg room, but I was a resolute squatter and I held my ground.

Too cold to sleep, I listened to the symphony of taps, drips, and drumbeats of water pattering against the taut rubber ponchos. The corners of the ponchos were string-tied to boughs, and the weight of the water pooling in the sagging valleys of the shelter's roof was bending the boughs. When the boughs dipped low enough the water would cascade out and the poncho roof would suddenly rise. The same thing was happening in the crotches of the broadest leaves, and when the water was too weighty the leaves would tilt or flip over and I'd hear water splashing to the ground. Still, the tent roof was diverting the rain and my soaked blanket eventually captured enough body heat to take the chill off my body. I stopped shivering and lay awake a little longer, wondering if the noisy rain could mask the creeping approach of the NVA, and then I drifted into a restless sleep.

I awoke in the wet of a rainy morning, bleary from lack of sleep. I lay still as my shelter mates dismantled their tent. They freed one of the poncho corners and Sugar Bear chuckled when I had to duck my head under my blanket to escape the water that drained off of it.

"What the fuck are you doing? Can't a man get some rest around here?" I asked amiably.

Sugar Bear growled. "I ain't gonna git wet just so's you can lay around all day."

I watched the Mailman untie his poncho, shake the rain off, and slip it on. He hunched his shoulders against the wet and pulled the poncho's hood over his helmet. Wrapped from head to foot with the poncho cowled in front of his face he looked like a monk. I steeled myself to relinquish the little warmth my wet blanket was providing and climbed to my feet. On the verge of shivering again, I settled my steel helmet on my head, started a hissing C-4 fire, and sawed open my last C-ration tin. I heated and ate it, grateful to have something warm in my stomach.

It rained for two more days and two more nights, and on both nights I edged my upper body under a corner of their shelter, accepted hospitably, even by Sugar Bear. When the rain stopped I welcomed the heat that baked the chill out of my bones, but that didn't last. Our section of rain-soaked jungle stayed exceptionally muggy, and then we waded into shallow standing water. The water gradually deepened, and soon we were slogging knee or thigh-deep through flooded foliage. I kept expecting that the flat jungle floor would elevate a few feet and we'd reach dry ground, but it didn't. We pushed through hundreds of meters of swampy expanse with no end in sight and waded on, sometimes through water so deep that we had to hoist our packs and weapons overhead and transfer them hand over hand to those who'd pushed through to shallower water. Twice we reached small patches of soggy ground that barely nosed above the water. Neither was large enough for more than a few men to stand so we struggled ahead, knee-deep or deeper in stagnant water, feeling our way forward with our feet and breathing in the overheated and humid swamp-amplified air. That was bad, but that wasn't nearly the worst of it.

The swamp had spawned hordes of swarming mosquitoes that were sometimes so dense that they appeared as dark clouds that randomly shaped and reshaped, flowing like schools of ocean herrings or flocks of soaring birds. At their thickest, the millions of their tiny bodies created murky gray curtains that obscured the swampy jungle that lay just beyond them. There was no way to avoid passing through them, and when we did those of us who'd packed t-shirts draped them fully over their heads and necks. All I had was the shirt on my back, and I waded through the swarms exhaling explosively to try to expel the bugs that had been sucked into my mouth, nose, and lungs when I'd breathed. In other sections of the swamp they weren't swarming as liquid-thick but they were always there, filling the air with a high-pitched whine punctuated by the dive-bombing, whir-buzzing sounds of the individual bugs that were flying in and out of my ears, my eyes, my mouth, and my nose. Imprisoned in that wretched place, I swatted my way ahead minute by minute and then hour by hour, desperately wanting the men ahead of us to lead the way out of the hellhole that had spawned those bugs.

In the late afternoon the men ahead of us paused. The pause held for a few minutes and Quinlin and I used some hanging vines to climb one of the trees and look for higher ground. I couldn't see any signs of dry land, but the hordes of mosquitoes and no-see-ums were swarming a few feet above the water so I stayed in the tree. When men ahead of us started moving I climbed down and checked for leeches. I'd string-tied my pants legs tightly over my boots but several blood-swollen leeches had found their way through and fastened onto me. Ripping them off almost guaranteed that their suction sites would get infected with jungle rot, but enticing them to release their grips by touching the lit end of a cigarette to them or drenching them with bug juice took time. The thought of them gorging on my blood was too repulsive and, one at a time, I worked a finger between the two attached ends and pulled until one end ripped free. I had to grip their slimy bodies hard to pull the other ends free, and when I finished I had blood-speckled patches on my legs where they'd been attached. I re-tied my pants to my boots as tightly as I could and rejoined the long line of men who were doggedly flapping and cursing their way through bug-infested swamp water that was amplifying the cloying humidity, hearing their muffled edge-of-breaking curses and wondering how long it would be before one of us couldn't bear it any longer.

The lead platoon changed course several times but in the early evening we were still trapped waist-deep in the murky water. They called in a marker round that exploded a hundred meters away, and we changed course. Our new course didn't lead us to higher ground and another marker round whistled in. We altered course again but the swamp didn't get any shallower. As the light began to wane it seemed we'd be trapped in waist-deep water all night, but about 20 minutes before nightfall we waded into mid-calf-deep water and gradually climbed to a damp dirt island that was just large enough to allow all of us to huddle out of the water.

I folded my body into a fetal position and wrapped my liner around my head to escape the maddening swarms of bugs. The air inside the damp blanket was suffocating close and I had to constantly flap it open to allow in fresh air. The bugs thinned out at full dark and I unwrapped from my liner, slopped on as much bug repellent as I could, and checked for leeches. I ate a cold C-ration and lay back in the darkness then, wondering how many leeches would crawl off the damp ground and fasten onto me while I slept. After a few hours of interrupted sleep I awoke with itching leech bites, surrounded by faces swollen from mosquito bites and stained dark from the refuse of bug-swatted body parts.

A half-hour later we waded through the last of the swamp and left that unholy place behind us, our path through it now just a dotted line that some clueless rear echelon officer had charted on the face of his pristine grid map. And, of course, there were no NVA there.

Dead Log

We were in the column traveling directly behind Captain Jones' command clique when they slowed to a stop. We hadn't moved far enough to have linked up with the lead platoon and Captain Jones and his contingent were on high alert, all of them holding their rifles at the ready and facing out at a narrow section of jungle on our right that had been napalmed or burned clear by natural fire. I hadn't detected a threat there but I scanned it again. The only thing that drew my eye was a grayish log lying on the ground about 40 meters to the right of our path. The tall dark-haired E-6 who'd attached himself to Jones, or Jones to him, was whispering to Jones, and I slipped up to find out what they'd seen.

"What do you see?" I asked when the E-6 glanced my way.

"We've got a body out there."

"Where?"

He motioned in the direction of the log with the barrel of his rifle.

"It's a log," I said.

"No, it's a body," he replied.

"OK."

"I'm going to check it out," he said to Jones, and then he set off on an exaggerated sneak, walking upright through the open ground with his M-16 snugged up against his shoulder in a TV-dramatic, ready-to-fire position. I searched through the terrain again. There was just that log, lying lifeless and wooden on the ground, but he continued his pause-and-start stalk of the log with his rifle at his shoulder as if he was expecting something lethal to appear. I was giving him the benefit of the doubt, thinking that if his eyesight wasn't very sharp he might have been uncertain about the log, but I knew he'd been putting on an act when he snuck up to within a couple of paces of the log before he *discovered* it was just a log.

And Captain Jones? The man who'd turned and ran in abject terror when the tracker dog had alerted was holding his ground and trying to look tough. *Were they trying to fool us or were they trying to fool themselves?* I wasn't sure, but if they'd been trying to impress us they'd failed miserably because all they'd done was make fools of themselves.

They'd have probably spared themselves that embarrassment if Buc had been with them but Buc was gone. One rumor had the Viet Cong killing him when he'd visited one of the multiple wives he reputedly had, but Buc was wary and I doubted that. He could have gone anywhere. He might have even gotten a better offer from the NVA or the VC, but whatever the reason I didn't miss his presence. I hadn't known any of our Kit Carson scouts well enough to develop any trust in them, and that was even more true after we'd caught one of them dropping notes on our back trail for the NVA. It hadn't been Buc but Buc had been too deadly and I hadn't wanted him lurking behind me. In the end his absence was just a side note because Buc and Captain Jones were well outside my circle of awareness which seemed to have narrowed to just my squad, my platoon, and the jungle we were walking.

In the morning I was walking point in a ground-hugging fog that was wafting with the movements of the air, softly white against the greens and browns of the foliage, both hauntingly beautiful and unnervingly obscuring. The seam I was following dead-ended in a tangle of interlocking vines and branches and I had to backtrack. The next seam I tried petered out quickly, and I ignored the pricks and scratches and pushed through to the end of the thicket, leaving one of my squad members to hack out a trail with the machete. Sugar Bear would bitch about me not cutting trail but the others wouldn't complain. Within an hour the fog dissipated and the jungle foliage showed clearly. It ended up being a hot, humid, wearying, thirsty, and hungry no-NVA day on point, a good day.

The Leaf Toter Ant

I'd spent several minutes watching an ant trying to tote an oversized leaf fragment over some bug-sized obstacles when "Saddle up- saddle up- saddle up," came whispering down the unseen line of men ahead of me. I passed the message on, and the quiet of the jungle gave way to the soft rustlings and clunks of men strapping on their packs and climbing to their feet. I slipped a pack strap over one of my shoulders and stood, and then I slipped in my other arm and cinched my lap belt tight. The hard-working ant was still struggling to hump that piece of leaf that was a lot larger than he was. I thought he'd bitten off more than he could handle but I could see that he wasn't about to give up, so I braced my feet against the weight of my pack, leaned over, and pinched a finger hold on a corner of his segment of leaf. I lifted it into the air, and when the ant gamely held his grip I deposited him and his leafy burden gently to the side of our trail facing in the direction he'd appeared to have been headed. As if such events were too insignificant to interrupt his important task, he rotated the sliver of leaf, fastened a new pincer hold, and renewed his journey to wherever it was that he was so determined to tote it.

I'd removed him from the crushing path of our boots but I worried that moving him off the trail he'd been following might make him lose his way, and then I wondered why that mattered to me. I'd read that there were places where all life was considered sacred, but we were hunting and killing other men and I couldn't imagine that anyone here would think twice about the death of a bug. I guessed I didn't care that much either because if I'd seen that ant as I'd walked down the trail I might have stepped on it intentionally. *But not this one*, I thought, *I'd watched this ant work long enough to feel that I knew him*. As odd as it seemed, I felt like I understood more about the heart and soul of that hard-working ant than I did about the hearts and souls of the men we were hunting.

Sick Jungle

We worked our way into a stretch of jungle where the leaves hung limply and some of the foliage was so drained of color that it appeared almost transparent. I rubbed a couple of the pale leaves between my thumb and index finger. They left a slimy residue, and I wiped my fingers clean, wondering what could have attacked the jungle so broadly. *Maybe a fungus*, I guessed. The sickness appeared to have disrupted the jungle's moisture cycle because the ground stayed so wet that the seat of my pants got soaked wherever I sat. The animals appeared to have abandoned this piece of jungle and the flying insects had thinned out, but there were leeches inching all over the moist jungle floor. My body's sentience could usually detect the leaches before they sprang their anesthetic ambushes, even in my sleep, but another insect slipped past it.

The tiny gold ring that had connected my ivory pendant to its leather cord had worn thin, and one day the cord was there, the pendant was lost in the jungle somewhere, and a lump was swelling in the hollow of my throat where the pendant had rested. The lump continued to grow and I kept exploring it with my fingers. When it reached the size of a small marble I borrowed a little mirror to get a look at it. The mirror showed an angry-looking red protuberance with a small opening at the tip like a tiny pink volcano. I pinched the lump between my thumb and forefinger and something pale appeared at the opening. I thought it was infectious material and I kept pressing with my thumb and finger to force it out. All I got was a little blood but I kept at it, and after about an hour something squeezed through the opening. I caught it with my other hand and looked down at the grub-like larva that was about the size and color of a maggot squirming in my hand. The lump was still there, seemingly as big as before, and I kept squeezing and pinching at it for the rest of the day. I guess it was the only one because nothing popped out.

A couple of days later we came to a small clearing that was marked with two bomb craters. Every bomb crater I'd seen had been filled with algae-green murky or muddy water but the water in the two craters was crystal clear. I felt uneasy about drinking groundwater in this sick jungle but my thirst got the better of me. The water tasted OK, and I refilled my empty canteens and drank that water for a day and a half, too ignorant to realize that the foliage was sick and the water was clear because they'd sprayed it with Agent Orange.

We moved on to a section of vibrant green jungle that was once again teeming with animals and insects struggling to secure their place among the many species that walked, flew, crawled, and inched through the vegetation. One day we passed by a thick-bodied snake that had to have been more than 10 feet long. That muscular snake ignored us, and we'd returned the favor by giving it plenty of room. In another place we'd happened upon two stubby foot-long snakes that were so intertwined in the branches of a short bush that they were almost invisible. The little snakes didn't appear agitated or aggressive but they could have killed us with one bite, and as we approached each of us warned the man behind us, gesturing toward them and whispering, "Bamboo vipers."

Those snakes hadn't spooked me but I'd met one that had. Its coloring, skin patterns, and triangular head shape shape were similar to the rattlesnakes back home, but it hadn't had any rattles and it had been much thicker and longer than the biggest rattlesnake I'd ever seen. The size of the snake had been scary enough but what had set it apart was its arrogance. It had seen me approaching and it had lain in my path and faced me down, staying coiled to strike and staring at me with its unblinking snake eyes. Some of the big timber rattlers I'd killed in my grandmother's orchard had been a little threatening but I'd never felt anything close to the level of menace I'd felt when that thick snake's lifeless eyes had been fixed on me. I'd heeded its warning and led my squad in a wide detour around it, not daring to provoke it and risk finding out why that snake had been so assured of its deadliness.

Some of the jungle's bugs demanded healthy respect too. The mosquitoes, flies, and ants were constant aggravations, but there were insects with much bigger bites. It wasn't unusual to come across inches-long tarantulas, big centipedes, and scorpions that looked scary as hell. There'd been some good-natured disputes regarding which of those was the toughest bug, and on one evening perimeter some guys from another platoon collected a big tarantula, a big scorpion, and a big centipede and stick-nudged them into a bare-dirt ring they'd cleared on the jungle floor. All three of the bugs looked fierce but no matter how many times they stick-rolled them on top of each other the insects weren't interested in fighting, just surviving. I watched the bugs crawling away from each other seeking a place to hide, reminded of the time Jay had told me of one of our squads letting some shell-shocked NVA pass by unmolested. I thought there was a lot of wisdom in what that squad may have done and in what those bugs were doing, but I couldn't imagine a realistic scenario where hesitating to engage with able-bodied NVA wouldn't end up getting some of us killed.

And refusing to fight didn't keep those three bugs alive, either. When the stick rollers realized that the insects weren't going to attack each other they stomped them to death. That's who we were, men quick to kill anything we feared, I guessed that's who we needed to be.

Chapter 15

Rising Out of the Jungle

A week or so later the choppers came for us, a gaggle of beautifully oily and noisy machines with room in their bellies to carry us to safety. I knew that another flight would be delivering us back to the jungle soon enough but at that moment there wasn't a finer sight than the circling, thumping choppers that were dropping into the clearing with their open doorways inviting us in.

I'd done this enough to appreciate the high that was coming. The kind of high you might have if you had no place to stay, no food to eat, and no hopes for a better future, and then you learned that you'd inherited a mansion in the sun and an income for the rest of your life, and the only thing you were thinking was *I never want to forget how this feels, ever*. I experienced something like that sitting in the windswept open doorway of a chopper soaring high above the roof of the sauna-hot foliage that had blanketed us for weeks, euphoric that it was hammering us to comfort and safety.

And there was more to come. We were men who'd held up under the never-relenting threat of being wounded or dying in pain. We'd lived hungry, tired, and wet in bug-ridden and heat-filled conditions that had sometimes bordered on unbearable, and all the while we'd been holding death in our hands and pitting our strength against deadly foes who were intent on killing us. The level of dread that created had brought some of us awake screaming in the dark of the jungle's night but we'd feel 10 feet tall and bulletproof on the LZ, and we'd walk among the LZ's regulars knowing we were elite. It didn't matter if they saw us that way, it was enough that we knew we were bad-ass motherfuckers in the baddest place in the universe. I understood how inane that macho-thinking was but as I soared high above the jungle with the cool air in my face I was as caught up in it as the rest of them.

Stolen Steaks

We alighted from the choppers, surged through the LZ's gate, and split off to our past hooches. I shed the pack, bandoleers, and pistol belt that had weighted my steps for so many weeks and hurried to the mess tent. Others followed, calling out to each other with non-whispery voices and seizing on any excuse to be noisy after our many weeks of hushed silence. The clamor assured us that we'd arrived at a place of safety, but the expressions on the faces of the artillerymen, battalion support staff, and the others waiting in line with us said they were seeing just another rough-looking bunch of grunts newly returned from the jungle. *Did they have any idea what it was like out there? Were any of them wondering if some of us hadn't made it back this time?*

That evening I was winding my way through some interior bunkers on my way to the mess tent. An aproned soldier was standing inside an open-sided lean-to barbecuing steaks on a grate, and I stopped and watched him forking cooked steaks off the grill into a half-filled ammo can. When the grill was empty he locked down the ammo can lid and started forking raw steaks on the grill. I thought we'd be eating steaks for dinner but they were serving shrunken hamburger patties on buns at the mess tent; the steaks were for officers or some favored group of REMFs.

After I ate I wound my way back to the little lean-to. The cook was offloading another batch of steaks into the ammo can. He closed the lid, and when he turned back and started forking raw steaks on the grill I stepped to the side of the lean-to, hefted the ammo can onto my shoulder, and walked unhurriedly away. I was expecting the cook to sound an alarm but I guess he never saw me walking away with them, or maybe he assumed that I'd been assigned to deliver the steaks, or maybe he was happy to see me confiscating them, I don't know because I never looked back. I stashed the ammo can behind the packs that littered our hooch, and in the dark of the night many of us ate like feudal kings of old, gripping the greasy still-warm steaks in our hands and tearing off mouthfuls of the rich calorie-laden meat with our teeth. I think those steaks would have been delicious even if we hadn't been half-starved grunts but the fact that we'd liberated them from the REMFs, maybe even the very REMFs who'd been sending us hard-boiled eggs and half-warmed bacon for our log day hot meals, made them the best steaks I'd ever eaten.

I was on night guard duty atop our platform when a flare whistled into the air. It popped open just beyond the perimeter and lit the wired area and part of the LZ with its bright light. A moderate breeze was blowing steadily and the flare followed a wind-driven downward arc, swaying back and forth beneath its parachute with a plume of white smoke trailing behind it. At first it burned so brightly that the heavens disappeared behind its brilliant halo, and then the searing white light faded to a shrinking orb of pale yellow and the black backdrop of the night sky began to reappear. The sight of the sideways drifting yellow orb trailing whitish smoke across that expanding black background created the illusion that the flare was fixed in the sky and our perimeter was spinning like a giant merry-go-round. As the flare grew dimmer the illusion grew stronger, and just before it burned out it was saluted with a series of prolonged "wooоowwwww maaans!" from guards up and down the perimeter who were high on weed. Having guards who were a little screwed up on weed wasn't something I'd have chosen, but giving them a few moments to feel they were riding around the LZ on a sky-darkened carousel was, I thought, a pretty fair trade.

Sniper School

The midafternoon downpour lasted for almost an hour, and then the clouds evaporated and the humidity lessened. Scattered shots and an occasional burst of full-auto firing sounded from the area outside the LZ that served as a firing range, and I decided that this low-humidity late afternoon was as good a time as any to zero in my M-16. I picked up a few cigarette butts as I walked through the LZ. I rolled them between my thumb and index finger to loosen the papers, and then I peeled the papers off the two least-stained filters and stuffed them in my ears to muffle the cracks of my shots. As I neared the shooting area I saw 4 or 5 guys from one of our other platoons taking turns shooting at a C-ration can that was resting about 40 meters in front of them. Roger Allred, one of the guys who'd come to the company with Rene and me, was with them, and I walked up, smiled, and said, "You aren't trying to kill that can, are you?"

I'd said it lightheartedly, but the guy standing beside Roger turned my way and said testily, "Let's see you shoot it if it's so easy."

Sugar Bear had been saying that guys in the other platoons had been complaining that our platoon wasn't as good as everybody thought it was so maybe I'd touched a nerve, or maybe I just hadn't realized how I'd come across. Either way, I wasn't going to let it pass. I chambered a round, clicked the firing selector to semi-automatic, and shifted to face the can at a 45-degree angle. I was almost certain that my M-16's sights weren't dialed in but I'd done a lot of instinctive shooting with a .22 rifle and a BB gun and my M-16 had been in my hands for weeks. When I flicked it to my shoulder it felt like a part of me and I squeezed the trigger as it came level. The can skittered away. The recoil propelled the end of my barrel up slightly, and when it dropped level I fired and the can jumped again. After my second shot I had the rhythm of the recoil and I was triggering the M-16 just as the barrel dropped back to level. At the end of my 18-round clip I was firing as fast as I could squeeze the trigger and the M-16 was chattering almost like it was firing on fully automatic. At that tempo it was impossible to tell which shots had hit the can and which may have missed, but the can never stopped leaping away.

The bolt of my M-16 locked open on the empty clip, and the can skittered to a stop a long way out. In the silence that followed I said, "**That's** how you kill a can," and when I turned and walked away one of them whispered, "*Shiiiit.*"

In the morning Lt. Jones came to tell me that a battalion-level officer had seen me at the range and he'd instructed my company to offer sniper training "to the guy who'd done the shooting." He asked if I was interested and I didn't know how to answer. The prospect of becoming a sniper made me think of a deer I'd shot when my dad had been between jobs and we'd needed meat. I'd been hunting about a mile above my grandmother's cabin and I'd seen a deer standing a very long way down a slope. I'd taken the shot, and my bullet had hit high on its back above its shoulder. The deer had dropped and as I'd scrambled down the mountain to put it out of its misery it had been bleating human-sounding pain-filled screams. Those cries had troubled me for a long time, and now the thought of putting a long-distance bullet through someone reminded me of the last tortured moments of that dying deer's existence. I couldn't see myself inflicting that on someone who wasn't threatening me but tickets out of the deadly jungle were too precious to throw away.

I told Lt. Jones that I'd have to think about it and then I ran it by Ron Belin. Ron told me that if I accepted it they'd send me to sniper school and I'd probably get posted on an LZ. I'd been pretty sure I wasn't going to take it but Lt. Jones had said that he'd been told to offer it to *the guy who'd done the shooting*, so I went back and asked if he could offer it to someone else if I turned it down. He thought it over carefully, and when he nodded soberly and said that he thought he could I asked him to offer it to Rene. A couple of hours later Rene came by to tell me that Lt. Jones had offered him sniper training. He wanted to know what I thought about that, and I repeated the information Ron had given me and encouraged him to take it. Others were telling him that it was too good to pass up, and Rene finally decided that he'd take it and after he completed sniper training he'd request a reassignment back to our platoon.

He left never knowing that I'd turned it down. I regretted that. It was the only time I hadn't been brutally straightforward with a fellow grunt about anything, big or little, but I'd worried that he'd have stayed in the jungle if he'd known. I hadn't wanted that, and especially not for Rene. In many ways the other guys were like family, and in other ways they were temporary men with stick-figure pasts and blank futures, but not Rene. Maybe it was because of his innate decency, courage, and bighearted nature, or maybe I'd just allowed myself to get too close to him before I'd fully grasped how tenuous our lives were here, I didn't know, but the possibility of seeing Rene wrapped in one of those fucking ponchos had been weighing on me from the night we'd huddled in our foxhole in that meadow off LZ Grant.

I'd miss Rene, but I rode the chopper back to the jungle relieved that he wasn't riding out with us.

Chapter 16

Return to the Jungle

The roof of the canopy flowing beneath our chopper created a frontier where our technological advantages over the NVA ended, and we dropped below that ceiling and reentered that foliage-choked realm where bullets fired by enemies just meters away could tear our bodies apart. My squad had the first cut, the one where every enemy within a 2,000-meter diameter circle would surely know we'd arrived. *Was death lurking there for one of us, maybe for me?* I wondered, and then I was slipping from cover to cover, pumping adrenaline and seeing myself creeping through sightlines that some part of my mind had reconstructed. I heard the tattletale animal's calls that warned of our presence that day, but only ours, and death wasn't lurking, not for me, not for any of us.

Days of hard humping followed with little respite from the thick overheated air, the buzzing, biting bugs, and the night-watch sleep-interrupted nights. We survived on whatever quantity of food and water we were willing to carry on our backs or forage from the jungle, and on log days we were supplied ample water, C-rations, one cold drink and a cold beer, and a *hot meal*. A calorie-laden hot meal would have been a huge deal but the ammo cans they offloaded were always half-filled with warm bacon and hard-boiled eggs, fitting companions to the sour "Squelch" sodas they invariably sent with them.

They'd done it again and Sugar Bear was furious. He'd been playing old hand to an FNG he'd nicknamed, *Baby Huey,* and as we waited our turn he was bitching, "They're selling the good stuff themselves an spendin' the money they git on whores. I'd like to see them pricks out here eating hard-boiled eggs and drinkin' that green piss. They're low-life motherfuckers that don't give a shit about anyone but their own lifer selves. Them bastards would screw their mothers if it would make em a buck."

I was standing behind them and in a kindly tone I suggested, "Sugar Bear, you should stop complaining and start thanking this man's army for the free food and a warm place to sleep at night."

Sugar Bear spun around and sneered, "Fuck you, you lifer," and then he turned back to Baby Huey and muttered, "Free food, my ass, I hope he chokes on them eggs."

Baby Huey was too new to know who he was dealing with. He asked hopefully, "Hey Sugar Bear, if you don't want em can I have your eggs?" and Sugar Bear snapped back viciously, "Fuck you, you dink! **I'm not givin' my hot meal to some goddamn FNG!**"

I laughed, but the shocked look on Baby Huey's face made it clear that he didn't have a clue what he'd done to deserve a tongue-lashing. And of course he hadn't done anything. I'd been the one that had lit Sugar Bear up, and a red-faced Sugar Bear made that clear by turning his back to me and hissing over his shoulder, "Fuck you, you dink."

He was so livid that I passed up the opportunity to suggest that Baby Huey ask about the availability of Sugar Bear's bacon. I carried my two eggs and three strips of bacon to the edge of the log site. The egg whites stuck to their shells, and when I finished peeling them I was left with two very small eggs. I sprinkled a packet of salt and ate each egg in one mouthful. I skimmed the thin layers of egg whites from the shell fragments with my front teeth and finished the sparse meal with the three limp strips of bacon, certain that Sugar Bear was right; the REMFs sending us these meals were *"low-life motherfuckers that didn't give a shit about anyone but their own lifer selves."*

An Army of Pillaging Ants

I slowed my overheated panting breathing and focused on the wide columns of army ants that were flowing through the debris about 3 meters to my right. Some of the leading ants had half-inch-long bodies equipped with oversized heads and massive pinchers. There weren't many of those, but the smaller ants marching behind them were so numerous that they were painting black swaths across the mottled greys, browns, and greens of the jungle's carpet.

The big-pincered ants flushed a 3-inch-long centipede out from under some debris, and a line of smaller ants closed in to hold the centipede at bay. The centipede's powerful mandibles decimated the first ants that engaged it, but within seconds a stream of ants split off from one of the main swaths and a dark shadow began to darken around the big centipede. The centipede was soon encircled by an inches-deep ring of the smaller army ants, and then, as if a distinct signal had commanded them, the masses of surrounding ants swarmed over the centipede. Its strong body curled and twisted under their onslaught but it was already blackened by hundreds of biting ants. It began to still, and before it stopped twitching the ants were dismantling it. I watched those army ants savage and devour everything that couldn't outrun them, dispassionately obeying the timeless laws of a jungle that played no favorites and granted no mercy to anything or anyone.

When we started up again we discovered that Jim Quinlin's squad hadn't made a full cut, and I heard Jim's whispering voice saying, "I tole y'all I dint wan nobody runnin up ahint me. Doan nobody wanna lissen? Keep gettin up ahint me an' you'll git us all kilt with thet racket. I ain't gonna die jus' cus someone doan lissen."

Quinlin had been walking point when someone in his squad had clanked their rifle against their canteen, and he'd stopped, called in the end of the cut, and waited for us to work our way up and lead on. He was still complaining when they radioed instructions for us to stop for the night.

Sam

Sam had told me that he'd applied for a hardship leave to return home and deal with a personal issue. He hadn't volunteered more, but it must have been serious because a few days later he'd ridden out on a resupply bird. I'd been surprised at how good I'd felt when he'd left, even if it was only for a short while. Getting any kind of a ticket back to the world was a huge fucking deal and Sam's mysterious departure had generated a beehive buzz of whispered conjectures, but when Sam returned on another log bird he offered no explanations and kept to himself. He never told me whether the issue he'd gone back to address had been resolved but he did say that he'd filed a complaint with his congressman about the *hot* meals they'd been sending out and his congressman had initiated an investigation. That must have carried a lot of weight because they started sending us ammo cans loaded with the kinds of meals they'd served on the LZ.

Sam told me that he'd also filed a complaint with the Army's Inspector General requesting a hardship discharge or a reassignment, and a few days later he climbed on another resupply chopper. Our previously morose Sam was smiling at me when the chopper lifted off, and that smile stayed on his narrow face as he ascended through the canopy into the mid-morning sky and made good his escape. I watched him go, thinking of how much had changed in the short time I'd been here. Three-and-a-half months earlier I'd been a raw FNG sitting in the sticky monsoon heat of LZ Grant listening to Sam and Jay's war stories, and now I was the squad leader, John was the platoon sergeant, Ron was packing a radio for the Lt., Jay was somewhere in the rear, and Sam was riding high in the air never to return. Walt the Mailman had been with us for a while, but of the guys in my original squad only Gramps, Sugar Bear, Big Jack, and I were left. I thought back on the faces of the men who'd been killed or wounded and a wave of wanting swept through me. I wanted to see every guy in my squad climb on a chopper and rise into the sky with a smile on his face, like Sam had, all of them, the originals and our FNGs. The feeling was so powerful that it seemed I could hold it so tightly that it couldn't escape, but I wasn't one of the handful of men who had that power. I let it wash through me, and then I returned to my pack and started rummaging through the company's discards in search of precious pound cakes that might have slipped through the hands of the others; a lowly grunt doing what he could to survive.

Chapter 17

The New Lt.

The 1st Cav's line officers served six-month combat tours, and when Lt. Jones neared the end of his officer's tour he left with no fanfare and no farewells, or at least not to me. His replacement arrived on the log bird, and when I spotted the new face I asked Sugar Bear who he was. Sugar Bear smirked, "It's the new Lt., you don't know much, do you?" I told him I hadn't needed to know because I didn't have any interest in kissing the new Lt.'s ass. That sent him into another sibilant tirade about me being the biggest kiss-ass in the company but I was too busy reading the new Lt. to give it the attention it deserved. We'd all been new guys once, and when a new guy showed up most of us watched the way he moved, the way he held his head, the way his eyes met ours, and how quickly he incorporated the way we were doing things. I could see the guys at the log site doing that now, reading the new Lt.'s body language, weighing his words, and wondering *can this platoon leader help us survive?*

We'd know soon. You could put on airs and embellish who you were in the rear but the jungle scrubbed away facades. It did it with hunger, thirst, biting bugs, heat, stickiness, wetness, itching, filth, sleeplessness, and loneliness, but mostly it did it with a never-ending weariness and a deep fear of death that overrode vanities. *And who could you hope to fool?* We all knew that our survival might someday rest on the actions of one of us and we were almost always attuned to what others could or couldn't do, and what they would or wouldn't do, reading the real them and not some construct they might have created to boost their egos.

This Lt. was circulating among the grunts in the log site area, a mid-to-late 20s dark-haired and round-faced man about 6 feet tall with a fleshy build. Like any new guy he was being met with tentative looks and guarded body language but he seemed oblivious to the cautious reception he was getting, and he kept pushing his way from place to place like a politician at a rally, talking more than he was listening and trying too hard. I watched him trying to chum up with guys who'd be trusting what their guts would be telling them, ever more certain that the impressions they were forming wouldn't be favorable. Mine weren't, and over the next days that didn't change.

About a week after his arrival, I was on our evening perimeter heating a C-ration meal over a hissing C-4 fire when a movement caught my eye. I looked up and watched the new Lt. pass through our perimeter and disappear in the leafy vegetation with a Colt .45 pistol waving in his right hand and packets of toilet paper clutched in his left. There'd been no whispered *"man out"* warnings, and when he rustled some brush guys were suddenly staring at the area where he'd disappeared with their M-16s in their hands. I passed word that the new Lt. had exited the perimeter without alerting anyone. My news was greeted with universal disgust and when the new Lt. reappeared several of us had our M-16s leveled at him to drive a lesson home. His steps hesitated but he recovered quickly and continued in, laughing it off like it was just a little thing. None of us were laughing with him, the grumbling had become too rampant, the view too universal, and the verdict too clear; *Someday that guy's gonna get somebody killed!* I looked at his still-smiling face, wondering if I'd someday regret the warning I'd given.

The Inspection

Our company had two no-casualty contacts that didn't directly involve our platoon and then the choppers pulled us out of the jungle again. LZ Grant was the same, stiflingly drab and, except for the booming artillery launches that unfailingly startled me now, placid. I had a squad leader's responsibilities and on our second morning Larry and Vern came to me complaining that the new Lt. had awakened them by touching them with his foot. They said he'd gotten "too friendly" and "watched us put our pants on." I told them that it wasn't a life and death issue but if he did anything like that again to let me know and I'd handle it. Their account left me uncertain whether they were unwilling to accept any degree of familiarity from a platoon leader they detested or if the new Lt.'s behavior had warranted their unease.

The next day all of the squad leaders were told that our battalion level officers were going to conduct a first-ever inspection of the LZ's perimeter and to make sure that the trash on our section of the perimeter was picked up.

My guys grumbled about having an inspection and having to pick up trash but most of them started gathering up the cigarette butts and the bits of trash that were scattered nearby. Larry and Vern hesitated, and then they pulled me aside and Larry said, "Cleaning up trash that has been mostly left by the REMFs is BS when we're out humping the jungle and they're just sitting on their asses,"

I agreed. I offered to convey their objections to the Lt. and they told me to go ahead. I asked if they were sure, and when they said they were I nodded my approval and started up the perimeter road to the new Lt.'s hooch. On my way past a few of our platoon's bunkers I paused to point out that they'd missed bits of debris here and there. The common response was a laughing suggestion that I should *go to hell*, or *mind my own damn business*, and I always responded by telling them that I was on my way to report Larry and Vern for neglecting their trash collection duties and that I'd be adding their names to the list.

I announced myself at the Lt.'s bunker. He said to come in, and I passed through the blanketed doorway and found him standing in front of a small mirror wearing a freshly pressed uniform and running a comb through his wetted hair.

He barely glanced at me. "What is it?"

"We've got a problem. Two of my guys think it's unfair to make them clean up after the REMFs and they've refused to pick up around the bunkers."

"Well make them do it, you're their squad leader," he said, still running the comb through his hair.

"I agree with them. I'm not going to make them pick up and I'm not going to ask the other guys to carry their load."

His eyes never left the mirror. "That's **your** problem," he said dismissively.

"What did you say?"

"I said it's not **my** problem, it's **your** problem."

He was making a huge mistake. We were the guys who took the risks and did the fighting, and having us submit to an inspection and pick up trash on one of our handful of precious LZ days showed a lack of appreciation for the physically miserable and hazardous weeks we'd spent in the jungle. This was about the way the men who were facing death needed to view themselves, and it was about the regard they felt they merited from the men who commanded them. Ultimately it was about morale, not the *rah, rah, let us at em*, crap but morale that was grounded on a sense of self-worth, belonging, and appreciation, the kind of morale that would embolden men to continue risking their lives fighting a brutally lethal war.

I'd known that intuitively and I'd listened to Larry and Vern's objections, acknowledged their validity, and supported them. It wasn't hard, all the new Lt. had to do was give Larry and Vern an audience and then give them some reason why they should go along with this simple chore, or just call it bullshit and promise to work on getting it changed, to just show them a little fucking respect instead of treating them like nothings whose opinions didn't matter. But he wasn't giving them that, and he wasn't showing me any respect either.

I spit back, "**No**, it's **your** problem!" and I left him standing in front of that mirror wetting and combing his hair, a man tasked with life and death responsibilities he was ill-suited to handle.

Larry and Vern were squatting with their backs resting against the side of the bunker as I approached. They both had uncertain looks on their faces, maybe regretting taking a stand or maybe reading the anger that was raging in me. The others had deposited the trash in the 50-gallon barrel that sat between our two bunkers, and I walked past them, hefted the barrel high overhead, and dumped the entire contents in the dirt.

Sugar Bear shouted, "Ed! What the fuck are you doing?" and I kicked the pile apart and said, "Leave it there. We're not picking up their fucking trash."

Sugar Bear looked like he was going to throw a fit, and then he smiled, maybe liking the idea of telling them to go to hell or maybe just happy that I'd be taking the heat for it. The others nodded wordlessly, and then we sat and waited. The new Lt. must have been watching when the inspectors rounded into view because he came sauntering down the perimeter road looking parade-ground immaculate in his pressed uniform. He appeared to be quite pleased with himself, and then he saw the trash scattered throughout our bunker area and his steps faltered.

"What's this? What's this mess? We've got to get this picked up!" he yelped, appearing far more alarmed than he'd been when he'd left the perimeter unannounced and returned to face the leveled barrels of our M-16s.

I said, "It's **your** problem," and we watched him scramble around gathering up trash with both arms and stuffing it in the barrel, all the while voicing distressed sounds.

He got most of it, clapped the dust off his hands, tucked and straightened his uniform, and, without a word or a glance in our direction, he scurried off to greet the battalion and company officers; men whose esteem he clearly valued far more than ours.

I waited for one of the inspectors to notice the debris that had escaped his hasty cleanup so I'd have an opening to say that we shouldn't be assigned menial details on our handful of days out of the jungle. No one did, and the inspection moved on.

Patrol off LZ Grant

Shortly after that they sent our platoon to patrol off Grant, and in the early midmorning we passed through the LZ's gate and headed southwest. We traveled about a klick and a half through the patchy semi-open terrain that extended from the base of the Black Virgin Mountain and stopped for a break in a small brush-edged meadow. I saw shadowy outlines of what appeared to be depressions just inside the brushy vegetation that edged the meadow, and when I moved closer a multitude of bare dirt holes took shape deeper in the foliage. There'd been no signs that anyone had walked this meadow recently, and I signaled where I'd be and meandered among the holes.

They were configured in wandering lines with the longer sides of the rectangular excavations generally facing in the same direction. The exceptions had been dug in the two areas where the ground was slightly elevated. The holes in the little rises were spaced further apart and positioned like hand-shuffled dominoes pointing in every direction. There was nothing to indicate that any of the holes had been used, and there were no footpaths, discarded trash, or footprints. I walked to the far reaches of the many excavations without picking up a single clue to indicate why they were there. I surveyed the large expanse of holes again, picturing the number of men it would have taken to dig them and knowing they had to have had a reason.

The walls of some of the holes had eroded a little but most of the shovel-blade marked walls were largely intact. I guessed that they might have gone through one wet season, and that made me think of the large NVA force that had attacked LZ Grant during the spring of the year. The timing was probably right but why would the NVA have dug holes so far from the LZ, and why didn't the layout of the holes make any strategic sense? I looked out over the holes that dotted virtually the entire low-treed expanse trying to discern a pattern that might suggest an answer. Nothing made any sense, and then the graveyard configuration of the excavations crystallized in my mind's eye. I might have been wrong, but the only explanation I could find to explain the existence and the configuration of those holes was that the NVA who'd attacked LZ Grant had stopped here to dig their own graves.

I stood in the rising heat, hearing the quiet sounds of my fellow soldiers and the stirrings of the listless midday wind and picturing this spot those many months ago; resolute men digging deeply into the dirt at each hole, each of them knowing that he'd soon be launching his body into the teeth of a fully manned and artillery-armed LZ ringed with concertina wire and laced with flesh-shredding claymore mines. The scene reeked of wretched desolation and despair, and I imagined that sadness had been dripping from their sweating bodies and soaking the soil beneath my boots.

Had they been crying tears for their loved ones who'd live on without them? Had they believed that they'd be forever revered for their sacrifice? I didn't know how those men thought, but if they'd expected this graveyard to stand as a testament to their courage and their sacrifice they'd been wrong; the hundreds of them who'd died attacking LZ Grant had been bulldozed into a common hole and buried near the LZ. These would remain forever empty, but I stood among the empty holes they'd dug certain that they were a testament to something the REMFs who'd planned our strategy were unable to comprehend; that a war of attrition strategy predicated on the premise that we could hunt and kill enough of these men to make them stop fighting was doomed to fail.

We left that forsaken place and traveled another half-klick to a small meadow. There was a small stream flowing a few steps inside the trees at its northern edge, and we found a small NVA trail there with a plastic baggie nestled in the dirt alongside it. A tiny Loach chopper buzzed in and hovered overhead, and the pilot radioed down that they'd spotted two NVA there a day earlier. The Loach buzzed away and the new Lt. directed us into the meadow and motioned for us to gather around him. I pulled my squad back from the inviting cluster he was creating and signaled them to spread out. I'd expected that every instinct of the men who were crowding together would be screaming at them to do the same, but Quinlin was the only one who separated out with us. The others stayed huddled around the new Lt., listening to him say that we were waiting for a *team* the battalion was sending out. When he finished talking the group of them settled on the ground, still clustered in the meadow and still inviting an attack on all of us.

I'd been deeply impassioned by the sacrifices and the commitment of the NVA who'd dug those holes and I'd been reminded of the lethality of men who were willing to die for a cause. Maybe that's why seeing most of our platoon heedless of the perils we were facing and putting my life at risk made me feel the way I'd felt when the E-6 patrol leader had told me to stay in the bomb crater. A word from me would have spaced them properly but I was so disgusted and so coldly angry that I made the same decision I'd made when I'd stepped to the lip of the bomb crater on my first day in the jungle; I resolved that my squad and Quinlin had made our choices and they'd have to live with theirs.

They were still clustered in the open meadow when a Huey chopper landed. Four men wrapped in bulletproof Kevlar vests climbed out of it and the group in the meadow packed themselves even more tightly around them. I kept scanning the nearby tree line, anticipating that something deadly might fly out of it at any moment. Nothing did, and after they'd talked things over with the new Lt. the four-man team headed to the tree line. They sniffed around a little, and then the four of them started slowly up the trail moving about an arm's length apart. Their point man was holding a shotgun in two hands, his backup was carrying a heavy-caliber automatic rifle, the third man back had a grenade launcher, and the fourth was carrying an M-16. They must have scripted their roles because the point man was invariably facing ahead, the second man was facing to the right, the third man was facing to the left, and the last man was facing forward.

That puzzled me. The way they'd armed and aligned themselves would give them quick-reaction firepower but putting bullets out was the easy part, not getting ripped apart by NVA bullets was the hard part. The heavy Kevlar vests they were wearing might protect their torsos but large areas of their bodies were unprotected, and they were so tightly grouped that a single burst of AK-47 bullets might put all four of them down before they could get off a shot. I didn't feel comfortable walking behind them, and I let the rest of our platoon move up the trail and then my squad and Quinlin trailed.

We were only 30 meters into the tree line when I heard something sloshing through the water ahead of me on my left. I hissed. The hiss was passed forward, and soon our entire column was frozen in place. Fuji, a newly arrived E-7 sergeant from Guam with a Fu Manchu mustache, worked his way back to me. I pointed to the place where the sloshing had sounded, and then I hand-signed walking steps and whispered, *"In the water."* Using Guamanian accented whispers and hand signals, Fuji conveyed that the trail doubled back and our guys had made the noises. I nodded my understanding, Fuji headed back up the column, and we started moving again. When we were parallel to the area where the sloshing had sounded I discovered the shocking fact that the trail didn't double back and the water-wading noises hadn't been ours.

When we moved further up the trail I saw the place where the NVA had constructed an ambush site by thinning the foliage below mid-calf level from about 7 meters to about 30 meters back on the right side of the trail. The taller growth and the first 7 meters of low foliage camouflaged the sight line they'd created for anyone looking from a head-high view but something had pulled at my eyes. I'd leaned low, traced it to where they'd have lain in ambush, and moved on, expecting that the four-man team had checked it out. We'd gone on a little further, and when we'd returned to the meadow and been waiting for the chopper to pick up the tracker team I'd asked the guy who'd walked point about that ambush site.

With an *oh shit* look on his face, he'd told me they hadn't seen it, and that was the last straw for me. We were facing enemies who'd dig their own graves and attack a deadly LZ head-on, and yet my platoon had invited an attack by congregating in the meadow, I'd followed behind men who'd failed to detect someone hiding in the stream, I'd taken the word of Fuji on something I should have confirmed for myself, and the specialized team our battalion had sent out had unknowingly walked us through the kill zone of a potentially lethal ambush site. Throughout the day, the only ones who'd seemed capable of recognizing and responding to the threats we were facing had been the men in my squad and Quinlin, the others had been so oblivious that they'd endangered the rest of us. And I couldn't envision things getting better. Little Joe and some of the other reliable old hands were gone, Barry had been replaced by Fuji, a career sergeant who'd attested to a vital fact he couldn't have been certain of, and the new Lt. was a huge liability. It was all too clear; in the space of less than a month we'd become a platoon that would allow a dumb-shit Lt. to turn us into targets, to turn me into a target, and I'd been just as dumb. Maybe it wasn't that bad, maybe all those self-dug graves had just made the enemy seem more real, but that's how it felt.

The Loach Pilot

After we returned to the LZ I couldn't shake the thought of us stumbling around until we blundered into something deadly. I'd made a friend of getting killed walking point because no matter how well you did that it was almost certain that you'd get killed if you did it long enough, but the prospect of getting killed because of someone's abject stupidity incensed me. That anger persisted that evening as I stood with about twenty guys listening to a Loach chopper pilot who was standing on the roof of a perimeter bunker telling us he needed a door gunner. Those pint-sized Loach choppers were usually called mosquitoes because they'd buzz in overhead and hover at the very tops of the canopies with their door gunners leaning out of their open doorways and peering into the jungle. The tempting targets they'd presented had sometimes elicited enemy fire, and the army had started using them as bait for the Cobra choppers we called Snakes. The large, narrow-bodied Snakes were armed with miniguns and rockets, and if the Loach drew fire the Cobra would come barreling in over the canopy's horizon firing rockets and torrents of minigun bullets. Those hunter-killer tandems had proven effective in smoking out and killing NVA, but the arrival of the deadly gunship didn't guarantee that the Loach's door gunner or pilot wouldn't have been killed in the initial contact, and I wasn't surprised when the pilot told us that his last door gunner had been killed. He added that he was a good pilot, but he had to know it wasn't the most uplifting sales pitch for a guy looking for a replacement door gunner. Still, the way he'd said he was a good pilot rang true, and I appreciated him putting that death in stark terms without sugarcoating it. Another thing that impressed me was that he'd had the good sense to fly to a remote LZ and search for a door gunner among grunts; the men who'd be most likely to recognize what they were seeing when they peered through the foliage to the jungle floor.

I'd only stopped to learn what the attraction had been and I'd stayed because I was curious, but it was more than that now. The pilot's confident manner and directness presented a sharp contrast to the keystone cops fiasco I'd witnessed during the day, and the longer I listened the more seriously I considered taking that door gunner ride. The risks didn't deter me. I didn't expect to survive walking point and if I got killed in the open doorway of a chopper I'd have avoided being eaten by more leeches and bugs, jungle rot, and prickly heat rash, I'd have had all the water I could drink, enough food to eat, access to showers, and a chance to sleep through a night without sleep-listening for creeping enemies and waking for my turn on night watch. Those things were drawing me but mostly it was the pilot. The thought of putting the day's debacle behind me and partnering with him in a little Loach was tempting, and when he asked those of us who were interested to stick around I was among the seven or eight who did.

I was standing at the back of the group but the pilot jumped off the roof of the bunker, walked straight to me, and introduced himself. He never acknowledged the others, and as we spoke they drifted away until the two of us were alone in the fading light. He had the innate assurance and authenticity of Barry Frost and I knew he'd offer me the ride. He did, telling me that he thought we'd make a good team. I felt a little hesitant but I'd invited that by staying and he'd made me his only option. I made a snap decision and told him that I'd give it a try. We shook hands, and then he headed to the battalion command bunker to secure my release and I walked to our hooch to collect my gear.

I'd been focused on my reasons for leaving, but as I walked the road to our bunker the prospect of leaving my squad got very real. I wished I'd spent more time deciding before I'd given my word, but I hadn't. I thought I was stuck with the choice I'd made, and then the pilot arrived at my bunker and told me that he'd tried everything but my company had refused to release me. His frustration was evident but I was relieved that fate had intervened.

We shook hands and wished each other good luck, and I watched him walk away thinking that if I hadn't been color blind I might have been the one searching for a jungle-savvy grunt willing to ride door gunner for me. I guess there were a lot of things I could have been but I knew who I was now; a grunt who'd learned how duty-bound he was to the grunts who'd walked the jungle with him.

I wasn't done learning that lesson.

Chapter 18

A Ticket Out of the Jungle

I was standing in Grant's open-air shower letting the thin stream of sun-heated water trickle over the lightly jungle-rotted skin on my neck and shoulders. A movement caught my eye, and I glanced up and saw an officer walking the road with captain's bars pinned on the lapel of his shirt. He had a belly so he had to be a REMF or an FNG officer, and I smiled, thinking that he'd sweat that belly off pretty quickly if he was assigned to a grunt outfit. I guessed he'd seen the smile because he stopped and stood on the road surveying me thoughtfully.

After an awkward interval he walked closer and asked brusquely, "What company are you with?"

I paused long enough to let him know I was choosing to answer, and then I said that I was with B Company.

"What's your job?"

"I'm a squad leader."

"That could be a problem," he said, "How long have you been in-country?"

I said that I had four or five months in-country. He paused, and then he said, "The battalion commander needs an orderly. Go talk to him at 1500 hours tomorrow. What's your name?"

I gave him my name and he said "OK" and continued down the perimeter road, leaving me wondering why the battalion commander would need an orderly on our barren LZ, and why he'd offer an interview to a random guy standing naked in a shower. Underlying all that was my certainty that the 4-5 months I'd spent in-country didn't justify my getting a ticket out of the jungle. I knew that categorically, we all did. I'd heard far too many discussions about a grunt wrangling one of the limited numbers of rear jobs that were available to us, and whenever someone had gotten one I'd listened to heated debates concerning how fair the selection had been. In every instance the sole benchmark used to weigh fairness had been the amount of time a grunt had spent in the jungle, and my handful of months fell far, far short of that mark.

Still, he'd offered, and I returned from the shower and told Big Jack, Gramps, and Ron that I'd been asked to interview for a job as the colonel's orderly. Their first reaction was, "Shit, you don't have any time in-country!" but their second response was, "That's the best job in the battalion and you'd be crazy not to go for it."

I'd felt miserable when I'd thought I'd committed myself to leave for the door gunner ride, but I didn't expect to survive the months of walking point that lay ahead of me if I stayed in the jungle. That's how stark the choices were, stay and walk point for my guys or grab onto the dedicated lifeline that the orderly job represented. My head was telling me I'd be a fool not to reach for that lifeline but the prospect of leaving my guys created a sick feeling in the pit of my stomach. I thought it over many times, and when I couldn't find an answer that made sense and still felt right I decided to interview and let fate decide. I'd thought laying it off on fate would make me feel better, and when it didn't I decided that I'd attend the interview but I wouldn't make any effort to get selected for the job. That felt right.

The next afternoon I made my way past faceless REMFs to the battalion headquarters. The battalion sergeant major introduced himself and escorted me to the outsized battalion command bunker. The colonel was seated behind a desk. He rose to his feet, an even-featured man in his early thirties with crew-cut brown hair. The sergeant major introduced him as Colonel Ordway, gave him my name, and told him that I was with Bravo Company. I nodded at the colonel and said a casual, "Hello." Apparently unconcerned with my disregard for military protocol, the colonel extended his hand and invited me to sit down. The sergeant major excused himself, and the colonel asked where I was from, how long I'd served in the army, and a few questions about my training. I responded with short, unenthusiastic answers until he asked how things were going in the field. The question mattered to all of us, and I leaned forward and said, "Our new Lt.'s a problem." Without waiting for him to ask, I recounted some of the things I'd witnessed that illustrated the Lt.'s inherent inability to serve as a platoon leader in the jungle. The colonel listened attentively, and when I finished he asked a few follow-up questions. I answered as objectively as I could and then he thanked me, shook my hand, and ended the interview.

I felt uneasy when I left, not because I'd passed up the opportunity to be an orderly but because ratting out the new Lt. made me feel tarnished. I regretted doing it behind the Lt.'s back but the colonel had opened the door and I'd rushed through it because the new Lt.'s continued command could become a life and death issue for us. When my guys asked how the interview had gone I said that I'd told the colonel that our new Lt. was worthless. *Damn straight!* Pretty well summed up their responses. They asked if I'd gotten the job, and I told them that we hadn't even discussed what an orderly's duties were and I was sure I hadn't. I believed that, but the next day we learned that the new Lt. had been relieved of his command, and a few hours later the sergeant major sent word that the colonel had selected me to be his orderly. A chance encounter on the perimeter road had ended my time in the jungle, and now I'd never slip down that dim jungle path that I'd so many times envisioned would lead to my death. I should have felt euphoric, or at least relieved, but emotions don't hinge on *should have felts,* and the feeling I had was the one you get when something really bad has happened.

Just one day later I was standing in the dirt outside Grant's perimeter gate watching my guys climb onto the slicks that were taking them back to the jungle. When the birds lifted into the air some of my guys were looking down at me and waving, still connected, but I knew that within the hour they'd be submerged in the overpowering reality of the jungle and I'd fade away. I'd been anticipating this moment but it felt worse than I'd imagined, and as the dust stirred by the choppers' churning blades drifted to me I ignored my watering eyes and watched them rise higher, tormented with a sense of self-loathing that brought to mind a shameful thing I'd done long ago.

At the age of 14 I'd met a warm and generous young couple named Charlie and Judy Brown. They'd camped on the Trinity River just upstream from my grandmother's bridge for the 10 days of their honeymoon and I'd shown them how to fish the river. At the end of their stay they'd invited me to spend a few days at their San Jose home to see how people lived in the city, and I'd called home and gotten permission. My grandmother's mouser had birthed a litter of Manx kittens and we'd taken the little kitten that I'd chosen as a pet with us but when they'd driven me to the Greyhound bus depot to catch a ride home we'd discovered that they didn't allow animals on the buses. We'd thought no one would care if I snuck a little kitten onto the bus, and I'd cut holes in a little cardboard box for it and boarded.

The little Manx had been quiet until the bus had started moving, and then he'd yowled, tried to claw his way out, and voided inside the box. The stench had permeated the air, and I'd sat surrounded by unsympathetic passengers with no way to calm the kitten or clean up the mess. When the bus had made another stop I'd carried the box off the bus and down a nearby alley. The alley had led to the back door of a restaurant, and I'd turned the little kitten loose there and walked away. There'd been the smell of food and the possibility that someone might pick him up to put a hopeful light on what I'd done, but the stark reality had been a tiny little yellow Manx kitten standing terrified on shaking legs, left helpless and abandoned to merciless whims and forces that were totally beyond his control.

I could picture him still, that wide-eyed, frightened little kitten that I'd left to fend for himself, and as I stood in the dirt outside LZ Grant watching the choppers carry my guys into the distance I felt the way I'd felt when I'd walked away from that kitten and reboarded that bus. The deadly enemies I'd so many times pictured lying in wait for us would surely be there one day, but it wouldn't be me leading my squad into them, it would be one of my guys... *And which of them could feel their way through a stretch of vine-twisted and leaf-covered deadly jungle, almost trancelike and knowing things that couldn't be explained? Who the fuck could do that?* I'd let go of the rope to save myself, and with my face hot with shame I turned back to a heat-glared and foul-smelling LZ that had become a place where colorless men did little things, and then I wiped the tears from my eyes and passed through the gate to join them.

The Colonel's Orderly

The orderly's responsibilities were to bring the colonel breakfast, lunch, and dinner trays from the mess tent, tidy up his bunker, and polish his shoes. That was it. Those simple tasks took less than an hour a day but the sergeant major had me job-shadow the current orderly who was scheduled to return to his hometown of Chicago in less than a week. On my second day the orderly started talking about the Jews in Chicago, saying you could identify them by their shoes, their hair, and their long noses. My German-Jewish mother had rarely spoken of her heritage and I was curious to hear what he'd say so I let him go on for a long while. He'd dug a pretty deep hole for himself when I told him I was half-Jewish. He mumbled that I didn't look Jewish and I let it drop, thinking he was more ignorant than hateful and wondering why he'd be so fixated on the Jews in Chicago.

While I was job-shadowing the orderly I crossed paths with the colonel twice. On both occasions he said, "Hi Ed, how are you doing?" and each time I answered, "Fine, how are you?" On the third day the job was mine. In the morning I carried a breakfast tray from the mess tent to the colonel. I ate breakfast and returned to his hooch to buff his shoes and straighten things up the way the last orderly had. I could have completed those tasks in a few minutes but I hesitated in the entryway, held there by something that wouldn't let go. I stood there for a long while, and when the feeling didn't let up I decided that he could take care of his own shoes and pick up his own things, and left. I didn't bring him a lunch tray or a dinner tray. I was pretty sure he missed lunch but I saw him hurrying to the mess tent just before they stopped serving dinner.

I couldn't have explained why I was making those decisions. I don't even know if I'd call them decisions because I wasn't thinking them through, I was just balking at doing things that *felt* wrong. That sense of wrong didn't change, and other than bringing him a breakfast tray on that first morning I never did a thing for the colonel. I was certain the sergeant major was going to arrive at any moment and tell me that I hadn't worked out, but the hours turned into a day, and then another, and then several more, and he didn't show up. It felt eerily strange when no one seemed to notice my failure to do the job, and it seemed even more bizarre when I crossed paths with the colonel a couple of times and he nodded and said "*hello,*" as if everything was fine. I nodded back each time, baffled by why they'd be overlooking my refusal to perform the simple tasks I'd been given.

One afternoon I overheard someone saying that one of our companies was getting shot up and I rushed to the battalion radio bunker to find out if it was my company. It wasn't, but the stress-laden voices of the RTOs calling for artillery and reporting the action gave me the adrenalin shakes. I couldn't stop my body from quivering, and when the shooting ended I left wondering how long I'd have to wait before the colonel sent me back. He'd been at the radio tent too, and he'd looked grief-stricken when the RTOs had reported that two of their guys were confirmed dead. Seeing that made me believe I could have had a meaningful conversation with him. I could have told him that I appreciated him giving me the orderly job but I hadn't earned one of the precious tickets out of the jungle and my guys needed me. Maybe I could have told him how the jungle neutralized the tactics we were employing or recounted the events I'd witnessed that illustrated the deep-seated resolve of the NVA we were fighting. I think he might have listened but I was a low-level enlisted man with a chip on his shoulder and he was a battalion-level officer, and all we shared were those casual greetings.

During the handful of days I'd been back I'd never had a conversation with any of the guys stationed on the LZ. I imagine I was as faceless to them as they were to me, and I spent hours at my hooch, sleeping or reading any book I could get my hands on to distract me from the sick feeling that I ought to be in the jungle. I hated feeling that I'd done something wrong but I didn't ask to be sent back to my platoon. If I went back I'd be walking point and I worried that the people who loved me might learn that I'd volunteered to go back and passed up a chance to live. I didn't want to leave them wondering *why* and agonizing over whether they could have said or done anything that might have caused me to make a different choice, so I kept waiting for the colonel to decide for me. I thought that day had come when the sergeant major arrived at my hooch, but it hadn't. The sergeant major told me that our battalion was moving to a newly established LZ in the Central Highlands that was linked to a special forces camp and a Montagnard village by a drivable path. They were having a jeep delivered for the colonel's use and he informed me that I was being reassigned as the colonel's driver.

The Colonel's Driver

"LZ Lee" was situated in the center of a huge grassy knoll that had been cleared of brush by nature or by the generations-long cultivation of the Montagnard people whose village was situated 2 or 3 kilometers to the northwest. When I arrived the perimeter bunkers were completed but they were still fortifying the half-culverts that formed the skeletons of the interior bunkers. I helped them fill and place sandbags until a Chinook chopper delivered the "mail jeep" and the "colonel's jeep." The minute they hit the ground the sergeant major handed me the keys to the colonel's jeep and instructed me to drive him and an interpreter to the village.

I hadn't had a steering wheel in my hands in months and driving down that little dirt road was a pleasure. The road forked about a klick from the LZ. The right-hand branch extended another klick or so to the Yard village and the left branch climbed about a klick of hillside and terminated at a special forces camp that overlooked the village. I turned right at the fork and continued to where the road was lined with huts. When I stopped a few village men began milling around the jeep and a man who could have been the head of the village stepped forward and ceremoniously greeted the sergeant major. The sergeant major stayed just long enough to introduce himself through the interpreter, and then he directed me to drive back to the fork. I turned uphill at the fork and continued to the special forces camp. We met the three special forces guys who were manning the camp, and after the sergeant major had a short conversation with them I drove back to the LZ.

I ate a meal at the mess tent and then I climbed back in the jeep and drove to the special forces camp. I stayed there for two days, drinking beer and sharing stories with the SF guys, and on the morning of the third day I drove back to LZ Lee. I made certain that the sergeant major saw that I was back but no one said anything about my absence. I had an open invitation from the special forces guys to come back and stay as long as I wanted, and I took the colonel's jeep and drove back to their camp again. The next morning Colonel Ordway arrived in the mail jeep.

I expected him to say something about my taking off in his jeep but, as always, he said, "How are you doing Ed?" and, as always, I answered, "Fine, how are you?"

He met with the special forces guys, and as he was leaving he warned, "Be careful driving at night. We don't know what's out there,"

"Yeah, I'll be alright," I said nonchalantly.

I think that response might have finally tipped the scales because I drove back to LZ Lee the next morning and a few minutes after I arrived the sergeant major approached and said regretfully, "Ed, the colonel really likes you but I'm going to have to send you back out."

"It's fine," I said.

In a kindly voice, he said, "You don't need to leave today, you can take the next resupply out in three days."

I nodded and turned away. The look on his face suggested that he'd expected me to have more to say but I'd just learned that we were getting resupplied today and I wanted to be on that log bird.

My M-16 was cleaned and oiled, my bandoleers were filled with loaded clips, and my grenades were fastened onto my pistol belt and pack. Feeling bigger than I had in days, I settled the familiar weight of my steel helmet on my head and ran to the chopper pad with my rifle in my hand and my pack bouncing on my back. The blades of a Huey were turning lazily in the mid-morning sun, and I yelled over the noise of the engine and asked the door gunner if he was logging B Company. He nodded, and I shoved my pack inside, stepped on the skid, and pivoted to my usual spot in the right-side front corner of the doorway. A few minutes later the blades started spinning in earnest, and then the chopper sprang into the air and it was done.

I felt a little like I'd felt an instant before I'd leaped off one of the high bridges that crossed over Lake Shasta, the drop to the water breathtakingly long and the landing uncertain, a little lightheaded and a little scared. A sense of guilt was pressing against the back of my head, too, because I'd just opened a door to suffering for the people who loved me. But as I looked down at the mesmerizing green jungle flowing beneath me that back-home world didn't feel real. The one that lay below me did, and I was flying back to fill the gap I'd left in it when I'd let my guys leave without me. I didn't know how that would end but I'd been feeling a deep sense of wrongness and doing this felt very, very right.

Part Two, The Central Highlands

Chapter 19

Rejoining My Platoon

The pressure of the hard deck lessened as we eased lower. The pilot zig-zagged just above the canopy, and then an opening appeared and the chopper reared nose-up, hovered, and descended into it. The skids touched the jungle's floor and I stepped off the slick and started circling through the brush that bordered the log site. Baby Huey saw me. His surprise registered on his face, and I said, "I didn't do much of a job as the colonel's orderly so they sent me back out." I asked where Sugar Bear was, and then I wound my way in the direction he'd indicated. The menthol scent of the cigarettes Sugar Bear smoked drifted to my nose, and I followed it to where Sugar Bear was bending over his pack with his dirt-darkened, dishwater blond hair framing his somber face. Jim Quinlin was beside him, sitting on his helmet and facing out at the jungle with tendrils of smoke wafting from the cigarette that was hanging between the nicotine-stained index and middle fingers of his left hand.

The ever-vigilant Quinlin turned my way, and I said casually, "You need another guy?"

Jim's eyes widened, and then he masked his surprise and drawled, "I rekin so."

Sugar Bear straightened and stared at me crazy-eyed. "Hell no!" he barked, "We got enuf FNG's widout taken on one what don't look too smart anyways," and then he asked, "What're **you** doin here?"

I said, "They made me the colonel's driver cause I didn't do much of a job as his orderly, and then I took off in his jeep and drank too much beer with some special forces guys so they sent me back."

Sugar Bear said happily, "What a dumb shit."

Quinlin shook his head, "I hope ya dun drunk sum good beer with them boys," and that was it, I was back.

Sugar Bear told me that after I'd left our old squad had lost so many guys that they'd disbanded it. Larry and Vern had discovered that the army would let grunts buy their way out of the field in return for extending their enlistments, and the two of them, Sugar Bear, and Quinlin had applied and gone to the rear to take a qualifying test. Vern and Larry had passed, extended, and disappeared, but Sugar Bear said that he and Quinlin had failed intentionally. Ron was carrying the radio for the new CO and Walter was carrying the radio for the Lt. I hadn't met, and after losing those four guys and me their new Lt. had merged my remaining guys into the other three squads. Sugar Bear had ended up with Quinlin and Big Jack and Gramps had gone to one of the other squads.

Sugar Bear said pointedly, "Our squad's the biggest in the platoon," and I replied, "It just got bigger."

They told me that our company's new commanding officer, Captain Peter Valtz, had served a combat tour as an enlisted man, received a battlefield commission, and commanded our battalion's weapons platoon before he'd taken over our company. I didn't tell them that I'd met Valtz when he'd hopped a log day chopper ride to LZ Lee and hunted me up. He was a quick-eyed and confident sandy-haired man of average height in his late 20s or early 30s, slim but not skinny. He'd introduced himself and told me that he'd only had a couple of minutes because the log bird was waiting, and then he'd said, "From what I've heard you belong in the field. Why don't you come back out?"

I'd smiled and told him that I wasn't crazy enough to volunteer for that, and he'd returned my smile and said confidently, "You'll be back." We'd both known he was right but no one could say I'd volunteered, not even him.

Sugar Bear ran out of news, and I moved off and squatted at the far edge of our log day perimeter, looking and listening out at the jungle. The bugs were buzzing and crawling, the leaves were barely stirring in the midday heat, and the calls that sounded in the distance were familiar, almost beckoning. I heard Sugar Bear and Quinlin whispering with someone and a minute or two later their squad leader, Steve, walked over. Steve was a short, athletically built, and very blond guy with an engaging smile. He told me that he'd grown up near the ocean in Florida, and I could picture him standing on a sunny beach holding a long surfboard. We talked until I heard the stirring sounds of men saddling up their packs. I walked back and slung my pack, and when the column started moving I found my place in line and followed, once again just another link in a long chain of men moving up to reconnect with the point platoon.

That evening I sat in the shadowed jungle listening to the hums of mosquitoes, the buzzing of flies, and the whisperings of men crouched over hissing C-4 fires. The last three weeks had seemed like a slow-motion dream and now I was awake, back with my guys, what was left of them anyway, Sugar Bear, Quinlin, and I in the same squad, Big Jack packing his heavy M-60 in another with gentle Gramps alongside him, John Glasshof our platoon sergeant, Ron carrying the radio for the new CO and Walter carrying one for the Lt. I hadn't yet met, all of us doing our share. That's what mattered, not the whys of this war, not the empty hearts and minds of the faceless men who were continuing it, and not the sordidness of the killing mission they'd tasked us with. Fuck that, what I cared about was us, only us.

Lt. Colclough

I'd hoped for more time to cement my place in the squad before the new platoon leader learned I'd come back, but just before dark Quinlin nodded at a guy who was working his way toward us and whispered, "Thet's the Lt."

Lt. Colclough was tall, gangly, red-headed, and after just 3 weeks in the field, painfully thin. He had the freckled face of a teenager but he spoke with the assurance of a confident adult. He told me he was glad that I'd come back and he asked if I wanted to take over the squad. I told him that I didn't want to be a squad leader and then we talked for another two or three minutes. I think he might have stayed longer but I'd always been socially aloof with anyone in authority and I might have been signaling that I wasn't going to be one of the guys who were eager to please their officers. If he read that he took it in stride, repeating that he was happy I'd returned, nodding to Jim and Sugar Bear, and leaving.

Lts. were important, and this one worried me. His eyes had been measuring me the entire time we'd spoken and his expressions and words had matched the responses I'd given, including the unspoken ones. A thoughtful platoon leader with the ability to read people could be a plus or a negative. Sugar Bear had said that this beanpole-skinny Lt. had gutted his way through the army's famously rigorous Ranger training and I'd heard that they cultivated gung-ho leadership attitudes there. An intelligent gung-ho platoon leader

My grandmother's cabin and bridge in Trinity.

Barbara and me a few days before I left for Vietnam.

A deep jungle setting.

Bottom up view of an NVA constructed Jolley trail trestle.

who tried to control everything could be a problem and I kept running our brief interaction through my mind, wondering, *When he gets his feet on the ground who will he be?*

I pictured his measuring eyes and I didn't have an answer.

Jim Quinlin and Me

I'd been certain that I'd be walking point when I came back, but I'd never anticipated that Jim Quinlin and I would end up in the same squad. Jim wasn't just another guy who'd taken a few turns walking point, he'd voluntarily taken over the point walking position for his squad shortly after I'd done the same for mine and from that time forward neither of us had followed behind another point man. That was going to have to change and I looked at Jim sitting sweat-soaked in the shadows with a cigarette in his hand, wondering, *Will we alternate turns, will I take it over, will Jim? How good is he?*

That evening I squatted beside him. We whispered for a minute or two and when the conversation lagged I let the silence extend, waiting for him to talk about how we were going to handle tomorrow's day on point. He raised his cigarette slowly to his lips, cupped his off hand to shield the glow, and sucked in a deep lungful of smoke. Faint lines of red showed between his fingers, and then he pulled the cigarette away quickly and exhaled the smoke. He kept puffing, and when I got tired of waiting I asked if he'd thought about how we were going to handle walking point. He asked what I thought, and when I said that maybe we ought to start by alternating turns he nodded his head and told me that's what he'd been thinking.

Quinlin was taking the morning's first turn on point, and as the last of our squad finished strapping up he was leaning slightly forward beneath the weight of his pack, a proud, dirt-encrusted, and sun-darkened man with a cigarette trailing smoke in one hand and a rifle in the other. The look of him conjured up an image of a century-ago buckskin-clad man standing near a Kentucky cabin with a powder horn and a muzzleloader, the kind of frontiersman you'd have trusted to lead you safely through hostile Indian territories. And in many ways Quinlin had been doing just that for the better part of the last 4 months, taking the lead on so many next steps that could have been his last.

He flipped his cigarette away, and when he led into the looming jungle I followed closely behind, watching him work. His feet landed quietly in all the right places, he found passable seams through the growth, and he constantly scanned the ground, the overhead canopy, and the eye-level jungle. Before we'd covered 50 meters I knew that he was far more adept at walking point than anyone I'd followed. My respect for his skills grew as we continued, and when I saw his body tense at the cusp of a sightline the thought popped into my head that I was glad Jim was walking point, and if one of us was going to get killed I wanted it to be him instead of me. I didn't like myself for that, but that's what I was feeling.

As we moved on I started noticing some subtle things that worried me. I never saw him sniff for scents, not even when a tattletale wind rustled through the foliage and made its way to us. He angled his ears toward likely danger areas less often than I would have, and he hadn't paused before he'd stepped into some sightlines that had opened back at us. Those little things made me uneasy, and I started paying more attention to the jungle that stretched in front of him.

Something at the upper edge of my vision drew my eyes, and when I looked up I saw that a section of the upper canopy wasn't swaying naturally with the wind. I hissed. Jim looked back, startled, and I hand signaled to where the taller foliage had been tied off. A long while later Jim started creeping forward. I followed. I glimpsed a tiny segment of an NVA trail, and I hissed again and moved up to join him. We crept the rest of the way up to a trail the NVA had hidden from aerial view by vine-tethering the overhead foliage together. The trail showed no signs of recent use, and we pushed on to the end of Jim's cut.

When my turn came I led out with my lightweight pack riding snugly on my back, my two bandoleers of ammo crisscrossed over my chest, and my trigger finger resting lightly on the trigger guard of my M-16. All those things had been almost as natural to me as breathing but my first steps felt awkward, maybe because I knew Jim would be watching my every move the way I'd watched his. After I'd moved through 30-40 meters of foliage that awkward feeling disappeared and there was just the jungle. Nothing remarkable occurred on my cut; no spooky noises or silences, no warning scents, and no unexplained nudges, but long before it ended I knew I hadn't lost anything when it came to walking point.

Quinlin was about to step out and take the lead on our next cut, and then he hesitated and met my eyes. I wouldn't have been certain what that meant once but wordless things spoke clearly here, and I nodded my agreement, stepped past Jim, and took the point. We never spoke of that moment of silent understanding, not even peripherally, we didn't need to. Walking point had a lot of things bound up in it, pride, status, adrenalin, and more, but mostly it had life and death in it and that little NVA trail had carried a message from the jungle. Both of us had read that message and neither of us was reckless enough to ignore it. From that time forward if Jim and I were in the jungle together I walked point and Jim walked backup.

Jim was amazingly adept at that. He rarely rustled the foliage and when I'd alert he'd hunker down motionless, his perceptive brown eyes scanning ahead, his M-16's selector set on fully automatic, and his reactions honed to a razor's edge. I'd felt alone when I'd led through sections of forbidding jungle but with Jim behind me I felt like we were two shadowy shapes inching through an immense jungle together, me and my jungle-savvy buddy Jim Quinlin. That's how I viewed it but Jim had lost some of his swagger. That was another thing we never talked about but I knew how much being a point man had meant to him. I think he felt like he'd taken a step back but I didn't see it that way. I viewed the two of us as a point team of equals, and to make that clear to Jim and everyone else I started every reference to anything that involved walking point with the phrase, "Jim and I," or "Quinlin and I," even when it hadn't involved him. I don't know if that helped but it wasn't long before Jim recaptured his assured and slightly boastful demeanor that let everyone know that in this perilous place Jim Quinlin knew how special he was.

The New Squad

The last time I'd joined a squad I'd been a new guy figuring out who I was, how I'd fit in, and what I was facing. I'd learned those things about myself, and now I was weighing the others and trying to decide what kind of squad we could be.

I was going to miss Walter's steadfastness and intelligence and Ron's insightfulness, the same qualities that had led to them being selected as our platoon and company RTOs. And I was going to miss Big Jack. Jack might get blown away on weed during our stays on the LZ but he was no easy-going stoner. He weighed people critically and if he thought they fell short he'd let them know without sugarcoating it, sometimes with a stern look and sometimes with a sarcastic grin. He was just as demanding of himself, and those qualities together with his proficiency with the M-60 machine gun made him almost irreplaceable. I'd learned that early on when some shooting had started and Big Jack had sprinted up and dived in head-first beside me. Within two or three seconds he'd flipped open the 60's tripod, set the gun, loaded the rounds, buried his face in the dirt, and triggered shots. He'd kept his head buried in the dirt but his heavy M-60 bullets had stitched through the vegetation in a knee-high arc so unvarying that I wouldn't have believed it if I hadn't seen it.

You couldn't replace guys like those, but after a week or two of jungle time I wasn't complaining about the guys in our squad. They were a mix of educated and uneducated men who'd grown up in a vastly different mix of economic, educational, and social environments. I thought we were about as motley a crew as you could imagine but during our first week together most of us had organically assumed roles that paired our innate abilities to the critical needs of our squad. My arrival had generated the most noticeable adjustments in roles, mostly from Quinlin, and then it all settled in and I knew who we were.

Hootie was from rural West Virginia, a tall, thin, long-faced, lanky, and uncomplaining young man in his late teens. He hadn't owned a pair of shoes until he'd entered the army and that, along with the fact that he was a little goofy, had inspired Sugar Bear to call him Hootie, a nickname he'd happily accepted. Hootie carried a rifle, and when we were on point he walked in the middle of the squad.

Baby Huey was a couple of inches over 6 foot tall, with narrow shoulders, broad hips, and long arms and legs. With his wispy thinning hair, large domed head, and thick glasses he looked like he'd have been an accountant but when you talked to him you'd realize pretty quickly that he wasn't that guy; he was the guy who'd skipped his high school classes and never planned much farther than the current day. Baby Huey packed the little M-79 grenade launcher and, hopefully, enough ammunition to keep it going when we needed it.

Freddy was from Puerto Rico. He was athletically built and he had warm and intelligent eyes, the kind of guy who'd surely had a lot of friends back home. I doubted that he was much older than 18 but he was full-grown-tough. Freddy carried a rifle, and when our squad was walking point he was gravitating closer and closer to the front of the squad.

Unmarried and devoutly religious *Cherry Instant* was a dark-haired, small, thin, and very private man. The basis for the *Cherry* part of his nickname was obvious to all of us, and the *Instant* part was because the army had sent him through shake and bake school, promoted him to sergeant, and sent him to Vietnam. None of that made the least bit of sense to me. Cherry Instant was so deeply spiritual and gentle that I couldn't picture him shooting an animal, much less another human being, and I doubted that he'd want to lead anyone to anything other than Christ. I wasn't sure where he walked in the squad and I didn't think it mattered. He should have been a medic.

Quiet and unsmiling *Billy Bass* was our M-60 gunner. Most guys packing that heavy gun and ammo were a lot bigger than Billy but he never complained about the load. He was always holding the M-60, cleaning it, sleeping with it, and connecting to it almost as though it was his lifeline. I didn't know why he'd be so connected but he was, and I couldn't picture him without that gun.

Blond, curly-headed, and medium-built *Kenny Martin* was from the farmlands of Ohio. Kenny had a boatload of positive energy and his face would sometimes light up with a sunny smile that would stand in stark contrast to the somber expressions that marked the in-jungle faces of most of the others. Kenny was quick, athletic, and what-the-hell daring, and if Jim and I hadn't been there Kenny or Freddy would have been walking point.

Our squad leader, *Steve*, was another shake-and-bake sergeant. He was a moderately short, athletic-appearing, and genuinely friendly guy who just wanted everyone to get along. He was more like a warm-hearted uncle than the guy who wanted to be in charge, and sometimes I'd see him with a concerned look on his face lending an ear to one of the guys.

Sugar Bear, Quinlin, and I filled out our squad, and we were an unlikely threesome. Quinlin had been born and raised in rural Kentucky and his formal education had ended at about the 3rd grade. He'd never learned to read or write but he had a very good mind. He wanted everyone to know that, and he never passed up an opportunity to make it clear that he knew more about something than someone else did. That might not have been well received in some circles, but Jim had a lot to offer and he was well-liked and well-respected in our platoon.

Sugar Bear was still so mercurial that you could never predict what was going to come flying out of his mouth. Far too often it was based on anger, envy, spite, or even hatefulness, but lurking beneath his ill-tempered behaviors was a deep craving for acceptance that he tried to hide. Despite his alternating bouts of awkward fawning and lashing outs, or maybe because of them, I felt a genuine affection for Sugar Bear. I was pretty sure he knew that but I was never sure how he felt about me. He'd occasionally surprised me with a self-deprecating comment, flashes of sober humility, or, very, very rarely, something that might have been warmth, but he'd never acknowledged that he'd felt any sense of friendship. That was typical of him and, with the exception of Quinlin, he'd rarely done or said anything that would indicate he trusted anyone to be his friend. His saving graces were that his nastiness was open and honest, he had a sly sense of humor and he loved to gossip. Every resupply day he'd wander around commiserating about our latest miseries and then return with news and rumors, and the Lairn who'd once been treated like an outcast had grown into the guy everyone knew as Sugar Bear.

I'd largely assumed the role I'd had before I'd left but I was far less social. I had a few whispered conversations with Quinlin and Sugar Bear, and an occasional game of spades on a log day site, but in many ways my most intimate companion was the jungle. I viewed it as an entity that could be my most dominant adversary or my most powerful ally, and like a mathematician searching for a solution to a perplexing problem with numbers and equations flying through his or her head my mind was almost always occupied with its sights, scents, sounds, and feels. I'd need that because there'd soon be times and places where I'd need everything I'd learned to have a chance of surviving.

The Central Highland Jungle

Much of the near sea-level elevation jungle off LZ Grant had been double or triple-canopy dense and during the height of the monsoon season the hothouse-like conditions had bordered on being unbearable. The higher altitude Central Highlands jungle off LZ Lee wasn't as foliage-choked and the monsoon season was nearing an end. The heat and humidity weren't as miserable and we suffered less jungle rot, ringworm, and prickly heat rash. The mosquitoes and blood-sucking leeches weren't as numerous either, but the downside was that jungle water was harder to find.

I'd gone a day or more without eating and each time my hunger pains had lessened after a few hours, but going without water was just the opposite. I'd learned that lesson because I'd previously gone several hours without water in the midday heat followed by a waterless night, and all I'd thought about was water; hot water, evil-tasting water, water that would make you sick, I didn't care, just any kind of water. We'd been searching for a place to land the log bird that next morning when our column had stopped near a slight swale. I'd thought I'd scented water and I'd dropped into the swale and found a pig wallow filled with a few inches of murky water at the lowest point of the hollow. I hadn't known what was in that dark water and I'd been so desperate for water that I hadn't cared; I'd buried my mouth and sucked it in, spitting out solids and swallowing what was left. I know I'd spit out pig droppings and swallowed microorganisms and aquatic bugs, but my years of drinking from puddles, springs, streams, and rivers must have generated immunities because I hadn't gotten sick.

Despite that, I'd kept carrying just 4 quarts of water, and yesterday morning I'd finished off my last few swallows of water. That had been our scheduled resupply day and I'd have been fine if they'd found a place to bring the resupply chopper in. They hadn't, and I'd gone without water the rest of yesterday, all night, and this morning. My thirst had kept me awake for most of the night, clawing at me ever more insistently, and I'd tilted my four canteens to my lips one by one several times this morning hoping that a drop of canteen-beaded moisture might fall into my mouth. The only thing that had touched my tongue had been hot air but they still hadn't found a place to land a log chopper and now we were trying to cut an opening in a bamboo thicket big enough to set one down. I was lying in the shade at the fringe of the cut, worrying that we wouldn't get it done in time and our resupply chopper would get diverted.

I saw one of our cutters slowing down and I climbed to my feet and relieved him. My cuts were stirring clouds of mosquitoes so I buttoned my shirt to keep them off my stomach and chest. I was lucky I did because the thudding impact of one of my next cuts provoked a nest of red ants that kamikazed out of the overhead leaves and started biting into my skin. I brushed off some of the ones that were fastened onto my head and neck and then I peeled out of my shirt and shook it hard. When I checked to make sure I'd gotten the ants off I saw that I'd gotten so dehydrated that my shirt wasn't even damp.

I ignored the bites and started hacking again. My cuts were so feeble that my machete kept binding in the stalks but I kept at it until I started seeing spots. I was afraid I'd pass out and I walked to the edge of the opening and handed off the machete. I was lying there when the Mailman walked my way carrying his pack. I heard water sloshing in the big plastic container he stowed inside it but I lay quietly as he passed by. Walter would have shared if I'd asked but that water was his insurance against the thirst I was suffering and I'd medevac out before I'd beg a drink from anyone.

Bamboo stalks were scattered like cordwood on the jungle floor but I didn't allow myself to count on resupply water until I heard the distant strumming of the resupply bird's blades. That beautiful green chopper hovered to a stop overhead, and then it mirrored the movements of the Mailman's guiding hands and seesawed down the opening we'd created. The clouds of cuttings sucked up by the backwash of its blades almost fully obscured it and then it settled to the ground, its rotors slowed, and precious water was within reach.

My sense of desperation lessened, and I let myself envision spinning a soda can on the block of ice the log bird was carrying and then swallowing it down in no-breath gulps. The thought was so tempting that I decided to end my thirst with that icy-cold drink, and when they unloaded the block of ice and sodas I walked light-headed into the full burn of the sun and took my place in line. I selected my soda, and then I spun the can on top of the ice block until it felt frigid-cold in my hand. With the assurance of a long-distance runner expending the last of his energy on a sprint to the finish line, I rolled it a little longer to guarantee it would be as icy cold as I'd imagined, and then I moved off a few steps, sat flat on the ground, and pulled my P-38 can opener out of a blousy pants pocket. I punched two holes on opposite sides of the top of the can, raised that icy-cold soda slowly to my cracked lips, closed my eyes, and sucked in a mouthful of chilled contents. I'd envisioned swallowing it in blissful gulps but my throat constricted. I drank it sip by sip until the can was half empty, and then my throat opened and I swallowed what was left in two or three gulps.

My thirst was still raging, and I filled a canteen with the bladder's water and drank it dry. The warm rubber-tasting water was more satisfying than the sweet cold soda, and I refilled my four canteens and sat in the shade sipping water while they set up the hot meal. They started dishing it out of the ammo cans, and I took my place in line and collected enough food to fill my shrunken stomach. They'd sent out clean socks, shirts, and pants, and after I finished eating I joined the naked and half-naked guys who were sorting through the jumbled wad of pants and fatigue shirts they'd dumped on the ground. I found a fatigue shirt and tugged on a pair of size 29 pants that hung loosely on the hard bones of my hips, and then I lay unmoving in the shade. When the lightheaded feeling ebbed I collected my C-rations, scavenged for pound cakes, traded away my beer for another pound cake, and refilled my canteens.

I left the log site with a stomach full of food and water, a poundcake-enabled lightweight pack, and just 4 canteens of water. That might have seemed a poor choice but I was willing to risk another thirst rather than add one more canteen. That was partly because I was associating every additional pound of weight I was carrying with a lessening of my chances of surviving and partly because I didn't want to change my luck. There was another reason too. I'd waited for that soda because I'd wanted to prove to myself that the jungle might kill me but it wasn't going to break my will. I couldn't have justified that to an earlier version of myself but I functioned differently now. Doing what *felt* right had kept me alive and packing 4 canteens felt right.

Walking the NVA's Trails

Our squad leader, Steve, was gone. I didn't know why he'd left or where he went. His replacement was Dennis Rydgren, another shake-and-bake sergeant. Dennis was a couple of years older than most of us, a brown-haired, light-eyed, and medium-short guy with the build of a long-distance runner. Shortly after he arrived there'd been some shooting that hadn't involved our platoon. I'd seen Dennis' reaction, and that evening I squatted beside him and asked if he'd been scared. He told me that he had, and I said that I'd been scared too but he was a squad leader and it was important not to let the guys see it. He knew what I meant and he nodded his understanding without any hint of defensiveness or false bravado. I had his measure then, and over the next days he proved me right by doing the squad leader things well and leaving the rest alone; a serious and resolute guy who'd picked things up quickly.

That was everything I wanted to know about Dennis because our before-Vietnam yesterdays weren't significant here, not his and not my own. On the other hand, the sights, sounds, scents, and feels that I'd experienced during my time in the jungle had immense survival value, and I was constantly comparing them to those that existed in each new piece of the jungle we were walking. My memory of such things had stayed so clear that I believed I could have retraced my steps from tree to tree, bush to bush, and leaf to leaf through many of the stretches of jungle that I'd walked, but if I'd been asked to pinpoint those locales on a map I'd have failed. The only topography that mattered to me extended no farther than the distance the NVA could reach out for us, and that distance was usually 30 steps or less; a perilous circle in a massive jungle that was the relative size of a drop of rain splashing into a huge lake.

The fact that our footprint in the jungle was so minuscule might have suggested that the random azimuths we were following were unlikely to lead us to the jungle-shrouded NVA soldiers; that no matter how desperately the REMFs directing our movements wanted to guide us to the NVA or how intent the NVA were on ambushing us, our convergence might never trigger the lethal power that lay dormant in the weapons we carried, but that wasn't the reality. The REMFs had eyes in the sky and intelligence from captured and surrendered NVAs that they could use to guide us near the NVA. If they did then our noisy insertions and intrusive presence in the jungle wouldn't go unnoticed by any aggressive NVA, or maybe our paths would intersect by chance. Those possibilities were daunting enough, but the likelihood of a deadly encounter with the NVA grew far greater when our Captain Valtz-led company reinstituted a previously discredited tactic; one it might not have been able to employ if Quinlin and I had made a different decision as I'd squatted beside a freshly traveled NVA trail.

I read the prints on the trail, knowing that the jungle wasn't a trackless maze and that our paths and those of the NVA didn't have to remain random. The narrow footpath that was inches in front of my face would connect to another NVA avenue, and that one would intersect with another, and on and on it went, a myriad of deep jungle trails that were branching into more trails, some bigger, some smaller, and all of them forming a spider-webbed network of paths that would lead to the NVA. The REMFs understood that, and in previous years they'd sent grunt companies up those trails to seek the NVA. Those earlier companies had quickly learned that the NVA trails they were walking led to deadly ambush sites, camouflaged bunker complexes, and spider hole positions that were strategically configured to enable smaller forces to decimate larger ones. That had happened, and the collective casualties of those ill-fated grunt companies had proven so costly that our predecessor grunts had deemed the practice of walking NVA trails *suicide*. Some of them had refused to travel the NVA's trails, and over time their refusals had grown so widespread that the REMFs had been forced to abandon the tactic. That had been a long time ago, but their wisdom had been passed down to us through a succession of adamant warnings that walking the NVA's trails was suicidal.

And that's why I was surprised when Lt. Colclough moved up beside me and said, "Ed, Valtz wants to know if you'd take us up the trail a hundred meters or so to see where it's heading?"

The way he'd phrased it and the hesitancy in his voice invited me to decline, but I looked up the track-scarred path and considered it. The line of it was rattling danger like one of the thick-bodied rattlesnakes coiled at home, its hissing rattles warning, *Here I am! I'm deadly! Stay away*! But I was hooked on adrenaline, or maybe I wanted to impress someone, maybe the guys, maybe Lt. Colclough who'd left it to me to decide, maybe our real-deal grunt CO, Valtz who'd invited me back to the jungle, or maybe myself. I didn't know but I'd crossed a lot of pulse-stirring NVA passageways and I wanted to slip down this one and read its messages the way I'd read that first bunker complex.

I had another breathless dive-off-a-bridge moment, and then I angled my face to Quinlin's and like some puffed-up character in a third-rate movie I whispered, "Fuck it. It's a good day to die. What do you think?"

Jim's eyes widened, and then he nodded and said huskily, "Good uh day as eny, I reckin."

I took to the trail, melting in and out of the foliage and sensing for any hint of an NVA presence. Everything but the trail faded away, and then I paused at the threshold of a short stretch of straight trail hearing the quiet footfalls of Quinlin landing on the sandal-worn surface of the trail behind me. I envisioned a column of NVA soldiers approaching just as silently, men facing the same risks and surely feeling what I was feeling, but the trail that connected us lay empty. I moved ahead, knowing that the odds of meeting the NVA increased with every step we took, and I was lost in those moments. A hiss from Jim brought me back. I turned, and when Quinlin hand-signaled that we'd traveled far enough I was vaguely disappointed to have left so much undiscovered.

Lt. had told us that Captain Valtz had wanted us to walk the trail to see where it was heading but I didn't think it was that. I think he'd read Quinlin and me and he'd been testing our willingness to walk the NVA's trails because that's what we started doing. A firm refusal from Quinlin and me might have prevented that but I didn't protest. I rationalized that I could travel their trails so stealthily that my survival odds would be more evenly balanced with those of any NVA I might encounter, but I think I did it partly because I wanted the adrenaline rush that I'd experienced walking that trail and partly because of a dark desire that had grown like a weed in a garden. I'd spent months analyzing the *what ifs* of how I'd react to the sudden jungle presence of silent reapers whose tearing bullets could darken our lives forever. I think those visualizations, the casualties we'd suffered, and my near-fatal experiences had kindled a deadliness in me, and in the solitude of a late evening perimeter I told Quinlin, "I want to kill a gook."

My mind recoiled at the words I'd spoken, but they were true and I couldn't take them back. Quinlin cocked his head the way he did when he was pondering something, and then he nodded once and said somberly, "I do too."

Saying those words had shocked me but I didn't question the fervor I'd voiced. An unhesitant deadliness might one day gain me a fraction of a second and I wasn't sacrificing that to alleviate a pang of moral disquiet.

Chapter 20

Christmas in the Jungle off LZ Lee

I felt like I'd spent half of my life in Vietnam but it had been just 6 months, and now it was Christmas Day. Nothing changed. There was no goodwill to man fellowship, no baby in the manger celebration, and no good cheer, just our everyday heat, filth, and the never relenting possibility of sudden death. There weren't many gifts, either. The chopper that had been hauling most of our Christmas mail had crashed and burned on the LZ's helipad, and the care packages we received from home were few and far between. The only one I got was from my sister, Evelyn, and I unwrapped it and found a single fir bough. I don't know how she could have known, but the little green bough she'd sent brought Christmas halfway around the world to Vietnam.

When I'd been a small boy we'd spent a lot of Christmases in Trinity, and the scent of our Christmas tree and the sweet aroma of my grandfather's pipe had filled the cabin. Sometimes other members of our family had been there, and every evening the grownups had sent Evelyn and me to our beds in the attic while they'd sat in the woodstove-warmed living room and told stories about old times. They'd considered those adult conversations, but Evelyn and I had always snuck back to the walled-in alcove at the top of the stairs and listened to my grandfather's oratorical accounts of incidents that had occurred decades ago. Almost all of his tales had been humorous and his punch lines had been amazingly funny. We'd tried not to laugh but we couldn't, no one could have, and at the sounds of our stifled laughter my dad had hollered, "You kids go to bed up there."

We'd always made a big show of opening and shutting the attic door without passing through it, and then we'd resumed our perches on the two hidden top steps. That was Christmas for me, and the fresh scent of that little fir bough brought it all flooding back; the anticipation of the magic of Christmas, my grandfather's storytelling voice, and the collective warmth and merriment of the people I loved. It was like a drug and I couldn't stop breathing it in. And it wasn't just me, I shared it with Sugar Bear and Quinlin and they kept raising it to their noses with faraway looks on their faces.

That evening I string-tied the bough to a branch that hung about four steps from my sleeping nook so that others could come by and smell it. I don't know how the news could have spread so quickly but within minutes a procession of guys started drifting up and bringing it to their noses, some for long minutes. Word of it must have circulated throughout the entire perimeter because at near full dark they were still coming, my guys and guys from the other platoons, every one of them caught up in his memories with no thanks, no words, no nothing, just shapeless shadows emerging out of the growing darkness, breathing the scent of that little fir bough deep into their souls, and then melting away into the dark of the night. I believe that most of the men in my company visited the shrine that little fir bough created in the deep jungle of Vietnam, many of them more than once, it was that powerful.

Chapter 21

An Instant of Forever

The choppers dropped us into a new section of jungle that was characterized by well-traveled NVA trails marked with recent use. On our second day there some guys in another platoon spotted an NVA riding a bicycle down one of the trails. The quickest reacting one pulled up the M-79 he was holding and fired a grenade that hit the NVA dead center. When Sugar Bear heard about it he and a few others went to view the body. He came back saying that the middle of the NVA had been blown out clear to his spine and that I ought to go and see it. I told him I wasn't going and he gave me his smug *what a wimp* smile. I shook my head, they could look if they wanted but I didn't want that ghoulish image rattling around in my head.

The next day my company was lined up along a flat bench of land that overlooked an area of dense foliage when the sounds of a machete reached us. The sounds were coming nearer and Lt. Colclough and my squad slipped back to set up an ambush. I sound-tracked the angle of the oncoming sounds, and when we were on a line with their course we dropped partway down the slope to get deeper views into the foliage where they'd emerge. The others spread out to create shooting avenues and Quinlin and I moved a little lower so we'd get an earlier look and know when to start the shooting. And then we waited.

I'd walked point through a lot of klicks of jungle knowing that any next instant the jungle might be filled with bullets fired by hidden ambushers, and now we were ambushing from the high ground and the NVA were approaching unaware. The circumstances could hardly have been more favorable but bullets could fly both ways, and if it turned into a firefight we'd need the foliage-piercing power of Billy Bass' M-60. He was a little uphill from me on my left, and when I glanced back I saw him lying flat with his finger resting on the trigger of his tripod-supported M-60. His often-grave face was tight and scared but it was the right kind of scared, not the turn and run kind, and

I looked away and lay silently with the others, all of us hearing the nearing NVA and steeling ourselves to take their lives, or at least I was. They were about 20 meters short of the place where they'd appear when a harshly imperious voice barked out a one-word command, and with barely a pause in his cutting the NVA who was wielding the machete turned 90 degrees to our left and started cutting at an angle that would keep them hidden.

I'd been prepared to kill faceless enemies but when I heard that NVA's contemptuous voice spit out that dismissive command I wanted to kill him, and I thought I could do it. They were cutting at an angle that would lead below the main body of our company and when our guys shot down at them they'd almost surely flee back up the trail they'd cut. I wanted to be there, and I slipped up to Lt. Colclough and whispered that Quinlin and I could move downslope, get eyes on their trail, and cut them down if they came running back. He thought it over, and then he shook his head because he didn't want to risk Quinlin and me getting hit by bullets fired by our company. It was hard to argue with an officer who was more concerned about my safety than I was, and I didn't.

A few minutes later the company stared shooting, and then the pounding footsteps of NVAs running up the trail sounded. None of us fired a shot, and they rounded the corner and ran off. I was fine with the hard-working NVA who'd been doing the cutting escaping but I deeply regretted the survival of the NVA who'd barked that order. The tone of that command had triggered my anger at men who'd contemptuously command others to take deadly risks, and that anger must have run deep because I'd have been down there waiting for them if Lt. Colclough hadn't been with us.

A day later I was on point tracking vague lines of travel that a few individuals wandering their way to a common destination at different times might have left. I followed their composite paths to a stand of slender-stalked bamboo clumps that were separated by meandering corridors of slightly yellowed knee-high grasses. The traces I was following thinned out ahead of me. I relaxed my eyes to allow everything in, and the overturned leaves, crushed grasses, and oddly positioned twigs suddenly coalesced into patterns that unveiled where the individual walkers had melted into grass avenues and moved on. They'd turned at various places but all of them had turned to my right, almost surely on their way to a nearby destination. I was pretty sure what that was, and

I melted into the cover of one of the bamboo clumps, held as still as I could, controlled my breathing, and listened.

A wispy wind wafted from the direction they'd gone. It whispered through the foliage and moved on. A second one rattled the bamboo stalks, and then the foliage quieted and the indistinct noises of the jungle came again. I opened my mouth and rotated my lower jaw slowly. Crackling noises sounded, and then the jungle's tiny sounds came more clearly. I raised my left hand and cupped my ear to bring the noises in closer, and then I angled my left ear in the direction the walkers had traveled and waited. A swirling wisp of wind carried a faint scent I associated with bunkers but I wasn't certain where the wind had picked up the scent. Minutes later a faint sound registered in my ears. It had been too soft to identify but I'd *felt* it was the cackle of a chicken. The noise had come from the direction the travelers had turned, and I squatted in the quiet of the sun-dappled bamboo slice of jungle that had sent me a faint scent on the wind and the maybe-cackle of a chicken with one question pressing on my mind; *would they know we were here?* We hadn't crossed any long sight lines, we hadn't made much noise, and I was almost fully obscured by the stalks of bamboo and the tall grasses. *Nearly invisible*, I thought, and then I pictured my silhouette unveiled by the random stirrings of the wind-driven foliage and I knew I wasn't.

Quinlin had settled about 20 meters back. I nodded to my right to warn him that something might be there, and then I motioned him up. He sent me a questioning look. I repeated the signal and he started, crouching low and moving with well-placed, silent steps like a hunted animal. I reached out to the jungle and sensed for a reaction as he moved forward. Careful to avoid brushing the slender shafts of the bamboo and revealing our presence with its shudder, Quinlin took a knee slightly behind me on my right. His eyes were flitting through the foliage searching for silhouettes or movements. I let him scan, and when he was satisfied he leaned in close to hear what I'd say. Sweat was dripping off his nose and chin and he smelled hot and wet, more sweet than sour, and when I placed my mouth near his ear, I could see tiny dark dots in the skin of his cheek and nose where dirt was trapped in his pores.

I motioned to our right with the barrel of my M-16 and whispered, "Chicken noise there. Smells like bunkers."

Our bodies weren't touching but I could have sworn I felt his pulse quicken. His eyes were darting through the sight lines again. I gave him a moment and then I whispered, "I'm thinking let's go someplace else."

He nodded and that was it, we'd decided for all of us. I focused into the jungle feeling for changes, and then I backtracked and angled off in a direction that would bypass the deadliness I feared was awaiting us where that half-heard cackle of a chicken had sounded.

I slipped through about 70 meters of foliage to a snaking NVA trail that was about a half meter wide and dished deep by long use. Dennis radioed the discovery back, and a few minutes later Lt. Colclough worked his way up to tell us that Captain Valtz wanted to travel it. The righthand course of the trail pointed toward the area where I was certain the NVA had a bunker complex but we got lucky; Captain Valtz wanted to go left.

I knew they'd want us walking point up the trail and I dropped my pack and steel helmet at the edge of it. Carrying the pack would diminish my quickness and the helmet could restrict my field of vision or possibly mute a tickle of a warning sound, but that's not why I did it. I'd envisioned countless scenarios where I'd encountered NVAs and reacted, and each time I'd done that I'd had a sight picture of an NVA soldier in my head. I was certain the most dangerous NVA fighters would have done the same, and if they were like me then the instant a silhouette of a grunt flashed in their eyes they'd react with lightning speed. I knew that sight picture would be a green-clad and steel-helmeted grunt with a pack on his back and a rifle in his hands and I was hoping that the sight of a bareheaded man unburdened by a pack wouldn't trigger their reflexive reactions. The possibility of that gaining me a fraction of a second was more valuable than the protection the steel helmet offered and I'd been dropping my pack and helmet when I'd walked point up trails. I'd talked about it with Jim and he'd been dropping his too.

And now a handful of daylight hours remained and another trail was waiting for me, this one marked with the fresh sandal prints of several NVA soldiers who'd traveled it in the direction we were going. *They'd have come from the bunkers. Would they be returning before nightfall?* They'd be there or they wouldn't and I glanced back at faces that were shadowed with dread, even Kenny's, and I nodded, confidently I hoped, and then I took in a deep breath and started up that well-used trail that was honest with its menace, every next meter portending thunderous noise and death, for me, for us, or maybe for the Ho Chi Minh-sandaled NVA who'd traveled it ahead of us, their tire-tread tracks midmorning fresh.

The vegetation was only moderately dense, leaving me too exposed, but after 50 meters the foliage thickened and I could slip from bush to bush, maybe unnoticed. I flitted to each piece of cover with my feet spaced wide, balanced to spring aside or dive to the ground at any hint of life ahead. My footfalls were landing silently on the worn dirt surface but I took care to place them gently, convinced that the pressure of a heavier footfall might carry ahead to someone as attuned to the jungle as I was. I paused after short intervals, squatting or kneeling in the shadows and slowly turning my head a few degrees from one side to the other, listening into the depths of the foliage for the telltale sounds of an ambusher brushing away an insect or repositioning himself to ease an ache where his body pressed against the ground, sniffing for NVA scents, and searching for any fragment of a jungle-foreign object that might lie hidden in the mass of vegetation that had changed with every step. I was aware that I was doing those things, but mostly I just relaxed my thoughts, sensing intuitively with no thinking, no deciding, and no questioning, at times bemused at myself watching another me finding its way through the jungle.

A ridgeline began to swell on the left of the trail, meters low at first and then gradually rising higher. The trail held to the base of that ridge, and as the ridge climbed higher the number of foliage-masked sightlines that peered down through the foliage that filled its slope increased. Those sightlines created avenues that could fill with bullets fired down at me, and as I moved down the trail they were sometimes opening and closing from one step to the next. I searched for a less exposed path forward but the only option that afforded a stealthy passage was the trail and I stayed on it, slipping noiselessly through the unnerving avenues that opened down from the ridge on my left.

The wind had stilled and I squatted beside the trail, attuned to any sounds or the absence of sounds that should have been there. I didn't know how long I'd been there when a whisper of sound from the right of the trail sent my adrenaline surging. Everything but that noise seemed to disappear. It came again, and then a third time, moving from higher to lower. I didn't hear it hit, but before it landed I knew it was a broad leaf brushing against other leaves or branches on its tumbling descent to the jungle floor. For a moment I was back in my head, amazed that I'd isolated the wispy sounds of a falling leaf, and then I was lost in the moments again, a tiny presence seeing myself slipping up the trail.

I kept ghosting to wherever it felt right whenever it felt right, vaguely aware of the heat radiating from my body and the slow, powerful beating of my heart, and then something changed! I didn't know what it was but the jungle felt different, forebodingly different. I sensed through the branches and leaves for it, and when I didn't find anything I crept to the threshold of the next corner and squatted in the green and browns of the foliage that lined the trail. On the other side of the corner the trail ran virtually straight along the base of the ridge for more than 70 meters. A big log had fallen across the trail at the end of the straight and my eyes reached down to the log, the area beside it, and the area beyond it. I didn't detect any movement. I listened past the log. I didn't hear anything but I *felt* something. I didn't know what that meant and I squatted for long minutes, sensing for a hint of whatever it might be. That stretch of trail seemed to be looking back and warning me. *Was that because the end of the straight was too distant for my ears to touch?*

I was so intent that I didn't know Quinlin was moving up until he appeared in the corner of my right eye. I turned my head slightly and saw that Sugar Bear, Dennis, and Lt. Colclough had come up with him.

Lt. Colclough edged slowly up to my right side and whispered very softly, "*Have you got something?*"

I was turning his way to whisper a reply, and then an ethereal vision of two NVAs rising from behind the log materialized in my mind! The image was isolated on the far-left edge of my peripheral vision but I knew their AK-47s were touching their shoulders and their barrels were an inch or two short of level and snapping up fast. And then it seemed the hands of time slipped a cog because the rise of their bodies and the movements of their rifles stopped so seamlessly and instantaneously that the part of me that was seeing it felt it couldn't be real. At the same instant their faces came into sharp focus, growing larger and closer until I was seeing their features with amazing clarity. I'd envisioned ambushers with hate-filled visages but the expressions frozen on their faces were tight and scared. I was surprised at that, and then I was surprised that in this fateful instant I was aware of being surprised, but even as those stray thoughts were drifting through my mind my body was reacting at a speed that my conscious brain couldn't follow.

I had a flashing image of myself suspended in the air. I knew I was spinning to my left and that my hands were flipping my M-16 up to the right shoulder that was coming to meet it. I could feel my finger squeezing the trigger very gently, sending its bullets from low left to upper right at the body of the NVA on the right. And then my hands were guiding the barrel down to the one on the left, two shots on the first, three on the second. I didn't register the sounds but I could feel the M-16 tapping at my shoulder, the taps coming so slowly that it seemed the lightning-quick M-16's action was barely moving, and with each tap I knew where the bullet had gone.

The expressions on the faces of the two NVAs were melting as my body hit the ground, and then their bodies were collapsing so limply that I was thinking they looked like puppets whose strings had been snipped.

It seemed like time restarted. Quinlin was sprawling to the ground. The others followed. AK-47s started firing down at us from high on the ridge and a moment later we were taking fire from up the trail.

I yelled, "On the left! Cover the ridge!" and behind us weapons opened up in that direction.

Lt. Colclough moved to the right to cover our right flank and started shooting into the foliage. He was yelling for someone to bring the gun up and Big Jack sprinted up, dived in, and started firing his M-60's heavy bullets up the trail. His ammo carrier, Howard Hellman, was with him, and then Henry and Joe Bunch came running up from farther back and dove in behind us. Henry started spraying bullets up the ridge in the direction of the shooters who'd targeted him on his way up, joining the rest of us spitting back bullets to suppress the shooting from the NVA ambushers.

I thought they might creep up through the dense foliage in front of us and I decided to frag it. I found the seam I was going to throw through, rose to a knee, pulled the pin on my grenade, and took a powerful step forward as I released the spoon, intending to make a long throw. My left foot landed and my right arm rocketed forward, and then my grenade slipped through my sweat-slickened hand and everything went into slow motion; the spoon spinning away to my right and the grenade hanging in the air behind me. It seemed to hang suspended for one pregnant moment, and then my turning head watched its slow-motion descent. It landed, recoiled a fraction of an inch off the springy humus-covered earth, and came to rest less than a meter from Dennis' head. Dennis had a desperate "*oh no!*" look on his face, and I watched him start burying his helmeted head nose-down in the dirt and wrapping his arms around his helmet.

My momentum was carrying me forward and as my right boot came down I spiked my heel in the dirt, spun on it, and leaped back. I pulled my knees up to bring my hand closer to the grenade and landed squatted, already twisting back to my left. I knew the frag was about to explode but I was spinning fast and I couldn't risk fumbling it again. I slowed my right hand and reached out, and when I felt it settle firmly in my hand I uncoiled and sprang away. I used the propulsion of my still-spinning body and extended arm to wrist-flip it underhanded in the direction I'd intended to toss it. I watched it leave my hand, and then my foot landed and I spun back again and dove away. I heard it explode, and then I landed flat with a searing pain in my left butt cheek.

The NVA shooting trailed off and stopped, and we quit shooting and assessed our losses. Joe Bunch and I had picked up minor shrapnel wounds from my grenade. Somehow we were the only ones who'd been wounded, and after taking a few minutes to regroup we started pushing up the dense foliage on the right side of the trail with the others further to my right and keying off me. I was about halfway to the ambush site when I stepped over a small log. I hadn't compensated by leaning low and I was shocked when my head bobbed up. I couldn't understand why my instincts had failed me, and then I realized that I felt like I'd taken a blow to the head. And it wasn't just that I felt dazed; images of those melting bodies and thoughts of what I'd find on the other side of that log were racing through my mind. I knew how vulnerable that made me but it seemed right that I'd pay a price for what I'd done, and I continued moving toward whatever was lying behind that log.

When I'd moved past where the log would be I angled back to my left. The line of the trail took shape and I sight-tracked its path to the log. There was a body behind the log and there were marks on the trail where they'd dragged the other away. His still-beating heart had spurted blood 2 or 3 feet to the right of those drag marks for the first few meters, and then his body had weakened and his blood had fallen in the drag marks. I followed the lessening spoor another 50 or so meters to the place where they'd abandoned his body. A smaller blood trail extended further but we stopped there.

I spread my nylon blanket a little to the left of the trail and Quinlin and Sugar Bear set up beside me. The rest of the company circled into a perimeter behind us, and the three of us sat unspeaking in the quasi-darkness. A few steps from us the NVA lay where they'd dropped him: a featureless shape dimming in the fading light. I took care not to look at him but no matter where I faced his body seemed to hover on the edge of my vision.

I'd never smoked cigarettes, but when Sugar Bear and Quinlin lit up I bummed a menthol off Quinlin. He held out the glowing end of his, and I lit mine off it and sucked the smoke carefully into my lungs, holding back coughs and welcoming the lightheaded feeling it generated. After we'd smoked for a few minutes Quinlin volunteered that he'd been facing my way when it started but he hadn't seen me move. I heard the question in his voice but I couldn't explain, and I didn't try.

Sugar Bear whispered bitingly, "I told you you was gonna git someone killed with them goddamned frags," and then we were done talking about it.

A couple of guys slipped up to ask what happened and I said what I always said about anything that happened on point; that Quinlin and I had shot a couple of gooks. What else was there to say? I'd done what I'd so many times envisioned myself doing, we were alive, and it was over. I tried to tell myself, "*Fuck it, it don't mean nuthin,*" but I hadn't anticipated the intimacy I'd felt when their frightened faces had gone slack and their bodies had melted.

His body was there in the gray light of dawn, still shrunken into the jungle floor. Someone had rifled through his pockets, maybe looking for useful intelligence or maybe just morbidly curious, but it hadn't been me. I'd never looked directly at him and I couldn't have said which of the NVA faces had belonged to him. Another platoon took the lead, and when we retraced our steps down the trail I saw the body of the second NVA propped up against the log in a sitting position. They'd marker-penned his left eye black, and they'd placed a cigarette in his mouth and a beer can in his hand and written, "I fucked with the Cav," on his now-bare chest. I hated seeing that.

The bunker complex I'd foreseen was there, a big one dug on the fringes of a meadow less than 150 meters from the place where I'd angled away. It was just-abandoned and the stuff they'd left behind indicated they'd left in a hurry. As I waited for them to check out the complex I heard a couple of chickens cackle on the fringes of the nearby meadow. They weren't very loud or talkative, those chickens, just one soft cackle and one soft answer. I guessed they were survivor chickens that had been too cautious to catch. I like to think they were, and I hope they went wild and that their progeny will forever cackle warnings in the head-high grasses of that meadow, wherever the fuck that is.

I'd seen that meadow when I'd been riding in on the lead chopper a few days earlier. We'd dipped down toward it and I'd thought we were dropping there, but the pilot had pulled up at the last minute and inserted us several klicks away. I'd thought he'd been making a phantom drop to disguise the location of our actual insertion site then, but it was more likely that he'd seen something on the way in. If he had then the REMFs had known those bunkers were there and they'd guided us back to them. That's how divergent our goals were; the REMFs trying to walk us into that complex and create NVA kill count opportunities and us trying to bypass those deadly NVA bunkers and avoid becoming KIAs.

My cigarette habit didn't last. The smoke had been dulling my sense of smell and I wasn't going nose dumb for whatever those cigarettes were feeding my brain. I'd never planned on staying a smoker anyway. My dad had chain-smoked Camel cigarettes and I'd hated the smell when our car had been hazed with smoke. He'd smoked inside the cabin at Trinity too, and I remembered how clean the mountain air had been when I'd stepped onto the cable bridge over the river. In the fly-droning heat of another jungle day my memory of that clean mountain air made me recall when I'd been an untroubled boy sitting on the sunlit side of a high mountain with a warm breeze whispering through the fragrant fir boughs. I pictured myself leaning back into the caress of that high mountain with no thoughts of anyone lurking behind me with killing eyes, and then I thought of the girl and I knew I was tormenting myself.

I'd done what I'd done and I'd become who I was, and when the man ahead of me stepped out I turned away from thoughts of another time and another me, slung my feather-light pack over my shoulders, and followed him up the trail.

Chapter 22

Malaria

They flew us to LZ Lee for a long-overdue reprieve from the jungle. Our section of the perimeter looked out on empty grasslands and distant tree lines, and the only thing that changed was the occasional appearance of a troupe of Montagnard who were heading to or from someplace to gather food, farm, or do whatever it was that they did to survive. When I'd driven the sergeant major to the nearby village I'd seen tin and wood buildings, outdoor vendors, and a few motorbikes, but the Yards who passed by the LZ appeared far more primitive. They moved along at unhurried paces with long walking sticks in their hands, and if they appeared during the heat of midday they'd sometimes disappear into one of the grass huts that dotted the meadow areas until the heat lessened. The men wore loincloths and many of the women were grass-skirted and bare-chested. Most of us hadn't seen a woman in months and the occasional far-off appearance of a bare-breasted woman would always create a rush to the perimeter and generate catcalls. I thought those calls were insulting but the passing Yards never seemed to pay the LZ any heed; continuing their trek as though we were little more than fleeting disruptions to their ancient ways of living.

I got feverish while we were on the LZ, and when Doc checked my temperature it read so high that they called in a medevac to fly me to the aid station in Củ Chi. The medics there tried to keep my fever down with aspirins and cold packs but it kept spiking. I assured them that I'd taken every malaria pill but they kept poking my fingers for blood to send in for malaria testing, and when one of the tests came back positive they transferred me to the army hospital in Saigon.

I arrived there feverish and exhausted, and I tugged off my filthy pants and shirt, pulled on the blue pajama bottoms they'd laid out for me, and collapsed onto my cot. A nurse came by with a food tray. She took my temperature and I fell asleep without eating. I don't know how long I'd slept when a Donut

Dolly volunteer appeared at my bedside. I was the first bed she stopped at, and although I was feverish and darkened with jungle dirt that kind-eyed Oregon girl stayed at my bedside and talked with me until her Donut Dolly buddies came to tell her that she had to leave. Her angelic presence had been so unexpected and unfamiliar that when she left I wasn't certain I hadn't fever-dreamed her.

I ate breakfast off a tray and slept fitfully for the rest of the day, waking only to eat lunch and dinner. That night I dreamed that my temperature was so high that if I didn't bring it down I'd be brain damaged. I tried to come fully awake but I couldn't break free of that in-between state of consciousness where things seem both eerily real and unreal. The dream persisted and I willed myself to sit up. Nothing changed. I tried harder, but my body didn't respond and I lay as unmoving as if I was paralyzed. I desperately wanted the nurse to make her night rounds but I could hear her flirting with someone at the nurse's station and their conversation didn't seem to be winding down. My fear that my temperature was dangerously high grew stronger but no matter how hard I willed myself to move I couldn't get a muscle to twitch.

The nurse's and the man's voices talked on and on and my sense of urgency rose higher and higher. I wasn't aware that I was moving until I found myself sitting on the edge of my bed. I knew that it wasn't a nightmare then, and I placed my hands on the mattress, gathered my strength, and levered myself to my feet. When the room stopped spinning I oriented myself, let go of the bed, and old-man walked to the nurse's station.

The officer was leaning against the counter talking to the nurse, and I leaned in beside him and waited for the nurse to acknowledge me. She continued conversing with the officer as if I wasn't there. I waited longer, and when she finally appeared to notice me she stared at me silently, her expression not friendly.

"My temperature's really high."

"Your temperature's not that high."

"I've had fevers before. It's high."

"I'll take your temperature when I make my rounds. Go back to your bed!"

"If you just give me a thermometer I'll take it myself."

"**Go back to your bed!**"

I'd never spoken roughly to a woman but my anger was unconstrained and my words were raw. **"Give me a fucking thermometer!"**

"**Here!**" she said, thrusting one at me, "Take your temperature if you want, but it's not that high."

I placed the thermometer under my tongue and then, too soon for an accurate measurement, I thought, she yanked it out of my mouth. She looked down at it, and then she started yelling for aids to help her get me to the shower room. They hustled me there, stripped me naked, and sat me on the shower floor with cold water running over me. The nurse left and returned with an armful of ice packs. She placed them under my armpits and between my thighs, and minutes later my temperature dropped and I was thinking clearly.

When I was toweled off and wearing dry pajamas I asked her what the thermometer had registered, and she answered matter of factly, "107," with no hint of apology in her voice.

The 1970 State of the Union Address

The only television I'd seen in Vietnam was hanging on one of the walls of our ward, and it was about to broadcast President Nixon's 1970 State of the Union address. We'd heard that Nixon was drawing down American troops and letting the South Vietnamese ARVN forces assume more of the fighting but nothing seemed to have changed. They were still sending us into new jungle areas to hunt the NVA and hundreds of Americans were being reported as KIAs every month.

I was anxious to hear what he was going to say about that but I had no idea how his words would impassion me. I should have. Like all of the grunts in my platoon, I'd internalized some immensely disturbing experiences and I think we needed something or somebody to vent our negative emotions on. We had the REMFs but they weren't our only scapegoats. A few of us focused our bitterness on the young men our age who'd fled to Canada to avoid the draft. Others detested the college-enrolled, well-off or well-connected people who'd finagled their way out of serving. Some focused on the "liberal" politicians who were purportedly blocking the military from bombing the entirety of North Vietnam into a wasteland to "end the war." For others it was the anti-war people who were portrayed as blaming us for the carnage. Many resented all of those factions, and some probably had scapegoats I hadn't considered.

I had my share of anger and sadness buried inside me but my bitterness was directed at the powerful men who were sitting in their safe perches, wrapping themselves in our flag, and spouting brave talk about how heroic we were as the number of our dead and wounded climbed higher. I understood that about myself, but I didn't realize how deeply those emotions ran until I lay on my hospital bed listening to Nixon's 1970 State of the Union Address:

> When we speak of America's priorities the first priority must always be peace for America and the world.
>
> The major immediate goal of our foreign policy is to bring an end to the war in Vietnam in a way that our generation will be remembered not so much as the generation that suffered in war, but more for the fact that we had the courage and character to win the kind of a just peace that the next generation was able to keep.
>
> We are making progress toward that goal.
>
> The prospects for peace are far greater today than they were a year ago.
>
> A major part of the credit for this development goes to the Members of this Congress who, despite their differences on the conduct of the war, have overwhelmingly indicated their support of a just peace. By this action, you have completely demolished the enemy's hopes that they can gain in Washington the victory our fighting men have denied them in Vietnam.

The inferences hidden in those loaded phrases spoke clearly to me, and I was wondering whether I'd put a bullet through him if I'd had my M-16 in my hands and he'd been within shooting distance. He wasn't, and I lay in that hospital ward quivering with adrenalin and trying to push those overpowering emotions back into some walled-off place where maybe they'd lie dormant and never take me down with them, only that.

Cam Rahn Bay

My appetite returned and I asked one of the ward nurses if there was some way I could get more food. She asked if I was strong enough to walk to the hospital cafeteria. I assured her that I was, and on her break she took me to the cafeteria and ordered food for me. She smuggled me in again on her next shift and both times I filled up with real food, and then they transferred me to the Army's Rehab Center at Cam Rahn Bay.

When the friendly clerk at the reception desk asked what my rank was I realized that I didn't know. I'd been promoted in Vietnam but I didn't know whether the article 15 demotion in rank that I'd been given in Oakland had caught up with me. I decided it didn't matter and I told him, "Put me down for an E-5."

"OK sarge," he said cheerfully, "step over to the desk there and we'll get you a pay advance."

They assigned me to one of the tin buildings that squatted on the South China Sea's dunes. Mine housed malaria patients and most of the 70 or so cots that filled the open floor were occupied. I selected a cot, and then I changed into the pajama outfit they'd provided and surveyed my spacious surroundings. A small crowd was gathered around a poker game, and when one of the players lost his stake I took his seat. A procession of players came and went throughout the night, and in the early morning I hit a lucky streak that busted the other players and ended up winning close to $300 and a couple of radios. I was exhausted, and I went to sleep, woke for lunch, dozed through the afternoon, woke for dinner, and slept through the night.

In the morning I walked the short distance across the undulating dunes to the blue waters of the South China Sea. A few patients were on the beach or in the water wearing the green boxer underwear they'd given us as swimsuits, and I stripped down to mine and stepped into the sea. The water was bathwater warm and the sand beneath my feet felt feathery soft. The seabed was so flat that I had to wade far from shore before I reached waist-deep water. I kept going until I was chest-deep, and then I spread my arms wide and let the gentle waves float my body up and down, feeling weightless and hearing only the gentle sounds of the surging water.

As the heat climbed dozens of sun-darkened patients filtered onto the beach, and when the waves picked up several of them started body surfing. I tried it but the waves were weak and my technique was so poor that I ended up spending most of my time waiting neck-deep in water for a wave that might be strong enough to compensate for my ineptitude. A lot of those waves passed beneath me but I finally managed to catch a few, including one perfect wave that propelled me all the way to the fine white sand of the beach. That's when I learned to bail out of a wave before it dragged my body across the abrasive, wet-packed beach sand and filled my ears and eyes with grit.

The rehab center was an oasis of civilization. There were no weapons and no foliage to conceal deadly men, just the open dunes, the sea, the patients, and the medical personnel. Every morning American nurses circulated through our barracks charting our temperatures and administering antimalarial medications. Tall, short, thin, heavy, magazine-pretty or not, every one of them embodied softness, gentleness, and warmth, and whenever they were present I felt an awed sense of reverence.

We didn't know anything about the lives of the nurses who appeared briefly in our ward with one exception. A sign was posted just north of our swimming area that read, "No enlisted men beyond this point." That posted section of the beach was rarely occupied and that made the daily arrival of the brunette nurse and the young officer who accompanied her noteworthy. Their appearance would always generate a buzz of conversation and eyes would keep glancing their way. They must have known that but their sadly loving looks and gentle touches made it seem that they were caught up in a world of their own. It was rumored that they each had spouses back in the world, and their unwavering solemnity made me wonder if one of them was scheduled to leave Vietnam soon. Vietnam was filled with bitter accounts of the betrayals of back-home wives or girlfriends but I never heard a Cam Rahn Bay patient begrudge those two their romance. I know I didn't. I think it was because they were such poignant reminders that lives could be filled with tenderness and love.

One night the sound of music drew me to the tennis courts that were located on the off-beach side of our compound. Local officers and nurses were crowded on the courts dancing, socializing, and drinking beverages served from a folding table. Just a few meters away pajama-clad patients were pressed three-deep against the chain-link fencing like night-flying insects fluttering against lit windows on a warm summer's night, wanting in and just as ignored. The music held me there but I was too proud to stand in the shadows of those who'd fenced us out. A long culvert was lying on the ground nearby, and I crawled into the middle of it, closed my eyes, and let the melodies, lyrics, and rhythmic beats of the music evoke poignant memories of the gentle touch and fragrance of the deep-eyed girl who still materialized in my dreams. I'd pushed those away for months but the music kept playing and memories of her pulsed through me like surges of passion in the embrace of a gentle lover.

On another night I was posted to stand guard on one of the high dunes that rose beyond the nurses' trailers, and I sat on the sand with the warm night's wind whispering against my face and the moonlight sparkling off the sea's rolling waves appreciating how peaceful it was. I think that calm scene typified my stay in Cam Rahn Bay. During the handful of days I spent there the soft waves of the South China Sea were a metronome that marked my idle hours, their rhythmic slaps and murmurs creating an unambiguous affirmation that the savage war in the jungle was far away.

My last day at Cam Rahn Bay was the hottest. I spent a lot of it bobbing weightlessly in the warm waters of the sea, but the war felt very near again. In the morning the guy who'd checked me in checked me out, and he remembered me, saying, "Good luck, sarge." He gave me directions to the place where I could catch a bus for the first leg of my trip back to the Cav and I made it there and waited, wondering what might have happened to my guys during the days I'd been gone.

The Colonel on the Bus

The bus slowed to a stop with squealing brakes and a belch of sooty diesel fumes wafted in its wake. I held my breath until the wind carried the exhaust away, and when the doors opened I climbed the three steps and surveyed the exhaust-tinged interior of the bus. It was crammed to capacity with unacclimated FNGs who were sitting red-faced and sweat-soaked, their uncertain looks cataloging them as unmistakably as their unfaded uniforms. A few were seated two across with their gear piled high on the seat beside them, but most of the bench seats held three men with their gear spread on their laps, shoved into the isles, and stuffed beneath their feet. The lone exception was sitting alone in the front row right-side seat with his gear resting on the seat beside him. He had Lt. Colonel's insignia pinned on his lapel and he was studiously avoiding looking my way.

My anger must have registered when I asked, "Is this your gear?"

He flinched, and his head turned my way. Without waiting for an answer I said, "Here, I'll move it for you," and I lifted his duffel bag off the seat with my right hand, reached across his legs, and let it drop. He hunched forward when the heavy duffel landed on his feet. I took a seat beside him as the bus started forward. He sat rigidly, not liking the contemptuous way he'd been treated but not objecting.

I could have left it there but I didn't. He wasn't personally responsible for the army's policy of providing better clubs, latrines, quarters, and food for the officer core but lacking the common decency to share a seat with enlisted men in such miserably hot and crowded conditions wasn't army policy, that had been his choice. And what really angered me was the near certainty that some of the men he'd left sitting crowded and overheated behind him had a much poorer chance of living through the next year than he did.

I said curtly, "Where you from?"

He hesitated for so long that I thought he wasn't going to answer, and then he said, "Fort Polk."

I said derisively, "You weren't born in the army, were you? What's your home state?"

I'd dropped his gear on his feet and now I was taunting him. The flush that suffused his thick neck traveled all the way to his ears but he was isolated from the safeguards his rank afforded him, and I was an unknown soldier with a don't-give-a-damn attitude in a lawless place where someone like me could do him harm and disappear into the anonymity of hundreds of thousands of faceless soldiers. The arrogance of rank that had led him to believe he was entitled to a full seat evaporated and he mumbled the name of his home state.

I ignored him and slouched low in my seat with my eyes half-closed against the glare of the sunlight that was piercing through the wire-screened windows. There were occasional hums of conversations behind me but I didn't turn to look back, not once. Some of those FNGs would be grunts on the first leg of their journey to the jungle. I'd been there once but I couldn't help them, I didn't want to see their faces or know their stories, and I sure as hell didn't want to think about the days and months they'd have ahead of them. At the end of our long ride I was the first one off the bus, scanning the smoke-smudged skies and tracking the choppers to where they were rising and landing.

As I neared the chopper pad a captain came walking my way. He fixed me with a power look that suggested he was expecting something, probably a salute. My anger at the arrogance of the bus colonel lingered and I made a point of staring through him as we passed. He meant nothing to me, nor did this place. The buildings, the sandbag-covered bunkers, and the men scurrying about were little more to me than shadows; the rounded tops of the bunkers and their bowed heads emblematic of a stifling existence that I abhorred. I was from another place, one that honed men to their core and one where tiny things held immense significance, and I continued on with ground-eating strides that were carrying me ever closer to the jungle.

At the chopper pad a sandy-haired guy was making his way toward a nearby chopper. I yelled above the din to ask if anything was heading to Quần Lợi and he gestured toward some choppers. A door gunner on one of them said that they'd be making a run there in an hour or so. I asked if he had space for me, he nodded, I had my ride, and the next morning I was back at my company waiting for them to load our log day chopper. A Hispanic guy from one of our other platoons was also waiting. I asked where he was from, and when he said he was from a Texas border town I asked what it was like there. He'd seemed a little guarded but he grew more and more relaxed as he talked about the food, the festivals, and his friends. I was picturing what it was like when he stopped mid-sentence, looked straight at me, and told me that back home he and his friends fought with the white guys. He said it was like a war with shootings and knifings and that they hated the white guys enough to kill them if they got the chance. In the same breath, he said that the Hispanic guys in our company didn't trust many of the white guys but they liked me. His face flushed when he told me that they called me "Hombre" because my name was Mann.

I hadn't understood why he'd been telling me those things but I did now. He'd let his guard down talking about his home but he had too much pride to let me think he was someone he wasn't so he'd told me who he was, no secrets and no lies. It was a lot to take in. I hadn't had any idea that the Hispanics in our company felt alienated from some of the white guys. I'd thought of all of us as grunts and I hadn't cared about race or who we'd been back in the world. I still didn't, and he and his friends being at war with white guys in Texas wasn't important to me. I'd seen the respect his guys had given him, and I'd read him myself. He was one of *us*, and that was what mattered to me. I could have just said that but he'd spoken to me on a deeply personal level and I wanted to give him something about me that ran deeper than words, so I said that the vice president of my high school class had been Al Valdivia, my good friend. He nodded, and that was it; no need for more words.

We talked about little things, and when the bird was loaded we climbed in and flew back to the company. The chopper circled, descended into a whirlwind of flying leaves and debris, bounced once, and settled with a lurch. The two of us picked up our M-16s, slung our packs, nodded, and headed off in opposite directions on the log day's perimeter. I'd catch a glimpse of him at times but we'd orbit with the guys in our respective squads and platoons. That was fine with me; I didn't need to get closer to a guy who might not live very long.

I'd worried that my platoon might have suffered casualties but they hadn't seen any signs of an NVA presence in the piece of jungle they'd been working. I imagine that's why Baby Huey and some of the others felt comfortable exchanging their steel helmets for floppy boonie hats when our squad went on a patrol. Giving up the protection of the steel pots was a matter of personal choice but I didn't like it. When I'd first arrived I'd heard about a NVA with a handful of battle citations in his pack who'd walked into a scared-shitless FNG and gotten himself shot dead. I'd marked that as a reminder that no matter how capable you were just one careless moment could get you killed, and I thought I was seeing a few of my guys who didn't feel it would happen to them. That was bad enough, but what bothered me more was that any NVA who got a look at us would be seeing a motley crew of overly confident targets moving jauntily through the jungle. I couldn't get that image of our squad out of my head, and that evening I circulated among the guys in my squad telling them that if any gooks got eyes on us we'd want them to see the kind of fully equipped and lethal-looking grunts they'd want to steer clear of. I told them it was their choice but the next time we went on patrol steel helmets were riding on every head.

We were still there when Dennis relayed that some high-ranking officers were planning to chopper out to the jungle and they wanted us to shave and clean up as best we could. I wasn't willing to pretend that things in the jungle were different than they truly were and I told Dennis that I wouldn't shave and play soldier. Quinlin decided that he wouldn't either, and when the day of their visit arrived we were the only ones who weren't clean-shaven. I would have held my ground but Lt. Colclough asked very gently if we'd shave as a favor to him. Lt. Colclough was a special platoon leader, the kind who'd ask you rather than order you and you'd know that if you said "no" he'd do all he could to make it work for you anyway, so we did it for him. It turned out that it didn't matter because the high-ranking officers never showed up.

Sugar Bear's Stolen 3-day RxR

I watched Quinlin make his way back from the log bird site, not ambling like he usually did but moving like a guy who needed to get somewhere. He made a beeline to where Sugar Bear and I were sitting and stopped at Sugar Bear's feet.

Without pausing he said, "Bar, thar's ah three-day, in contry RxR on the 20th an she goes ta the one thet's the shortist...[has the least time left on their tour.] If you doan wan her, she's mine."

He was standing stiffly and the pace of his drawl had quickened, wanting that 3-day RxR badly, I guessed. Sugar Bear read that, and without hesitating he said, "I got my 7-day RxR on the 21st. You take it."

Quinlin spun on his heel and left without another word, and Sugar Bear watched him walk away with a trace of a smile on his face, basking in the glow of a good deed done for his best buddy. That didn't last. The resupply chopper's blades started churning the thick air and Sugar Bear looked up and barked, "Where's **HE** goin?"

I glanced at the chopper, and when I saw Quinlin on the log bird I knew why he'd been in such a hurry. I said as innocently as I could, "He's riding the bird out for that 3-day RxR on the 20th, remember, you told him to take it cause your 7-day RxR was on the 21st?"

Sugar Bear's reddened face twisted, and he turned to me and snapped, "The 21st of **next** month, **you ass**! That dink never told me it was for **this** month!"

I tried to put a sympathetic look on my face but he didn't buy it, and cursing every step of the way he stormed off to complain to someone, probably the Lt., about Quinlin stealing his 3-day RxR.

Sugar Bear stayed in a foul mood the entire 6 days Quinlin was gone, and when Quinlin returned and climbed off the log bird I was waiting to see what Sugar Bear would do. Jim was appraising Sugar Bear warily but a stony-faced Sugar Bear wouldn't even glance at him. I'd been anticipating this moment for the entire time Jim had been gone, and when Quinlin was a few steps away I smothered a smile and asked cheerfully, "So how was your 3-day RxR?"

Quinlin knew I wasn't being helpful. He gave me a sharp glance and replied tersely, "It whar OK."

There was an awkward silence before Jim took a big risk and asked Sugar Bear what was new. It was the opening Sugar Bear had been waiting for and he pounced like a cat on a mouse, snapping his head in my direction and hissing, "Tell **HIMMM** that he's a prick an I ain't gonna forgit it!"

"What the hell," I thought, and I turned to Quinlin and said, "You're a fucking prick and he's not going to forget it."

Quinlin said, "Fuck it then,"

Sugar Bear pretended he hadn't heard, so I turned to him and whispered, "He said fuck it then."

"Tell **HIMMM** that **I** don't care what **HE** says," Sugar Bear replied.

"He doesn't care what **YOU** say," I repeated dutifully, and that was the start of Sugar Bear's shunning of Jim. More accurately, it was the start of his semi-shunning of Jim because at odd times Sugar Bear would insist that I relay snippy messages Quinlin's way. Jim was always within earshot but Sugar Bear never wavered in his pretense that Jim couldn't hear anything he'd said and that he couldn't hear anything Jim had said, and I took advantage of my go-between role by garbling or embellishing Sugar Bear's snippy messages and Jim's terse responses. Jim never commented on my distortions but Sugar Bear would give me long disgusted looks and repeat his messages **very** slowly to make it clear to me that he thought I was a simpleton, and then he'd instruct me to tell **"HIMMM** exactly" what he'd said. Sometimes I'd re-relay the messages accurately but at other times I'd mangle them even more or add comments that he hadn't made.

Sugar Bear was too pissed and Quinlin was too dour to appreciate my contributions, but I considered some of my embellishments immensely entertaining and I never let their sour dispositions deter me from garbling their exchanges. Sadly, Sugar Bear got madder at me for garbling his messages than he was at Quinlan for screwing him out of the RxR and in the quiet of a late evening he glared at me hatefully, and then he leaned in and whispered to Quinlin, "Ed's a real asshole, ain't he?" Quinlin grunted, and that was the end of it, they'd made their peace.

I missed the fun of it, and an hour later I invented a snippy message from Sugar Bear and whispered it to Quinlin. In the fading light of the approaching night they somberly shook their heads in unison, as though I merited their sympathy, and I had to choke back laughter at the thought that they'd consider me the peculiar one, almost surely reinforcing their views that among the three of us, I was.

Combat Leader's Course

I told Quinlin and Sugar Bear that they were sending me to the rear for Combat Leader's Course training. Jim didn't like it but he didn't say anything. Sugar Bear sneered. "**Some** people, who knows who **they** are, sure knows how to brown-nose outa the bush," and I told him that if brown-nosing was what it took then "**some**" people would have gotten out a long time ago.

Two days later I was sitting in the cavernous interior of a high-ceilinged tin building. Every company of the 1st Cav Division that had been able to arrange transportation had sent one E-3 to E-5 ranked grunt here, and about 50 of us were seated on rows of folding chairs in front of a portable chalkboard and a pull-down screen. I listened to the murmured conversations and scanned the faces of the men sitting with me, reading them the way I'd read the FNGs who'd arrived at our company. Most of them looked like levelheaded men who wouldn't stray too far from the line; the kind of dependable men most officers would want as squad leaders. I knew that I didn't fit that mold but I was sitting on a real chair inside a real building and I wasn't complaining.

Two NCOs arrived. They stepped briskly in front of us and everyone quieted. One gave a no-nonsense introduction, telling us that we'd been selected because we'd demonstrated leadership potential in the field and been considered capable of becoming team and squad leaders. He said they were going to teach us small unit tactics, air assault techniques, map reading, communication procedures, and first aid and leadership skills. He was still outlining the program when a nearby artillery battery fired off a barrage. Most of us were just a day or two out of the boonies and we dove to the floor and sent chairs skittering in every direction.

"It's just the artillery battery next door," the instructor said sympathetically, but the amused look he was trying to hide said he'd known what was coming. Several guys were sprawled on top of me at odd angles, and when they climbed off me I rose, retrieved my chair, and sat, wondering if I'd end up like one of our combat-shattered drill instructors in basic training who'd had an uncontrollable startle reaction to any unexpected noise.

I'd been living almost wordless days and thinking in impressions for months, and now I was suddenly barraged by hours of words. Keeping up exhausted me, and I'd often find my mind flicking through jungle scenes. I'd try to pay attention but the room would always slip away and I'd once again realize that I'd been revisiting the sights and sounds of the jungle. I'd expected that many of them would have trouble adjusting to word-thinking but I'd see them concentrating and taking notes. That made me feel a little like an outlier in the classroom but I never felt that way when we gathered at the nearby service club. A lot of the others had shared their experiences there and every one of them had done it respectfully and humbly with no hero stories and no macho talk. It was another reminder of how clearly the jungle revealed the character of men and I wasn't surprised when I learned that most of them were already squad leaders.

They gave us a Sunday off near the end of our ten days of training. The nearby service club was closed on Sundays so five of us hitched a ride to a special forces' PX to buy alcohol. It turned out to be a drab building with mostly empty shelves. The only liquor was labeled *Taylor's Pink Champagne*, and each of us bought two quart-sized bottles, stepped outside, and twisted the plastic caps off. The champagne fizzed over the lips of the bottles and we tipped them back and drank the tangy foam, and then we gulped the sweet contents down like it was Kool-Aid.

We weren't strangers to walking and we headed back on foot, 5 high-spirited grunts tipping back our champagne and drinking so greedily that our first bottles were soon empty. I felt amazingly young and carefree, and then we rounded a corner to the wired-off compound that stretched along the right side of the street. About a dozen Vietnamese men were standing or sitting in groups of twos and threes in the pen's open air or under the open-sided lean-to that was inside the wire. At least half of them were amputees, others were swathed in fluid-seeped bandages and some had plaster-cast appendages. They were NVA and we were grunts, and on some primal level we recognized each other at first sight. It froze us in our tracks, all of us, and I stood staring into the glowering eyes of one of my enemies with eyes equally as hateful.

One of the guys with me began to parody the gait of a one-legged amputee, and soon others were pointing at various crippled soldiers in the pen and mimicking their disabilities. Their laughter had an insane, feverish, quality. I didn't parody anyone but my own laughter built until I thought tears might fill my eyes. But I didn't cry. The NVA glared back, silent and unbroken, and we walked on, passing them by as we surely had in the jungle, each of us carrying hatreds born of fears. Those hatreds hadn't sprouted from seeds we'd planted but they'd found fertile ground in us, and, like indentured laborers compelled to their work, we harvested that bitter crop in this place we no longer considered a part of the world. I went directly to bed when we arrived, and the next morning I woke with a pounding headache. The headache eased but my memories of the baleful men in the pen and the shameful echoes of my laughter didn't.

Our CLC training ended a couple of days later. The lecturers selected a lanky redheaded guy who'd been my closest acquaintance as the outstanding soldier of the cycle, and my classmates voted me the outstanding leader. I'd been relatively quiet but I think I may have stood out because I was a little different. Whatever their reasons, I felt deeply honored by those old-for-their-years grunts.

I made my way to a chopper pad and found one that was heading in the right direction. I asked the door gunner if he had room for me, and I was once again invited in with no questions. Chopper flight paths constituted South Vietnam's highway system, running south to Saigon, north to the coast, and to Bien Hoa and LZs like Lee and Grant. Any chopper might be called upon to fly anywhere at any time, and for the pilots, crew chiefs, and gunners it must have seemed like the old west where a chopper was like a horse you could saddle up whenever you wanted. Those crews didn't have anyone looking over their shoulders and when they recognized one of us who had a *been-there and done-that* bearing they'd take us on if they had enough room. That opened up the entire chopper highway for me, and I knew I could have gone anywhere and stayed for a while without worrying about any repercussions from Capt. Valtz or Lt. Colclough. I liked knowing that, but someone had been shouldering my share of the risks while I'd been gone, and I made it back to LZ Lee in one day and caught a ride out on the log bird's first run.

Henry and Kenny were standing 20 meters off the tail side of the chopper, and when it landed Kenny said, "Look who's back," with his always-ready grin on his face. I found Quinlin and Sugar Bear sitting on packs stuffed pillow-full of three days' supplies of food. Empty boxes and cans littering the brush near them. Their uniforms were as dirty and grimy as the canvas of their packs, and both were infused with the smell of C-4 cooking fires, cigarettes, and unwashed clothes. They were playing two-handed spades with the same raggedy-edged deck of cards we'd been using when I'd left, the 5 of diamonds missing its upper left-hand corner and the top right-hand corner of the jack of clubs creased, or maybe torn off by now. Intent on the game, Sugar Bear flipped down a card. He lost the trick. A frown flitted across his face as Quinlin's left hand snatched up the cards. It was like every log day card game before I'd left except this one was two-handed. I slowed my steps and their eyes came up.

"Where the fuck you bin for so long?" Sugar Bear said, genuinely pissed.

His being pissed at me for something wasn't unusual but I'd just spent a few days with a different kind of men and it struck me wrong. I stared at him until he dropped his eyes.

Jim slid his pack aside. "Do ya thank ya still knows how ta play cards or did ya furgit whilst ya was out chasin whores an eatin hot suppers?"

Fuck Sugar Bear, I thought, and I took my place at the corner of the triangle.

A slight movement of the air brought the scent of log day food. Flies were droning all around but the mosquitoes weren't too bad, maybe clinging on the underside of leaves to wait out the worst heat of the day. Ants and crawling bugs were feasting on bits of scattered C-ration food, the calorie-rich bounty a respite from the hard living they'd been eking out of the jungle floor, and some birds or monkeys were calling amiably in the distance. I didn't know their faces but I knew their voices well.

I shuffled the cards. The jungle-weathered deck riffled familiarly in my hands, and I leaned forward and dealt, certain of who I was in this place of unrelenting discomfort and uncertain futures. This was my jungle and these were my people. I owned them, or maybe they owned me, it was the same either way.

Chapter 23

Mad Dog

A week or so later we were resupplied in two small meadows that were linked by a narrow vine-choked avenue. The resupply chopper had already lifted off and we were marking time waiting to leapfrog up the trail the point squad was creating. I was squatting beside my pack in the lower meadow. My shirt was hanging on a nearby bush to dry and I could feel the sun's radiant heat burning onto my shoulders, portending another hot, bug-droning, and hard-humping day. I saw Dennis meandering from guy to guy in our squad, and I wondered idly what news he was sharing and why I was apparently going to be last on his list.

When he finally wound his way to me he said, "Ed, you know the guys have been bitching about packing the shovel, right?"

"No, I didn't know."

"Well, they have. I gave it to a couple of the guys to take turns carrying, but they felt that wasn't fair so I decided that we'd all take turns humping it."

He'd chosen his words carefully and I chose mine just as carefully, "Dennis, I don't pack enough food or water for three days. I go hungry and thirsty because if I get tired walking point I'll get killed. I take a larger share of the risk and I think someone else can take a larger share of packing the load."

"Ed, I've already told the guys," Dennis said.

There'd been a hint of a question in his voice but I wasn't going to help him find an out. I said, "That's fine Dennis, but the day I start packing the shovel is the day we start taking turns walking point."

I could see him running alternatives through his agile mind, and then the heavy steps of our newly arrived platoon sergeant, *Mad Dog*, sounded behind me. I pivoted a half turn and he stopped an arm's length away, his eyes challenging, his hands clenched into fists and his body leaning forward.

He'd joined our platoon when I'd been at the Combat Leader's Course, a big, athletic-looking E-7 in his late 20s or early 30s who had *lifer* imprinted on him as clearly as if he'd tattooed it on his forehead. Sugar Bear said he'd been a drill sergeant back in the world, and that rang true. He had the aggressive *shut your mouth and pay attention* demeanor that most of them affected, and he'd rarely bypassed an opportunity to issue housekeeping orders in an imperious manner; trying to establish that he was in charge, I guessed. The thing he hadn't seemed to have learned was that out here age was measured by time spent in the jungle and authority was earned by demonstrating competence. Judged by those metrics he hadn't proven himself and I'd been waiting for someone to tell him to shut the fuck up. No one had; his testosterone-fueled assertiveness and his size were too intimidating and he'd remained an unchecked and disruptive presence.

I'd known we were destined to clash the minute I'd arrived back from CLC and he'd known it too, keeping his distance and measuring me, each of us anticipating this moment. He hissed. "Did he tell you to do something?"

A huge surge of blood coursed through my body. I had an immense sense of physical power and I positioned my right foot slightly behind my left and stared directly into his eyes. "Yes," I said, the single word coming from deep inside my lungs.

"Are you going to do it?"

"No."

"Yes, you are," he said in a voice that rang with certainty.

"No, I'm not," I said, my anger barely restrained.

"Yes, you are, or I'm going to give you that to do and something else too."

"I won't do that either."

"Yes, you will."

"No, I won't."

"Yes, you will."

"No, I won't."

"Yes, you will."

The back and forth was juvenile but the issue was deadly serious. The only thing Mad Dog understood was that an E-6 squad leader had gotten into a minor disagreement with someone he'd recognized as a threat to his authority. He'd seen this as an opportunity to establish himself as the top dog and the right or the wrong of the issue didn't matter to him. I didn't give a damn about that either. This was about him and me and I wasn't going to let it pass.

I made myself slow the words, "Why don't you tell me to do something **right now,** and we'll see if I do it?"

My words infuriated him. His left shoulder turned a little, his feet lined up, and I saw the muscles of his right arm tighten. The point of his jaw was within the coiled reach of my right fist and I willed him to do what he was leaning into. He almost did, and then he seemed to see something in me.

His eyes widened and he stepped back and said, "Come with me. We're going to see the Lt."

Not so tough after all, I thought derisively as I pushed through the vine-choked avenue to the other clearing, still so furious that I didn't feel the *wait-a-minute* thorns tearing through the skin of my shoulders and back.

Lt. Colclough was standing at the edge of the second meadow talking on the radio. Mad Dog walked straight to him but Lt. read our faces and turned away. I listened to him prolonging the call, and then he signed off, turned, and said, "What's the problem, Ed?"

Mad Dog started to sputter something but I talked over him, "It's Mad Dog. He's ordering the guys around but he doesn't know what he's doing and he's too stupid to wait until he learns. He's too goddamn dangerous to have around."

Mad Dog started to say something but Lt. ignored him and asked, "What can I do about it?"

That wasn't what I wanted to hear. I said, "I'll talk to someone who can," and I wheeled and walked away.

Captain Valtz's alert eyes were watching my angered approach from the far side of the meadow. Without a preamble, I repeated almost word for word what I'd said to Lt. When I finished all he said was, "I'll take care of it."

When I returned to my pack Mad Dog was out of sight, maybe with the Lt., maybe not, *but he'd better stay the fuck away from me.*

From that log day to the next Mad Dog stopped barking orders. He never even glanced in my direction, either, but I was sure we weren't finished with each other. I was wrong. The tempo of our next log day chopper's blades picked up and Sugar Bear nodded toward it and said, "Mad Dog's on the bird."

I looked up and saw Mad Dog sitting in its open belly with his M-16 and his pack resting beside him. I realized that they were sending him out of the jungle and I said loudly and bitingly, "Going somewhere, Mad Dog?"

His jaw clenched, and then a wide smile transformed his face and he said reverently, "Yes. **YES I AM!**"

He'd risen too high to hear my voice but I surprised myself by nodding my head and returning a smile of my own, one equally as spontaneous and equally as genuine, no longer angry and both of us free to walk our separate paths to whatever fates awaited us. As the chopper rose higher our eyes stayed locked and our smiles held, and when the chopper wheeled away I silently wished him well.

Dennis came up with some plan for packing the shovel that didn't involve Jim or me and, once again, my only adversaries were the deadly men hidden in the jungle.

I don't know if they'd actually sent Mad Dog out of the jungle because of that incident, but at the time I thought they had and I didn't have any misgivings about it. I'd viewed Mad Dog as a hyper-alpha male who hadn't had enough sense to wait and find his place organically, but I think my view of the world was far too narrow. Mad Dog was a Black man. I'd known that some of the men with us were racists but it had never occurred to me that the common dangers and miseries we shared wouldn't override their prejudices. I think that might have happened over time but I'd never been on either end of that kind of thinking, and Mad Dog surely had. Maybe he'd believed that he'd needed to bark orders and prove himself a force to be reckoned with to gain the respect of men who'd grown up believing that black people shouldn't be given authority over them, and maybe he'd been right.

The contrast between the Mad Dog I'd clashed with and the one I'd glimpsed as he'd ridden the chopper out with that smile on his face had remained in my memory but it was much, much, later before I'd consider things in a different light. I regret that. I wish I'd been wiser and more emotionally insightful into how difficult it would be to function among people who viewed me through the lens of deep-seated prejudices. If I had then maybe I'd have tried to find a way to make things work for us. I imagine it wouldn't have panned out, that I was too reactive to anyone who attempted to exercise any control over me and that Mad Dog was too conditioned by the army's chain of command protocols and too new to the jungle to have backed off, but I wish I'd tried.

Under a Distant Star

I had the first watch, the one where the sounds of someone feeling his way a few steps along the early night perimeter or the soft whisperings of a nearby voice were safe ones. Reassured, I turned my face to the heavens. The dense canopy obscured the night sky and then the earth rotated a fraction of a degree and a pinpoint of light from a solitary star found its way through a tiny gap. I watched it flicker thinking of the summer nights I'd spent in the loft of my grandmother's cabin trying to spotlight a deer sneaking into her orchard. Sometimes layers behind layers of distant suns had glistened overhead like shining jewels, each one sending its starlight across countless years of space and time, and then through the clear mountain air to the orchard in Trinity, and on no-moon cloudless nights their collective luminance had bathed the orchard in a pale glow that had been bright enough to reveal the shadowy movements of a deer sneaking apples.

I'd read a lot and on some nights I'd imagined an intelligent being looking down and seeing me gazing up. I'd thought that our shared sentience and curiosity would connect us and I'd felt a sense of kinship with that cosmic life form that had raised my spirits then, but I couldn't recapture that feeling as I watched that little star's light flicker down at me. *If any being could see me doing this he'd forever turn away*, I thought, but no one would see. We were hidden beneath a jungle canopy that extended in every direction, *throwaway men whose fates rested in the hands of men who'd long ago accepted our deaths.*

I felt so alienated that I couldn't imagine that little star shining above my grandmother's cabin when the earth turned, and when the noises behind me changed to sleep noises I pushed away childish fantasies and searched for stealthy movements in the shadowed foliage. The whys of things might matter elsewhere but they sure as hell didn't matter here.

The Fruit Tree

When our column slowed and stopped I was standing under a huge, bushy tree. A gaggle of mid-sized birds were hopping from branch to branch overhead, squawking noisily and feeding on something. Several pieces of purple-skinned fruit were lying half-buried in the leaf-littered debris and I pulled one from its nesting spot. It was about the size of an apricot and it had the color and firmness of a nearly ripe plum. I peeled back its tough skin and exposed a thin layer of golden-tinged flesh overlaying an oversized pit. I looked up to make certain the birds were eating what I was holding, and then I placed my tongue against the inside of the purple skin. The skin was extremely tart but the golden flesh beneath it rested deliciously sweet against my tongue. The still-feasting birds bode well and I bit into it. I'd planned to be cautious and eat just one or two but they were delicious and I was so starved that I ate the skin and flesh of every one I could find. I would have shared but when I held up one of the fruits and shrugged a question the nearby guys shook their heads emphatically. Sugar Bear went further, moving his right hand to his throat in a choking gesture and then pointing at me with a malicious smile pasted on his face.

They had no idea what they were missing. I'd thrived on apples, grapes, strawberries, plums, and peaches from my grandmother's orchard but I'd never eaten anything as delicious as the golden flesh of the fruit I found lying beneath a wild plum tree in the middle of an untracked piece of jungle.

A Second Gramps

Our original Gramps, Jerry, had wrangled a rear job. I liked to think of him safely back in the rear with his childlike smile imprinted on his open face, happily doing whatever job they'd given him. His nickname had found a new home in a FNG who'd been dubbed, "Gramps 2." Gramps 2 was a drawling brown-haired Southerner who was three or four years older than most of us. I think most people would have considered him handsome although he sometimes pursed his mouth in a way that gave him an old man look. Maybe that's what made the Gramps 2 name such a natural fit, or maybe it was because he tended to air his views in a slightly superior tone that suggested he considered himself very wise.

A week or two after Gramps 2 joined us we were patrolling single file down a gently descending ridgeline that was dotted with towering trees. The dimness beneath the trees had thinned out the undergrowth and created long sightlines that reached back at us from the long ridgeline that stretched ahead. An NVA spotted us from far downslope and opened up with his AK-47. I leaped behind the trunk of a big tree, and then I reached around the side of it and sprayed some bullets down the ridge. Some of the guys behind me joined in and fired a few rounds in his general direction. The shooter emptied about half a magazine's bullets, and when he stopped shooting we did too. None of his bullets had hit anywhere close so maybe he'd been a bad shot, but the distance he'd chosen to fire from and his wide misses made me suspect he'd been sending a "keep away!" warning. I was fine with being warned off, and I backtracked up the ridge slipping from cover to cover and collecting guys nestled behind the trunks of big trees.

Gramps had been walking at the tail end of our squad, and I found him burrowed between two root tendons that swelled into the trunk of a huge tree. I don't know why that brief encounter had terrified Gramps but it had. The back of his head was pressed tightly against the main trunk, his feet were outstretched in the dirt, his body was rigid, his face was drained of color, his eyes were unfocused and his breathing was rapid and shallow. The acrid odor of urine filled my nose and I saw that the front of his pants was piss-darkened from his crotch to his knees. Hootie was kneeling behind an adjacent tree. I sent a questioning glance his way and he shrugged his shoulders with an *I don't know?* expression on his guileless face. I turned back to the mess that was Gramps. I had an impulse to help him to his feet and lend him a shoulder but if I'd been in his situation I'd have wanted a chance to climb out of that dark hole on my own, and I wasn't going to take that from him.

I kept any hint of sympathy out of my voice and said, "We're moving out. I need someone to walk flank for me. Can you do it?"

There was no sign that he'd heard anything I'd said but I leaned in closer and repeated the question. A flicker of awareness crossed his face. His head started to shake "no," and then his eyes started to focus. They locked on mine, and then his head tilted back almost convulsively and his pupils rolled so far into his head that the whites of his eyes were all that showed. I thought he was surely passing out, and then he took in a shuddering breath and clenched his jaw. He released that breath, and then he reached across his chest with his right hand, rolled onto his left side to a crawling position, and tried to stand. His legs were too shaky-weak to support him so he reached up, gripped the bark of the tree, and tried to pull himself erect. When he couldn't do it he fumbled a grip on the barrel of his M-16, planted the stock on the ground, and tried to lever himself upright. By pushing down on the M-16 and pulling up on the tree he made it to his feet and stood in the crotch of the root tendons with his knees wobbling like those of a baby standing unsupported for the first time.

I pointed to the right side of our ridgeline and said, "Over there."

Gramps took another shuddery breath, and using his rifle as a crutch he moved away on rubbery legs, his contorted face as white as a sheet and his pants drenched with urine. I led up 60 or 70 meters of the ridge at a snail's pace, expecting him to collapse on any next step, and when I stopped Gramps collapsed into a panting heap a few meters to the side of us. Sugar Bear was staring at him curiously but the others studiously ignored him, out of courtesy, I thought. Gramp's panting started to ease and after a few minutes he sat up. I gave him a little more time, and when we started up the ridge again Gramps took his place at the tail end of our squad, not needing the M-16 for a crutch and his legs not wobbling, one of us again.

I've heard people speak of courage. I know that it means different things to different people but whenever I hear that word I can see Gramps filled with terror, soaked with urine, sensing death, and walking wobbly-legged up that ridge alongside us because death-be-damned, a man can choose who he will be.

Chapter 24

An Ending Written in Bones

They plucked us out of one small clearing and flew us a long distance toward another. The chopper began its gradual descent and I grabbed a handhold and leaned out of the doorway to get a fuller view of the jungle. Just ahead a circular area of flat jungle was bordered on 2/3 of its periphery by steep slopes that rose to flat terraces. Dominant trees rose imperiously out of the thick growth that covered the terraces overlooking the lower jungle but the roof of the more thinly vegetated lower jungle was as uniformly flat as the ground that lay beneath it.

They were inserting us at the edge of the low bowl and I stepped off the skids, dropped through the short grass, and made my way to the rest of my platoon. The last chopper's blades ticked into silence and another platoon's point squad separated out to cut trail. I listened for the cautious animal calls to return but the jungle was still silent when our column moved ahead to reconnect with the point platoon. Over the next hours we penetrated further into the interior of the bowl and the animal calls that should have carried in the stillness of the jungle came rarely and only from afar. The bubble of quiet that was hovering over the entire section of the lower jungle kept pressing at the back of my mind. *Did it signify an NVA presence?* I'd seen cuttings where bamboo sprouts had been harvested but none of them had been fresh and the one small trail we'd found hadn't shown signs of any recent use. I glanced at Quinlin, wondering if he was feeling as uneasy as I was. If he was it didn't show.

A few thin and truncated calls echoed down from the terraces in the evening but if any animals were sharing the lower jungle with us they weren't talking. That was spooky, and it got spookier near dark when some fuck you lizards added their voices to the weirdness of this place,

fuk yuuuuuuuu!

        fuk yuuuu!

     fuk yuuuuuuuuuu!

There were no other calls from the huge area of the lower jungle, just those fuck you lizards.

In the morning we pushed further into the eerily muted area without encountering any evidence of an NVA presence.

The next day I was walking point when I detected a minor NVA trail that was limb-littered and leaf-burdened from long disuse. It was pointing in the direction of the azimuth I'd been given, and I walked about 100 meters of it through single canopy jungle filled with brush and hanging vines. The trail passed through a slight dip, and when I ghosted to the bottom of the dip something made my breath catch. Heart hammering, I slow-motion lowered to a squat. Almost immediately, my eyes guided my mindfulness through 30 meters of leaves, branches, and vines to a few inches of thin line that was suspended horizontally. I focused my ears there, and when I didn't hear anything I shifted a few inches to open up a wider sight avenue. I could see the line extending further and I shifted again, sensing for lurking danger and finding only a stretch of thin line that was suspended too horizontally to appear natural.

I crept closer. The outline of a hammock hanging unmoving in the stillness of the jungle materialized, and then the shapes of other hammocks and the shadows of foxhole depressions began to appear through the branches and vines. I didn't sense any life, and I moved the rest of the way up to the foliage-suspended, sun-faded hammocks that were hanging inertly in the jungle. About half of them were empty, and the others cradled the bones of the men who'd died in them. The foxholes dug alongside them were moldy and dank. Some held human remains. My nose wrinkled in anticipation of the stench of death, but the armies of voracious insects had done their jobs well and the only scents that reached my nose were the musty odors of moist dirt and decomposing leaves.

The rest of my platoon moved up and secured their ill-fated perimeter, and I wandered through it reading the history the jungle had recorded. A company of twenty-five or thirty men had established this perimeter. The depth of their foxholes indicated that they'd considered this section of jungle perilous but their sentries hadn't detected the tiny sounds the night-cloaked NVA would have made as they'd inch-crawled in on them. Those attackers had worked their way perilously close and fired swarms of bullets into the section of the perimeter I'd detected. Many of the men there had died in their hammocks, and in the bullet-laced darkness the attackers had penetrated their perimeter. A few of the men on the far side of the perimeter had rolled out of their hammocks and made it to their foxholes but there'd been too few of them to repel the attack.

I'd heard of grunt companies that had been overrun in night attacks and this place of death depicted that terrifying reality all too clearly. I could picture the last survivors cowering in the phantom protection of their foxholes with the screams of the wounded sounding in their ears and the muzzle flashes of the heavy AK-47s firing at point-blank range flashing in their eyes. One or two would have survived until an aggressive attacker had moved in close and fired a burst of bullets or tossed a frag into their foxhole, but the attack had likely been over in minutes. What followed would have been the stuff of nightmares with the sounds of the moans and the exhalations of air escaping from the lungs of the mortally wounded, the stench of explosives mixing with the odors of blood, urine, excrement, bile, and gases released from the punctured bodies of the dead, and sights of the dead and dying surely creating memories that would forever haunt the darkness of their killers' dreams.

But the gruesome site was peaceful now. The bones that nosed into the dirt at the bottom of the foxholes were dark with mold but the air-dried bones were a lighter shade of gray than the weathered, once-black hammocks that still cradled bodies partially shrouded in the remnants of rotting uniforms. A corner of a plastic-wrapped wallet was poking out of one of those rotting uniforms and I tugged it free and opened it. There were pages written in Asian script inside it along with some Asian currency notes and a photograph taken against the backdrop of a farming village. The photo showed a young man, a young woman, and a girl and boy who looked to be about 7 or 8 years of age posing arm in arm in front of a hut. All four of them had been smiling happily, blissfully unaware that deep in the jungles of Vietnam I'd one day be standing beside the fluid-stained hammock that held the young man's bones with that picture in my hand. *Did they know he was dead or were they still praying that someday, somehow, they'd see him walk back through the huts of that village and return to them?*

I carried photographs too, but there was nothing I could do for them. I placed the wallet and its contents back in his hammock and we melted away from that site as silently as we'd come, leaving their bones lying undisturbed and un-honored in the shadows of the dank foxholes and cradled in the gray hammocks that hung unmoving in a stillness disturbed only by the insects that inched on them or near them. As that doomed perimeter disappeared a few meters behind me I wondered how long it would be before the jungle swallowed our sign and then all of it, leaving the gruesome events that had happened there known only to those who couldn't forget.

I wasn't sure who those overrun soldiers had been but I knew who'd killed them. Before we left that eerie place we encountered a handful of NVA on the extreme edge of the sterile swath of low jungle. It was the Tet holiday season and they must have been high because Earl's squad came across them incautiously dancing around a North Vietnamese flag. They spotted Earl's squad and fled, no shots fired, and Earl and Sam reportedly rushed in and grabbed the flag and some other souvenirs. I thought Earl and Sam's rushing in to grab those souvenirs was as reckless as the NVA getting high and dancing around a flag. It left me wondering if none of us getting killed for a while had made them careless but I didn't say anything; the lives they'd risked had been their own and it had turned out OK.

I left carrying the mystery of why that low jungle bowl had been so devoid of animal calls. I took another thing too; an empty hammock I'd found hanging beside the foxhole that had held its previous owner's skeletal remains. The nylon-netted hammock compressed to the size of an orange and weighed just a few ounces and yet it was strong enough to support my weight. I was too tall for it but I could string it between a couple of sturdy branches and when it rained I could hang above the wet ground, wrap my nylon blanket around me, and stay a little warmer. It was a good plan but I'd seen how easily death could seek out a target hanging in the air and I knew that hammock hadn't brought its last owner any luck. My unease didn't lessen, and I tossed the hammock in the brush and walked away. That night I shifted my body to conform to the curves of the bug-tracked earth and fell asleep tucked into the debris-cushioned jungle floor with no regrets.

A few days later our company was moving along the rim of a high bench that dropped steeply to the bottom of a deep ravine, and when we stopped they designated our squad to work our way to the bottom of the gully. I could hear water splashing and gurgling far below, and I dropped off the rim and started winding my way lower as cautiously as a prey animal approaching a water hole. It wasn't easy. The thinly vegetated clay-like ground was steep and slippery, and I was grabbing onto any foliage I could find to stop myself from sliding. I'd made it about halfway to the bottom of the ravine when I heard a noise above me, and I looked up and saw Gramps sliding feet first and picking up speed. I took a couple of lateral steps to try to intersect his path but before he reached me his foot caught in a bush that yanked him to a sudden stop.

Dennis worked his way down to Gramps while I climbed up to him. When we reached him he told us that he'd hurt his ankle and he didn't think he could walk. Dennis radioed that to the company and Ron radioed back, asking if we could get him up to the rim. Gramps said he was willing to give it a try, and wincing with pain he started up the steep rise with one arm over Quinlin's shoulder and another over Kenny's. I held back to catch them if they came sliding back, and after they'd made it partway up the slope I slung Gramp's heavy pack over my light one, grabbed his M-16 in my off-hand, and started trailing them up. The load felt leaden for a few steps and then I caught my second wind. I'd long ago learned to conserve every ounce of energy but I got on a runner's high and climbed harder than I needed to, thrilled that after recovering from malaria my lean body held that much power.

It was evident that Gramp's ankle had loosened up enough for him to start bearing more of his weight but he was still leaning heavily on Jim and Kenny. I wondered if he was trying to make sure he didn't give up an injury ticket out of the jungle or if he was still hurting that much, but either way it didn't matter to me. Sugar Bear saw it differently, and before we crested the rim he dropped back and whispered maliciously that Gramps was "faking it." Sugar Bear had chosen to stay in the jungle with us when his ringworm could have gotten him a free ride out, but this was Gramp's call and I didn't think it was any of Sugar Bear's business. I asked why in the hell he cared and he launched into an out-of-breath, puffing, tirade about what an asshole I was. I knew how eloquent he could be on that topic but I'd heard it many times, and I stepped past him and moved on.

Captain Valtz gave up on scouting the bottom of the ravine and we started moving along the rim again. There was no place to land a medevac chopper, and when Gramps saddled up his pack and started limping along with us Sugar Bear shot me a triumphant look to let me know that he'd read Gramps right. I guess he thought he'd proved something but the only thing that look told me was that Sugar Bear was never going to stop being Sugar Bear.

The alluring sound of that gurgling water faded behind me but I wasn't sorry. Running water was nectar in the jungle and who knew what might have been awaiting us at the bottom of that shadowy ravine?

Letters From Home

I'd been getting an occasional letter from my friends, Mike Iverson, Phil Lewis, and Jim Webb, and more often there'd been a letter from my sister Evelyn or my mom. My dad had written two or three very brief letters too, but most of my letters had come from Barbara. She'd written almost every day but she mailed them in batches, and on log day's mail call Ron Belin handed me an inch-thick packet of her letters. She'd sprinkled them with her perfume, and when I walked past the guys who were waiting on their mail the scent of her perfume generated some soft good-natured hoots.

The weeks-long no-mail interval had sometimes made me question whether she'd been hesitant to write because she'd met another guy. I wouldn't have faulted her if she had. She knew I might not return and that if I did I might not be the right guy for her, and I'd sometimes wondered if it wouldn't be better for her if she had moved on to someone else.

I didn't want to lose her but my remorse for the suffering I thought my death would cause her made me want to have been loved by no one and free to do whatever felt right without having to worry about who I'd hurt or what I'd lose. That wasn't possible but I'd distanced myself after suffering those dark days by accepting death. I still *thought* of returning home at times but it never *felt* real, or maybe I never let it feel real. What felt real was the lifelike image I had of myself slipping down a shadowy jungle trail to the specific light-dappled place where my life would end. Accepting that had cleared my mind and lessened my fears, and I wasn't going back.

That's how I wanted it to be; just Vietnam with no distractions, and then Barbara's letters would pull me in like the scent of the fragrant fir bough my sister had sent at Christmas and the world I'd left behind would come alive again. I didn't think it through at the time, but I think her gentle written voice was nurturing a resilient thread that stretched halfway across the sphere of the earth to the girl I'd seen standing on the other side of a dance floor three years earlier. And I think those letters helped the part of me that was thoughtful and humane rein in the part of me that resonated so unreservedly with the powerful drumbeat of conflict and danger.

I knew what was coming, and I waited until we'd set up our evening perimeter to read her letters. She'd written of running into my friend Phil Lewis at the Chico State College campus, the three part-time jobs she was working to put herself through college, her plans to visit her mother and stepdad in Washington State during the Christmas break, and news of her roommate Chris Bergie. I envisaged my friend Phil's exuberance, Barbara's graceful presence working as a waitress and a secretary, and her long drive up the I-5 freeway to Washington, all everyday events in the lives of people who were living incredibly distinct lives from the ones we were living. *They'd be foreseeable one-year-older versions of themselves but who would any of us be after this year?* I'd had that thought before but I wasn't pondering that as I burned her letters one by one, I was pushing back against the pain of yearnings and hopes.

Gramps and the Quiet

It was another day on point. I saddled up my pack, picked up my rifle, and started toward the perimeter. Quinlin pulled hard on his cigarette, flicked it away, and pivoted to follow. The others would fill in behind him. Gramps was still walking last and he'd be dropping leaflets of toilet paper behind us that the platoon could track when we radioed them up. He was standing splay-legged with a tight look on his face when I passed him by and led into the foliage. I slipped through about 300 meters of moderately dense jungle and paused. It was reassuringly quiet ahead, and I turned and noise-tracked the rest of my squad as they closed up behind me. The intermittent scuffs and rustles that reached my ears weren't too loud, and then noises sounded that would have carried past me to a sharp-eared NVA waiting in the jungle ahead. The noises had come from somewhere near the end of our squad and I had a pretty good idea who'd have made them.

I rarely initiated a whispered conversation with anyone other than Quinlin and Sugar Bear but that evening I squatted beside Gramps and whispered about the bugs and when we might get back to the LZ. When it felt right I said, "Gramps, I need you to do something for me."

Gramps nodded, suddenly serious, and I said, "I've heard noises behind me when I was walking point. I sneak around up there trying not to make a sound so I won't get killed, and I figure that whoever is making the noise doesn't understand how important it is for them to stay quiet. I'd hate to get zipped because someone was careless with noise."

He nodded, and I said, "You've been around for a while now, would you do me a favor and keep an eye on things and remind the guys to step quietly, tie their stuff down, or do whatever needs doing?"

Gramps sat up straight, looked me in the eye, and said solemnly, "I'll make sure Ed. There won't be no noise behind you."

I'd often been so laser-absorbed by the jungle that lay ahead that I hadn't heard the subtle sounds behind me, but the next few times I walked point I made sure to listen back, and each time my squad was moving quietly. I wasn't certain that Gramps had been the noisy one but I knew he'd helped stop it when Sugar Bear started saying that Gramps was "a pain in the ass" and complaining bitterly, "That dink, he's always telling everyone they're too noisy. I'm tired of his shit."

"If you weren't so noisy he wouldn't be telling you anything," I pointed out.

I don't know who could argue with that but he lit up, snapping, "Keep it up and I'll show you noisy!"

God in the Jungle

The others, almost all of them, were gathered for an extremely rare service with the chaplain, father, rabbi, or whichever man of God had ridden this resupply chopper out to the jungle to offer a few minutes of worship. The denomination wouldn't matter to men who knew they could be one fateful next step from a face-to-face meeting with their Lord and they'd be listening to his words of faith, hope, and love, and praying fervently for their own survival, and all the while their killing weapons would be cradled in their arms or resting within easy reach.

I wasn't one of them. I'd once believed that a benevolent God was watching over me and offering the gift of a joyful afterlife but as I'd gotten older I'd become less certain, and now I was sitting isolated among the packs that dotted my section of the perimeter. I'd heard men of God defending unanswered prayers and tragic losses by proclaiming that God worked in mysterious ways but I wasn't buying it. The others could pray for God's protection and their salvation but there were no words powerful enough to penetrate the hardening shell of my angry rejection of faith.

Chapter 25

The Jolley Trail

The choppers thundered in over another green horizon and dipped into the little meadow to collect us. Our turn came and Sugar Bear, Quinlin, Hootie, Cherry Instant, Kenny, Baby Huey, and I hustled out and climbed on. I took my customary spot in the chopper's front right-side doorway with my feet anchored on the skid as the pilot revved the engine to a roar. He powered our loaded bird high enough to tilt its nose down, and then he started skimming the grasses toward the tree line that loomed at the end of the clearing. As the trees sped closer it seemed our chopper was destined to crash, but at the last moment the pilot converted our lateral momentum to vertical lift and the chopper sling-shotted toward the sky. The G forces pressed me hard against the metal floor, and then the skids brushed the tiptop of the foliage and we were clear.

Speeding high above the overheated terrain we'd labored through had lifted our spirits, but not this time. Sugar Bear had returned from his log day rounds saying that they were inserting us into a "no-fly" piece of jungle that was beyond the reach of our artillery support. The rumor had taken hold and I could see a few guys on the nearby choppers scribbling letters, almost surely penning what might be their last words that they wanted forwarded home if they didn't survive. *Had Sugar Bear gotten it right?* Walter or Ron would have told me but I hadn't needed to know. I was as prepared as I was going to get, re-acclimated to subsistence levels of food and water and adept at conserving energy until I needed it. I was usually fatalistic too, living in the moments and letting go of things I couldn't control, but seeing those guys writing shaky letters in the noisy bellies of our choppers gave me a sense of foreboding. *Would this be the dim place I'd envisioned? Would I die here?* There was nothing to be gained by wondering, and I grabbed a handhold on the doorway's frame, leaned into the wind, and watched the green-carpeted roof of the jungle flowing thousands of feet beneath us.

Our birds hammered their way over kilometers of rolling terrain, and then the land started rising into the most mountainous terrain I'd seen in Vietnam. The topography continued to elevate and soon we were flying above sunlit peaks and shadowed ravines. Our fleet of choppers leveled out high above the canyons and then they dropped down and flew just above the higher ridgelines. The pilots altered course a couple of times and flew to an insertion site that was situated on the side of a ridge. My chopper hovered several feet in the air to keep the tips of its blades clear of the upper side of the gentle slope, and I tossed my pack out and stepped off the uphill skid. I two-foot landed on flexed legs, retrieved my pack, and climbed to the crest of the ridgeline. The last of the choppers disgorged its human cargo and hammered into the distance. A squad from one of the other platoons started moving down the crest of the ridge, their platoon followed, and when the last man of their platoon passed by our platoon we joined the column and followed them down the ridge.

After we'd traveled 200 or 300 meters the ridgeline widened. It was late afternoon, and we stopped there and established an elongated night perimeter that overlapped both sides of the ridge. I found a wrinkle on our side of the crest that would keep me from rolling downhill, and I dropped my pack there to claim it. Unburdened, I moved further down to get a clearer view of the terrain beneath our ridge's right-side slope, and then I settled on my inverted helmet and surveyed the broken land below. The shadows created by the setting sun highlighted the contours of the terrain and I took note of the still-sunlit main ridgelines, the secondary ridges that fingered off their crests, and the shadowed lines of the gullies and ravines that separated them. As the minutes passed the flattening rays of the falling sun began to paint the higher crests a golden, almost effervescent, yellow, and the courses of the winding ravines showed even more starkly. The sun dropped lower, and when everything turned to shadows I relaxed into the calls of the animals of these higher elevations, absorbing the progressions of their shrieks, whistles, and hoots and their ending notes, and trying to sense whether any of them were signaling alarms.

The dusk deepened to dark and a sliver of a moon cast a pale light that barely illuminated the land below. The scents and silence of the darkened jungle had a primordial aura that nudged warily at some corner of my mind. I waited, listening for clues, but the early night jungle kept its secrets. I was about to return to my sleeping nook when a shocking expulsion of air from massive lungs echoed up from the canyons far below, a coughing sound so immensely deep and powerful that I could sense it passing through me. My M-16 was in my hands but that sound resonated in some primitive recess of my brain that felt powerless to defend itself from the beast that had voiced it. I could feel my heart hammering, and I deliberately slowed my breathing and reached out to the lowland where it had originated. Over the next minutes coughing explosions of sound came twice more, the arrogant challenges of a beast announcing its dominance throughout kilometers of the night-silent jungle. A long period of silence followed, and I made my way back to my pack and sawed open a can of C-rations. I ate them cold and settled onto my nylon blanket, wondering whether even an animal as dominant as that would have so brazenly voiced its presence if the NVA were hidden in broken terrain below.

The heat-soaked earth kept me warm for most of the night, but I was on the verge of shivering when Kenny tapped me for my early morning watch. I slipped through the shadowed night and waited for the dawn with my lightweight blanket liner wrapped around my shoulders. The jungle slowly turned lighter shades of gray, and then the light grew stronger and the majesty of the highland jungle was unveiled. I'd spent years climbing to ridge crests that had opened up new vistas, and now the terrain below me was nearly as broken as the land I'd so stealthily walked back home. The sight of it lifted my spirits and I stayed at the perimeter listening to the morning screeches and hoots of the animals as the sunlight climbed to the ridge crests. Most of the others had eaten and packed up when I turned away, and I dry brushed my teeth, stuffed my lightweight blanket in my pack, and waited for word to move.

I'd expected that they'd want our squad to walk point but another platoon led down the crown of the ridgeline. The sun edged higher, heating the moist hollows and generating hazy white mists that wafted lazily in the nooks and crevices below. The mists slowly evaporated as we moved lower, and about an hour later our ridge dead-ended into a dominant ridgeline that intersected ours at a sharp angle. I'd thought the challenging call of the animal that had so openly announced its presence was a sign that we wouldn't find any NVA here but when we reached that new ridge I discovered that I'd been wrong, really wrong.

A many-times-traveled NVA trail more than a meter wide was running atop its rounded crest. Finding a major NVA trail was scary but what really spooked me was that they'd left the wide course of that trail fully exposed to our eyes in the sky. Their leaving that major trail so open to detection was eerily reminiscent of the impression I'd had of the dominance of the massive animal who'd issued its arrogant coughs in the early night. I couldn't imagine that a lone infantry company isolated in a vast section of mountainous jungle that was a long distance from any support would go on the offensive, but whoever was making the decisions, probably Captain Valtz, decided to send two of our platoons walking the trail to our right and my platoon walking the trail in the other direction. Splitting the company was about the last thing I'd have wanted to do, but that's what we did.

I was sure I'd need the jungle's help to get to the end of another day and as I slipped down that fucking NVA highway I wasn't getting it. The trail's wide path and long straights created sight avenues that extended beyond the reach of any subtle scents or sounds that might have alerted me to the presence of any NVA lying in wait. I had to rely on my eyes, but eyes could see both ways and I crossed through wide sections of the trail knowing I could be stepping into the view of NVA ambushers. Ever aware that my first warning might be a flash of movement or the crack of a bullet, I freed my eyes to isolate any flicker of movement in the long sight lines that were opening back at me and worked my way down the gradually descending trail without focusing on anything.

I made it through several sweeping curves and long straights to a sun-bleached and slightly curved section of trail that dropped into a low swale and then climbed to the backbone of a sky-lined ridge. I traced every step of its 150-meter path through the dip and rise to the place where the trail turned sharply left and disappeared over the crown of that crest, and then I gathered my nerve and slipped into the swale. When I reached the bottom of the swale I took a knee and reached out with my ears for any sounds that might emanate from the hidden side of that crest. The only thing I heard was a deep and heavy silence, and I edged back to the trail and crept up the rise. A few meters short of the crest, I squatted alongside the trail, stilled my breathing, and sensed into the void on the other side of the ridge.

It stayed silent. I signaled Quinlin up, and when I knew he had eyes on the site where the trail crossed the ridge I leaned in close to the sharp-edged Ho Chi Minh sandal track that had printed in the loose dirt at the edge of the trail. It was so fresh that it hadn't been marked by the tiny trail of a crawling insect and the wind hadn't blunted its sharp edges. I sniffed the air for the scent of the NVA who'd left it, and when I didn't smell him I duck-walked up the trail to the AK-47 casing I'd seen glinting in the debris at the side of it. Part of the casing had oxidized to a dull hue but the section that had nestled snugly in the rifle's chamber was a brighter coppery color. I brought it to my nose, and when no scent of gunpowder lingered I traced the line of scuff marks that extended from the sandal print to where the trail crossed over the ridge, almost certain that the NVA who'd left those marks had sent that spent casing spinning to the side of the trail. He'd had to have kept it in his rifle for a long while for part of it to have oxidized to such a dull hue, and then minutes ago he'd chambered a live round and crossed over that crest. He'd marked us. *Had he kept moving? Was he alone? Was something waiting silently on the other side?* The only thing that showed beyond the crest was the sun-lit eastern sky.

I squatted motionless in the quiet and reached out with my ears. The silence wasn't telling me anything and I backtracked to Quinlin, angled off the trail, and started side-hilling the slope on our side of the ridgeline. Quinlin trailed a few steps back and the others filled in behind him, all of us staying far enough beneath the crest to avoid sky-lighting ourselves. I continued past the place where I thought an ambush might target the site where the trail crossed over the ridge, and then I stopped and looked back. Most of my platoon was spaced out on the NVA trail but about a dozen of us were lined up below the ridge. I waited for their breathing to steady, and then I started creeping straight up to the crest. When I was a couple of steps short of it I reached out with my ears. I didn't sense anything. I moved up another step and the far-distant lowlands began to appear. I climbed another step. I could see the trail crossing over the ridge and angling below me but the terrain beneath me was hidden. I straightened out of my crouch to elevate my head, and when the section of the trail below me still wasn't visible I took a step higher. A section of the trail dropping down toward a thickly vegetated gully on my left appeared. Lower down I could see traces of the trail doubling back to my right. The angles of the upper and lower sections of the trail were pointing to a convergence in the brushy gully but the place where the trail switched back was screened by the foliage. I let my eyes wander through the foliage there, and when I didn't detect anything I moved a half step higher.

He'd been hidden in the V of the switchback. Maybe he'd seen something or maybe he gotten spooked when we hadn't appeared when he'd thought we would. Whatever it was, something made him bolt down the lower leg of the trail. He was a uniformed figure as big as an American, and he was moving at a full sprint when he flashed into a 2-meter gap in the foliage but he filled my eyes as clearly as if I'd been standing a few feet away. He'd sweated a diamond-shaped dark patch between his shoulder blades and as he disappeared through that gap my M-16 spit two bullets into the spot where that diamond-shaped stain would be. I didn't fire again; I knew where his next step would have carried him and I knew where those two bullets had gone.

I waited for my ears to recover from the cracks of the shots. I didn't hear anything moving but I waited longer to be sure, and then we crossed over the ridge and started down the slope. Nothing stirred, and I crossed the upper leg of the trail, dropped to the lower leg, and crept along it in the direction he'd been running. I knew he could have been fleeing toward other ambushers and I listened into the foliage where he'd disappeared. The silence held, and I slipped closer to the place where he'd be lying and held my breath, listening for the rasps of breathing. I didn't detect any sounds of life, and I slipped through the last veil of vegetation expecting to see his body lying on the trail or alongside it.

There was a meter-long gouge where the butt of his rifle had plowed through the dirt but no dead body. I slipped further down the trail to make sure the jungle was clear and then I returned and checked the ground for signs. I didn't find a blood trail and there was nothing in the debris that lined the trail to indicate that he'd tumbled away wounded, just that furrow in the trail. I couldn't shake my certainty that my bullets had gone where he'd have been so I climbed up to the precise spot where I'd been standing when I'd triggered the shots and marked the gap he'd flashed through. I kept that gap in sight as I worked my way back down, and I stepped onto the trail at the spot where he'd disappeared from view and turned in the direction he'd been sprinting. One long step ahead of me the trail doglegged slightly to the left. It wasn't much of a change but he'd had to alter his line of flight to stay on the trail, and if my bullets had gone where I thought they had that slight change had probably saved his life.

I was fighting a war I didn't believe in against men I didn't hate, but when I looked at that furrow in the trail I felt a strong sense of disappointment. We were two men born and raised half a world apart who were now linked by our shared survival instead of the death of one of us at the hands of the other, and yet I stood on that spot regretting that he wasn't lying dead on the trail in front of me. I knew how perverse that was but that's what I was feeling.

I was still standing on the lower section of the trail when the sounds of frenetic shooting came from the area where the rest of our company would be. It stopped after a handful of minutes and Lt. Colclough relayed that we were linking up with them. We took to the trail and started back, and when I reached the switchback I saw the runner's narrow sight line to the spot where the trail crossed over the ridge. He'd selected a nearly perfect hit-and-run ambush site but the place where the trail crested the ridge was an obvious danger point and he should have anticipated that I'd work my way up my side of the ridge and crest it above him. He'd been lucky that little dogleg had been there, but it wasn't just luck that had kept him alive. He'd recognized the trap he'd created for himself and he'd acted decisively and bolted down that trail as if death had been on his heels. He'd been gutsy and smart, and I paused before I crossed the trail over the ridge and looked back at the broken terrain that dropped to the flat jungle in the far distance, knowing he was there somewhere and thinking of how tenuous the line that separated our living or dying had been.

We found the company spread out in the foliage above a place where the trail climbed out of a gully. They'd heard my shots and they'd been waiting for us to radio in when a squad of NVA had hurried out of the gully, almost surely to investigate my shots. They'd let them walk into the open and then they'd started shooting, and there were two NVA bodies lying on the trail and blood trails where wounded NVA had crawled away. I tracked one of the blood trails to the body of an NVA with a single bullet wound in his thigh. I wouldn't have expected it to have been fatal but he'd bled out the last moments of his life in the dim light at the bottom of the ravine. I heard that they'd found two more blood trails that led to bodies but I'd seen enough.

We established a night perimeter on the rise overlooking the body-strewn gully, and late that evening I sat on my inverted steel helmet listening to the *night-is-coming* calls of the animals. I'd been rationing my water hard and I uncapped one of my canteens and treated myself to a deep swig of its rubber-tasting tepid water. It wasn't good water but I swallowed it gratefully. The ending of this day was like that; all of us settling on the bug-tracked earth, enduring buzz-bombing blood-sucking bugs and fingering dirt-encrusted skin, many of us hungry and thirsty but each of us one day closer to that magical ticket on a freedom bird that might one day take us out of here. It hadn't been a good day but it was another day of life, and, like that rubber-tasting water, I swallowed it gratefully.

Two of the bodies that had lain in the gully were gone in the morning, and I marveled at the stealth and daring of the NVA who'd crept in to retrieve them. We packed up and walked the trail past the remaining bodies in a company-long column. The trail climbed the other side of the gully, crested a low ridge, and dropped into a deep ravine. The steep sections of the trail's path down that ravine were inlaid with woven stalks of split bamboo that formed a matted walking surface that would support the transport of heavy loads when the monsoon downpours turned everything to mud. We continued to the bottom of the ravine and discovered that they'd bridged the deep wash at the bottom of it with a trestle that was about 15 feet high at its midpoint. The jungle had supplied every part of the matted surface and the trestle bridge, including the logs they'd used for piers and cross members, the several inches in diameter bamboo stems they'd used for the structural members, the supple jungle vines they'd used to tie them together, and the split bamboo stalks they'd used to construct a deck strong enough to support a heavily loaded transport. I crossed the trestle and climbed the bamboo-matted highway up the far side of the gully, considering how valuable this trail must be and wondering how much worse things were going to get.

The trail turned left near the top of the ravine and continued slightly uphill through canopy shadowed jungle foliage. We set a tripwire-activated ambush to cover our back trail there and moved on. About an hour later the ambush exploded and we turned back to check it out. I'd expected that the NVA had triggered it but we found a huge tiger so unmarked that it seemed it might suddenly spring to life. I'd seen slack-bodied and undersized zoo tigers but the muscle-bulging animal lying dead on the trail looked like a survivor from the time of the saber-toothed tigers. Awed, I stood before the carcass of that massive carnivore with its lethally clawed oversized paws and the inches-long still-glistening fangs that protruded from its grimacing jaws, suffused with the inborn dread I'd felt when its apex call had echoed up the ridge and vibrated through me. And then I pictured it padding noiselessly through the night with a dead NVA soldier in its jaws like a wolf mouthing a rabbit. I might have been wrong but if we cut into its stomach I thought we'd find human flesh.

Captain Valtz wanted that tiger's hide and he was willing to freeze us in place for the time it took to remove it. I didn't want anything to do with that but Quinlin must have seen things differently because he volunteered to help Lt. Colclough skin it. I watched Jim and a couple of others struggle to reposition the hundreds of pounds of carcass. They got it done, and when Lt. started skinning the tiger Sam and Earl started machete hacking at the tiger's jaw to cut out its lethal fangs. The *thunk-thunking* sounds of the machete and the thick scent of the tiger's blood sickened me, and I picked up my gear and moved up the trail. Quinlin came up later, sweat-drenched and reeking of the tiger's carcass. He dropped his pack beside mine, settled wearily on the ground, and lit a cigarette. A few minutes later Ron Belin showed up asking for salt to preserve the hide, and Jim delved into his pack and offered a couple of packets. I heard they sprinkled the little salt they'd collected on the fleshy side of the hide, and then they rolled it and tied it into a weighty bundle that someone would have to carry. I was starved, especially for meat, and I returned to the carcass and cut some strips from the tiger's backstrap, and after we retraveled the trail to the place where we'd been when the ambush had exploded we set up for the night and I built a smokeless wood fire and roasted tiger steaks. The meat tasted OK but the tiger's flesh was so sinewy that I always ended up with a mouthful of rubbery gristle that I couldn't bite through.

I'd thought that the death of that apex predator had left a huge void in the jungle but early that night another coughing call sounded. The lungs that had generated it hadn't created the shock wave of sound I'd heard that first night and I'd sensed that it had ended with a questioning note but I knew another night-stalking tiger was nearby. It felt right that a tiger would still be prowling the primeval jungle's nights; a fearsome predator that would have stood high atop the jungle's vast pyramid of deadly life if not for the lethal weapons we carried.

The NVA were carrying lethal weapons too. They knew we were walking their trail and they'd a full day to prepare an ambush, but when the next day dawned we learned that Captain Valtz wanted our platoon to lead the way further up that NVA highway. I knew that my squad would lead out and stay on point. No one had ever put that into words but in spooky places that's what we'd always done. I guess we'd become known for that because Sugar Bear had been telling Quinlin and me that some of the guys in our company resented the reputation our squad had earned, and I wondered wryly how many of them would want to trade places with us for a chance to earn that reputation here. I knew the answer, but as crazy as it seemed if we were going to walk this trail I wanted to lead.

I dropped my pack and helmet and moved to the head of the trail. When I passed Quinlin he looked away, maybe not wanting me to read what was in his eyes, and I pulled in a lungful of the morning cool high mountain air, steadied my breathing, and started. Quinlin waited for a gap to develop, and then he followed. The rest of our squad, our platoon, and then our company filled in behind us, forming a column of almost a hundred men moving up that huge NVA trail. I knew those men were behind me, and I knew that not one of them could help me survive. Ten thousand men could have been trailing me and I'd have been just as alone on that trail. It was always that way, and I kept moving.

The trail emerged from the shadowed growth and continued atop the extended line of a bamboo-greened ridge. The sun-heated air that was rising from the lowlands was pushing against the light-green new bamboo shoots and the darker mature leaves, and the gray-green stalks that edged the trail were swaying in the breeze. I envisioned myself moving up the sunlit course of that wide trail, and then I freed my eyes to seek out any unnatural lines or any movements of the foliage that didn't conform to the tugs and releases of the wind. My eyes found nothing, and I used the shadows cast by the windswept bamboo and flitted from spot to spot up the too-straight and too-wide section of trail. When I made it to the next shallow curve I looked back at the stretch I'd covered, thinking that if they'd passed up an ambush site like this then a more lethal would lie ahead. I continued on, slipping along the crests of flat or gradually climbing ridgelines that all pointed in the general direction of a high peak a few klicks distant.

The morning grew hotter and the winds rising from the sun-heated lowlands grew more powerful and insistent, whipping and releasing the willowy crowns of the bamboo and creating an ever-nosier cacophony of clanks, rustles, hisses, and knocks. In a few places I walked point knowing that some part of me was reading the jungle but in other places the sight lines were too long, the vegetation was too noisy, and the wind pressing against my back was carrying the sounds and scents away. With no jungle whispers to warn me I had to think my way ahead, reading the terrain and considering where I'd be if I were them, and then darting from cover to cover trying to detect any unnatural shapes or movements. I did that again and again and the labyrinth of dancing vegetation that framed the NVA trail always stretched ahead, darkly enigmatic, and too often unreadable. I was transfixed by it, slipping through curves, straights, inclines, and dips as countless heartbeats of time and distance passed unnoticed.

Late in the morning, I made it to the end of another long section of straight trail, and I took a knee and looked back for the first time in I didn't know how long. Quinlin was just rounding the corner almost 100 meters back. He spotted me, settled into deep cover, and waited. I'd told him that I didn't need him following me into the kill zone of an ambush but seeing him trailing that far back was unsettling, someone walking on your grave kind of unsettling. But it made sense, and I turned away, slipped around the corner, and started working my way down another long stretch of straight trail.

Sometime later, I crouched motionless at the cusp of a long stretch of trail that was lined with extremely dense cover. The overhead sun was beating down on my helmetless head, and I pulled my lone canteen from my pistol belt, took a deep swig, and re-sheathed it. I checked behind again and spotted Quinlin peeking out at me from far back. He'd be wondering how much farther I'd make it, or maybe not but that's what I was wondering. Distant vistas opened down on the trail from afar, and I knew they'd have eyes up there watching us move up the trail they'd spent many thousands of hours creating. They'd thought we wouldn't come and now we were here daring them to ambush us. Each time I'd made it through another likely ambush site I'd been certain they'd be waiting in a more lethal site ahead, and I kept looking for it as I moved on like a wary mouse caught up in a deadly cat-and-mouse game.

Early in the afternoon I reached a 150-meter section of the trail that undulated a little left through two shallow depressions and then curved sharply right and disappeared into the base of a slope that was forested with vibrant bamboo. In the mountains at home every wrinkle in the topography, every change in the topsoil, and every sun-exposed or sun-shielded face of a slope could grow different vegetation, and that's what I was seeing where the trail disappeared. The ridgeline courses of the trail had been brushy and the ravines that had dropped down from them had grown thick foliage, but the slope that the trail disappeared into was facing south and the bamboo on it had grown tall and lush. The difference was striking, and I took a knee and spent a long time searching for any hint of the ambush I'd been anticipating. I didn't find anything, and I slipped through the two dips and melted into cover near the base of the bamboo slope.

I didn't detect any presence, and I moved into the shadowed foliage. Ahead of me, a very gently rounded slope that was only about 60 meters wide rose steeply. Both sides of it were edged by brush-choked drop-offs but the narrow slope was dotted with by far the biggest bamboo clumps I'd seen. The multiple thick stalks that arrowed out of those clumps were so tall and leafy that they'd shaded out the undergrowth and created damp leaf-littered avenues between the dense clusters. The NVA trail climbed through those avenues, traversing the slope diagonally to the left and then switching back and toward the right side drop-off. I traced the line of the trail higher and saw where it switched back again. I could see a few meters of it running left in the center of the slope and then I lost sight of it. Before I'd dropped through the dips I'd seen the bamboo-covered rise terminate at the line of another of the dominant ridgelines so I knew that ridge crest wasn't far above me but I couldn't see to the top of the slope.

I moved up and crouched at the bottom of it. The bases of the inches-wide bamboo stalks were swaying gently but their willowy ends were knocking and rattling in the hissing wind and masking any soft noises that might have carried from higher up the rise. I waited longer, searching for any reason why the NVA would have chosen this as an ambush site rather than the others I'd passed through. I was still there when Quinlin worked his way up. He settled close behind me and started scanning the slope with his quick eyes. The rest of our squad worked their way in behind us and waited for me to move. Having the high ground looking down on me and the steep and brushy drop-offs funnelling me up the narrow confines of that slope made the prospect of working my way up that rise unnerving, but I thought I could do it.

The trail was doubling back and traversing the steep slope diagonally to reduce the incline but I wasn't going to make a target of myself by appearing in the middle of the slope, and I crept to the extreme edge of the left side's drop-off and started straight up the steepest slope of the hillside. I climbed ten steps up the damp humus ground without slipping back, and then I kneeled behind one of the bamboo clusters and cleared my thoughts. The clusters were creating hidden nooks above me and their wind-stirred crowns were generating a din of dissonant sounds that would drown out telltale noises. I waited, hoping the wind would still for a moment, and when it didn't I continued climbing the steepest part of the knocking, rattling, bamboo-obstructed slope with my squad trailing close behind. Staying as far left as I could, I reached the elevation where the trail switched back from the right-side drop-off and started running toward the middle of the narrowing bamboo avenue. I climbed another 10 meters and a shallow dip that was running across the slope like a long wrinkle on a bed blanket appeared. The line of it stretched across the full width of the slope above me, rising gradually higher on its way to the right-side drop-off. The bases of the bamboo clusters growing just beyond it were hidden in the dip but I couldn't tell if it was deep enough to hide ambushers.

I stilled my breath and focused my ears along the line of it, needing the wind to let up so I could hear what was there. It didn't, and I gave up and climbed higher. The location where the NVA trail crossed through the dip appeared. There was an extremely dense clump of bamboo growing just below and to the left of it. I climbed the far left side of the slope until I had about a 30-degree angle of approach, and when I didn't detect anything I veered right and sidehilled up toward it using that clump of bamboo to screen me from the view of any NVA who might be hidden where the trail crossed the dip. I covered the last 20 meters to the big clump in one quick move. I waited a split second to see if anything jumped out at me, and when nothing did I dropped to a knee in the 2 or 3-inch deep saucer-shaped depression that dimpled the ground there. I was just short of the elevation that would give me a view into the dip. I listened intently and all I heard was the wind-driven rustling, knocking, and rattling of the vegetation. I thought, *I guess this isn't it*, and I was about to creep up and get a look at whatever was in the dip when the Puerto Rican-accented voice of Freddy uttered a shocking, "**guh!**"

I was flat on the ground as he finished warning, "**guh, guh, goo, GOOKS!**"

I searched above frantically, and when my darting eyes didn't find them I glanced back to where his voice had sounded. Freddy was kneeling just below where I'd angled off, and his eyes were riveted on the left side of my bamboo clump.

No one was shooting so they'd circled behind the bamboo. *Would they keep circling and appear on my right?* I got a knee under me, angled my body in that direction, and waited.

Every other time I'd been in combat I'd experienced the gift of slow-motion clarity, but when the instants passed and they didn't appear everything began to move faster; my heart beating more rapidly, my mind buzzing, and my perspective shrinking until there was nothing but that clump of bamboo stalks and the NVA lurking on the other side of it. They hadn't charged around it so they'd be hunkered down waiting for me to appear, the way I was waiting for them, but *what would they do when they decided I wasn't coming?*

I envisioned them slipping unseen along the dip, flanking me, and then popping up and shooting into me. That's what I'd have done, but they'd probably wait a little longer to make sure I wasn't going to come around that clump and shoot into them. My eyes fixed on the right edge of the bamboo clump where a single bamboo stalk had grown away from the main cluster. The lower portion of the outlying stalk extended semi-horizontally above the ground for about half a meter, and then it curved to vertical and reached straight into the sky. An image flashed in my mind, and without a thought I pulled a frag off my pistol belt, popped the spoon, and sprang toward the right side of the lone stalk like a sprinter exploding off the starting line. I'd been a couple of steps short of the downhill edge of the clump but I reached it in one bound and gripped the stalk with my left hand. My momentum was spinning me around it, and when I was halfway there I extended my right arm as far as I could and let the frag arc to the back side of the clump. It took all the strength I had in my left arm to suck my spinning body back into a gap about the width of my body. I wasn't sure I'd make it, and then my right shoulder brushed bamboo and I cleared, planted my right foot, and dove back to my shallow depression. I was on the ground when the grenade exploded.

I was still fixated on the NVA that were lurking on the other side of the clump and I scrambled head-uphill again and leaped back to the bamboo stalk with another grenade. I spun again, released the grenade, and made it through the gap cleanly.

There was a stinging sensation on my cheek as I landed, and when I reached up and touched the bamboo splinters that were sticking out of my cheek I felt like I'd come out of a trance. I had a sudden memory of shots fired from my right and bullets spitting into the bamboo as I'd spun around the stalk, and the shooting hadn't stopped. The NVA were lined up all across the dip and firing a barrage so relentless that it was drowning out the sounds of the fusillade of shots coming from my guys below.

I realized that I'd been flanked from the moment I'd arrived here, and I turned onto my back and raised my head to watch for anyone who might pop up from the dip on my right and shoot into me. I couldn't see the shooters but bullets started biting into the dirt beside me. I'd landed with my head downhill, and I slammed it on the ground an instant before a literal wall of bullets came snapping, buzzing, and wasping just inches above my body. I desperately wanted to reposition my head uphill to get a line of sight at the shooters but I could feel the paths of those snapping bullets. I knew that if I elevated an inch or two higher they'd start tearing into me so I sucked in my stomach and lay as still as I could. Bullets started splintering the bamboo stalks in front of my feet. I turned my toes to the ground so the tops of my feet wouldn't get blown off, and then I lay motionless in the slight depression hoping they'd think they'd killed me.

The sounds of NVA's shooting grew so incessant that I could no longer distinguish individual bursts of firing, just a rolling thunder of noise. They weren't all fired at me but bullets continued to wasp and snap mere inches above my body. I didn't dare to move, and then I felt the jolt of a bullet digging into the dirt beside me and I reached down to my pistol belt and fumbled my last frag into my hand. I didn't have the courage to risk elevating my arm into the paths of their bullets so I swung my right arm parallel to the ground and released the frag. My side-armed effort was so feeble that the frag bounced once, tumbled a couple of meters, and exploded on my side of the crest.

I'd always known what to do when I'd been endangered but for what seemed to have been minutes I lay motionless with my head downhill, frozen in place by the bullets cracking overhead with no plan, no way out, and one thought flashing through my mind, *this is it*!

A flash of movement registered in the corner of my right eye, and I angled my head slightly and saw Earl bent over and moving slowly uphill about

25 meters to my right. He was just a few meters beneath the crescendo of heavy-caliber gunfire that was coming from behind the dip, and the words, "*GIT DOWN! GIT DOWN!*" just exploded out of me. Before he could have reacted a bullet slammed into his thigh and the force of the impact propelled his leg directly over his head. For a moment his body seemed to be suspended with his wounded leg pointing straight to the sky and his head almost touching the knee of his standing leg, and then his overhead leg completed its circular path and Earl cartwheeled over. He landed on his back with his head downhill, screaming in pain.

I yelled, "*GIT HIM!*"

It was the kind of moment where if you took the time to think about it you probably weren't going, and in the charged instants that followed no one appeared. I'd long ago settled it in my mind that I'd try to pull someone in if they needed it, and I told myself, *don't think about it,* let go of my rifle, rolled to my right, and started rising. I was amazed that bullets weren't ripping through me, and then I was dismayed at the time it was taking to get my feet under me. When I finally made it to my feet the roar of gunfire was so deafening that I didn't think I'd make it one step, and then I was sprinting across the slope a few meters below the little dip in plain view of any shooters who'd risen high enough to see over it.

I felt like cement blocks were weighing down my feet and I was traveling in slow motion but I made it to where Earl was writhing on the ground screaming. I kept running, grabbed a hold on his pants leg, and started dragging him downhill. It was his ruined leg. He let out a high-pitched primal scream but I kept pulling the full weight of him on that torn leg with his body sliding and bouncing behind me, running us out of their kill zone and away from the bullets I thought were coming. I made it about 10 or 12 meters, and then he hung up on something and I lost my grip on his blood-soaked leg. My momentum carried me two or three steps before I could dig in my heels and stop, and then I leaped back to Earl and tried to lift him into my arms. Earl was oblivious to everything but the pain and he twisted and bucked so violently that I couldn't.

I dropped to a knee to secure him in a fireman's carry position but he fought me again, screaming; "Oh God! It hurts! It hurts! Leave me, **Ed, just leave me!**"

I snatched his head in both hands, placed my face inches from his, and hissed, "**Earl**! Do you want to see your wife again?"

He gasped a shuddery breath, and then he reached up to help me get him onto my shoulders. When I felt his weight settle I spun off a knee and sprinted straight downhill with my bootheels plowing furrows at the end of every long stride and Earl's body bouncing on my shoulders, his ruined leg spurting blood and surely sending waves of nerve-shattered pain to his brain but Earl not screaming, just moaning, the sounds a testament to the pain he was holding inside. I ran us full speed all the way off the hill and through the company to where Doc was waiting. Three guys lifted Earl off my shoulders. They laid him on the ground where Doc was kneeling with a vial of morphine and bandages to staunch the blood that was spurting from his leg, and suddenly it was like stepping into the eye of a hurricane where the violent storm lets up, it gets quiet, and the whole world seems to have changed.

I knew that I needed to get back to my guys but something held me there, something powerful. Earl and I hadn't been close but the last moments had connected us in a way I couldn't have envisioned, both of us back from the precipice of death and now imbued with images, emotions, and fears that were ours, and only ours. Those created a soaring high that the two of us could share and I knelt beside him, not wanting to let go of it.

His body tightened with a spasm of pain but his eyes held mine when he said "I'm going home, Ed. I'm going home to my wife."

Bloody, bullet-shattered, almost been killed, might lose a leg or limp for the rest of his life, midwestern-stoic Earl, smiling the biggest smile I'd ever seen him smile, and saying it again, more certainly now, "I'm going home to my wife, Ed, **I'm going home to my wife!**" And me nodding with him, my smile nearly as wide.

He'd been through the worst moments of his life and this was the best. I wanted to stand close and bask in the glorious light of it but the still-raging firefight was calling and I couldn't. I had an impulse to reach out and squeeze Earl's shoulder but I wasn't able to break through whatever it was that was keeping me from that, so I just smiled and said, "Good luck. Earl, I've got to get back up there."

He nodded his understanding but the light had left his face and he was just Earl again. Maybe it was the morphine that had darkened the light, or maybe, like me, it was the guys on the hill.

My blood-drenched bandoleers were still strung across my chest but I'd left my rifle on the ground at the base of the bamboo cluster. I said I needed to borrow a M-16 and one of the guys standing nearby extended his. Without noting who he was, I snatched the rifle out of his hand and sprinted up the hill, rushing past platoon members burrowed here and there on the leaf-littered earth until I reached Lt. Colclough. He said that Valtz wanted us to push up and take the hill, and then he paused. Lt. knew I'd been up there and that I'd know what we were facing, and I think he thought I'd have an idea. If that was true then he was right. I knew the little wrinkle that crossed the slope was blocking our bullets and I knew how it was configured. We couldn't shoot into them if they stayed below it and they couldn't effectively aim down at us without rising and exposing themselves. They'd proven that they weren't willing to take that risk because they'd fired countless bullets and the only one of us they'd hit had been Earl when he'd climbed near the lip of the dip. If we put enough bullets at the dip I doubted that they'd rise high enough to shoot into us, and if we maintained that level of fire the entire way up to the dip they'd get killed if they did. I thought we could do that.

We started up with me on the trail directing traffic and the rest of our platoon divided evenly on my left and my right. Each side alternated turns lying flat and shooting into the crest while the other advanced a few meters. We gained ground with each jump, and as we neared the dip the NVA stopped shooting. When I walked the trail over the lip of the dip the bamboo cluster I'd been pinned behind was on my left and Dennis was a few meters to my right. No one shot at us, and we pushed past their ambush site and climbed to the relatively flat low-brushed ridgeline that marked the ultimate top of the rise.

The trail continued atop that new ridgeline, and we established a small defensive perimeter on a wide spot and waited for the rest of the company to climb the rise and link up. Gramps brought me the pack I'd dropped so many hours ago and the rifle and pistol belt I'd abandoned when I'd gone for Earl. The pistol grip of my M-16 was bullet-shattered and one of the metal fasteners had been shot off my pistol belt. I was pretty sure the pistol belt had been lying on the ground when it had taken that bullet but I had a vague sense of the M-16 being in my hand when the bullet had shattered the pistol grip. I'd been utterly terrified then but I leaned back against my pack in the insect droning heat of our shocked-into-silence-ridge and gazed up through the wind-whipped crowns of bamboo to the floating-clouds-sky, not feeling it now.

I'd heard a chopper fly in somewhere below and hammer away, so Earl was on his way home. He'd arrive at an aid station and get shipped out to a hospital in Japan or one back home where they'd piece that leg together. If history held true we'd never hear from him, but that didn't matter to me now, nothing did, not the trail, not the NVA, nothing. I understood how bizarre that was, especially for me, but I was out of adrenalin, or maybe I was euphoric with adrenalin, and I went with it, ignoring the sight lines and gazing up at a few cottony clouds drifting across patches of blue sky.

My blood-soaked shirt kept sticking to my skin and drawing flies, and when I couldn't ignore it any longer I tugged it free from my skin and tossed it over a nearby bush. I spread my bandoleers on the ground too, hoping the gummy blood would dry and flake off. Quinlin was watching, sucking hard on his cigarette and pulling it away with that snatching movement I'd worried might someday draw a shooter's eye. He volunteered that he'd seen me start out after Earl and he'd stood up and emptied a full magazine at the crest. I was still pissed that no one had gone to get to Earl when I'd yelled and I didn't reply. Sugar Bear met eyes with me and mouthed, "Earl?" I whispered that Earl had been smiling about going home and Sugar Bear hissed, "That lucky bastard." I knew he meant it. Earl might lose that leg but I was certain that a lot of the guys out here with us would have willingly paid that price for a guaranteed one-way ticket back to the world.

I pictured Earl walking up the hill toward that barrage of bullets. I had no idea why he'd done that but I was lucky he had. I'd made a near-fatal mistake by fixating on the NVA on the other side of the bamboo cluster, and by the time I'd realized there were NVA dug in all across the crest I'd been so pinned down that I hadn't had the nerve to move. If Earl hadn't come up I'd probably have cowered in that little earthen depression until their bullets had found me. He'd given me a reason to risk getting up, and he'd probably diverted their shooting or I wouldn't survived that. The guys would be saying that I'd yanked Earl out of a bad place but the truth was that we'd probably saved each other.

Sugar Bear had wandered off, and a few minutes later I saw him dive in behind the M-60 Billy Bass had left pointing up the trail. I rolled to my stomach with my M-16 in my hands looking for the threat as Sugar Bear jammed the ammo belt in the 60, slammed the lid shut, and yanked on the trigger. He'd loaded the ammo backward so the gun didn't fire. Red-faced and breathless, he whispered that he'd seen two or three gooks coming down the trail and they'd spotted us and ran off. That encounter could have been lethal but I was strangely unperturbed, as though it was happening to someone else.

C-4 fires started hissing and soon the aromatic scents of heating C-rations filled the air. I didn't want to break the spell I was under but I'd burned a lot of energy and I knew I needed to eat. I pulled my small tin of canned chicken out of my pack, sawed it open, and ate it cold. I was leaning back against my pack when I saw Dennis striding purposefully up the trail. He headed directly toward me, and I took one look at his somber face and knew he was going to tell me that Captain Valtz wanted us to push further up that fucking trail. Our crazy captain wasn't asking me to do something he wouldn't have done but I wouldn't have asked that of us, not here and not now. Still, Quinlin and I had opened the door when we'd traveled that first NVA trail, and I looked into his *the worst is going to happen* face and said, "OK."

The trail's new ridgeline ran toward the high peak we'd been nearing all day. Secondary ridges were fingering off both sides of it and the wind was still tugging noisily at the low brush and bamboo that edged it. The long straights were there too, and I kept slipping through those stretches of trail like a canary carried ever deeper into a mine shaft, inviting the bullets that would alert the others that death was lurking ahead.

In the late afternoon, I arrived at a very long stretch of curving trail that sloped gently down to the base of the dominant mountain the trail had been pointing to. I scanned for shapes or movements on its steep and heavily vegetated mountainside and listened for animal alarms, and then I started down the incline knowing I'd be nakedly exposed to anyone watching the trail from that high mountain. I was about 70 meters short of it when I squatted in the brush and took a long look at the mountain that towered in front of me. I could see the line of the trail climbing its slopes down low, and sections of it showed through gaps in the foliage up higher. I knew it would wrap around the side of the mountain somewhere short of the summit but the summit was a long way up and that left a lot of trail to cover. I pictured myself inching along its switchbacks with likely ambushers waiting above, and then I took another look at that mountain and decided that we'd gone far enough.

Quinlin was peering out from behind a screen of leaves and branches. I hand signaled him up and then I turned back to see if anything stirred when he moved. When I looked back he was still there. I motioned again and he started forward, moving like a man who knew I might have overlooked a trap that was waiting for more men to step into its teeth before it snapped shut.

He slipped in beside me. I waited for his rasping breathing to settle, surprised at how comforting it felt to have my buddy Quinlin huddling beside me, and then I whispered, "Jim, we're going to see some gooks and start shooting."

The look on his face told me that he'd taken my words literally but I didn't want to say anything he might be asked to repeat, so I said. "Jim, we're going to spot some gooks and start a firefight **right here, instead of moving up the side of that mountain**. Do you see them?"

He nodded once and whispered, "Ah thank ah sees em, up et thet cornah whar them trees is."

We flattened on the ground, and when I triggered my M-16 at the side of the mountain Jim's shots joined with mine. We emptied our clips, popped in new ones, and shot them empty. It wouldn't have surprised me if we'd drawn return fire, but we didn't. Others in our squad ran up and I pointed Billy Bass toward the place where we'd *seen* NVA. He opened up with his M-60 and the rest of us sprayed bullets from our M-16s. We stopped shooting and Sugar Bear worked his way up to tell us that Captain Valtz had a fixed-wing bomber on the way. I heard its droning approach about 15 minutes later and we popped smoke to mark our location. I used the training I'd received at the Combat Leader's Course and radioed the azimuth and distance from our smoke to the phantom ambush site. The little bomber made two runs over the top of us and both bombs landed on the phantom ambush site. The bomber flew off, and when they radioed that they were pulling us out we backtracked and rejoined the rest of the company.

Lt. Colclough told me that our extraction point was far down our back trail and that if we didn't get there with enough daylight left to land the choppers we'd be stuck here for another day. He asked if I thought we could make it in time but I was pretty sure he was asking if I was willing to lead down that trail at the pace we'd have to travel to do that. I weighed the risks of spending another night and part of another day here against the risks of rushing headlong into any NVA who might be trailing us. The bombs and the shooting would have marked our current position but any NVA trailing us wouldn't be expecting us to reverse course, and if I covered a lot of ground fast I might be on top of them before they could react. *And what difference would it make anyway?* I'd never found a strategic way to negotiate that NVA highway at any pace so what would I lose by traveling it fast now instead of slower later? Those were the justifications that were flashing through my logical mind but I'd known what I was going to do from the moment he'd asked. I'd had an increasingly terrifying premonition that an overwhelming deadliness was descending on us and I was going try to get us there in time no matter how risky it was.

I said that I thought we could make it, retrieved my pack, and saddled up. Minutes later our platoon hurried past the long line of men who were stretched out on our backtrail. We cleared the last of them, and then we ran down that terrifying fucking trail as if we owned it, the corners, the ambush site, the lush bamboo slope, the undulating ridgeline, the ravines, and the long straights rushing by in a kaleidoscope of greens and browns with my pack bouncing on my back and my helmet bobbing on my head...just two eyes and a rifle charging down that deadly NVA highway with a full company strung out further and further behind me.

And fate was kind, there were no NVA there, or at least none that wanted to engage us, and we climbed into those beautifully ugly choppers and rode them into the safety of the sky, every one of us, and all of us alive.

Chapter 26

Malaria Relapse

As we flew from the Jolley Trail I lay in the belly of the chopper with my back pressed against the iron-plated deck and my face angled toward the door gunner. He was sitting on a crate behind an ungripped M-60 that was dangling from its harness and one or more flak jackets were under his butt, maybe to stop a bullet from taking his balls. The guys in my squad were vibrating to the thumps of the chopper's blades and all of them had old man looks on their faces, near the ends of their ropes like me I guessed, but it was going to get better. They'd said they were flying us to the Michelin Rubber Plantation, a place reportedly so pacified that Vietnamese civilians would appear out of nowhere selling food and drinks, something I could hardly imagine.

The place we'd been was so remote that they had to drop us in a meadow and fly off to refuel. As we waited there was a lot of talk about the time we'd spend on the plantation, but I was too tired to care. I thought I'd gotten exhausted, and then I got the chills. Doc took my temperature, read it, and radioed in for a medevac. I knew my fever was too high but I didn't have the will to bear the misery of the chills, and I moved into the open meadow and let the lessening heat of the setting sun soak into my chilled body. Sugar Bear was there when I climbed into the medevac, asking, "How long ya gonna skate this time?" Quinlin was behind him with a cigarette in his hand, his face impassive, the rubber plantation awaiting and my being gone not that big of a deal.

They flew me to an aid station and one of the medics directed me to a cot. I was half asleep when two corpsmen ran in carrying a shrieking soldier on a stretcher. They transferred him to a hospital bed, repacked his wounds, and injected him with morphine, and then they walked away and left him on the cot shrieking. It had probably been less than an hour since he'd taken a bullet in his right armpit and the medics had to know that he'd be frantic with pain and fear, but I could hear them laughing about some whores they'd hooked up with in Saigon so I rolled off my cot, walked over, and knelt at the head of his bed. I told him he'd been shot in the shoulder and that they'd be able to fix him up, and when his shrieking didn't let up I asked him where he was from and who'd be waiting for him when he got home. He started gasping out short answers between panting breaths, and I stayed and talked with him until the medics rolled him off to a screened-off section of the tent where a doctor was surely waiting. I'd intended to tell the two of them how fucked up they were for leaving him screaming but I barely made it back to my cot before I was fever dreaming of phantom firefights and men screaming in pain.

My malaria test came back positive, and when my fever came down a little they returned me directly to the rehab center at Cam Ranh Bay. The cheerful clerk who'd checked me in and out the last time said happily, "Hey, sarge is back!" I got another pay advance and moved back into the malaria tent but the events of the last few days were fresh in my mind, and I think that's why the serene beaches and the blue waters of the South China Sea had lost their magic. I read a few paperback books and waited restlessly for my release but I didn't have to wait long; whatever new medicine they were giving me took hold quickly and after three or four days I told them I was fine. The nurse insisted it was too soon to release me but I got one of the doctors to write a medical discharge effective the next day.

I didn't want to get stuck on another bus ride filled with uncertain FNGs so I made my way to a chopper pad. I couldn't find a chopper heading in the right direction, and when I knew I was stuck for the night I stopped at a club to kill some time. The narrow interior had a few tables and a bar that stretched the full length of one of the walls, and it was empty except for the Vietnamese bartender, several Vietnamese bar girls, and a couple of GIs who were drinking quietly at the far table. I took a stool at the bar and one of the bar girls hurried over, smiled invitingly, and asked me to buy her a Saigon tea. I'd seen desperately lonely soldiers spend all their money buying colored-water drinks to secure the company of bar girls who'd left as soon as their money was gone, but I wasn't that guy. I smiled, shook my head, and said, "no thanks."

She complained loudly and left, and then the other bar girls started arriving one by one, each of them demanding, begging, or trying to embarrass me into buying her a tea. I declined each request politely until one of them yelled shrilly, "You number 10, you cheap GI!"

I didn't like that, and I nodded to the wrinkled older woman who'd been mopping the floor and said, "I'll buy you a tea."

She must have understood because she beamed a wide smile that exposed a few teeth blackened by years of betel nut chewing, leaned the mop handle against the bar, and climbed nimbly onto the stool beside me. The bar girls were spitting angry sounding words at the bartender but he harangued them back and set the drink in front of the mop lady. The poisonous looks the bar girls were giving her made me question whether I was doing her any favors but she couldn't stop grinning, and when she finished that drink I bought her another. She drank the second slowly, sitting quietly beside me with a wide bezel nut-tinted grin on her face. She finished the second tea and I smiled and told her I was leaving. I was worried that I was abandoning her to face the hostility of the bar girls alone but when I looked back from the doorway her face was joyously triumphant.

Some Things Have to Be Lived With

On my chopper ride back from Cam Ranh Bay I asked the pilot if he knew anything about the Jolley Trail. It was just a shot in the dark, but he told me that they'd pulled a full army division out of the rice lands of the Delta and inserted them on that jungle trail. He said the division had started taking casualties almost immediately and that over the next several days they hadn't had enough choppers to retrieve all of the dead and wounded. According to him, after they'd finally gotten them out they'd sent what was left of that division back to the Delta and conceded that piece of high jungle to the NVA. I felt sorry for those flatland grunts but mostly I was glad that we hadn't been left there to contend with the hornet's nest we'd poked.

I found my company scattered along a red clay road in an area so pacified that I saw two Vietnamese civilians come down the road pushing a cart carrying hot food and ice chests filled with cold drinks. I traded some MPC for one of the sodas and sucked out the sugary contents. Several others were eating the hot food but I wasn't willing to risk eating something they could have contaminated.

Things had changed while I'd been gone. Captain Valtz had sent Ron Belin to Saigon to deliver the tiger hide to a taxidermist and Walter had filled in for

Ron as Captain Valtz's RTO. Ron had returned but Captain Valtz had kept Walter on as his RTO and allowed Ron to stay with his command group. That had left Lt. Colclough needing an RTO, and there was some history involving Sugar Bear and that RTO slot.

The worthless new Lt. had been our platoon leader the last time that job had become vacant and Sugar Bear had really wanted the radio. He'd asked for the job, and then he'd tried to improve his chances by fawning over the new Lt. Watching his clumsy attempts to be the Lt.'s *helper* had been both embarrassing and entertaining. I hadn't hesitated to point that out to Sugar Bear but he'd been determined and he'd ignored me and kept at it for a couple of days. Unfortunately he was Sugar Bear, and one day he lit up over something minor and lashed out at the new Lt. The possibility that he'd blown his chances had sent him into a day and a half of surly depression, and it turned out that he had because Walter had been given the job. I don't believe Walter had made any attempt to get the radio but Sugar Bear hadn't cared about that. He'd bitterly accused Walter of being a "kiss ass," and whenever Walter had been nearby and his RTO duties had pulled him away Sugar Bear had taunted him in a childish voice, saying, "Walter, your daddy's calling you."

I didn't know how he'd managed to pull it off this time but Sugar Bear was packing the radio for Lt. Colclough. He was surprisingly good with the radio, and he was still making time for his log day rounds and spreading rumors. I'd asked how things had gone in the Michelin Rubber Plantation and he'd grinned slyly and told me that a handful of prostitutes had shown up on one of their evening perimeters and slipped into the bushes with anyone who'd wanted to trade a few MPC notes for sex. They must have had a few takers because, according to Sugar Bear, the gonorrhea epidemic that followed had been pervasive enough that they'd pulled our company back to the rear to treat the infected guys. Sugar Bear was convinced that the diseased prostitutes had been sent by the local Viet Cong but he wasn't holding any grudges. It might have been germ warfare but it had gotten them a few days in the rear and he viewed the VC as having done them a favor.

Sugar Bear's mood was surprisingly upbeat but Quinlin wasn't himself. I thought he must have gotten some bad news from home until one of the guys told me quietly about an incident in the Michelin Plantation. The plantation was far less threatening than any of the other jungle areas we'd worked but it was still lethal enough to have been designated a free-fire zone, and Jim had been walking point when he'd detected movement. He'd triggered his M-16 and checked and found a woman and child lying dead in the foliage.

Some things are so gut-wrenching they make you question everything, but I didn't blame Quinlin. We'd spent months in jungle areas that had been populated by NVA intent on killing us, and for all those months Jim had been prepared to react lethally to any hint of a human presence. The movements had surely triggered him to respond the way his survival instincts had conditioned him to react but that evening I watched a cheerless Quinlin bitty-punching lines through the lid of his C-ration can, sure that he'd be questioning everything he'd done. I'd have talked with him if he and Sugar Bear hadn't avoided telling me, but they had. I wasn't sure why, but Jim was a grown man and I decided that I wouldn't say anything unless he brought it up, *and besides, what the fuck could I say that would make anything better?*

Colonel Ordway and his sergeant major had moved on. The battalion's new command team was choppering out to address us and our full company was waiting in a no-shade section of the red-dirt road when their Huey landed. Our officers hurried over to greet the men who climbed out, and after they'd conferred for a few minutes the new arrivals stepped in front of us and started giving short speeches that were filled with the typical *looking forward to working with you men and I've heard good things about you* refrains. And then one of them said "I know you men are anxious for some action" and I felt like my head exploded. He was talking like this was a game and I wanted to throw his words back at him, to hit him so brutally hard with the truth that he'd never again make the mistake of thinking that men who'd seen their fellow soldiers die painful deaths would view "some action" the way he thought we did. I only hesitated because I knew that what I was going to say would reflect on Lt. Colclough and Captain Valtz, and then the moment had passed and I sat in the hot sun regretting my silence.

While we were in that red clay road area I tracked some sandal prints that led to a couple of long-existing spider holes. Their trap doors might have opened to tunnels but I left them uninspected and unreported, resolving that if any Viet Cong in the area were willing to live and let live then so was I. Our truce, if that's what it was, held until a flight of choppers dropped us back into the deep jungle. The minute we set foot in that shadowy foliage we resumed our long-practiced behaviors, packing full loads, steeling ourselves to endure successions of hot and exhausting treks to each next night's perimeter, and functioning on a few hours of restless sleep interrupted by night watches; once again a cavalcade of skinny, bug-bitten and whispering men walking hollow-eyed under the camo wrapped steel helmets we'd donned for so long that we no longer noticed they were there.

We didn't find any signs of an NVA presence and the mood grew less tense. Quinlin was becoming his customary boastful self and there were a few more social interactions. Sugar Bear was a big part of that. Initially detested, he'd become one of the most talked-to guys in our platoon and maybe the entire company, and it wasn't because he'd changed much. He was still caustic and grouchy but his tongue lashings were rarely taken personally, and in many ways I think it was just the opposite, that his cantankerous personality, his occasional tirades, and especially his complaining added a dash of color to our austere days as he whispered the latest gossip and bitched about things so eloquently that at times you'd actually find yourself thinking, *Hey, it's not that bad!*

I think I'd taken a turn in the opposite direction. I'd been more sociable when I'd arrived but most of the guys I'd socialized with then were gone. Of the ones that remained, John Glasshof was a platoon sergeant walking with Lt. Colclough, Walter and Ron Belin were with Valtz, and Big Jack and Gramps were in another squad. If I crossed paths with any of them we'd say a few words but I never tried to make that happen. Maybe that was because of lives being short out here and not wanting to get too close, or maybe Sugar Bear and Quinlin were providing all the socialization I needed. Whatever it was, it wasn't purposeful, it was just the way things had turned out.

Sugar Bear still sought out Jim and me whenever he was free, and on log day he was laying on the ground beside me with his head resting on his pack. His sweat-beaded face was marked with a grim expression and his hands were so grimed with dirt that they appeared black against the printed pages of the *Stars and Stripes* newspaper he was holding. His unbuttoned shirt revealed a once-chubby stomach shrunken almost flat and Jim and I were even leaner, the two of us subsisting on meager meals and navigating more than our share of the risks. We'd come a long way to get here, rolling with the threats, the weather, and the bugs, and now we were old hands still running lucky. Everything that scene evoked was so deeply etched in my mind that I couldn't envision it changing.

Chapter 27

A Place Called Bù Gia Mập

The choppers came to pluck us out of one section of the jungle and deposit us in another. I settled in my customary spot in the right-side doorway with my feet resting on the skids. The door gunner was perched over my right shoulder sitting on a wooden crate filled with belts of M-60 ammo, and the seven of us and our gear covered nearly every other inch of the Huey's armor-plated deck. The sturdy little slick struggled our heavy load into the air, climbed high, and leveled out toward our destination. One of the choppers flying ahead of us caught a downdraft and dropped out of sight, and an instant later it felt like our chopper fell out from under us. It was a spooky sensation but no one grabbed for a handhold; we'd ridden a lot of choppers and none of us wanted to see smirks on the faces of door gunners who'd be watching for our reactions. Our chopper caught with a jerk, and when we reached calm air I braced my feet firmly on the rails and leaned out to get a fuller view down to the jungle.

Far below, the shadows cast by our choppers were running ahead and slightly to the right of our path, elongating immensely and then shrinking back abruptly as they passed over the leafy crowns of the centuries-old jungle giants that towered above the lower canopy. Speeding more than 100 mph over terrain we'd have had to inch our way through on foot, I was struck by how remarkable it was for us to have progressed from horse and buggy days to skies filled with supersonic jetliners in less than 100 years. And it wasn't just air travel, our technology had advanced so rapidly that tasks that had required months or years to finish could be completed in days or hours, and sometimes even in seconds. A month after I'd set foot in Vietnam I'd learned that our astronauts had left their footprints on the very surface of the moon, and yet here we were, sky-riding our amazing flying machines into the depths of a primeval jungle where we'd hunt and kill other men as savagely as our primitive ancestors had. Viewed from the sky that seemed inanely stupid but it was what it was. The NVA eyes looking up at our choppers wouldn't be awed by mankind's amazing progress, they'd be seeing fearsome machines transporting men who'd kill them on sight, deadly men like me, or maybe this time they'd kill me.

They were sending us into a place the army viewed as one of the last NVA strongholds in III Corps. It was a place that they'd left nearly untouched for years but all we'd heard was that they were dropping us into another NVA-dominated no-fly section of jungle. I pictured them poring over aerial photos and bending over their cleanly lined grid maps penciling in azimuths that we'd have to follow, but those aerial photos couldn't begin to convey the multifaceted reality of the green-closeted maze of three-dimensional foliage teeming with scents, sights, and sounds that awaited us. You'd have to experience that environment as human prey to appreciate how vulnerable we'd be when we set foot in that maze. I had, and I knew it intimately; the dim jungle's short sight lines, its hidden bunkers, its cleverly designed trails, and its foliage that could hide deadly men lying in wait a few steps away. Entire companies had been wiped out in NVA dominated jungle like that, and I'd heard of guys faking rat bites to get held back for rabies shots or simply refusing to go when they'd known they were headed there, but all of us were on these choppers.

I think each of us felt he owed that to the rest of us. I wasn't sure if I'd call that brotherhood, family, clan, gang, tribe, or something else, but I knew how strong that bond was. It was one of the reasons I'd come back from the rear but I wasn't fooling myself into believing I was martyring myself for the good of the others. I was repulsed by the senselessness and savagery of the war and saddened by the price it exacted but I was seduced by it too; proud to be performing an important role in a deadly fight for survival and lured by the adrenaline rushes. I'd done a pretty good job of making a friend of dying too, but I'd never fully vanquished that fear and as we flew to what was rumored to be another deadly section of jungle I was wondering, *will this be the place?*

The roof of the flat jungle began to wrinkle into mountainous terrain that rose higher as we flew on, and then the shadow of a spectacular gorge appeared. I had a brief glimpse into its river-run canyon, and then we circled beyond the edge of the gorge and paralleled its course. I leaned out to look at the broad swath of semi-flat terrain that stretched from the side of the rim. Directly below us bushy ridges were wandering through savannah-like grasslands like green lines drawn on a yellowing page. After a minute or two the ridge-lined grassy bench of land that extended from the rim of the gorge changed to low canopied undulating jungle. We flew above the rolling terrain briefly, and then our choppers started dipping into a small meadow. My chopper flared to a midair stop, and I dropped my pack, stepped off the rail, and plunged through the wind-buffeted grasses. I landed on flexed knees, collected my gear, and hustled toward the edge of the meadow. As I neared it I saw traces of an NVA trail peeking through the bamboo, and when I reached the meadow's edge I saw that all the edible bamboo shoots had been harvested. Some of the cuts looked like they were days old but most had healed over months or years ago, and I knew then that rumors were true.

We settled on the fringe of the meadow and waited for the second wave of choppers to insert the rest of our company. One of the guys coming in on the second wave got hurt bailing out of his chopper. That lucky grunt got a ticket back to the rear. The others filled in beside us, and the choppers thumped away leaving us with whatever number of NVA had harvested all the bamboo sprouts that had grown here.

Day 1

Any NVA who'd heard or seen our choppers flying over this no-fly swath of high jungle would have been alerted but that didn't deter Capt. Valtz from sending us down the NVA trail that was running just beyond the edge of the meadow. A very solemn Dennis showed up to let us know that they wanted our squad to walk point. Quinlin and I left our packs and the others saddled up. When we passed by another platoon one of their guys caught my eye and nodded soberly. I knew what he meant and I nodded back, thanking him.

The ¾ of a meter wide trail was so well-traveled that its bare dirt surface was dished in the center. It didn't show the fresh smudges of someone who'd fled our insertion but I knew that any NVA within a day's walking distance would have been forewarned. I scanned the path of the trail through the no-wind foliage, knowing that we'd stay on point and that every step we took could be deadly. The odds of walking kilometers of those steps and surviving were unnerving but I told myself I didn't have to survive all those kilometers at once; I just had to survive a few meters to the next piece of cover, and then a few meters to the next, to just feel my way down that trail step by step. *Just the next few meters,* I thought, and I looked up at a handful of semi-translucent clouds drifting high in the blue sky, quieted my mind, and started down the NVA's trail.

I soft-footed through 200 shadowy meters of the trail's meandering path along a gently rounded and moderately foliaged ridge. The ridge started to narrow, and I paused and sensed ahead. I didn't sense any presence but I held longer, getting a feel for this new piece of jungle. A few small birds were talking amiably but it was quiet overall, maybe a heat of the day quiet, maybe a cautious quiet that was lingering in the aftermath of our noisy arrival, or maybe something darker. The jungle wasn't telling me much but trails could talk. The thicket choked and doubling back on themselves NVA paths in the lowland jungles off LZ Grant had hinted of the patient, deadly, and clever NVA we'd found there. The trail where Earl had taken a bullet had reeked of arrogance and overconfidence and the NVA we'd encountered there had been less prepared. This was another no-fly section of jungle that the NVA had controlled for a long while but these NVA had created a hidden rabbit-warren trail that provided avenues for ambushes; the kind of trail that men who'd learned caution through deadly lessons would have built. I envisioned combat hardened men waiting ahead and then I started moving again, getting out of my head and flitting to any next piece of cover when it *felt* right.

Later, a gentle wisp of wind rustled through the foliage. I breathed it deeply into my nose. It carried no warning sounds or scents and I moved on, slipping ahead in small increments with my body pumping adrenalin, my ears registering the tiniest whispers of sounds, my unfettered eyes finding their way through the foliage and gathering mosaic bits and pieces that some part of my brain was assembling into identifiable shapes and forms, my nose scenting the air for danger; a hunted animal strung as tightly as the two bucks I'd seen peeking their antlered heads above a late afternoon ridgeline in the mountains of Trinity. At times my conscious awareness was so threadlike that I felt I was a part of the living jungle, and then something changed. An instant later my eyes guided my awareness through a tangle of foliage to a few inches of foliage-obscured trail. I turned my head slowly and tracked traces of its brown hue down the slope of the ravine ahead of me on my left. I took a knee and listened down the line of it. Everything was quiet and still, maybe lifeless or maybe hiding NVA that were as unmoving as I was.

I heard a little gust of wind come whispering through the foliage. A perfectly rounded head-high bush was just ahead of me and a little to my right. A beam of sunlight was shining down on the silver-dollar-sized leaves that adorned it, and when the little breeze reached the bush the leaves started to stir. The breeze gusted stronger, and the white inner sides and dark outer sides of the leaves started flipping over and springing back so that the bush seemed to come alive and shimmer like a dancer in a silver sequined dress. Some primal part of me was sensing out for deadly threats but another part of my brain recorded every detail of that magical moment of that just right breeze hitting at that just right angle at that just right moment to make that bush shimmy and dance like it was bedecked in silver sequins, and then the breeze passed, the bush stilled, and there was just the trail climbing out of the gully, maybe lifeless, maybe deadly.

I rotated my jaw to crackle my ear canals fully open and tiny sounds came even clearer. I raised my left hand slowly, cupped my left ear, and angled it at the likely location where the two trails would intersect. Everything stayed quiet and I uncupped my ear, quieted my mind, and knelt unmoving on one knee waiting for any tiny nudge of unease that might be telling me something my thinking brain couldn't know. I was idly aware of the thin line of ants that were marching toward my left boot. I felt the tiny sting of a mosquito on the inner side of my exposed left forearm and I inched my left arm slowly toward my side. The hungry mosquito held fast and I crushed it into a tiny smear of mosquito parts and blood, and then I regripped the fore end of my M-16 and listened to the high-pitched hums of mosquitoes, the intermittent drones of flies, and the twitters and flutters of a few small birds flitting in the low brush.

I slipped silently up to the intersection of the trails. The trail rising out of the ravine was a well-used branch of the trail we were traveling. It side-hilled far down the slope of the ridge we were on to a large area of secreted jungle but the section that reached up to me felt lifeless. I moved just beyond the junction and waited for the squad that was trailing ours to move up. When they had eyes on the trail rising out of the ravine I moved on, covering a few meters at a time and then pausing and reaching out to the jungle. I did that again and again, often little more than a detached watcher trusting a far more instinctual me to sense the jungle and know things I couldn't.

Our trail's ridgeline began to slope down gently and then it branched into two distinct ridgelines. The left branch dropped gradually beneath the right branch, and the thin brown line of the NVA trail showed on the lower branch. My eyes were probing the two ridgelines when two bursts of M-16 fire erupted behind us. The shooting was too distant to pose an immediate threat to our squad but we knew the men behind us had encountered the NVA. Everything stayed quiet for a handful of minutes and, then we heard the roar of an explosion followed by the chattering reports of M-16s and the deeper reports of M-60s or AK-47s.

The shooting persisted. We set up a small defensive perimeter at the head of the trail and I backtracked to where Walt was manning the company radio. Walter told me that the first shooting had been one of our guys firing at an NVA who'd been sneaking below our column, and the explosion that followed had been the NVA tripping an automatic ambush we'd set on the trail out of the ravine. The automatic's claymores had killed 7 or 8 NVA and wounded a couple of others. One of the wounded NVA soldiers wanted to surrender but the other NVA was shooting at our guys and trying to kill the NVA who was trying to surrender. I was continuing up the trail toward the firefight when a frenzied burst of firing erupted. It lasted for about a minute, and when I started moving again a medic and a guy with a bandaged arm appeared on the trail. I stepped aside to let them pass. The wounded guy didn't seem to be in a lot of pain and his arm appeared to be intact. The shooting didn't resume and I was about to head back to my squad when two guys came down the trail carrying a wounded NVA soldier lying feet-first on a poncho strung between two bamboo poles. The guy at the back of the stretcher was bearing most of the load, and after they passed I moved up beside him and fastened a grip on the left rear pole. He released his hand, and I stutter-stepped to get in cadence and helped them carry the wounded NVA down the trail.

As we made our way down that narrow trail the NVA's head was a few inches in front of my right hand and his face was perpetually in my vision. He was in his late teens or his early 20s, so young and downy faced that he appeared almost effeminate. His clothes had been cut away or blown off by the force of the explosion and his wounds were fully exposed. He'd had to have been directly in front of the claymores when they'd exploded because the claymores' blast-driven pellets hadn't risen high enough to reach his upper body. His lower body had caught the full load of pellets and they'd produced a fluid-leaking, hamburger-like abomination below the line of his stomach that I couldn't have accepted as human if it hadn't been attached to the rest of him.

He was fully conscious, and after a few steps he raised his head and craned his neck to view the butchered remnants of his lower body. I watched a soul-sick mask of despair contort his features, and then his pupils rolled to the top of his head and he started slamming his head back against the taut rubber of the poncho stretcher. After three or four thumping drumbeats he squeezed his eyes tightly shut and twisted his head violently from side to side, the agony embodied in those silent cries unmistakable. The ghastly thing he'd seen was too graphic to question, but a few steps later his head stopped turning, a look of disbelief began to form, and he elevated his head again. The look of despair, the slamming of his head, and the silent "NOs!" came again. And it didn't stop. He kept raising his head to see and each time the looks of unbearable anguish would distort his features and he'd beat his head against the poncho as if he could somehow pound out the reality that his eyes had revealed.

His suffering terrified me, and I willed him to accept his fate, or pass out, or better yet *just fucking die*, but his shocked disbelief kept clawing its way back and the horrifying pattern kept repeating. I didn't want anything to do with it but his face was always there in front of me, so I distanced myself from his suffering by cultivating a sense of contempt because he couldn't accept what he'd become and because he hadn't found the courage to end his life at the site of the ambush.

We reached the site where they'd be bringing in the medevac and we lowered what was left of him to the ground. No one had spoken as we'd come down the trail, and I turned away wordlessly and continued toward my squad. The sickly-sweet scent of his blood that had shrouded me as we'd made our way down the trail was still there. I sucked in a lungful of the hot jungle air and expelled it through my nose as hard as I could but the blood scent seemed to follow me. The festering images of him craning his neck to view what he'd become were following me too. I told myself, *Fuck it, this day is three-quarters done*, and then my guys were there watching me approach, their unguarded faces haunted, a long stretch of foreboding trail behind us and more of it ahead, and, finally, I was living my reality and not that of a butchered young gook completing the irreversible trajectory of his horrifying death.

Less than an hour later I was stepping ahead so softly that my footfalls wouldn't nudge the awareness of an NVA who might be as attuned to the jungle as I was. I reached the lower branching ridge and traveled the trail another 250 or 300 meters to a charcoal-darkened patch of dirt that had been burned clear of foliage. A 30 meter long section of the trail dropped steeply through the burn to flat section of the jungle. I could see that it turned 90 degrees to my right through the open burn at the bottom of the drop, and then it disappeared in the thick foliage that filled the lower section of jungle. I moved closer and listened into the quiet below. I felt an odd something, like a vague pressure, and I melted into the foliage on the left of the burn and started working my way down. Cringing at the soft sounds I couldn't avoid creating, I made it to the bottom of the drop and squatted in the thick vegetation's humid air, and then I took a deep breath and stole through the shadows to the near edge of the burn. Nothing appeared to have changed, and I hand signaled Quinlin down.

When he was situated I moved into the open burn and leaned in close to the tire-tread impression that had been pulling at my eyes. The NVA who'd left that print had stepped out from the cover at the bottom of the burned patch and pivoted down the trail, and the sandal he'd pivoted on had pushed up a well-defined ridge of the dirt that was just-made sharp. The spacing of scuff marks he'd left as he'd continued down the trail revealed that he'd been running, and now I was sure. He'd been a spotter placed there to alert other NVA that we were approaching and I was almost certain that the ones he'd alerted were waiting in ambush close ahead.

I felt my pulse strengthen, becoming more powerful but not disruptive as I surveyed the jungle where the trail led, grateful for the thickness of the foliage there. I envisioned myself moving through it more silently and more invisibly than they'd anticipate, flitting from shadow to shadow with my ears sensing beyond the reach of their eyes and detecting whispers of sounds or unnatural zones of silence that would unmask the place where they'd be hidden. I believed I could do that, and I rested my finger lightly on the trigger of my M-16 and moved into that thickness. I felt a little lightheaded for a moment, and then the feeling passed and I was lost in the feel of the jungle.

Time meant nothing to me and I used it, harmonizing my movements with the wind-stirred pulses of the jungle and waiting in shadowed places for seemingly timeless intervals as my senses crept slowly through the veiled growth like feelers searching for life, and then, finding nothing, inching on in an adrenalin fed almost trance-like, state. The tiny watching part of me was seeing a hunter slipping one loose-limbed glide to cover and then another, aware that I was balancing delicately on the edge of a forever void. It had questioned the whys of that at times but the cerebral me was all in now, seduced by the danger and committed to seeing it through to the end, one way or the other. There were a lot of reasons why that didn't make sense but that's how it was.

In several places I squatted in brushy cover reaching out for sights, smells, or sounds that didn't belong or for those that should have been there and weren't. And then I was crouching in the cloaking embrace of a broad-leafed bush and sensing through the few meters of slightly thinner foliage that the trail passed through. It felt empty on the other side, and I slipped up to within a couple of meters of the semi-open area and crouched longer, feeling for any slight oddness in the jungle. I didn't detect it, and I mapped a broken course that would take me through the exposed section so quickly that an NVA with his finger on his trigger might not have time to get an accurate shot.

I'd planned every footfall, and I took my first step intending to slip through it like a flickering shadow. That was the only thought in my head, and then I was standing one step into that open section of trail with a sense of impending death that couldn't have been greater if I'd been one step short of the path of a Freightliner bearing down on me at 60 mph! An instant later the image of an impossibly huge semi-translucent Asian face formed high in the forefront of the foliage ahead. The specter was like something half-seen on the extreme edge of my peripheral vision, and then his pitiless features solidified into a coldly intelligent face that was calculating but not brutal. I felt like I was seeing myself through his calculating eyes, and I could feel his dispassionate hunger, for me. Every survival instinct I'd honed should have sent me diving back for cover but the dread that had frozen me one step into that opening wasn't letting go, and I just stood motionless in a semi-open section of a trail I was certain was ambushed.

Some part of me knew that I couldn't stand there forever but another part of me was seeing myself through eyes that hungered to kill me. I sensed that any movement might trigger that deadly intent, and a lot of heartbeats passed before I mustered enough courage to inch back like a timorous mouse in the presence of a coiled snake watching with deadly eyes. I reached my previous cover, knelt, and peered back at the trail. The apparition was gone but my sense of dread was undiminished, and I had to regather my nerve to slip further back. I reached out again from my new vantage point, and when I found nothing I retreated further.

Quinlin was close behind when I stopped. His darting eyes were seeking whatever had spooked me back, and I surveyed the section of trail I'd retreated through and answered his unspoken question, whispering, "I've got a bad feeling and I'm not going any farther."

Quinlin acknowledged my words with a barely perceptible nod, and then he dropped back to let the others know we were stopping. I waited there, feeling the vestiges of that great dread, sensing up that trail, and wondering. Minutes later Dennis crept up to ask what I'd found. I told him that it was just a bad feeling. I didn't expect him to question me, and he didn't. He left, and a short time later Lt. Colclough slipped up to ask if I'd seen or heard anything at all. I told him that I hadn't, that it was just a bad feeling, and Lt. nodded and left. I thought it was settled until Dennis crept back up to tell me that Captain Valtz had radioed that we couldn't stop here and that we had to move on to a more defensible night position.

The thought of doing that never entered my mind. They'd called on our squad to lead them through some bad sections of the jungle where a lot of us could have been killed. We'd always done it, and in every instance the route we'd taken and the pace we'd traveled had been left to me with no suggestions given and no questions asked, not even a whisper. That wasn't going to change, and especially not now, and I hissed at Dennis to go back and tell them that if they wanted to move ahead they could come up and walk point, "**because I'm not taking another fucking step.**"

Dennis nodded soberly and left, maybe in agreement or maybe just a go-between. Alone again, I surveyed the jungle that stretched beyond where I'd stopped, morbidly certain that if they found anyone who'd be willing to lead them there he'd die. They didn't find anyone, or maybe they didn't try, and soon the rest of the company was keying off our squad and spreading through the dense foliage to form as close to a circle as they could. After we'd created a perimeter the guys who always dug foxholes started digging in deeply, and those who didn't normally dig were digging just as deeply. I didn't expend the calories it took to dig foxholes, and I spread my blanket liner into a hint of a swale, folded it to create a bed, and lay flat on the ground, too spent to do more.

At the tail end of the day I was heating a C-ration tin over a hissing C-4 flame. Quinlin was sucking on his before-dark cigarette and both of us were facing out at the sight avenues that reached back at us from the night-dimming jungle. The sense of relative safety that almost always came after we'd spent an uneventful hour or so on an evening perimeter was so lacking that everyone was defecating inside the perimeter to avoid venturing even a few meters into the shadowy jungle. I felt it too, and I looked down the darkening line of the NVA trail that ran beyond our section of the perimeter, thinking of the NVA bodies we'd left in our wake and wondering what dark vengeance would be gathering in the foreboding expanse of jungle that reached beyond our fragile perimeter; the place where I'd had that incredibly eerie experience.

    I'd felt inexplicable warnings before, things like my sense of someone seeing the downed tree shudder on the day I'd been bullet grazed and the many little nudges and tugs of unease or assurances that had come to me. I'd assumed that was because some enigmatic corner of my mind could detect patterns in the jungle's sounds, sights, and smells that had been too subtle or too fleeting to register in my conscious mind, but I couldn't explain this experience that way. My certainty that if I took *one more step I'd be a dead man* hadn't been a nudge, it had arrived fully formed and terrifyingly specific. Even more inexplicable was the apparition I'd seen and sensed. If my mind had been filled with thoughts that might have stimulated me to imagine what I'd seen and felt then I could have attributed it to an overactive imagination heightened by fear, but it hadn't been. I'd stepped into that open stretch of trail with nothing in my head but those planned footfalls, and a fraction of a second later I'd been standing in that semi-open stretch of trail, shocked, confused, and frozen in place by that overpowering premonition of death. As the huge Asian face had solidified into a calculating visage a voice had been whispering in my head that he couldn't be real but I'd seen what I'd seen and I'd known what I'd known.

    I still couldn't accept that he hadn't been real. I couldn't explain that either, and I didn't try to. I'd grown up in a world where words were essential tools and logic could often predict outcomes but things were different here. The ancient jungle reigned supreme and its ever-changing scents, sounds, sights, and feels were forever creating mercurial threads of meanings that were too fluid, too subtle, or too fleeting for my logical mind to grasp. I'd sensed that early on and I'd heeded ancient instincts that were telling me that the shadowy touches of my intuitive mind were the keys to survival here; to just read the fucking tea leaves and get my plodding word mind the hell out of the way. Those instincts had kept me alive and I heeded them again, never questioning my certainty that I'd have died if I hadn't trusted that warning and, as incredible as it seemed even then, never discounting the possibility that the cold-eyed visage I'd seen might have mirrored the flesh and blood face of the NVA soldier who'd have ended my life if I'd traveled down that trail.

It was fully dark when I pulled my liner up to my chest, brushed my fingers over the selector switch of the M-16 that was pressed against my side, and wriggled into a comfortable position. I was almost asleep when the roar of a powerful diesel engine shattered the quiet, coming from about a klick away and a little to the left of the direction the trail was pointing. The engine worked at half to full throttle for a few minutes, and then it stopped and the night was unnaturally silent. Wide awake, I lay in the darkness wondering how they'd gotten a piece of heavy equipment into this high section of jungle and why they'd have exposed it when they'd known we were nearby.

What was in here? The NVA who'd triggered the automatic ambush had come up the trail that climbed out of the ravine, there was an NVA presence where that engine fired up, and the harvesting and wear on the main NVA trail indicated a probable NVA site was behind us. Those points formed the outline of a triangle with our company situated inside it. What made it even spookier was that the NVA here weren't the run-and-hide kind. The NVA soldier who'd lurked at the bottom of the burn had almost surely been part of an ambush and the squad of NVA who'd triggered the claymores had been stalking us. One of them had been so hardcore that he'd died trying to kill the young NVA I'd helped carry down the trail, and a guy that tough and committed would almost surely have found his way to a combat unit. I knew I was just guessing but I drifted into an uneasy sleep picturing our company in the middle of an unknown number of battle-hardened NVA soldiers.

I awoke to the booming echo of an explosion. I rolled off my blanket and waited with my M-16 in my hands to see if it foreshadowed a night attack, and when it stayed quiet I grabbed my bandoleers and moved to the perimeter. Others joined us. The night was too dark to reveal movements so we listened in silence. The sound of the boom had come from the area where Dennis had wired the trail with a battery triggered claymore, and a handful of minutes later a muffled "*pffi*" noise sounded there. There were no further sounds, and after about a half hour of quiet I made my way to my blanket thinking that the pfft sound must have been from an NVA triggering a dirt-clogged rifle or a bullet that had misfired.

Sometime later I came wide awake with my heart hammering in my chest. I knew something was very wrong and I lay perfectly still, stopped breathing, and reached out with my ears. My heart jumped higher when I heard the sounds of sleep breathing coming from where our guy on watch should be. The night was so black that I could barely distinguish the shadowy shape of a poncho shelter a few steps away, and I pulled in a lungful of air, held my breath, and focused my ears in very, very close. I didn't hear any nearby movements so I listened beyond our perimeter. The night air wasn't moving and it was quiet out there. And then I heard a tiny rustling noise. One noise didn't tell me what I needed to know but the ones that followed did. They were so soft and so random that they could have gone undetected, but I'd been night-listening for those specific sounds since the morning of my second day in the jungle when I'd found that Ho Chi Minh sandal track imprinted in the dirt beside my claymore; they were the sounds of men inching across the debris-carpeted floor of a night darkened jungle.

I gently thumbed the firing selector of my M-16 two clicks to automatic, and then I lay still to determine whether the clicks had targeted me to a creeper who'd penetrated our perimeter. I didn't hear anything, and when the shadows didn't waver I inched off my blanket liner, rolled to my stomach, and waited. Nothing seemed to have changed, so I crawled to where Hootie and another guy, maybe Kenny, were sleeping. They awoke at my touch, immediately alert. I whispered that we had movement outside the perimeter and the three of us crawled off to spread the word. Within minutes our entire platoon was lined up along our section of the perimeter. We'd made enough noise to warn the crawlers that we'd detected them but Lt. Colclough wasn't taking any chances. We opened up on his signal and lit up the night with our muzzle flashes and the frenzied sounds of M-16s firing on fully automatic. There was no return fire but after a short pause Lt. Colclough called for another *mad minute*. It ended, and when the bullet-clipped vegetation stopped moving the area beyond the perimeter stayed silent.

I returned to my blanket and slept until I was awakened for my turn at watch. A sliver of a moon had risen above the canopy but very little of its dim light was reaching down to the floor of the jungle. I knew what was out there and I spent my watch listening intently into the dimness. A couple of *maybe* noises made my heart jump but the sounds never formed the patterns I associated with a creeping man, and at the end of my watch I returned to my blanket and slept for another hour or so. I awoke as the light of the not-yet-risen sun was beginning to turn the jungle a hazy gray, and I slipped out from under my poncho liner and moved to the perimeter to see if our bullets had found human targets. The jungle brightened, and when I didn't see any bodies I wondered if any wounded NVA had crawled off or if any bodies had been pulled away. I would like to have known but I wasn't curious enough to venture out and search for blood trails or bodies in the foliage, none of us were.

Day 2

The sun had risen when I led our squad up the trail toward the place where our automatic ambush had exploded. As I neared it the low silhouette of something lying on the trail appeared, and I moved ahead and stopped about 15 meters short of the still form of an NVA soldier who was lying on his back with his face angled up at the patches of sky that showed through the broken canopy. An AK-47 was resting across his chest, and I watched intently to see if his chest was rising and falling. When I was certain he wasn't breathing I slipped past him to see if any sharp-witted gooks were ambushing our ambush site. They weren't, and I turned back and squatted beside his body.

Like the obscenely wounded NVA we'd carried down the trail yesterday, he'd been almost on top of the claymore when he'd triggered the ambush. The force of the explosion had propelled him onto his back, or maybe he'd still had enough strength to roll onto his back and face the night-skied canopy. The pellets had savaged his lower body but he'd lived a little longer. He'd have been deafened by the explosion and he'd surely been terrified that we'd be creeping up on him but he'd been too wounded to crawl away, or maybe he'd known how badly he was hurt, or maybe his pain had been unbearable. The sign he'd left couldn't answer those questions, but the AK-47 lying across his chest had stayed in his hands or landed within his reach and in the brief interval between the explosion and the "*pffi*" sound he'd wrapped his mouth around the barrel of that pristine AK-47 and pulled the trigger, forever ending his terror and his pain.

I'd avoided looking directly at his upturned face but I'd seen more than I'd wanted. The recoil of the AK-47 had blown the barrel back out of his mouth so the entrance wound was hidden and his face was intact. There wasn't any expression on it, just the vacant look of death, but I imagined he'd said his silent goodbyes before he'd done what he'd needed to do, and I squatted beside his body and nodded my head in approval, respecting a soldier who'd known it was his time to die and been strong enough to accept it. The thoughts stirred empathetic feelings I didn't need, and I pulled back by telling myself, *he's just another dead gook.*

Half of his pack was pinned beneath his back and the rest was exposed. I could see that something had leaked out of his pack and pooled on the exposed portion of his pack, and I assumed it was the fermented fish sauce I'd heard the NVA carried to flavor their rice. I'd always wanted to know why the NVA had the distinctive smell that identified them to me, and I pulled my finger through the liquid and raised it to my nose. I'd expected it to have a pungent odor, and when it didn't I touched my finger to my tongue. The liquid was tasteless. I was still wondering what it could be when Dennis turned the body over and my color-insensitive eyes traced the trail of liquid from the hole in the back of his head to the place where it had pooled. Trying desperately to avoid forming words that might forever inscribe a memory of what I'd done, I pulled my canteen from my pistol belt and emptied half of it rinsing my mouth and spitting out mouthfuls of precious water.

An hour later we trailed another platoon to the semi-open stretch of trail where I'd felt the touch of death. The setting was exactly as I'd remembered it but on this day there was no face hungering for me, and I felt no sense of immense dread as I walked slowly through the site I'd intended to flit through so quickly. The trail held to a generally straight line through another 40 or so meters of dense foliage, and then it made a 70-degree turn to the left and side-hilled a gentle slope for about 80 meters. At the end of the 80 meters of sidehill trail the vegetation transitioned to grassy areas spotted with brush. An NVA trail crossed over a low ridge crest about 100 meters to our right there. That trail dropped down to intersect our trail and the line of the intersecting trail pointed toward the location where the diesel engine had fired up. None of that explained the experience I had but the NVA who'd been there would have had plenty of time to cross over the ridge and go to ground on the uphill side of the 80 meters of the trail we'd been walking. I had no way of knowing whether they had but the NVA who'd waited at the bottom of that burn had been there for a reason, and if I'd wanted to set a major ambush that's the place I'd have chosen.

The guys walking point must have been making hard targets of themselves because they took a couple of rounds of sniper fire and no one got hit. They led another 300 or 400 meters to a large meadow, and we established a temporary perimeter on the edge of it where our trail entered. My platoon was the last one in and my squad set up on both sides of the trail. About 30 minutes later we learned that they were sending Alpha Company in, and shortly after that choppers started dropping into the other side of the meadow. About 15 minutes later I saw a line of soldiers walking toward us. I couldn't imagine that they'd be sending them back into the section of jungle we'd just escaped but the pack-burdened men of Alpha Company kept walking purposefully our way.

I knew that Alpha Company had suffered an appalling number of dead and wounded over the last months and I scanned their lead men as they neared, wondering if their losses had left them short of old hands. An alert-eyed brown-haired guy of average height was walking point. He had the look of a guy who'd been around, a confident, head up, and easy-striding young man. The guy walking backup for him was dark-haired and shorter. He had a more subdued walk and a more sober demeanor but both of them were carrying their M-16s resting flat on their right shoulders with the fore-ends of the barrels gripped in their right hands, whatever that meant. The fourth man back was a tall, lithe-limbed blonde guy packing a M-60 with a cocky-tough look on his face.

They looked like they'd made it through some bad places, and when their point man was about three strides away I uncoiled out of my squat and fixed my eyes on him. In the unspoken language of the jungle I was telling him I had something to say but he passed me by without pausing. That surprised me. If I'd been in his place I'd have stopped to ask about the terrain, the foliage, the locations and sizes of any NVA trails, and any estimates of the numbers, aggressiveness, and toughness of the NVA that might have been here. I'd have been so fucking anxious to get any little edge that I'd have asked a one-day FNG for information if I'd thought there was the slightest possibility he'd have known one tiny thing I could have used, but it was their point man's life and his choice.

That's what I told myself, but when he was two or three steps past me I thought *the hell with it!* and I said quietly, "Hey, we came in that way. It's bad. You'll likely get hit before you get out a hundred meters."

His steps hesitated slightly, and then he looked over his shoulder and said, "Yeah, we know what we're doing."

His backup shot me a sober look but he kept walking too. I turned to the 60 gunner. He still had the cocky-tough look plastered on his face, and I nodded, turned away, and reminded myself that it had nothing to do with me. I believed that, but as their column filed past us I glanced down the trail at times, thinking they were moving too fast and that every step they took was bringing them closer to the moment where they'd have to do every minuscule thing exactly right to survive. I didn't think they would, and the bright-eyed point man's words kept echoing in my head. "*Yeah, we know what we're doing,*" he'd said, a brave young man leading through a place where things could so quickly turn fatal.

I felt the anticipatory sorrow of his death, and I turned to Quinlin and said, "Those first two guys are gonna be dead within the next 20 minutes."

Quinlin took a deep pull on his cigarette and gazed down the trail where the point man and his backup had disappeared. Smoke wafted from his nose, and then he nodded and said solemnly, "I spect yer right."

I nodded, too, as if it didn't matter much, and maybe it didn't. Every week courageous young men like them were getting zipped into body bags and 400 or 500 more of us would be added this month. They'd just be two more but I was mentally cringing in anticipation of the rattle of gunfire I expected to erupt at any second. For long minutes it didn't come. I thought, *maybe this isn't their day to die,* but it was. The last of Alpha Company's men were still in the meadow when the AK-47s opened up. The M-16s started firing seconds later but the timing said it all; Alpha Company had walked into an ambush. When we learned that the point man and his backup were dead and another guy was wounded Quinlin looked at me and shook his head. I was dreading the sight of them packing back two lifeless bodies jostling limply in their ponchos and smelling of blood and death like Merle's had, but we weren't there when they did.

Whoever was running things was intent on sending Alpha Company further into that piece of jungle a second time and my first thought was that they'd walk into a bloodbath and get us pulled in with them. I guess Lt. Colclough and Cpt. Valtz felt the same way because Lt. asked me if I'd be willing to take over the point and create some distance between Alpha Company and us. The prospect of hurrying away from Alpha Company twinged at my conscience but my allegiance was to the men who'd walked the jungle with me and I never hesitated. We were walking point on back-to-back days but this time the terrain was the finger-ridged, savanna-like area I'd seen when we'd flown in. There was no trail to walk and no way to conceal our presence, and I moved through the open reading sign on the run, searching for movements or shapes in the brush of the low ridges that bisected the long grassy areas and hoping they wouldn't have time to set an ambush. I held to the center of the open areas when the brush line was distant enough to make uncertain targets of our fast-moving silhouettes, and in the narrower areas I crossed to one side or the other and paralleled the brush line, playing 50% odds that any NVA would be on the other brush line. After hours of that the flat terrain began to wrinkle and patches of brush were creeping into the open areas. I didn't like those brushy patches creating ambush sites and I slowed my pace and moved on more cautiously.

We stopped an hour or so before dark and established a night perimeter on the east edge of the plateau. My platoon was situated at the top of a little ridge with a small NVA trail on it that didn't appear to have been used in months. I didn't view it as a threat, and after two consecutive days of walking point I was ready to kick back a little and let someone watch out for me. Quinlin felt the same way, and we moved to the relative security of the middle of the perimeter and sat down with Walt the Mailman to eat C-rations. We were still there when a shrill whistle sounded. The pop of a small-caliber report followed on its heels, and suddenly NVA tracers were painting green lines high above our heads and M-16s were stuttering out bullets. The action was on our platoon's section of the perimeter, and Jim and I ran back and joined our squad. Henry's squad was dug in above the little ridge and they were putting out a lot of bullets. The green tracers eventually stopped coming but Henry and his squad kept up their frenetic shooting until Captain Valtz's voice yelled for them to stop firing and conserve ammunition. Their shooting trailed off, and then a voice yelled, "I've got movement!" and the shooting started up again. When it stopped the raw-throated screams of a wounded NVA sounded below us. He was so close that his screams marked him as an easy target but none of us fired at the pitiful sounds. He kept screaming for minutes and then another NVA pulled him out, or maybe he died or lost consciousness, and it stayed quiet.

Jim and I had missed most of it, but Sugar Bear told us that after the pistol shot signal the gooks had started moving up the ridge toward Henry and Big Al's squad. He said the NVA's bullets had been flying but when the NVA had gotten close Big Al Gilmore had stopped their advance by rising to his feet with one of our M-60s and cutting some of the attackers down. Al's courage must have been remarkable because our typically disparaging Sugar Bear was unreservedly awed by what Al had done.

The NVA who'd come up that ridge had been courageous too, but why would an NVA officer have prewarned a fully armed and dug-in infantry company and then ordered his men uphill into it? Captain Jones had sent us through an open meadow to the tree line of a stretch of NVA-occupied jungle and I guessed the NVA had incompetent officers too. This one had ordered his men to attempt a suicidal assault and an unknown number of them had paid the ultimate price. What a fucking waste of brave men, but at least it wasn't our dead. The men of my company had put another day behind them, evading bullets and the fallen's nightmarish recognition of impending death. I was one of those men, and I settled in on my bed of bug-tracked earth haloed in the acrid scent of bug repellent and enduring the buzz-bombing of blood-sucking bugs, grateful to be alive in a jungle that mercilessly devoured the unwary and the weak.

Days 3 and 4

Early the next morning we continued on the heading that would take us farther from A Company. We traveled a short distance and then our radios came alive with frantic voices reporting that Alpha Company had walked into a major ambush and suffered substantial casualties. They'd managed to pull back with their wounded but they'd left several of their dead behind, and they were ordering us back to help retrieve the bodies. I'd covered a lot of ground on the day we'd left Alpha Company and I knew that whoever would be walking point would have to lead us back at a full run to get us close before nightfall. He didn't, he led at a far more cautious pace for nearly a klick but that didn't save him. The flat cracks of shots fired in our direction came, and a few seconds later the pops of M-16s shooting away from us started. A short interval of intense shooting followed and when it ended word was passed from man to man that our point man was dead and his backup was hit hard; the probably not going to make it kind of hit hard. The point man who'd died had a Hispanic name. I'd never known the name of the proud Texan who'd shared a log day ride to the company with me one day, so it could have been him. I probably could have asked around and found out but I didn't want to learn that it was him and I didn't.

A medevac picked up the point man's body and his seriously wounded backup. It took another casualty too. Their squad leader was reportedly so profoundly shaken from witnessing the event that he was deemed incapable of remaining. Sugar Bear was incensed at that. He started ranting that the squad leader had deliberately gotten himself sent back, and I wasn't going to let that go unanswered. I didn't know what their squad leader had witnessed up there or how attached he'd been to the dead point man and the wounded backup but that didn't stop me from having the opposite opinion. I thought that anyone who'd had the guts to stay out with us deserved the benefit of our trust and I never doubted him. I'd have bet that if he'd been given the choice he'd have taken a survivable bullet instead of the injury that had shocked his mind so violently, and I told Sugar Bear that he didn't have any fucking idea what he was talking about. The look of hate that crossed his face spoke volumes, but he could add this to all the contradictory feelings he had buried in that mercurial head of his and live with it because this was about being a grunt's grunt and I couldn't have cared less.

The medevac left and we headed back again, still moving at a cautious pace. We covered about half the distance back to Alpha Company without running into the NVA, and I settled in for a night of sleep that was interrupted only by my turn on watch. We got an early morning start, got resupplied, and set up a night perimeter near Alpha Company's position. Just before dawn we were all awoken and told that a B-52 arc light run was heading our way and the bombs were going to hit close. We were warned to take cover, plug our ears, and open our mouths when we heard the B-52s coming, and when I heard the roar of the oncoming jets and the surprisingly noisy wind-whipping hissing of the bombs tumbling through the air I buried my helmeted head in the dirt, plugged my ears, and opened my mouth. My hands were covering my ears but the overlapping explosions were shockingly loud, and then the bombs stopped exploding and the earth trembled for a few moments. We thought it was over, and when the B-52s made a second bombing run the ear-pressuring blasts caught us by surprise. I heard that some guys had suffered perforated eardrums but I was OK.

Day 5

They decided to send Alpha Company to retrieve the bodies on their own so we moved closer and waited in a mid-sized meadow in case they needed us. There was a wide-spreading tree growing in the middle of the meadow and Captain Valtz decided to blast it down using C-4 explosives. He claimed he was doing it to create a bigger landing site in case we needed to bring in choppers but I thought he wanted to find out if he could topple a big tree with C-4. Either way, I wasn't sure he'd know what he was doing and I settled a safe distance from the tree. The sun circled overhead, and when I lost my shade I gathered my gear and walked along the edge of the meadow looking for another shaded nook. I passed about a dozen guys who were dozing, writing letters, or idly waiting out the uncertainty of whether we'd get called in to help Alpha Company.

And then the unmistakable "**thump**" of a mortar round launching off the bottom of a tube sounded and everything changed. I took two leaping steps and dived belly flat against the side of the decaying log that was lying in the meadow, and then I lay with my helmeted head planted face first in the dirt listening to the thumps of more mortars launching. I didn't know if my log would be too rotten to shield me from the blast of a mortar landing on the other side of it but it was out of my hands now. From the moment each of those mortar rounds had thumped off the bottom of its tube my survival had been indelibly encoded in the formula that determined the endpoint of its parabolic path, and as the whistles of the falling mortar rounds grew terrifyingly shriller I waited for fate to decide whether I lived or died.

The scream of the first mortar round grew so piercing that I feared it was going to land directly on me, and then it exploded about six steps ahead of me on the other side of the log. Clods of dirt pelted my body as the banshee shrieks of more incoming rounds screamed ever louder in my ears. I was terrified that one of those screaming rounds would have my name written in it but the second mortar exploded a few feet on the other side of my log, the third exploded behind me, and then the explosions were tracking further back and I could breathe again. A stress-tight voice started yelling, "*MEDIC! MEDIC!*" and seconds later Doc sprinted past me to where the first mortar had landed. And then it finally stopped.

It seemed to have lasted forever, and for one member of our squad it had. He was a new guy I'd seen climbing off the chopper, a dark-haired shake-and-bake sergeant who'd been walking with a hint of uncertainty but hadn't been overwhelmed by the tense situation he'd stepped into. I hadn't talked to him but I'd seen enough to feel sure that he'd make a good hand. He'd never have that chance. Lt. Colclough had helped Doc cut a hole in his throat for a trachea tube. They'd gotten it in but his body had been too shredded by shrapnel to survive. A medevac chopper hammered in, and when they lifted his body out I thought of the many times I'd heard grunts saying that if you were gonna die it was better to get zipped before you had to endure months of misery. *Fuck it, it's done,* I thought, wanting him to be a nameless no-family FNG that I could forget.

I think it was about midday when we learned that Alpha Company's survivors had retrieved the bodies of their dead without encountering the NVA, and now they were pulling them out. The site they'd chosen for the extraction was the same meadow we'd been in when Alpha Company had arrived, and they sent our company ahead to re-secure it. We made it there without incident, and after we'd established our perimeter Lt. Colclough sent our squad out to determine whether the section of jungle where the NVA trail ran was clear. I scouted out far enough to be reasonably certain it was but something was urging me on and I went with it, retracing the ill-fated steps of Alpha Company's point man up that deadly NVA trail. My squad followed, never questioning why I was doing it. I don't know what I'd have said if they'd asked. I'd wanted to know how their deaths had happened so maybe curiosity was pulling me up that trail, but I think it was something buried deeper. For months I'd envisioned myself bleeding out my last moments of life on some shadowed piece of jungle that would never be known to anyone who'd cared for me, the way Alpha Company's point man and his backup had, and I think I felt compelled to bear witness to the place where they'd so gamely died. Maybe it was more than that but if there was another reason I wasn't aware of it; I was just doing what felt right and I kept ghosting up that lethal fucking NVA trail searching for the site where their lives had ended.

About 50 meters short of the place where the trail that crossed over the ridge crest intersected our trail I found a patch of dirt where one of them had spilled a lot of himself. I stayed there for a long while, sensing into the places where the NVA might have been and where they might now be hidden. I didn't feel they were there, and I moved on to a blood-darkened stench-of-death patch of trail where buzzing blowflies were devouring the last bits of Alpha Company's bright-eyed point man. The many sight lines that the lethal NVA bullets might have reached through were pressing in on me but I crouched longer in the fly-buzzing stillness of that jungle trail taking it all in, and when I'd created a vivid memory to mark his passing I backed away and left the two of them there, remembered.

We were in a meadow when a column of exhausted Alpha Company men straggled into our perimeter bearing the corpses of their body-bagged comrades. A flight of choppers lifted them and their gruesome burdens away, and more than an hour later the choppers returned for my company. They loaded as many of us as they could carry, and when they realized that they hadn't sent enough choppers whoever was running the extraction told the birds to lift off anyway. They did, and the dozen or so of us who were left in the meadow melted into the grass.

The sounds of the choppers faded and everything got deathly quiet. We knew the surrounding jungle was crawling with NVA, and the minutes passed heartbeat by heartbeat as we lay hidden in the grass listening for the thumps of mortar launches or the sounds of enemies approaching. After thousands of those heartbeats the distant whispers of choppers reached us, and when the birds appeared above our grassy horizon two of us rose out of the grass and waved our arms. The pilots spotted us, adjusted their angles of approach, and dropped in hard and fast. We'd anticipated that the NVA might be waiting to mortar us when the choppers returned, and we sprinted toward the place where the choppers were landing and barreled through their open doorways like panicked rabbits fleeing to their burrows. When the last of us were inside the pilots jumped the two slicks into the air and lifted us away from that slice of highland jungle that would be forever stained with blood, theirs and ours.

As the high plateau slowly receded behind us I looked back one last time, wondering where the watching NVA were hidden and what they'd be feeling, and then I leaned heavily against the chopper's doorway, too fucking exhausted and emotionally numb to care.

Chapter 28

LZ Snuffy

We landed on a bulldozer-torn red-clay piece of ground near the Cambodian border, and they put us to work helping them build *LZ Snuffy*. The site was adjacent to a dirt landing strip that was rumored to have been used by NVA aircraft. I heard that they'd tried to construct an LZ there earlier and that the NVA had attacked it so relentlessly that they'd abandoned the effort. I guess that was true but all we had to deal with was a handful of incoming rockets.

I'd written to Barbara asking if she'd mail a pint of whiskey and the package arrived. The bottle had made it halfway around the world intact and in the late evening Henry, Kenny, and I were shuddering down gulps of straight whiskey. After weeks of bare subsistence living the alcohol took hold quickly and the three of us were laughing and talking like teenagers at a summer keg party. A warm evening rain started and after we finished off the bottle we stripped off our shirts and let the rain rinse over us. That felt good, and I pulled off my socks, boots, and pants, and hung my red-clay-soiled pants and shirt to let the rain rinse some of the dirt away.

One of the LZ's 4-wheeled open platform *mules* had been parked nearby, and we walked over to check it out. When we saw that they'd left the key in it there was no question that we were going to liberate it. The mule started right up, and in the dim light of the late evening I drove it at full throttle through the slick mud of the LZ. The little engine topped out and I spun the steering wheel hard left to get the back end sliding. The mule's top speed was so anemic that it wouldn't slide so I drove on, searching for slipperier mud and trying to get it to spin out with the three of us joy-riding that turtle-slow vehicle and Kenny and Henry hollering like we were on a heart-leaping carnival ride. We knew our noises were echoing throughout the LZ but we were far too wild to waylay, and we owned that LZ.

It was almost too dark to drive when we arrived back at our company's area. I shut down the mule and when I climbed off Henry and Kenny tackled me, pretending they were getting revenge for my scaring them with my crazy driving. We wrestled in the muddy clay laughing and yelling, and then a voice out of the dark barked, "**What's going on out there? Who's making all that noise?**"

The tone he'd used was one a parent might use to discipline his children and I replied, "Go fuck yourself."

"Do you know who this is?" the voice warned, "this is **Lieutenant ----**."

Yeah, I knew who he was. He was the just-arrived platoon leader of one of our other platoons and he hadn't spent a day in the jungle. He probably thought this was his opportunity to employ one of the imperatives they'd drilled into him in his OCS, West Point, or ROTC training, the one about establishing his authority over enlisted men, but if that's what he intended he was seriously mistaken. This wasn't a stateside army base and we weren't parade-ground soldiers, this was an LZ perched on the edge of the jungle and we were combat-seared men who sometimes functioned on the fringes of rationality.

Our three responses overlapped when we told him, "**Go fuck yourself!**"

There was a pause, and then the voice repeated hesitantly, "This is Lieutenant ----."

The transformation from smug arrogance to tentative hesitance sent us into fits of laughter, and when we stopped laughing he was gone, or at least his voice was. We'd been a little rough but I thought we'd done him a favor. If he was smart he'd learn the significance of the common grunt refrain, "What're they gonna do if I don't, send me to Nam?" and then he'd earn the respect of the pivotal grunts in his outfit or he wouldn't. We knew that you couldn't teach true leadership and we sat in the rain musing about how lucky we were to have Lt. Colclough and Captain Valtz. The conversation turned to the quality of the LZ's food and how much time we'd have before they'd send us back out, and then we ran out of things to talk about. Henry and Kenny wandered off but I sat longer, thinking. The rain turned colder, and I slicked most of the gummy mud off my body with my hands and made my way through the sucking muck to my bunker. I scraped the red clay off my feet and dried myself with the nylon blanket liner that had been with me through so many nights, and then I wrapped its sodden dampness around my chilled body and lowered myself onto my cot. My body generated a little warmth inside the damp blanket and I drifted off to sleep listening to the patter of the rain.

I awoke with a hangover, forced myself to eat breakfast, and spent the rest of the gray-skied morning filling sandbags with mud. For the next handful of days I showered, ate hot meals, drank my fill of water, and idled. I'd relaxed into that restful interlude on other LZ stays but this time was different. Memories of Bù Gia Mập kept flashing through my mind; the movements of the leaves, the calls of the animals, random scents, the hungry-eyed face that had hovered on the upper edge of my vision, the certainty of death I'd felt, the "*pffi*" noise that had marked the wounded NVA's escape from the nightmare of his living, thoughts of the deadly ambush that had ended so many of the Alpha Company men, the ever-shriller whistles of the incoming mortar rounds, the manic screams for the medic, the ever-forming looks of disbelief on the face of the stretcher gook and his soul-sick recognition each time he viewed the thing that had become him, the shrieks of the wounded gook who'd almost certainly suffered the last minutes of his life on the ridge below our perimeter, the maybe-death of the proud Hispanic guy I'd respected, and the hollow looks I'd seen perpetually etched on the faces of the men who'd lived through those things with me.

There were all of those and there was something else, something that I wouldn't have anticipated. I'd crossed paths with Alpha Company's bright-eyed point man for only a minute or two but I'd felt like I'd seen myself passing by that day. I needed to believe that our deaths counted for something and I couldn't find it, not for him, not for any of us. That made me angrier and more bitter, or maybe more despairing, and I didn't want that. I wanted to be grateful for the good things; our stays on the LZs, the respite of a cool evening rain, the sense of camaraderie that we shared, the pride of being an important part of our platoon, and even the dark thrill that came from slipping through the shadowy jungle burning adrenalin like an ember glowing on a dark night. Those were still there but the grim memories were stronger and they kept coming.

I needed a break, and it came at the most opportune time.

RxR

I'd requested a seven-day RxR in Australia and my orders arrived while we were on LZ Snuffy. Captain Valtz made a point of finding me before I left.

He said that he knew I was a "hothead," and he told me that if I got into any trouble on RxR to make sure I made it back to the company so he could take care of it. I thought it was ironic that he'd tell me I was hotheaded. He might have gotten a battlefield commission but I never questioned that he'd refuse to follow any orders that might get us stupidly killed, and I didn't think that made him hotheaded. I didn't think I was either, but he wanted me to know he'd have my back and I smiled and said I would.

Reaching for Redemption

I hopped chopper rides to the RxR center on the Tan Son Nhut Air Base and when I arrived a day early I set off to explore the base. I heard music playing and I followed the sounds to a canopy-shaded enclosure where thirty to forty servicemen were sitting at tables listening to a South Vietnamese band. I surveyed the crowd, all air force guys, and then I walked inside and positioned a chair against the fence. The shade of the canopy didn't reach that far but having the fence behind me would prevent the uneasy feeling I always got when something might be lurking in my blind spot. One of the Vietnamese women who were working the bar at the side of the wooden stage arrived to take my drink order, and when she left I took a deep breath and turned back to the face I'd thought I'd buried.

The lead singer's resemblance to the first NVA I'd killed on the other side of that downed log was so remarkable that he could have been his identical twin. I couldn't look away, and I sat apart for long minutes seeing the expressive face that had once reached out to me with awareness and fear so filled with life. There were moments when I could believe that he hadn't died in that frozen instant on that shadowy trail, and at other times I watched him through blurred eyes, imagining the life he might have led if I hadn't taken it. Something inside of me built until I wanted to explode out of my chair and rip things apart, but I couldn't, and I forced myself to my feet and left him smiling and singing on that stage.

My anguish followed me to the RxR receiving center and I lay on my cot with raw emotions coursing through me as relentlessly as waves breaking on a beach. I felt that I'd done what I'd needed to do but that didn't lessen the heartsick grief I felt for taking the life of the young man I imagined he'd have been. I told myself, *if it has to be, it has to be*, but I wasn't as iron tough as my grandmother and I couldn't break free of it. For hours it seemed my grief would never ebb, and then in the early hours of the morning I was infused with a burning desire to lead a life that might begin to compensate for the life I'd traded for my own. That was my lifeline, and I reached for it and made wholehearted vows of atonement to the young man I'd killed. I knew it wasn't enough but it was all I had to give, and, finally, I collapsed into an exhausted sleep.

Sydney, Australia

Sydney was clean, bright, and beautiful with a blue water harbor floating massive oceangoing ships up the middle of the city. I took a cab to the University of Sydney, and it passed by botanical gardens filled with acres-large plots of ground-hugging flowers that created rainbows of vivid colors. It was a beautiful scene, but it didn't come close to matching the natural splendor of some of the green-hued jungle we'd walked through in Vietnam.

The old university was situated a long way out of the city. Its main building reached two stories high and covered an area that was probably the size of a full block. It was encircled by a wide swath of green lawn, and with its brick-walled exterior, gabled roofs, and the decorative spires that reached above the walls it looked more like a medieval castle than a university campus. A huge gate opened a way inside its walls but I bypassed the gate and circled the grassy expanse that bordered its ivy-covered brick walls on foot, taking my time and picturing the world of reason and intellect that I imagined was humming and bustling inside it.

I'd arrived with a hazy self-awareness that I was searching for some sign of a path that might lead a way out of the darkness of Vietnam. I think I'd expected it to happen the way it had in the jungle; that subtle cues would guide me and something would simply take shape, but as I walked those grounds all I was finding were doubts, insecurities, and fears. I'd earned a place for myself in a savage setting where strength, grit, and loyalty were highly valued, but I was certain the erudite people within those walls would value themselves based on their intellect and humanity. My doubts that I could measure up to those standards unnerved me but I felt driven to atone for the lives I'd taken, and I was done being a pawn in a larger game and taking orders from men who knew or cared too little. I knew that my path necessitated an education, and as I walked those grassy lawns I promised myself that I'd try. Those were the thoughts and emotions that were flying through my mind but I never found the courage to pass through the gates of that grand old university. I felt too coarse, or maybe I felt too stained, so I circled back to my waiting taxi and returned to the King's Cross section of Sydney, safeguarding myself from the sense of alienation I feared I'd feel if I tried to mingle with the scholarly men and women who studied there.

The King's Cross section of Sydney was filled with American servicemen on RxR, and one evening I ran into Dave Smedley, the younger brother of my high school friend, Doug. We shared a couple of drinks, and when I told them I was leaving Dave and the two guys he was with decided to share a cab with me. The driver didn't reset his meter, and when I pointed that out to him he told me not to worry, and that "It was OK." I'd taken the same route on an earlier cab ride, and when we arrived I knew he'd doubled the fare. I told him that we weren't going to pay twice what the ride should have cost and he lunged at me swinging. I put him on the ground with a punch. He scrambled to his feet cursing and screaming that he was going to the cops, and then he jumped in the cab, slammed it in reverse, and accelerated backward. I reached out and opened the rear passenger door as he passed, intending to get in a last word, but the door caught on a parking meter pole, tore free, and skittered a few feet along the sidewalk. He jumped out shaking his fist and yelling, and then he climbed back in and peeled away. We walked down the street, and when we heard a siren Dave and his buddies ran in one direction and I took off in the other.

I'd come here wanting to become more like our first medic, Doc White, the strong and gentle man who'd been genuinely prepared to accept death rather than kill a fellow human being. That's what I'd wanted but I could have handled the overcharge more gently, and when he'd charged me I could have stepped aside and asked him what he was doing. I hadn't done either. I was sick of savagery but I'd always resonated to the beat of it, and faced with the same situations I feared I'd react as I always had.

All my RxR days weren't so filled with melancholy reflections. On one memorable evening I ordered a steak and butter-dipped lobster dinner in a little bar and restaurant that turned out to be the best meal I'd ever eaten.

A very attractive Australian girl was seated at the adjacent bar and I watched a parade of guys drift over and offer to buy her drinks. She'd declined every offer, and when I finished my meal I walked over, leaned in beside her, and suggested that the next time someone offered to buy her a drink she should order a scotch and water. She glanced over her shoulder and said that she didn't drink scotch, and I smiled and said, "*No, I drink scotch and water.*" She laughed, and for the rest of the evening there were two or three drinks lined up in front of her whenever I wanted one.

A couple of grunts from the 2nd of the 7th Cav drifted in and I invited them to join me at one of the tables at the side of the small dance floor. An American couple in their early thirties arrived soon after and they took the table next to ours. The husband said he was in Australia on a business trip and I ended up spending a couple of hours drinking and talking with him and his wife. They were the first American civilians I'd spoken with since I'd left the States, and the short time I spent with them made it seem like home reached all the way to Australia. I would have stayed longer but the Cav grunts said they wanted to leave and I'd had enough free drinks to feel duty-bound to stick with them.

I thanked the girl for the drinks and told the couple I was leaving. The lady stood and hugged me like a sister, and the man clasped one of my hands in his and extended a thick roll of American currency in the other, saying earnestly that I was fighting for them in Vietnam and they wanted to do something for me. I told them that they'd done enough for me already and that the time I'd spent with them had meant more to me than they could ever know. Those words came straight from my heart. I'd been too fearful of rejection to pass through the walls of the university but that couple's warm acceptance of me and their heartfelt words made me feel that Vietnam hadn't doomed me to an outcast's existence and that if I survived I might someday mix with regular people and live a worthwhile life.

My week in Australia provided a safe place for me to begin processing the things I'd done, the person I'd become, and the person I wanted to be. I think my attempts to work through that and my uncertainty about what I might hear in her voice were the reasons I waited to call Barbara. The operator put the call out and there were several clicks as the call found its way to America, and then Barbara's phone buzzed and her melodic voice answered, "Hello."

The operator asked if she'd accept a call from me and my spirits lifted when I heard her enthusiastic, "Yes!" We talked for almost an hour, and I ended the call believing that her feelings hadn't changed. When I was flying back to Vietnam I didn't realize how much my time in Australia and that phone call had meant but I knew those unbidden thoughts of Bù Gia Mập and the NVA who'd died behind that log weren't popping into my head. I wasn't thinking of my days on RxR either, I was hearing Barbara's voice and, for the first time in months, I was envisioning a future filled with predictable outcomes and a lifetime of tomorrows.

Chapter 29

Return From RxR

After processing at the Ton Son Knut Air Base I stopped by the air force NCO club. Three senior air force sergeants saw that I was alone and they invited me to their table. After a drink or two, they told me that they hadn't run across many grunts and they asked how things were out in the field. I saw the concern on their faces when I explained how formidable the NVA were and what the conditions were in the jungle, and when I finished one of them said compassionately, "You're so fortunate to have your career NCOs out there to lead you." The other two nodded in agreement.

I thought about the bizarre collection of guys who'd been arbitrarily assigned to my platoon; can't read or write Quinlin who was full of native intelligence and common sense, capable, quick thinking, and competent Walter Morris who worked hand in hand with the officers they'd sent us, deeply religious and gentle Cherry Instant, city-raised guys like Rene and rural guys like Joe Bunch, Gramps, and barefooted most of his life-Hootie, solid Henry, fun loving Kenny and somber Billy Bass, impossible to categorize Sugar Bear, Dennis Rydgren, John Glasshof, and others who'd declined officer's candidate school training or been selected for shake and bake sergeant's courses because of their intellect and performance during training, Lt. Colclough who'd been drafted halfway through law school and was now packing a heavy law book through the jungle, and our audacious CO Peter Valtz who'd been granted a battlefield commission, all of them dropped literally out of thin air into a lethal environment so chaotic and mercurial you could rarely plan for anything.

There were no career NCOs leading my platoon in the jungle and there never had been. I was sure that competent career NCOs must be providing that leadership to units somewhere but I hadn't seen it, and I hadn't heard of it during my time at the Combat Leaders Course. I was confident that over the many years of war far too many of them had learned how deadly the jungle was, and I had to tell them, "They're not there. They don't come to the jungle because they don't want to get killed."

I saw bewildered looks on their faces, and I explained that in my company the only career NCO who'd come to the jungle with us was Sergeant Fuji from Guam and that the rest of us were rank-and-file soldiers who'd been drafted or enlisted for a single term of service. I was sure they believed me but I'd seen the pride those thoughtful air force NCOs felt in the role they believed their army counterparts were playing in units like mine and I was pretty sure they'd end up assuming that my company was an outlier. I could have tried harder to convince them but I knew that belief was important to them, and I didn't.

As I left they wished me heartfelt "good lucks" and "take care of yourselves" like uncles or fathers sending a tender young man out into a cruel world. I was probably as non-tender as anyone could get in the place where I was heading but I was touched by their concern and I played my part, assuring them that I'd be careful and that I'd be OK.

The Door Gunner

I caught a ride out of Ton Son Knut that brought me closer to my unit. I couldn't find one for the second leg of my return, and that evening I paused at the doorway of an enlisted man's club and surveyed an interior that was three-quarters full of guys who looked to be rear base regulars. The lone exception was sitting at a table with his back against the wall. I'd have joined him then but the look on his face made me wonder if he wanted to be alone. I found a vacant table and ordered a drink, and he arrived on its heels, asking, "Who you with? What kind of country you working? How much time you got in-country? Let me buy you a drink," his buddies off somewhere and him lonely for company, I guessed.

He told me he'd been a grunt in a line company and then he'd gotten a door gunner ride on a slick. When I asked how he liked that he told me that he'd shoot anything that moved, and then he laughed and said that one time he'd seen some figures running into the brush and he'd opened up on them. Two of them had been quick enough to make it to cover, he said, but the last one had been pregnant. His voice was laughing when he told me that she'd been too slow and he'd blown her away, but the eyes that hadn't left my face weren't laughing.

I'd been picturing him firing down at three fleeing enemies and the end of his account had shocked me. Here I sat with a guy who'd faced hard death, a fellow grunt who'd earned a combat infantryman's badge; *one of us*, and now one of us had gunned down a pregnant woman and he was trying to shine it on like it was OK. There'd been a time when I'd have felt unreserved condemnation and loathing for a man who'd shoot down a helpless woman but it wasn't that black and white for me now. I detested what he'd done and I felt a deep regret for the lives he'd shattered, but I was surprised at the deep reservoir of sympathy and understanding I was feeling, for him.

The words he'd used and the cavalier way he'd said them suggested that what he'd done didn't bother him, but if he believed that he was fooling himself. Ghostly question marks had hung at the ends of his sentences and the eyes that were reading my face had been searching for judgments. I understood; who else could he tell that he'd "wasted a pregnant gook," maybe from meanness or maybe just because she'd been running and he'd had his finger on the trigger? Who but a fellow grunt could fathom, really fathom, the depth of the fear and anger that he'd internalized in Vietnam, and who but another grunt might understand how that could transform a man who'd probably once been as decent as everyone else into the man who'd done what he'd done? I didn't know if he was searching for approval, forgiveness, indifference, or maybe condemnation, but I knew he'd dropped it on me to find out how one of *us* would judge it, and I weighed my words carefully.

The horrible thing he'd done couldn't be minimized with the standard, "*it doan mean nuthin*," dismissal that we'd so often used to put things that couldn't be undone behind us, and I gave it to him straight, one grunt to another, "You're fucking up. Those are real people. How you gonna feel back home if you don't stop?"

He leaned back and stared down at his beer for a long time. In the empty minutes that followed we ordered another drink and talked about nothing, trying to get a little beyond it. Neither of us could. He left. A gnawing sense of the darkness he carried was eating into the pit of my stomach and I stayed longer, alone in a crowd thinking about a deadly chopper hammering above a desperate woman fleeing for her life and remembering the look I'd seen on the face of the man who'd killed her. I'd read his remorse and I didn't want his story to end with that look on his face, so I pictured him returning to the world, attending church, raising a family, and coaching his kids in Little League; maybe locking everything away in nightmares and trying desperately to forget that in this hellishly brutal place he'd lost his moral compass and done horribly evil things.

And then my thoughts turned to the powerful men who were prolonging this war; willfully ignorant, incompetent, or immoral men who were wrapping themselves in our flag and doing it to boost their egos or for personal gain. I could forgive the door gunner who'd pulled that fucking trigger but I didn't believe I'd ever forgive those cold-hearted bastards for what they'd done to that pregnant Vietnamese woman and the American soldier who'd killed her.

Bravo Company Headquarters

I arrived back at Bravo Company's headquarters with a little over a month left on my tour. I'd expected that I'd be riding the next log day chopper out to my company but the new company sergeant told me that they'd decided I'd done enough and they were keeping me in the rear.

I felt numb. Many thousands of insects and a lot of leeches had sucked my blood and hunger and thirst had gnawed at me for almost every hour of every day I'd spent in the jungle. Larvae had hatched out of my flesh and jungle rot had eaten away my skin. I'd worn through the soles of two pairs of boots, gone weeks without bathing, and worn the same clothes for so long that they'd begun to rot off of me. I'd been so hot that I'd felt the heat boiling out of me, so cold that I'd shivered for hours, and wet for days at a time. I'd been so scared that the sounds of the blood coursing through the capillaries of my ears had threatened to drown out the sounds I'd desperately needed to hear and so miserable that I'd hardly cared whether I'd lived or died. I'd been bloodied by shrapnel and bullets, and I'd survived the kinds of close-quarter ambushes that most men hadn't. For months I'd expected to die here and I'd just been told that I wouldn't. I knew I should be feeling uplifted, or at least relieved, but I didn't.

I'd thought I'd return one more time to the murmuring whispers of the magnificent jungle and the camaraderie of the guys in my platoon, and that if I made it through the next weeks I'd have said my goodbyes. Those things were still pulling at me but another side of me was telling me that this time I'd earned a precious ticket on a freedom bird that would transport me home, and that part of me prevailed. Still, I didn't feel like thanking him, and I just nodded and turned away.

The Drowned Rat

Sometime in the night a *"thud-thumping"* sound started reverberating from somewhere behind my hooch. When it drummed on I decided it was probably a downer-drugged REMF beating on something, and I put the sounds in a corner of my mind and slept. The thumps were much softer when the morning began to gray, and the lapses between them grew so lengthy that I'd believe they'd stopped until another came. I was curious, and when it was fully light I circled behind my bunker to see what it was. Four REMFs were staring down at a corrugated washtub that was 3/4 filled with rainwater, and I moved up behind them and saw one of the rats that thrived among us lying on the bottom of the tub.

We weren't strangers to rats. Hordes of them nested and foraged in the fortifications we'd dug at the edges of the jungle. We viewed them as dangerous pests but they'd proven themselves far too cunning to be eradicated with poison or traps, and in many ways it seemed they owned the rear areas as much as we did. A few of them showed very little fear of us, and their boldness usually went unchallenged because a razor-toothed rat that was nearly the size of a small dog wasn't an animal you'd want to corner. The biggest and oldest rats seemed to sense the fear they generated, and if you stumbled across one of those it might fix you with its knowing red eyes before it ambled insolently away. Some of them were even more aggressive, and there were numerous accounts of rats biting chunks of flesh out of the bodies or faces of sleeping or stoned REMFs, accounts that were taken so seriously that even on miserably hot nights some REMFs slept with their faces buried under their blankets.

I thought the big rat on the bottom of the tub was dead until it kicked its hind legs weakly against the bottom of the tub. That feeble kick had barely enough force to propel the rat's nose above the surface of the water. I heard it suck in a sodden lungful of air, and then the rat went limp, sank slowly to the bottom of the tub, and lay unmoving. Somehow it had ended up in the tub and it hadn't been able to claw its way out. When it had gotten too exhausted to swim it had allowed itself to sink to the bottom of the tub, and throughout the night it had used its powerful hind legs to push to the surface for a lungful of air. The drumbeats of "*thud-thump*" noises had been from the flexing of the air-gapped bottom of the metal tub every time the rat had pushed off, and as the rat had weakened the intervals between the thumps had lengthened and the sounds had softened.

They had to know that the rat on the bottom of the tub was doomed to drown but the REMFs were animatedly discussing various ways of killing it. They settled on a plan, and one of them overturned the tub. The limp rat flooded out with the water, and when the water drained away the rat was standing on legs that quivered the way Gramp's legs had wobbled after he'd crutched himself up from the crotch of that big tree. One of the REMFs poured gasoline on the rat but the rat was so near death that it barely flinched. Another of the REMFs flicked a lit match at the rat and the gas ignited. Aflame, the rat mustered enough adrenalin to crawl toward a nearby bunker, and when it neared the bunker one of the REMFs bludgeoned it to death with a shovel. I watched the four of them laugh, vaguely disgusted with myself. I hadn't participated but I hadn't said anything either, and I turned away feeling more melancholy than I'd have expected. I think it was because I'd seen how much that rat had endured trying to stay alive and then, like so many of us, it had died a hard death anyway.

The Company Sergeant

Our new company sergeant was a medium-tall and muscular veteran of the Korean War who appeared to be in good shape. Every evening he'd drink beer with some of the men who were permanently attached to our headquarters and I'd hear them talking when I was in my hooch. As far as I knew he'd never ventured outside the wire in Vietnam but that didn't deter him from pontificating about how much tougher it had been for them in Korea than it was for us in Vietnam. He'd never done that when he'd known I was around but his tough-guy talk and his profound ignorance of the conditions in the jungle were wearing on me.

I wasn't trying to be one of his buddies and he started assigning me details while his drinking pals didn't pull any duty. On my third day there I'd had enough and I told him that I wasn't going to carry the load for guys who'd never spent a day in the field. He had a macho reputation to uphold and he stepped forward aggressively, barking something about **"draftees!"** The next thing I knew I had him slammed up against a sandbagged bunker with his feet inches off the ground. His eyes were very wide, his head was pulled back, and his hands were extended above his shoulders in an open-palmed non-threatening position. I felt the fabric of his shirt start to rip, and I let go and stepped back. He stumbled when his feet landed, and then he caught his balance and stood very still. I waited. Neither he nor his buddies spoke or moved, and I pivoted and walked away.

It was another resupply day and I gathered my M-16 and my gear, walked to the chopper pad, took my customary seat in the log bird's open doorway, and returned to the one place in the army where no one could own me.

Chapter 30

Back to the Jungle

In our platoon, and probably in all of our company, I was the last of us who'd arrived in the summer of 1969. One by one the others had melted away. Sugar Bear, Quinlin, Big Jack, Ron Belin, and the Mailman had left the jungle in the last two or three months, and when Capt. Valtz and Lt. Colclough had completed their 6-month officers' tours they'd paved the way for some of the guys I'd have considered new guys to leave with them. The closest thing to old hands left in the jungle now were Denny Laughter, Dennis Rydgren, Kenny Martin, Henry (David) Tedford, Jerry, Baby Huey, Cherry Instant, Joe Bunch, Billy Bass, and Freddy, and they were telling me to take the platoon sergeant slot that the Lt. who'd replaced Lt. Colclough had offered. I had to think about it, but I'd taken a mental step back when I'd allowed them to keep me in the rear and I agreed to move back with the new Lt. and his RTO.

Three days later our log day chopper started ratcheting its noisy way into the jungle, and I looked up and saw Rene riding the skids with his pack on his back and his sniper rifle in his hands. Memories flashed through my mind; Rene and I at the Cav training center, the two of us uncertain FNGs riding the chopper to LZ Grant, Rene's voice behind me at the bomb crater whispering, "Wait a minute Ed, I'm going with you," Rene's welcome voice asking if I was OK after I'd flopped in the foxhole and landed on Ralph, crazy-brave Rene with his head elevated in the naked light of the flares scanning for attacking NVA, Rene walking back up for me to the termite mound where I'd been bullet grazed and scanning through the arc light-mangled jungle foliage with his head up once again. I remembered how relieved I'd been when he'd left for sniper school and how much I'd missed my friend's presence on our evening perimeters.

The chopper settled and Rene bounded off and headed straight to me with his steel pot bobbling on his head and his smile lighting his face. He looked so pleased that I laughed.

"What are you doing here?"

"I heard you'd come back out and I decided to join you."

A lot of grunts would have thought he was crazy but I understood. Eleven months ago five wide-eyed FNGs had landed on the dusty chopper pad outside LZ Grant. Two of us were dead and Roger was safe in the rear, but I think it felt right to Rene that he and I would complete our one-year circle of the sun the way we'd begun it, two friends sharing the risks. That's how it felt to me but I didn't put it into words and neither did Rene.

That evening Rene told me that Sugar Bear had gotten a job driving a garbage truck, and then he'd run over and killed one of the moped-riding young Vietnamese they called *Saigon Cowboys*. Rene said that Sugar Bear was claiming it had been an accident but I'd seen Sugar Bear lash out at the smallest provocation and I wondered. Either way, Sugar Bear was facing court-martial proceedings that would keep him in Vietnam past the end of his tour date, and I was reminded of the many instances when he'd crowed to Quinlin and me that he'd be back home with our girls while we were, "getting your asses shot off in the frigging jungle," Quinlin had always replied, "*Ya best not stop fer a cupa coffee lest I pass yuh up*," and I could picture him shaking his head and saying, "*I tole yuh so.*"

Transitions

While I'd been on RxR my company had crossed the into Cambodia as part of a massive US incursion to disrupt the NVA's supply lines. That incursion must have hit the NVA hard because our division's casualties had dropped dramatically. That didn't mean the jungle was safe when I walked point for my old squad up a small NVA trail we'd come across. I'd thought it would be the way it always had been but it wasn't. I couldn't clear my mind of thoughts of how very close I'd come to surviving and I wasn't able to feel my way ahead. I knew how vulnerable that had made me, and that evening I thought about the people who were expecting me to arrive home in a few days and I resolved that I'd walked point for the last time.

I didn't know how much that decision would shake my sense of self until I made it. My willingness and ability to walk point had made me special but I was days away from returning to a life where the essential characteristics and skills that had set me apart weren't needed. Like an aging running back who'd valued himself based on his ability to power through anyone until one day he couldn't, I didn't know who I was anymore. In many ways it was ironic, I'd stepped into the jungle a wide-eyed and uncertain FNG facing deadly unknowns and then I'd gone full jungle and owned this place about as much as anyone could, and now I was about to leave it feeling nearly as uncertain as I'd felt when I'd arrived. The way I was feeling made me appreciate those simpler times when living another day had been the only thing that mattered and I'd played an important part in making that happen, but I wasn't going to stay.

The Last Lt.

I'd always socially distanced myself from our officers, even the good ones, but the Lt. I was walking with had no one to talk with except Rene, his RTO, and me. He had a wife and one child, and on an evening perimeter he told me how fearful he was that he might not survive to care for them. When I asked why he'd come to the jungle if he'd felt that way he told me that he hadn't had a choice. I remembered how Mad Dog had left, and I told him that a platoon leader who didn't get along with his company commander would probably get transferred out of the jungle pretty quickly.

He didn't say anything but mid-morning of the next day he was on the radio arguing doggedly with the by-the-book captain who'd replaced Captain Valtz, and after several days of that he rode the resupply chopper out and didn't return.

The Nightmare

On many a night I'd come awake to the blood-curdling screams of one of us who'd been caught up in a death nightmare. I'd never had one, and then just as I was about to leave one came that would follow me home.

I dreamed that our platoon was pinned down in an intense firefight that had lasted for more than an hour. I hadn't seen them die but I knew that Dennis, Hootie, and Gramps had been swept away in the first bullet-torn minutes. I'd heard the sounds of others dying but the thick foliage had screened them and I hadn't been able to put faces to their screams or the gasping rasps of their last breaths. More and more NVA had kept crawling in closer and killing more of my guys and there'd been nothing I could do to stop them. Sugar Bear had died nearby, terrified and in pain. Quinlin had been off to my left. His gun had gone silent and I'd called out to him but there'd been no answer, not from him, not from any of them, and I'd been alone.

Partially sheltered in a big clump of bamboo, my toy-like M-16 and my ability to shoot it had been my lifeline and the bodies of those I'd killed had been crumpled on the jungle floor all around me. Every time I'd seen a flash of movement I'd hit my target, but I'd had just a handful of shells left and bullets had been raking across my cover from unexpected angles, striking closer and driving my head into the dirt. With so many dead to stir their vengeance I'd known they weren't going to stop and all the opportunities to live that I'd thrown away had been flashing through my mind, and I'd come wide awake with a heaving chest and the bitter taste of fear and regret in my mouth.

I knew why the nightmare had found me. *I'm going to make it,* had been echoing in my head and the part of me that had accepted my death in the jungle was beginning to embrace a vastly different future than the one I'd been anticipating for months; a future where my blood would never soak the rich dirt of the sun-dappled stretch of trail I'd envisioned, and one where I'd once again gaze into the depths of Barbara's blue-green eyes, swim in the crystal clear waters of the Trinity River, and lean back on those high mountain slopes seeing the afternoon sun reflecting silvery off the threadlike course of the river murmuring so far below, observed only by a few cautious blue belly lizards doing their tiny pushups, just those watchful little lizards.

That soon to be a recurring nightmare had opened a wide window into an aspect of our time in the jungle that I hadn't wanted to think about. I'd moderated my fears by making a friend of my likely death but the terror I'd felt in the grip of my nightmare gave me a deeper appreciation of the long-enduring courage of the men spread throughout the brush of the nearby jungle. Rene and I would be leaving soon but they'd still be caught in this fearful web, maybe to die. My heart went out to them, and waves of sadness and anger followed at those who sanctioned this from afar, men who'd have ended this senseless war long ago if they'd been in our boots or if the rotting corpses coming home in body bags had been the corpses of their kids. But they weren't dying here and it would never be their kids, just us.

I tugged aside the worn nylon blanket liner that had comforted me through so many months of jungle nights and rose from the leaf-littered earth. I had 7 days and a wakeup left in Vietnam and I felt a sudden urge to escape the jungle.

Ending

Rene and I rose out of the jungle one last time, me riding the rail in one open doorway and Rene riding the rail in the other. We each had smoke canisters. His was yellow and mine was red. We were a couple of meters in the air when we popped them, and as we climbed higher their plumes of colored smoke trailed in our wake.

The chopper rocked from side to side as the pilot struggled to hold it within the confines of the vertical tunnel that opened out of the jungle, and I had a long while to see the distance between myself and the platoon widen. Baby Huey was standing almost directly beneath the chopper. He had his arms folded across his narrow chest and a beam of sunlight was shining through his thinning wispy-yellow hair. Peering through the thick lenses of his glasses, he caught my eye and nodded with a sad smile on his face. Billy Bass was sitting off to the side with his back resting against his pack. The M-60 was nestled against him like a sweetheart, the way it always did. His upturned face had its perpetually solemn look. He didn't smile and he didn't nod. Most of the others were looking up and nodding or waving, all of them silent, but I had to look for Kenny. Our chopper was near the tops of the trees when I spotted him, standing alone just inside the bamboo and looking up. I secured a solid handhold, stood with both feet on the skids, and leaned far out of the chopper. I dropped the dying smoke, and then I forced a grin and gave him a single wave with my right hand. His unsmiling face lit up and he raised his right arm high and waved at me. He had it raised when the pilot wheeled the chopper over and we hammered away. It's still up there.

He hasn't moved in decades.

None of them have.

Glossary

arc light. A B-52 bombing mission. The army's official code name, Arc Light, was apt because when the B-52's line of bombs exploded it created the appearance of an arc light weld sparking across a piece of metal.

ARVN. An acronym for the Army of the Republic of Vietnam, the South Vietnamese force that was trained and armed to take over our role in the war.

article 15. A summary courts martial proceeding that could fine and reduce a soldier in rank.

azimuth. A compass heading intended to lead from one place to another.

bloop gun. The name we used for the M-79 handheld grenade launcher was based on the "bloop" sound it made when one of its small grenades were fired. It was configured like a single shot break-open shotgun but with a barrel big enough for the plumb-sized explosive round it fired.

body bag. A heavy rubber bag used to enclose a body. It had a full length zipper that led some grunts to refer to getting killed as "getting zipped."

boonies. Along with "the bush," "outside the wire," and "the boondocks," a reference to the deadly areas where the enemy was hidden.

bunker. Ours were sandbagged shelters constructed inside the wire, our enemies' bunkers were earthen shelters dug into the jungle floor with above ground dirt walls and ceilings.

Chieu Hoi. The term for an enemy soldier who voluntarily surrendered pursuant to a program that encouraged them to defect.

CO. The commanding officer of an infantry company, usually an army captain.

DEROS. An acronym for "date estimated return from overseas" that marked the date you were eligible to leave Vietnam if you lasted that long.

Donut Dolly. A Red Cross volunteer whose role was to boost morale among the troops in Vietnam. Less than 700 of them reportedly served during the years of the war, visiting troops all throughout the country and bringing reminders of home with them.

enlisted men. Any soldier who wasn't an officer, regardless of whether that soldier was drafted or had volunteered.

fng. An acronym for a "funny new guy," or a "effen new guy."

frag. A grenade, whether theirs or ours.

freedom bird. The name given to the commercial airliners that flew soldiers home at the end of their tours. There were times in the jungle when the sun would gleam off the metal of one that was flying like a little speck in the sky, and faces would look up and men would whisper reverently, "Hey look, it's a freedom bird."

grunt. An infantryman's term for those infantrymen who ventured out and fought the enemy.

gunner. A common nickname given to the man who carried the M-60 machine gun along with its belts of ammo. The gun weighed about 23 pounds and thus it was sometimes called, "the pig."

hooch. Any temporary living quarter we used, typically a cot or a blanket laid inside a bunker when we were in the rear.

Huey. A UH-1 Huey helicopter. The Huey was by far the most used chopper in Vietnam, and it was commonly called a "slick" when the interior was emptied out and used to transport troops.

hump. The word used to denote the carrying of a heavy load, and often combined with bush, as in, "humpin the bush."

kill count. The metric used to weigh our losses versus the enemies' losses, purportedly to assess the success of the Army's war of attrition.

log. Log is shorthand for logistics. Any day we received food, water, ammo, and other supplies in the jungle was referred to as a "log day."

Loach. A "Light Observation & Command Helicopter" that was so tiny we called it a "mosquito."

mad minute. A defensive tactic where everyone opened up shooting on fully automatic for a minute or so.

Montagnard. South Vietnam's indigenous ethnic minority living in the central highlands of Vietnam. During the Vietnam war they were reliable allies of the Americans.

NVA. An acronym for "North Vietnamese Army," but it was also used as a term to describe an individual soldier serving in the North Vietnamese Army; as in, "a NVA." The NVA were distinct from the Viet Cong (VC) forces that consisted of South Vietnamese citizen fighters who supported the North Vietnamese, usually blending into the civilian population during the day and employing guerilla tactics.

PRC 25. The radio carried by an RTO in the field. The radio weighed about 25 lbs. and thus it was often referred to a the "Prick 25."

rear job. Grunts referred to any job that didn't involve venturing outside the wire as a "read job." Rear jobs were considered lifesavers and they were coveted no matter how miserable they were.

remf. An acronym for "rear echelon mother effer" that was commonly used by grunts to label anyone who had never walked the bush. It was used with varying degrees of reprobation depending on what negative impact that remf was viewed as having with respect to supplying, respecting, or risking the lives of grunts.

RPG. A grenade from a shoulder fired launcher, propelled by a rocket after launch, and exploding on impact.

RxR. A one week break from the war at various off-country sites. Married soldiers were allowed to select Hawaii as a designation so they could meet up with their spouses, others had to choose between various Asian designations or Australia.

RTO. An acronym for a radio telephone operator. The RTOs in the field carried the PRC 25 that added another 25 pounds to the heavy loads they were already packing.

short. The word used to describe how near a grunt was to the scheduled end of his tour. Everyone knew when a grunt was "gettin short" but it wasn't usually talked about with the grunt whose tour was nearing an end. There were many reports of guys who'd gotten killed just days before they were scheduled to leave and no one wanted to jinx him.